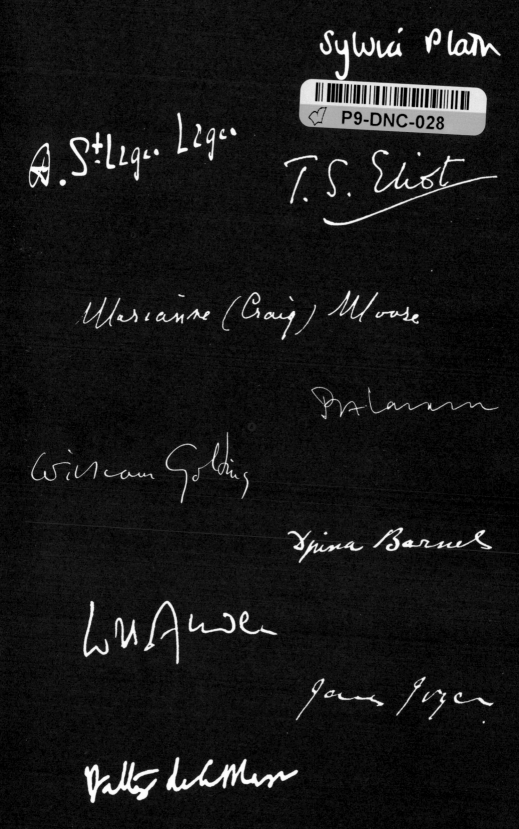

Faber & Faber

# FABER & FABER

## The Untold Story

### Toby Faber

FABER & FABER

First published in 2019
by Faber & Faber Limited
Bloomsbury House
74–77 Great Russell Street
London WC1B 3DA

Typeset by Faber & Faber Limited
Printed and bound by CPI Group (UK) Ltd, Croydon, CR0 4YY

The right of Toby Faber to be identified as author of this work
has been asserted in accordance with Section 77 of the Copyright,
Designs and Patents Act 1988

A CIP record for this book
is available from the British Library

ISBN 978–0–571–33904–4

2 4 6 8 10 9 7 5 3 1

To everyone who has ever worked for,
or been published by, Faber & Faber

# Contents

List of plates: A selection of Faber jacket designs     ix

Introduction     xi

1: 1924–1929
'She dislikes Elliott's poems very much'     1

2: 1929–1935
'The Russell Square Twins'     64

3: 1936–1939
'With a very real danger of war'     104

4: 1939–1945
'Riding high on the crest of the highest wave'     138

5: 1945–1950
'It taught me a valuable lesson'     182

6: 1951–1960
'Flair rather than taste'     200

7: 1960–1970
'People feel that we are smug'     259

8: 1971–1979
'A reasonable hope of survival'     319

9: 1980–1986
'Faber has been taken over by a different generation'     353

10: 1986–1990
'A week is a long time in publishing'     387

Afterword     399

Appendix: Faber & Faber Sales and                    403
    Profit History, 1929–1990
Acknowledgements                                     406
Index                                                411

# List of plates:
## A selection of Faber jacket designs

Spain in a Two Seater, 1925
Memoirs of a Fox-Hunting Man, 1928
Memoirs of an Infantry Officer, 1932
Good Food, 1932
Louder and Funnier, 1932
Guide to Kulchur, 1938
A Traveller in Time, 1939
Finnegans Wake, 1939
Old Possum's Book of Practical Cats, 1939
The White Goddess, 1948
Justine, 1957
The Hawk in the Rain, 1957
Cover Her Face, 1962
The Whitsun Weddings, 1964
Ariel, 1965
Death of a Naturalist, 1966
Rosencrantz and Guildenstern are Dead, 1967
The Iron Man, 1968
Slag, 1970
The Unbearable Lightness of Being, 1984
My Beautiful Laundrette, 1984
Spitting Image, 1984
Making Cocoa for Kingsley Amis, 1986
The New York Trilogy, 1987

# Introduction

'If you want to make a small fortune out of publishing, start off with a large one.' It is an old joke, but especially true of literary publishing. In choosing to invest in the company that became Faber & Faber, my grandfather Geoffrey picked a notoriously uncertain business.

Books start with authors of course, but it is the publisher who has to bring their work before the public and try to make it pay. A publisher like Faber makes the initial investment, paying for all aspects of a book's production and design, selling it to bookshops on 'sale or return' (i.e. on the basis that the publisher accepts the return of any unsold copies) and giving each title the marketing push that, it hopes, will lead to those copies being bought by actual readers. The publisher also pays the author an advance, to be earned out as the book earns royalties on each copy sold, but never to be paid back if the book fails to sell.

There are few guaranteed bestsellers. A literary publisher is dependent on the taste of its editors, who commission books in the hope that the reading public will agree with them. General acceptance of a writer might take years; it might never happen. If editorial judgement proves justified and an author develops a following, there is then no certainty that they will stay for their next book. When it comes to the poetry for which Faber is famous, T. S. Eliot, its first editor, knew that his objective was not to make money, but to lose as little as possible.

So there is already a story worth telling in the simple fact of Faber's survival as an independent company. In any industry, a firm which has lasted for three generations would be interesting. In literary publishing it is truly remarkable. There are numerous occasions in the book that follows when Faber was about to run out of money, when it might have folded quietly, or gratefully succumbed to the warm embrace of a larger competitor. If any good story requires jeopardy, then this one has it in spades.

Moreover, Faber & Faber has not just been any literary publisher. For most of the period since it was founded it has been THE literary publisher: midwife at the birth of modernism in the 1920s and 1930s, and reinventing itself at least twice in the period covered by this history. The story of Faber – of how it came to publish so many great writers – is part of the story of twentieth-century literature itself.

———

These days, a company controlled by the Faber family owns exactly half of Faber & Faber. During my childhood in the 1970s, it owned it all. My father was, essentially, an academic physicist, but he was also one of Faber's directors. Every few weeks, boxes of newly published books would arrive at our house in Cambridge. I grew up reading them and listening to discussions about the firm which produced them. My surname would leap out at me from the spines of books in shops and libraries. I scanned newspapers for reviews and heard stories from the parties which my parents occasionally attended. The connection did not, however, mean that we were rich. Once, my siblings and I boasted of it to some other children we met on holiday, only for a kindly but definitive rebuff. Our status had already been established by the Renault 4 in which we had arrived, four children squeezed together on the back seat: 'Don't be ridiculous. You'd be in a Rolls-Royce driven by a chauffeur.'

From 1996 to 2001 I worked full-time at Faber; since 2003 I have held a position similar to that occupied by my father forty years ago. I already knew when I started writing this book that there was a good story there waiting to be told. Now, having spent two years in the Faber archive, reading letters, memoranda, board minutes, diary entries and catalogues, I am even more in awe of the achievements of my predecessors. I feel as though I have eavesdropped on the arguments that began the business and on the conversations that led to the arrival of the authors who give the firm its literary status today. The letters have brought my father and grandmother alive for me again. I have discovered a personal side to authors whom I have only known before as a reader. I've grown to know my grandfather (who died before I was born) in a way not given to many grandsons.

——

As much as possible, I have told the story of Faber through these original documents. It is not just that the people writing them could turn a phrase with an elegance that makes them tremendously readable. It is also that they could not know how their story was going to turn out: the future importance of *Old Possum's Book of Practical Cats* and *Lord of the Flies*; why it was a bad idea to turn down *Animal Farm*. Their excitement, hopes, fears and frustration vibrate through these pages, giving the book a sense of immediacy that hindsight-laden commentary cannot.

My own contribution is limited to introducing each chapter, and then to occasional *italicised* asides, intended to explain what you have just read, highlight something that may not have been immediately apparent, or bring in a new theme. For these I have drawn on my own knowledge of both family stories and publishing, as well as other sources such as memoirs.

The narrative flow almost always dictates that I order extracts chronologically. This can lead to juxtapositions that I hope are not too disconcerting. For example, I think it is useful to see how, at the same time that Geoffrey Faber was engaging in crucial discussions with his fellow shareholders about the viability of the book publishing business, Richard de la Mare wrote to Siegfried Sassoon to take on *Memoirs of a Fox-Hunting Man* (the firm's first bestseller).

I am not slavish about this, however. Sometimes I let a theme reach its natural conclusion before hopping back a few months to follow a different strand of the plot.

Readability trumps academic respectability. On the rare occasions when I have had to guess an illegible word, I have done so, and have not alerted the reader to my actions. I have used a single date format for my headers, and a single way of denoting *titles*, despite the many different conventions used by my sources. I have expanded abbreviations and corrected spellings, where these seem to me to distract the reader, but left them in when they amuse me, or tell us something. I have, occasionally, corrected some of the more egregious examples of poor punctuation (but have preserved the stray commas for which William Golding was famous).

My aim throughout has been to cut out the boring bits, drawing single paragraphs from documents that may run to several pages. Any cuts between two extracts from the same source are indicated by [. . .] but there may be many more words both before and after an extract that have not been similarly signalled. This approach has its disadvantages, of course; I'm particularly sad not to be able to show the way relationships develop from 'Dear Sir' through 'Dear Faber' to 'Dear Geoffrey', but that sort of thing is probably best left to the published correspondence.

Forty years ago, many readers knew Faber for its magnificent list of art books. Its gardening, cookery and bridge lists were second to none; it pioneered books about the organic movement; science fiction was a real strength. For decades, the firm derived far more money from its medical list than from its poetry. Nevertheless you will find little relating to any of these books or their authors in the pages that follow, for the simple reason that they are no longer part of the Faber list. I regret the exclusion, but I have had to focus on the books which give Faber the character it has today. The children's list, by contrast, remains an important part of the firm – and I grew up reading it – but again I have not given its authors the space that they deserve, essentially because, with a few exceptions, I have not found the correspondence.

Finally, I hope what follows will evoke a sense of fun: both the fun that people (generally) had and (generally) still have while working for Faber, and the fun that I've had in writing the book. There are only two substantial letters in what follows that I have reproduced in their entirety – because every word was relevant. Both were spoofs written by T. S. Eliot to my grandfather. Those two men deserve this prominence for a reason. If one part of this history provides this book with its core, and gives Faber the character which it still has today, it is the relationship between them. So my first extract, of course, has to be from the letter in which T. S. Eliot introduced himself to Geoffrey Faber.

Toby Faber
London, 2019

# I: 1924–1929
## 'She dislikes Elliott's poems very much'

At thirty-four, Geoffrey Faber had still not settled on a career. Born in 1889, he had spent the First World War on the Western Front in the Post Office Rifles – surviving when his older brother did not. He had also published two volumes of poetry, the first to good reviews, notably from Walter de la Mare. His most distinguished achievement, however, had probably been to win, in 1919, a prize fellowship at All Souls College, Oxford (in the same election as T. E. Lawrence). A year later he had married Enid Richards, twelve years younger, and had become a director of Strong & Co., a brewing company in Hampshire that was owned by a Faber cousin. Their first child, Ann, was born in 1922.

Unfortunately, Geoffrey had little obvious talent for brewing. In 1923 he lost his job and the prospects which had allowed him to dream of becoming a beer magnate and Conservative MP. Supported only by the £600 salary he earned as Estates Bursar of All Souls (a post he continued to hold until the 1950s), he moved his young family to a small house in Campden Hill, London. As Enid later remembered, 'We had very small private means, and had cut down our staff to one cook and a young nanny for Ann. This felt quite meagre in those days. Geoffrey was writing unsuccessful plays.' He also wrote a novel satirising the state of modern fiction, *Elnovia*, which failed to interest any publishers.

Deliverance would come through Geoffrey's All Souls connections. The distinguished lawyer Maurice Gwyer was another Fellow, and his wife Alsina had inherited from her father Sir Henry Burdett an interest in a publishing business, the Scientific Press. This company had been founded in the 1880s, essentially around *The*

*Nursing Mirror*, a weekly magazine which had become the main way to advertise to nurses, although it also published a number of books on hospital management and nursing technique. By the time the Chairman, George Dibblee, resigned in 1923 the firm's annual profits were over £14,000 and it was paying a £10 dividend on every £10 share (so the owners were getting back their original investment every year).

George Dibblee had also been a Fellow of All Souls, and when looking for a replacement the Gwyers were not inclined to look any further. To add to the business experience he had from brewing, Geoffrey had also spent time in publishing: a not very distinguished couple of years working for Oxford University Press before the war. By April 1924, Geoffrey was installed as Chairman and Managing Director of the Scientific Press. In June he made his first appointment. Charles Stewart, who had also been at Oxford and worked for OUP (although not at the same time as Geoffrey), became General Manager.

The Gwyers had brought in Geoffrey not just to run the existing business but also to lead a diversification away from medical publishing. By August that year, Geoffrey had produced a memorandum explaining how he proposed to do that: a new focus on 'legal cram books' (an idea which doesn't seem to have led anywhere), novels, including translations of French and German fiction, and the publication of a literary magazine.

Maurice Gywer 'read with admiration your very convincing Memorandum', and Geoffrey began talking to people about his plans. One of them, the journalist and writer Charles Whibley, a frequent guest at the All Souls high table, was a regular contributor to a literary magazine that might serve Geoffrey's purpose: the *Criterion*. He suggested that Geoffrey might like to talk to its editor.

## T. S. Eliot to Geoffrey Faber, 25 November 1924

I understand from my friend Charles Whibley that he has conveyed to you his reasons for thinking that we should meet; and if you are so inclined, I should be happy to call upon you, if you would suggest an evening.

*A date was fixed, even though Enid was in hospital preparing for the birth of their second child, Richard.*

## Geoffrey Faber, diary entry, 1 December 1924

Bought wine for dinner. Then to see Enid. The preliminary operation was done at 11.15 – rubber bougies placed inside the womb. Involved anaesthetic.

Then home; where T. S. Eliot dined with me, and we had a long and interesting talk about the *Criterion*.

*Although Eliot had by this time already published much of his most celebrated poetry, including* The Waste Land, *I rather think Geoffrey had not heard of him. Nevertheless, he liked the fact that Eliot was not only a poet, editor and critic, but also – at the time – a banker, presumably with a head for business. More important than that, the two men got on very well. Geoffrey immediately started thinking how he might bring Eliot into the firm he was building, and for that he required testimonials to persuade the Gwyers.*

## Charles Whibley to Geoffrey Faber, 7 December 1924

I will gladly tell you what I know about Eliot. He is of American birth and is related to the Eliot Nortons & Norton Eliots of Boston & Harvard. (He is strongly anti American, as you would suppose, and is now being naturalised.) He was educated at Harvard & Oxford, and is at present in Lloyds' Bank, in the Foreign Department. The Bank thinks very highly of him, and I believe he is at the head of the Intelligence Department. So that you may take it that he has been trained in business. He has published several books – *The Sacred Wood* (prose), and *Poems* and *Wastelands*. As a critic, he is the best and most learned of his generation and is respected (and a little feared) by the young. As a poet he is obscure and allusive, but I have faith that he will come out of his obscurity and write something really fine.

I know him intimately and count him among my closest friends and I have a perfect belief in his star. He knows all the young writers and is well able to discriminate among them. He gave a lecture here in Cambridge not long since and met with a reception from the undergraduates which surprised me.

Is that the sort of thing you wanted to know?

## Geoffrey Faber to T. S. Eliot, 16 December 1924

I do not want to raise your hopes unduly, but I do think, if we go about things in the right way, that there is a fair chance of something emerging at the end.

> *Persuading the Gwyers about T. S. Eliot was one thing. Alsina Gwyer, however, was not the only shareholder in the Scientific Press. Her sister had an almost equally large shareholding. Confusingly, while Alsina was married to Maurice Gwyer, her sister Olive was married to George Maurice, a colonel in the Royal Army Medical Corps. This couple's view of the future of the Scientific Press was very different from the Gwyers'.*

## Colonel Maurice to Geoffrey Faber, 14 November 1924

You know that I think this policy of expansion is likely to be costly and to result in heavy losses and that the wise policy is to screw out of the concern year by year all possible and to sell as soon as danger signs are visible. But I have had to consent to the course I think less wise; greatly against my wish.

> The Maurices were prepared, however, to sell their shares. They even got as far as finding a possible external buyer – Hodder & Stoughton – but Geoffrey and the Gwyers would not allow a sale to a competitor. Instead, Geoffrey saw the Maurices' willingness to sell as an opportunity for him to buy a substantial stake in the company he chaired. The only problem was that he didn't have any money, just the eventual prospect of inheriting a share of the relatively large estate left by his father's cousin, Arthur Faber. For most of Arthur's life, Geoffrey's father Henry had expected to be his heir. Then, just before his death, Arthur married his nurse, Ishti. Henry would inherit nothing until she died, and she was considerably younger than he was. Henry's death in 1917 (only three days after his elder son's) meant that Geoffrey's mother Florence was now the 'reversioner', leaving Geoffrey and his sister Dorothy (who never married) with a very remote interest indeed.

## Geoffrey Faber to his mother Florence Faber, 3 February 1925

I am exceedingly anxious both (a) to get rid of the Maurices, with whom it is impossible to make any progress and (b) to buy at least half of those shares for myself – which means raising from £15,000 to £17,500.

How on earth, you will say, can this be done?

Well, this is my idea. The value of the Arthur Faber Trust Estate – of which the reversion is yours – is, . . . certainly <u>well over</u> £25,000. If Ishti (as life-tenant) and you (as reversioner) gave your consent, it would be possible to borrow (say) £15,000 either directly from the Estate (the money being raised by the sale of securities) or for the Estate to borrow the money from the Bank and relend it to me. In either case the shares would be handed over to be held by the Estate, until the whole of the loan was paid off. The Dividends would be applied (a) to paying interest on the loan (b) to paying off the loan itself year by year, by a sinking fund. With what I could put up myself, both at the outset, and year by year, the whole thing would be paid off probably inside ten years.

In the result <u>everybody</u> would benefit. Ishti would have had the benefit of the interest on the loan, which would be more than she gets on the securities now; the Estate would be intact at the end of the ten years; I should have acquired a valuable property, with a substantial income; and you, in your will, would feel yourself able to make a better provision for Dorothy than you would otherwise be able to do.

*Florence's response to her son gives some hint, perhaps, of the reason he always found their relationship rather difficult.*

### Florence Faber to Geoffrey Faber, 5 February 1925

I feel I cannot give you any answer yet about the scheme you are proposing with reference to the Arthur Faber Trust Estate. Not only must I wait for the details about it, but really do not know much about the 'Scientific Press' concern myself, as I have only had scraps of conversation with you about it, and actually know nothing of its <u>financial</u> condition – But I should like now to mention a few things about my views on the subject.

(1) Your Father left me a <u>very sacred trust</u>, in leaving me all
    his money unconditionally, and his sole executor, and
    in consequence I realise <u>profoundly</u> what an immense
    responsibility rests with me in <u>all</u> matters connected with it.

(2) He (your Father) had an intense dislike to breaking a Trust and rather than do it in the case of your Uncle Brace's marriage settlement he gave up the Trusteeship – I must say I sympathise in this view.

(3) Of course there cannot be any guarantee as to the repayment of the loan from the Faber Trust Estate, in either ten years or any other length of time, as you might not live long enough to accomplish this, or things might go wrong and then – what would happen?

(4) I think £15,000 or more, far too much money to be invested in <u>one</u> concern, unless it were a <u>recognised</u> Trustee Security – It is putting all 'one's eggs into one basket' – which I have always been taught is a fatal mistake – and I have come across several instances of the folly of doing this –

(5) I could never consent to <u>Dorothy's</u> half share of the Estate being sold out, as I could not agree on <u>her</u> behalf to an increase of income at the expense of security of capital.

It would cost a great deal to sell out and arrange the matter legally – Where would this money come from? It certainly ought not to be paid for out of the Estate itself – I feel it is far better to state my objections freely <u>now</u>, and if you still wish to risk <u>your</u> share of the Estate by selling out, I shall have to consider the matter further, but it will be against my inclinations altogether – I have resisted all idea of getting any <u>immediate</u> benefit myself from the Reversion, and I cannot but regret that you do not share this view with me – I would rather be poor than touch money left in Trust, or which does not yet belong to me.

I fear this will not please you, but I must be honest and speak my mind, and I <u>do</u> feel such a great responsibility in the matter.

I hope you will be led to act <u>wisely and rightly</u>, and to do what is best for your <u>children's</u> future, as well as for your own present good.

*A long letter from Geoffrey, together with a rapid consent from Ishti, then living in rural Ireland, combined to overcome his mother's misgivings, to the extent that both she and his sister Dorothy bought small shareholdings.*

### Dorothy Faber to Geoffrey Faber, 15 February 1925

We are converted, and I feel it will be very convenient to have a millionaire brother in the future! What I really want to say is – could you get me 3 shares if I were to raise the necessary £221?

### Geoffrey Faber to Colonel Maurice, 22 February 1925

I have been very hard put to it to obtain guarantors for an offer to purchase the 476 shares which you and Mrs Maurice are prepared to sell. I have, however, at last succeeded in getting authority to make you and Mrs Maurice an offer of £30,000 (Thirty thousand pounds) for the whole of the 476 shares. The transaction to be completed immediately (i.e. before March 25) and the purchasers to take all future dividends and bonuses.

*This offer was accepted. The necessary changes to the Arthur Faber Trust were handled by Florence's brother, Brace Colt, a solicitor.*

### Brace Colt to Geoffrey Faber, 2 March 1925

I must admit, as I have already verbally told you, that I am not very keen on the proposition at all, as it seems to me that you are taking a tremendous risk and so is the life tenant and also your mother, but I do not see how you can get out of it now, as you have definitely promised to purchase these shares from Maurice and he could go for specific performance of the Contract which you have entered into with him.

## Geoffrey Faber to Brace Colt, 3 March 1925

Thank you for your letter. I quite appreciate the fact that I am taking a certain amount of risk but 'There comes a tide in the affairs of man which, taken at the flood, leads on to fortune,' and I am convinced that this is an opportunity which it would be both cowardly and foolish to neglect.

## Ishti Faber to Brace Colt, 21 March 1925

The whole thing has been done rather hurriedly. I did not realise before that we were breaking the Trust. However, I rely on you and Geoffrey to do all that can be done to make things quite safe and as far as I can judge by the terms of the Deed you have done so. Therefore I do not think it necessary to employ further legal opinion. I am a day's journey from the nearest Solicitor so am unable to ask his opinion concerning the matter. I am sure everything is all right and agree to the loan made on the security set out in Deed.

*In a brief memoir Geoffrey wrote of his childhood he acknowledged Ishti's 'generous attitude'. It had enabled him to make his great gamble, buying £15,000 in shares, essentially with other people's money (although he paid a reasonable rate of interest on the loan). Apart from his mother and sister, the other purchasers included his friend Stanley Robinson (a distinguished numismatist) and Maurice Gwyer. Since his wife Alsina still held the largest shareholding, this meant the Gwyers now owned a majority of the shares with an implied right to veto policy and replace directors. Any problems that might cause were, however, in the future.*

*In the meantime, Geoffrey was making advances on a number of fronts. While holidaying at Eastbourne, where Enid was recovering after Richard's birth, Geoffrey had visited the public*

*library and worked out from the 1911 census that there were*
*probably 150,000 nannies in the UK. He at once wrote to Gwyer*
*about the possibility of a paper for them.*

## Geoffrey Faber to Maurice Gwyer, 1 January 1925

I think that it would be a mistake to try and lure in the nursing mother, or the nursery governess. If the paper is good enough, we can hope for a certain circulation amongst these. But that should come unsolicited; the <u>children's nurse,</u> whether institution trained or nursery trained, is the person the paper must definitely set out to please and serve. That provides the paper with a clear and definite policy from the outset, namely to raise the status and encourage the professional sense of children's nurses, provided that nothing is done or said to disturb the equanimity of mistresses.

*Gwyer's response was lukewarm, but a paper for children's nurses*
*was only one scheme. At another end of the publishing spectrum,*
*Geoffrey was starting to think more about the books the new firm*
*might publish, and still hoping to find a place for T. S. Eliot and*
*the literary periodical he already edited, the* Criterion.

## Geoffrey Faber to T. S. Eliot, 9 March 1925

The Publisher must be much more of an opportunist than the Editor, at any rate to begin with. In order to get going at all one may have to publish books which one would send elsewhere later on. At any rate I do set this standard that whatever we publish shall have some virtue in it, even though it may not be of the very first order. My tentative suggestion that, if we entered into an alliance for the publication of a quarterly magazine or review, you might join as a Director, would go a long way towards establishing the kind of organic connection between the paper and the books which I should hope to see grow up. [. . .]

One thing more before I close. I want to say again, as I have said once or twice already, that once the thing is launched I should withhold criticism unless it was asked for, and put full confidence in you. The man who is actually steering the ship has to take into account all sorts of things which the passengers know nothing about; but this being so I feel it to be essential that we should thoroughly under-stand what is at the back of each other's mind before we commit our-selves to the general undertaking; hence the length and, I am afraid, obscurity of this letter.

> *At this point the Scientific Press was based in Southampton Street, just off the Strand, where it also operated a bookshop, but the kind of expansion that Geoffrey planned would require larger premises.*

## Geoffrey Faber to J. J. Done,[1] 25 March 1925

The position of Russell Square is excellent, both from the general publishing, and from the Nurses' Bookshop point of view. It is easy to get at for the collectors from the big bookshops, and wholesalers, and there is a tendency on the part of publishing firms to move in that direction. It is more or less ringed with hospitals.

> *Geoffrey chose Bloomsbury not just for its literary connections, but also because it was convenient for the nurses who were the main customers of the Scientific Press.*

---

1   J. J. Done was surveyor to All Souls, and was eventually succeeded by his son. Geoffrey knew him from his own position as Estates Bursar, and came to rely on the Dones in everything to do with property in both his personal and professional life.

### Geoffrey Faber to T. S. Eliot, 6 April 1925

I am very glad to be able to tell you that at a meeting of our Board of Directors this afternoon, we decided to invite you to become the Editor of a new quarterly review, to be published by us, at a salary of £400 a year, to be reduced to £325 a year if it should be possible to offer you a seat on the Board of Directors at any time, carrying with it a remuneration of £150.

*By the end of April, Colonel Maurice had resigned his directorship and Eliot was formally appointed to the Board in his place. He might have been taken on because of the* Criterion, *but Geoffrey also included a provision in his service contract to the effect that Faber & Gwyer would publish his future books, which had previously gone to Leonard and Virginia Woolf at the Hogarth Press.*

### Geoffrey Faber to T. S. Eliot, 28 May 1925

I am very glad to have *The Waste Land*. You won't think it unkind of me to say that I am excitedly groping in it. You <u>are</u> obscure, you know! With an obscurity compared to which Meredith at his most bewildering (and he can baffle, too) is the purest ray serene. I wonder if you realize how difficult you are? And alternatively I wonder if I am specially stupid.

### Geoffrey Faber to Charles Whibley, 29 May 1925

I expect Eliot has told you about his arrangement with us; we are going to take him on as Editor of the *Criterion* or its successor, and he is also joining our Board of Directors. I want to say to you how very glad I am that you have made us acquainted. He is a most attractive fellow, and if only his health holds out I am convinced that he will make a considerable name for himself. I am running him for a research fellowship at All Souls next November, and with great difficulty got him to spend last Saturday with me at Oxford. His health really does rather alarm me; the strain of looking after his wife seems to be telling on him severely. I do hope now that he will soon be in the way of earning a reasonable income, by congenial means, that both he and she will climb rapidly out of the melancholy state they had got into.

All is going pretty well here. We are changing our name to 'Faber & Gwyer Ltd.', and are moving in September to new premises at 24 Russell Square. Rather a fine house; we have got to build up as fine a publishing business as we can to inhabit it!

*Future extracts will occasionally also mention T. S. Eliot's first wife Vivien. It was a famously unhappy marriage – certainly by this point in Eliot's life – which effectively ended with their separation in 1933, but formally continued until Vivien's early death, aged fifty-nine, in 1947.*

## Geoffrey Faber, diary entry, Sunday, 31 May 1925

I need one of my periodical moral pull-togethers. Business begins to take up too much room, and I am letting everything else slide. More method, and less indulgence; more genuine work and exercise! and more reading of decent literature.

## Geoffrey Faber to T. S. Eliot, 9 June 1925

I should certainly like to publish your poems in the Autumn, about the time when the *New Criterion* starts, and I am quite prepared to give you the terms offered by the Woolfs. I hope, however, that by complying with the conditions of our agreement you won't upset your relations with your friends. I should be very sorry to think that we had put you in such a position.

## FABER & GWYER LTD.

28-29 SOUTHAMPTON STREET
STRAND, LONDON, W.C.2.

WILL PUBLISH      DURING THE
THESE BOOKS                           AUTUMN, 1925

The Scientific Press changed its name to Faber & Gwyer on 26 June 1925, announcing its first list soon afterwards, including one book which was to set the course for the firm:

*Poems, 1909–1925*
By T. S. Eliot

Few poems have had so remarkable an effect upon their generation as *The Waste Land*. This poem, now out of print, together with many others no longer obtainable and some not previously collected, Mr. Eliot reproduces in this volume, which contains all his verse, so far published, which he wishes to preserve.

*The formation of an association of college trained nursery nurses led Geoffrey to revive the idea of a newspaper specifically aimed at nannies.*

## Geoffrey Faber to Maurice Gwyer, 15 July 1925

I enclose a memorandum on the subject of a nursery paper, which I think fully explains itself. Circumstances are without doubt forcing us to consider this question again, and to come to an early decision upon it, one way or the other.

## Alsina Gwyer to Geoffrey Faber, 17 July 1925

I am sending you this note to thank you for the memorandum received this morning and to say that could I be present at any of the discussions I should give the project my unhesitating support. I am all in favour of it now that we have a ready made public who can be reached in groups (the Colleges) as nuclei of the larger public we hope to gain.

> *Thus encouraged, Geoffrey pressed on with launching the new paper he had first suggested in January:* The Nursery World. *This would be another weekly magazine to complement* The Nursing Mirror. *He also soon had news of another recruit.*

## Geoffrey Faber to Alsina Gwyer, 30 September 1925

I have engaged Richard de la Mare, who is a son of Walter de la Mare, the poet, as an assistant to Stewart, at a commencing salary of £300 a year. [. . .]

Young de la Mare seems to have plenty of ordinary practical ability (as the sons of mystical poets very often do!) and I have every hope that he will be of great assistance to us. [. . .]

Not the least of the advantage which we may hope for from his accession to the firm is that the de la Mares have probably the largest literary acquaintanceship in England. [. . .]

As for Russell Square, things are beginning to move there at last. The steel work for the lift, which hung everything up for a long time, has been completed, and the installation of the lift itself begun. Painting too has begun and all the structural alterations of course are finished. I think we shall probably be able to move in during November.

### Geoffrey Faber to Alsina Gwyer, 9 October 1925

Eliot himself has been through a bad time, and has not yet been able to help me very much outside the *Criterion*; but he is getting together what will, I believe, prove to be an important and valuable series of monographs on Foreign writers, which we shall probably begin to publish next autumn. One or two other things are also coming to us through him – not money-makers, but reputation-makers.

### Alsina Gwyer to Geoffrey Faber, 12 October 1925

How quickly everything grows and advances – It seems almost incredible when one remembers the impasse we had reached 12 months ago – It is a source of the greatest delight and thankfulness to me. For you I hope that you will soon add to the pleasures of selection and creation, those also of fruition of all – or if not <u>all</u> at least <u>of</u> <u>most</u> – of your hopes.

### Geoffrey Faber to Alsina Gwyer, 15 October 1925

I am glad you liked the first two books of *The Modern Health Series*. There is a bad misprint in the preface which you will have discovered for yourself; it came from the substituting of the plural 'books' for the singular 'series'. You will probably by now also have got *Spain in a Two-seater*, of which I do not think the binding is very successful; but one must learn by mistakes.

Yes, the whole business is a great contrast now to what it was a year ago. I confess I have my moments of suspense about the future, but I (like you) am a gambler at heart!

### Geoffrey Faber to Alsina Gwyer, 9 November 1925

Eliot has been ordered off by his doctor to the south of France, and will not be back for about a month; I am very glad indeed that this has happened. He has been under terrible strain for a year or more through his wife's continual illness. She has now definitely gone to a nursing home, and the whole business has really been far too much for him. When he comes back I am confident that I shall get a good deal of help from him. The Eliot connection is already beginning to fructify; but more of this later. Mr de la Mare has taken to his job in a very promising way; he and Stewart hit it off together admirably.

## Geoffrey Faber to Alsina Gwyer, 18 November 1925

I am interested to hear about your opinion of the books. It is very much my own, though some people consider *A Flower in Rain*[2] better than *They Want their Wages*.[3] I fear that you will dislike *Siren*[4] very much indeed! It is an unpleasant book and told in a very modern way, but to my mind it is a remarkable book.

We are being very badly handicapped by the book-trade dispute, which has now been going on for about 3 weeks. Originally directed against Simpkins, the wholesalers, who have always under-paid their staff, it has developed into a fight between 'The Book trade Employers Federation' and 'The National Union of Printers and Paper Workers' or whatever they call themselves, over wages to be paid to packers and porters. [. . .]

The result is that practically all the publishers are now depending for sales on retail orders. The position is further complicated by the fact that there is a partial sympathetic strike of binders, and three or four of our books are consequently held up indefinitely, including

---

2  *A Flower in the Rain* was a novel by Lionel G. Short; according to the catalogue, 'A study of the industrial forces at conflict in our modern civilization, with a love story closely interwoven'.
3  *They Want their Wages*, a novel by Harry Colindale, was 'A moving story, told with an effortless distinction of style'.
4  *Siren*, a novel by C. Kay Scott: 'Its theme is the fate of a woman who took the world for her lover, Belle Harris, who was perhaps half-animal, half-saint, perhaps both in one person.'

my own book *Elnovia*. I am afraid it is almost inevitable that we shall drop money over our Autumn book-publishing list, but one must hope for the best and chance it.

> *One of the perks of having his own publishing company was that Geoffrey could publish his own books. In the case of Elnovia, however, he agreed to make good any losses, a promise he would come to regret.*

> *By early December Alsina Gwyer was in Italy. She was meant to be convalescing from some unspecified condition, but instead suffered a relapse that meant her husband rushed out to join her.*

### Geoffrey Faber to Alsina Gwyer, 3 December 1925

We think that we have started off very successfully with *The Nursery World*. We printed 32,000 copies of the first number, and have had a repeat order from Smiths which we are just about able to meet, so we are sold out. Of course the test will not really come till January, but the beginning is very promising. [. . .]

Everybody here is anxious to have more and better news of you.

### Maurice Gwyer to Geoffrey Faber, 7 December 1925

The news is better to-day. My wife has had a very good night and is decidedly stronger, tho still very, very weak. [. . .]

She asks me to tell you that she dislikes Elliott's poems very much, but that per contra she has a high opinion of *Siren*! *Minims*[5] has intrigued us all.

> *It took Maurice Gwyer a long time to learn how to spell 'Eliot'.*

---

5 *Minims* by Edmond X. Kapp; according to the catalogue, 'In this little book, which is bound in the brightest paper wrapper, Mr. Kapp, the eminent artist, has given rein to his imagination.'

# Vigorous Advertising Campaign

in leading Periodicals and Newspapers will create great demand for this

# NEW WEEKLY

On Sale December 2nd

THE

# NURSERY WORLD

FOR MOTHERS AND NURSES.

## CONTENTS OF FIRST ISSUE

1. *NURSERY TRAINING FOR SCHOOL-ROOM DAYS* By Viscountess Erleigh
2. *ABOUT NURSERY NURSES* By the Hon. Mrs. St. Aubyn
3. *THE "ANGEL CHILD"* By Dr. E. Sloan Chesser
4. *THAT MONTH OLD BABY* By Ethel A. Moon
5. *THE UNEXPECTED ADVENTURE* A New Serial by Philippa Preston
6. *AN ARTICLE By Dr. Kenneth Dickson*
7. *AN ILLUSTRATED ARTICLE ON MR. A. A. MILNE'S NURSERIES*

A CHILDREN'S SUPPLEMENT

And Articles on Nursery Furniture; Needle-work; What the Shops have to offer; Book Reviews; Fashions for Children and Cookery; Etc., Etc.

The Newsagent who thinks there are already enough weekly journals will admit at once that there is room for "The Nursery World." It is entirely different from any other journal It deals with the most important phase of home life, viz., the care of the children. It is brightly written, authoritative, and contains just the information that mothers and nurses need. A vigorous advertising campaign has been arranged for the eve of the publication of the first issue. In anticipation of a big demand Agents are asked to place their orders at once, so as to facilitate printing arrangements and prevent disappointment and loss of sales.

**2 D.**

EVERY WEDNESDAY

PUBLISHED BY

FABER and GWYER Ltd.
28, Southampton Street, Strand,
LONDON.

*Proprietors of "The Nursing Mirror."*

Geoffrey's first great entrepreneurial endeavour,
advertised in *The Nursing Mirror*.

## Geoffrey Faber to Maurice Gwyer, 8 December 1925

I am very much interested by her judgement of *Siren*. It has had a considerable slating in most of the few reviews which have already appeared, as you might expect; but the favourable note has not been absent and some interest does seem to be taken in the book. As for Eliot's poems I don't like them myself, and I don't think Eliot does either, but they are a genuine and not an imitation product.

Trade orders for *The Nursery World* have a little increased, and we are printing 32,000 again, the same number as the first week. Advertisements have been difficult to get for the second number, but we shall do all right in that line after Christmas.

## Geoffrey Faber to Alsina Gwyer, 28 December 1925

About the books. Reviewing our experience so far I have come to the conclusion that our sales arrangements are inadequate, and that what we have got to do is to get in from outside a man to act as Sales Manager; i.e. to run the travellers,[6] the circularisation of booksellers and of private persons, and generally to concentrate all the year round on marketing the books as well as the papers. The production side seems to me to be good and we are getting a lot of very interesting material; but we lack the professional touch in our relations with the trade, and I cannot see any other way of supplying it. Of course all our books came out much too late. Reviews are now coming along well, and most of them are very good indeed, but they were too late to affect Christmas sales, which have been undoubtedly very disappointing. It has, I believe, been a very disappointing season for publishers generally, partly on account of the strike, which is still wandering on, and partly because, for some reason or other, people are not spending money on books. I am, on the whole, very well satisfied with our start.

---

6  Nowadays the 'travellers' are called 'sales representatives' or just 'reps': the sales staff who travel around the bookshops selling books and taking orders.

I think we have made a good showing, and have laid the foundations well for the future, though I think that we shall have to write down our stock as low as we can afford to.

Another thing which I propose to do if I can possibly find time in the early part of the year is to visit the principal centres in the country, and call on the chief booksellers, simply introducing myself and having a general conversation about books and about the firm. The personal touch!

*A. J. B. Paterson was appointed as Faber and Gwyer's first sales manager soon afterwards, remaining until 1933.*

## Alsina Gwyer to Geoffrey Faber, 28 December 1925

Will you forgive me if as a 'constant reader' of *The Nursery World* I write once again to tell you how very uneasy I feel about it? It is so very thin and vague that I cannot imagine that if it continues on its present lines that it will ever be able to keep the circulation with which it started, much less to increase it. There is a lack of purpose about it, and no sign is given that it is directed by one who has any knowledge or love of children or real understanding of their needs. Also it is so snobbish. What does it matter whether Lady somebody has blue or pink or green or red in her nursery unless we are told the theory of the effect of colours upon nerves and the reasons why one is preferable to another? [...]

You have conclusively proved, contrary to my husband's expectation, that there is a large and eager public waiting for a paper of this kind. We do want to supply it with the very best – a paper on which to rely – such as *The Nursing Mirror* becomes increasingly to nurses under Mrs Colmer's[7] most able guidance.

---

7  Mrs Colmer was editor of *The Nursing Mirror*.

Faber & Gwyer moved into 24 Russell Square on 29 December 1925.
The position of its entrance – on the side and therefore outside the
square – was crucial: the landlord, the Bedford Estate, would not allow
trade to be conducted within the square.

*At the end of 1925, a young American author sent T. S. Eliot a*
*copy of his third novel, inscribed to 'T S Elliot / Greatest of our*
*living poets'. Eliot's response, from Faber & Gwyer, shows that*
*his instincts as a publisher were already well developed.*

## T. S. Eliot to F. Scott Fitzgerald, 31 December 1925

*The Great Gatsby* with your charming and overpowering inscription arrived the very morning that I was leaving in some haste for
a sea voyage advised by my doctor. I therefore left it behind and
only read it on my return a few days ago. I have, however, now
read it three times. I am not in the least influenced by your remark

about myself when I say that it has interested and excited me more than any new novel I have seen, either English or American, for a number of years. [. . .]

I have recently become associated in the capacity of a director with the publishing firm whose name you see above. May I ask you, if you have not already committed yourself to publish *The Great Gatsby* with some other publishing house in London, to let us take the matter up with you? I think that if we published the book we could do as well by you as anyone.

*Sadly, Fitzgerald had to reply that the book was already committed to Chatto and Windus.*

## Geoffrey Faber, diary entry, Thursday, 4 February 1926

Went with Enid to tea with the Eliots – Edith Sitwell, a satisfying person in a dark cloak with bright coloured collar-flap and cuffs, and a great long nose. She talked of her hatred of suffering, and of herself as 'useless'. Mrs. Patmore. Ramon Fernandez. A rather 'choked' little party.

## Maurice Gwyer to Geoffrey Faber, 15 February 1926

I have obtained some interesting information with regard to the *Woman's Pictorial* which I pass on to you, because it has perhaps a bearing on some of the criticism which I have heard made upon *The Nursery World*. [. . .]

It is a whole-hearted advocate of the Truby-King principle of dieting and all the answers to questions are prepared by Truby-King experts; and it is this which gives them their value & makes them so eagerly sought after. I don't wish to argue from this that the 'N.W.' should necessarily become an advocate of the same system itself, though I am myself a whole-hearted supporter of it and have no doubt at all that its general adoption would do more than anything else to reduce infant mortality in this country, as it has done in New Zealand; but I want to point it out as an example of the enormous advantage to a paper of standing for something <u>definite</u> (provided of course that it is something good).

### Geoffrey Faber to Maurice Gwyer, 17 February 1926

I don't pretend to be an authority on children's diet myself; but I understand that one of the essential features of the Truby King Method is that they do not permit the mixture of milk and water. A large number of people, including many doctors, entirely disagree with this. [...]

Now in my view it is much better for a paper like *The Nursery World* not to stand for a single more or less rigid scientific method, which can only be satisfactorily applied in hospitals and homes with well-equipped nurseries. It ought to stand for sound common-sense; but the sound common-sense must, of course, include all recognised advances in method, which are universally agreed to be good, and which are easily followed in ordinary and in poorer households.

### Maurice Gwyer to Geoffrey Faber, 18 February 1926

Where have you got your information from about Truby King and his methods?

### Geoffrey Faber to Maurice Gwyer, 19 February 1926

First of all let me repeat that my own knowledge of the matter if not quite nil is at any rate very small; all that I said came not at all from Mrs Edwards[8] but from my wife. It would appear either that she has

---

8  Mrs Edwards was the founding editor of *The Nursery World,* although she was soon to lose that position, as Mrs Colmer took over the editorship of both *The Nursing Mirror* and *The Nursery World.*

got hold of the wrong end of the stick (which knowing her I think very unlikely) or that I have.

## Maurice Gwyer to Geoffrey Faber, 2 March 1926

We seem by the way rather to have got off the subject of *The Nursery World* and embarked on a Truby King discussion; but you are right in thinking that I am full of zeal for the method and that must be my excuse.

## Geoffrey Faber to Maurice Gwyer, 3 March 1926

I want the Truby-King method to be fully described in *The Nursery World* whether by a series of articles or in whatever way. But in the meantime what I feel is that *The Nursery World* ought to stand for all forms of common-sense in the nursery, and not for one form above all others. [...]

I will frankly admit that my main object with *The Nursery World* is a commercial one. I want to bring into being a profit-earning paper, not for the purpose of increasing our dividends so much as for the purpose of enabling us to spend more money on extending the business. But of course I don't want the paper to be a bad or useless paper. Mrs Gwyer has a nobler object. She wants a paper as good as it can be made, without reference to the state of the public tastes.

*If that seems rather a lot of space to give to the discussion of an obscure and obsolete feeding system, all I can say is that the actual correspondence is a great deal longer. I just can't resist the thought of these two Fellows of All Souls expending so much energy on the subject. Meanwhile, a more serious threat to the business was raising its head: the General Strike.*

### Geoffrey Faber to Maurice Gwyer, 4 May 1926

You will of course realise that if the strike continues for more than a week or two the business outlook will be very grave indeed. It is not merely that we shall all the time be losing the revenue of *The Nursing Mirror*, but also that when it is over it will probably be found to have dried up to a very large extent the purchasing power of the country. Even a slippage of a week or two is bound to have a very unfavourable effect upon our half-year's Profit and Loss Account. Under these circumstances I profoundly hope that you will be able to face with comparative equanimity the serious curtailment and possibly even the complete suspension of the Interim Dividend in August. If matters come to this pass I shall do what I can myself to lighten the outgoings of the business, by resigning or postponing a part of my salary; and I have already warned the senior members of staff that we may be forced to make an all-round reduction in salaries and wages. [. . .]

It is the unkindest stroke of fate that our first and our second publishing seasons should be wrecked by industrial strife. There is one bright spot. If the strike doesn't last too long we shall probably have the rest of the summer clear for those of our books which are still unpublished, and it is quite possible we might do very well out of them. Most of the publishers have now finished the publication of their spring lists, and have no summer campaign before them. Cape is one exception, and we are another.

### Geoffrey Faber to Maurice Gwyer, 13 May 1926

Here we are not yet fully out of the wood. There is deadlock between the Master Printers and the Unions; the former saying that they can only take men on as they find room for them, and the latter saying that they will not come back if they cannot do so as a body. I hope to goodness this matter will be settled at once. [. . .]

We are not attempting to publish either *The Nursing Mirror* or *The Nursery World* this week, but we hope to make up lost time next week.

*Geoffrey put a great deal of effort into his attempt to have T. S. Eliot elected as a Fellow of All Souls. He had some support from other Fellows – one went so far as to remove* The Waste Land *from the Common Room, as he thought it might spoil Eliot's chances.*

## Geoffrey Faber, diary entry, Monday, 24 May 1926

A dreadfully long meeting. Eliot not elected. He only got 14 out of 35 votes. A very hard disappointment; unforgivable attacks by Lucas, Adams and Macgregor on his poetry as obscene and blasphemous!!

## Geoffrey Faber to T. S. Eliot, 'Whit Monday', 24 May 1926

I grieve to say that you have not been elected, and it is small consolation that none of your 3 rivals were elected either. The College was evenly divided, and the 2/3 majority necessary was not to be obtained. But I should like you to know that you had very warm support from the more enlightened half of the College, including the Warden. What did you in was alas! your Poems, which had shocked some professional old women; there was also the narrow angular opposition of the academic historians to any kind of research other than that which they themselves understand.

## Geoffrey Faber, diary entry, Monday, 26 July 1926

The position is a somewhat anxious one, and I find it hard to justify my buoyant self-confidence of last year. If this proves another failure I shall not again try to take on a big responsible job, for it will have proved me deficient in the qualities necessary for commercial success. Meantime I hope that is not so. Much hangs on the Coal Strike – and that is not in my control; but I ought, I think, to have foreseen trouble and gone more cautiously.

## Maurice Gwyer to Geoffrey Faber, 28 July 1926

Did I tell you that I saw Milford[9] the other day? He informed me that according to the gossip of the publishing world Faber and Gwyer are being financed by Elliot who, being a banker, is supposed to have large sums of money at his command. This will entertain both you and him.

## Geoffrey Faber to Maurice Gwyer, 29 July 1926

Milford's information about Eliot has given both him and me a good deal of amusement!

*There were to be few other opportunities for light relief in Geoffrey's correspondence with the Gwyers.*

## Geoffrey Faber to Maurice Gwyer, 3 August 1926

I am sorry you are disturbed by the half-year's Accounts. I agree that the loss on *The Nursery World* is a very big drain and that we cannot contemplate continuing it at that rate for very much longer. [. . .]

The Directors very carefully considered the position at the June Board Meeting. They were all of the opinion that we must certainly carry on at any rate until October, when it ought to begin to be possible to judge more accurately the future. I should think it myself a deplorable thing to have to give up the paper, and I should personally be prepared to make a further sacrifice of dividend in order to avoid that.

---

9  Humphrey Milford became head of Oxford University Press in 1913, and oversaw Geoffrey's introduction to publishing before the war.

*Given that Geoffrey depended on the dividend to pay the
interest on his loan from the Arthur Faber Estate, this is quite a
striking statement. A few weeks later, he found himself dealing
with a thorny managerial issue when he heard from A. J. B.
Paterson, his newly appointed Sales Manager, that a longstanding Scientific Press employee, H. E. Smithers, was causing
problems. He asked Paterson to make a formal statement.*

## Statement made by A. J. B. Paterson, 27 September 1926

I declare that the following statement is in every way correct.

That Mr Smithers [. . .] led me to deduce that Mrs Gwyer, being
jealous of Mr Smithers's friendship with the (then) Managing
Director, made arrangements whereby he (The Managing Director) was dismissed. Mr Faber was then appointed to the vacant position – this fact leading to Mr Smithers expressing the opinion that
'Mrs Gwyer was a bloody ass', and that she was swayed by the
charm of Mr Faber's manner. In addition he stated that Mrs Gwyer
'possessed no mental stability and no discernment, otherwise she
would not have made such a decision'. He contributed further
information that 'Mr Faber has no business brain, his only ability
being the preparation of statements and figures which were of no
use to anyone. In fact he is quite incapable of successfully running
a publishing business.' While pursuing his remarks in this direction, he mentioned that 'The Woman (Mrs Gwyer) was a bloody
fool' to have thrown away a perfectly good nest-egg for the whim
of a man whose only claim towards acumen was being a 'Fellow of
All Souls'.

## Geoffrey Faber to H. E. Smithers, 7 October 1926

I am desired by the Board to inform you that on behalf of the Company it has decided to dispense with your services as Advertising

Manager forthwith and that your employment as such under your agreement of July 16th 1924 is determined as from to-day's date.

*About a year later, after protracted legal proceedings, Smithers received compensation of £725 for loss of office.*

T. S. Eliot posing outside the Russell Square offices of Faber & Gwyer, 'in the way of earning a reasonable income, by congenial means'.

*The whole Smithers affair and the time it took up convinced Geoffrey that he needed more senior help running the books business. So only a few days later, he produced a memorandum making two key recommendations: that all books should be*

*taken on by a committee, not just himself alone, and that both*
*Charles Stewart and Richard de la Mare should be promoted to*
*the Board.*

## Geoffrey Faber, Memorandum, 12 October 1926

Obviously the Book Committee must include the management, as
well as the directorate. In my opinion it should consist of

a) All directors able and willing to attend it
b) The Manager (Stewart), the Production Manager (de la Mare),
   and the Sales Manager (Paterson), whether as full members of
   the Committee or in an advisory capacity only.

It must, of course, be under the Presidency of the Chairman of the
Company, or, in his absence, a Director.

The decision of the Committee should be authoritative and final
except that the Chairman of the Company should, I think, retain
the power of cancelling the decision of the Committee on his own
responsibility. I believe in the maxim that 'two heads are better than
one', but I also believe that no business ought to be under divided
control, and that the Head of a business must always have it in his
power to take what he believes to be the right decision, even against
his advisers. [ . . .]

Of the proposed new directors I have the following remarks to make:

Stewart is not brilliant, but he is very sound . . . While he will never
set the Thames on fire, he is an equably-minded competent all-round
man, who may be trusted to give his best to the business, and to keep
it going in fair weather and foul, without losing his head. I think he
deserves the encouragement which a directorship would give him,
and that it would increase his sense of responsibility and usefulness.
We must always look elsewhere for the touch of genius, which a
successful publishing business must have in it somewhere; but we

should not get that with the all-round steadiness which is equally wanted.

De la Mare is also very sound, and a very hard worker. He has brilliance, but his interests are more specialised than Stewart's. His real flair is for book-production; good judges think him in the first rank. His ability here is a great asset to us. He has also, I think, more subtlety of judgment than Stewart. I believe that he has that touch of genius which we want. Hitherto he has not had very much scope for the initiation of books. A directorship would give him great gratification, and help to enlist his interests and those of his family definitely on our side.

> *The Board of Faber & Gwyer now consisted of Geoffrey Faber, T. S. Eliot (still mainly focused on the* Criterion), *Charles Stewart and Richard de la Mare (known as Dick) as executive directors. There were two non-executives: T. M. Taylor (who resigned, to Geoffrey's regret, in 1927) and Alsina Gwyer (who therefore attended the Book Committee, when able). Maurice Gwyer owned a similar shareholding to his wife, but chose not to sit on the Board.*

### Geoffrey Faber, diary entry, Thursday, 4 November 1926

Book Committee – first meeting, over 4 hours.

### Maurice Gwyer to Geoffrey Faber, 8 November 1926

I am not clear whether the document headed 'draft minutes' represents a resolution already passed, but in any case the proposals it contains I could never agree to, any more than you would yourself if you were in my place. [. . .]

It is proposed to give to the new directors the right to call for the issue to them of a further 100 ordinary shares. This would mean that the control of the ordinary shares would at once pass from the hands of my wife and myself; and I do not need to point out to you the value of that control in certain contingencies (e.g. if anything happened to yourself). Indeed it seems to me so vital that I should feel bound to take any steps open to me to preserve it.

Richard de la Mare, the newly appointed director,
'seems to have plenty of ordinary practical ability (as the sons of
mystical poets very often do!)'.

*Maurice Gwyer had his way; the new directors were not given the right to acquire shares. This is probably the point at which Geoffrey ceased to enjoy the unquestioned backing of at least one of his shareholders. The relationship between 'Faber' and 'Gwyer' began to break down.*

## Geoffrey Faber, diary entry, Friday, 7 January 1927

Things are now looking at their most difficult for me: here are my troubles – most of my own making. (1) Myself! (2) *The Nursery World* (3) The Books (4) The coming accounts and future dividends (5) *The New Criterion* and Eliot (6) paying for Thomas, *Elnovia*, & Hadfield,[10] and learning to spend less and use my time better! May God help me to win through, for all our sakes: as I trust, with such help, I shall.

## T. S. Eliot to his cousin, Marguerite Caetani, 18 January 1927

Very many thanks for your New Year's letter and every good wish for you and the health of your family for another year. I delayed answering it until I could produce the necessary proof of my existence which is the complete translation of *Anabase* enclosed herewith. I have sent another copy to Léger together with thirty or forty notes of passages on which I want his opinion, and if, as I expect, I have no reply from him within two or three months I shall ask you to use strong pressure. I should like to get the book out in March or April but that will not be possible without his collaboration.

*The writer referred to in this letter, the French diplomat Alexis St-Léger Léger (pen name St-John Perse), would win Faber's second Nobel Prize in Literature in 1960 for his poetry.*

---

10 'Thomas' was the putative name for the third child Geoffrey and Enid were expecting in April. James Hadfield was taking Geoffrey through a long and expensive programme of psychotherapy.

## Maurice Gwyer to Geoffrey Faber, 12 April 1927

I have never concealed my opinion that the starting of *The Nursery World* in 1925 was precipitate and unwise. At any rate, if my opinion had been asked at the time, it would have been wholly adverse. Nothing that has happened since has caused me to change it.

## Geoffrey Faber to Maurice Gwyer, 13 April 1927

I appreciate your restrained, though firm, statement of your views about *The Nursery World*. Your letter will be read to the Directors at tomorrow's meeting

You will believe me when I say that I am doing my utmost to view the question impartially – and not to cling to *The Nursery World* merely because I am responsible for it, and therefore reluctant to drop it. If we should decide not to go on with it, it will be because the reasons for doing so appear to the Directors and to myself to be conclusive. [. . .]

My own advice tomorrow will be to continue up to the end of May, and if the results then obtained seem to warrant it, up to the end of June or July.

## T. S. Eliot to Geoffrey Faber, 14 April 1927

I believe in *The [Nursery] World* so long as it does not damage the facade of Faber & Gwyer. If the facade is too wide, that cannot be helped now, but it is partly my fault. The same problem, on a smaller scale, is the problem of the *Criterion*. I believe in it, in the long run; the question is, whether Faber & Gwyer can <u>afford</u> to give it a long run. And the Faber & Gwyer books too are merely a question of the long run; with a few blunders – not more than any publishers make – the list seems to me extremely well chosen; it is no fault of judgment, but wholly adverse and unpredictable circumstances, if they have not done better.

Enid Faber with the three children, Ann, Dick and baby Tom.

I imagine that you are under considerable strain for private reasons. But that, I hope and believe, will soon be happily ended; and a strain that ends is preferable to one in which no end can be seen. My sympathy to you and your wife.

> *After a very difficult (and expensive) labour, Thomas Faber (my father) was born on 25 April 1927.*

### Geoffrey Faber, diary entry, Wednesday, 4 May 1927

Dined, as Eliot's guest, at the Commercio restaurant in Frith Street, and we went on to the Albert Hall, where as Lady Rothermere's[11] guests we sat in a Grand Tier box and watched boxing. Amazing sight – crowd, lighting, organ, and the supple bodies of the boxers. Teddy Baldock beating Bell.

---

11  Lady Rothermere had been providing the *Criterion* with financial backing.

## Geoffrey Faber to Maurice Gwyer, 5 May 1927

Of the future of the book-publishing I have no doubt at all; though I do not expect (unless we have a 'winner' or two) to show profits as yet. Nor are the profits ever likely to compare with those derived from the *Mirror*. [. . .]

These figures are enough to show that – apart from *The Nursery World* – the business is in a perfectly satisfactory condition. We come now to that paper, and to the problems which it presents.

The position now is this. We have launched a circulation campaign covering the richest fields in the North and the Midlands, to be continued during May and June, with a less expensive 'fetch-up' round the sea-side in July and August. We have also embarked on a new 'editorial' policy – new cover, larger paper, free postage once a month. And we are driving as hard as we can go at the advertisers.

Now either these efforts are going to succeed, or fail. We provide ourselves with several possible halting-places. The first at the end of May. By that time we should be able to know pretty well how the circulation campaign is going, and what the advertisers' reaction to the new paper is. (Incidentally, we cannot expect a big increase in the advertising during May itself.) If things are obviously going badly we shall shut down all extra expenditure, call off the campaign, and try to sell the paper. [. . .]

I do not expect you to look upon this proposal with enthusiasm. But I do nevertheless most earnestly ask you to assent to it, with a full sense of my responsibility in doing so. Looking first at the <u>worst</u> that can happen. Suppose we spend up to the limit of our capacity in *The Nursery World*, and then have to close the paper without being able to sell it. We shall still be solvent – still able to pay our dividends, and find enough for the books, and have money over. I am not therefore proposing to run an unwarrantable risk.

### Geoffrey Faber to Maurice Gwyer, 5 May 1927

The first branch reports from Liverpool are very encouraging: the trade reception is described as 'remarkable', and a certain increased sale in that district of 1,000 copies next week is said to be assured. I am in the meantime taking steps to have the present market value of the paper estimated; and I hope to be in a position by next Tuesday to have two independent opinions of the price we could get for it. I am more and more certain that it would be a mistake of the first magnitude to give it up now, for lack of the courage to face a risk, which we can safely shoulder.

### Maurice Gwyer to Geoffrey Faber, 6 May 1927

I have read your letters very carefully and, so far from relieving my mind, they show that the financial position is worse than I had supposed. The essential profit making capacity of the Company is, of course, not permanently impaired, though it may easily become so unless steps are taken to liquidate the present position. But that its financial position is nothing like so sound as it was two years ago seems to me not open to doubt.

### Maurice Gwyer to Geoffrey Faber, 9 May 1927

It seems to me therefore that ever since February there has really been no policy at all except one of the kind which used to find favour with Mr Micawber.[12]

### Geoffrey Faber to Maurice Gwyer, May 1927

You choose your language with your usual care; but that you have lost your confidence in me, and in the Board, is something that the choice of words cannot cancel.

---

12  Charles Dickens, *David Copperfield*, 'something will turn up'.

I am quite clear that the policy I wish to follow is the right one, and if I am forced by the circumstances to accept your own fiat it is not a happy position for either of us.

In this unfortunate situation it is clear that no satisfactory solution can be found, except a separation of interests. A direct conflict of opinion on a matter of policy is bad enough; the lack of confidence which it brings in its train is worse. It would be better if either you or I disposed of our interest in the business. I venture, therefore, to ask you if you would be prepared to sell your ordinary shares, and if so what is the lowest price you would be willing to accept.

### Alsina Gwyer to Geoffrey Faber, 10 May 1927

Surely you are joking. Your suggestion seems too fantastic to be taken seriously. I can only think that you wrote hurriedly without having the full facts of the situation in mind.

> *This is part of a very short note to Geoffrey. I have assumed it is a response to Geoffrey's proposal that he should buy out the Gwyers and if so I can understand Mrs Gwyer's incredulity, given that she and her husband each held more shares than Geoffrey. At around the same time, she withdrew her support for* The Nursery World; *with a majority of the shareholders now against the venture, Faber & Gwyer had to cease publication.*

### Geoffrey Faber to Alsina Gwyer, 14 May 1927

I have given notice to the editorial staff; we have called off the circulation campaign, and are shutting down all avoidable expenditure; and, miracles excepted, the last issue of *The Nursery World* will be that of May 25. [. . .]

We drop the paper at the moment when its prospects are brighter than they have ever been. The first two weeks of the circulation campaign have put at least 2,000 on to the net circulation; and on the advertisement side, contracts have just, for the first time, been secured with Almata, Glaxo and Nestle – while the whole advertisement 'atmosphere' has undergone a complete change. To abandon it at this juncture, when there is a perfectly sound method of financing it, without any risk the business could not shoulder, is and will always be to me the most disheartening experience of my life.

## Alsina Gwyer to Geoffrey Faber, 16 May 1927

Are you the only one who has cause to feel hurt? How far you have travelled since the day when you hoped that our son might carry on the name when we were gone.

*Later in life, Geoffrey would certainly show his belief in the hereditary principle.*

## Geoffrey Faber, diary entry, Wednesday, 18 May 1927

In all this period, I feel life is not worth living: the business seems to present insuperable obstacles – anxieties become acute – the burden is too great to be carried much longer.

*Some respite was to come the next day, with an offer to buy* The Nursery World.

## Sir Ernest Benn, Managing Director of the publishers Benn Brothers, to Geoffrey Faber, 19 May 1927

I am up against a very old problem with me in *The Nursery World*. I have never been able to value a loss, or to see how a goodwill value could attach to a losing proposition. [...]

The only suggestion that I can make to you therefore is that we take the paper over on an agreement to pay to you for ten years a royalty of one farthing a copy on all sales over 10,000 an issue, and a commission of five percent upon all advertising revenues in excess of £50 a week.

*Geoffrey accepted the offer a week later, putting in a word for Elizabeth Fleur, up to then Assistant Editor, to stay on as Editor (Mrs Colmer remained with* The Nursing Mirror*). In the meantime, he had received an explanatory letter from Alsina Gwyer showing a level of self-awareness that I suspect Geoffrey did not appreciate.*

## Alsina Gwyer to Geoffrey Faber, 22 May 1927

Certain aspects of the present position have been gradually forcing themselves to the front of my mind and this morning I have awaked with the feeling that if there is to be any future association between us (or even if there is not) I must now set them forth plainly.

Financially my husband and I are equally involved but morally my responsibility is not only greater than his but utterly different in kind and it is because of my sense of my trustee-ship to my Father's work and memory that I now write.

Since his death in 1920 the business has been to me a living thing – almost another younger child – certainly an entity – whose interests have been committed to my care – Of course I have never been under the illusion that I possessed the experience or knowledge to guide its destinies myself, but few parents find themselves qualified personally to educate their children.

### Geoffrey Faber to Sir Ernest Benn, 31 May 1927

I am very glad you are taking on Miss Fleur and giving her a chance. She is, as I expect you saw, perhaps a little too conscious of being defenceless in a wicked world. But she is a really hard worker, and capable.

> *Geoffrey's first piece of entrepreneurship had ended in failure. I can understand the Gwyers' unwillingness to sink more money into a speculative venture, but I do feel bound to record, on my grandfather's behalf, that* The Nursery World *was soon profitable and is still being published (nowadays as* Nursery World*).*

### Geoffrey Faber, diary entry, Monday 18 July 1927

Back to lunch for christening. Eliot came up afterwards, and Thomas Erle was duly baptized by the Vicar Carnegie, in the Parish Church, present godfather T. S. Eliot and godmother Frances Duke, the other godfather Eric Beckett being in Geneva.

### Richard de la Mare to Geoffrey Faber, 24 August 1927

My dear Faber
(May I be so bold as to drop the 'Mr'?)

> *I rather like the happy juxtaposition which shows the different ways in which Geoffrey's relationships with his two co-directors were gradually deepening (he would eventually become godfather to Dick's son Giles).*
>
> *Dick de la Mare's confidence as a publisher was growing. That autumn he oversaw the publication of* The Ariel Poems *series. The initial list of eight poets included Thomas Hardy and Siegfried Sassoon, as well as, perhaps more obviously, T. S. Eliot and Dick's father Walter de la Mare.*

MESSRS FABER & GWYER'S AUTUMN
ANNOUNCEMENTS 1927

*The Ariel Poems*
This series of little booklets consists of single previously unpublished
poems each suitably decorated in colours and dressed in the gayest wrappers. It has been designed to take the place of Christmas cards and other
similar tokens that one sends for remembrance sake at certain seasons of
the year.

## T. S. Eliot to W. H. Auden, 9 September 1927

I must apologise for having kept your poems such a long time, but
I am very slow to make up my mind. I do not feel that any of the
enclosed is quite right, but I should be very interested to follow
your work. I am afraid that I am much too busy to give you any
detailed criticism that would do the poems justice, and I suggest that
whenever you happen to be in London you might let me know and I
should be very glad if you cared to come to see me.

> *This was, of course, only a temporary rejection and Auden was
> not disheartened by it, writing to Christopher Isherwood, 'On
> the whole coming from Eliot's reserve I think it is really quite
> complimentary.'*

## Geoffrey Faber, diary entry, Tuesday, 27 September 1927

Took Eliot to lunch at club. Heard much about his wife, who is now
in a sanatorium in Paris. Eliot said 'For a long time it has been just as
much as I could do to keep going. I'm like a man who can just keep
his head above the water by treading water but can't begin to think of
swimming.' Had Turkish Bath in evening: and got home after dinner.

> *Geoffrey liked his Turkish baths, and would take them two or
> three times a week.*

*Having forced Geoffrey to sell* The Nursery World, *the Gwyers now started to question the book-publishing business. In December 1927 Geoffrey produced a memorandum on the subject, suggesting the books would require a maximum further investment of £30,000 (in addition to the £20,000 already spent) before starting to turn a profit. From the point of view of Geoffrey and the rest of the Board, this was easily affordable because of the continuing profitability of* The Nursing Mirror. *Nevertheless, the clarification helped crystallise the Gwyers' opposition. Geoffrey responded with another attempt to persuade them to sell him their shares. On 19 January 1928, Mrs Gwyer refused for herself and told Geoffrey that her husband would be writing on his own behalf.*

## Maurice Gwyer to Geoffrey Faber, January 1928

I think that it is agreed that the Board wants strengthening, and I have suggested that a competent and intelligent chartered accountant would be a very useful member of it. I adhere to that view. I believe you would find him an invaluable coadjutor who would ease your burdens in many ways. You speak of adding someone else with publishing experience, and I should raise no objection; but it seems to me that in that case the Board might become unduly large. I would like, therefore, to put this suggestion before you. As you know, I have always regarded the appointment to the Board of Stewart and De la Mare as premature, and I think you are not now disposed to think their presence on it adds to its strength. I understand also that they are seeking an increase of salary which I am not surprised to hear. Would it not be possible to tell them that they may have an increase, but that they will in future be known as Joint Managers and will cease to be Directors? It would scarcely be possible to take them off the Board without giving them a quid pro quo, and the above suggestion is offered for your consideration as a solution of the difficulty.

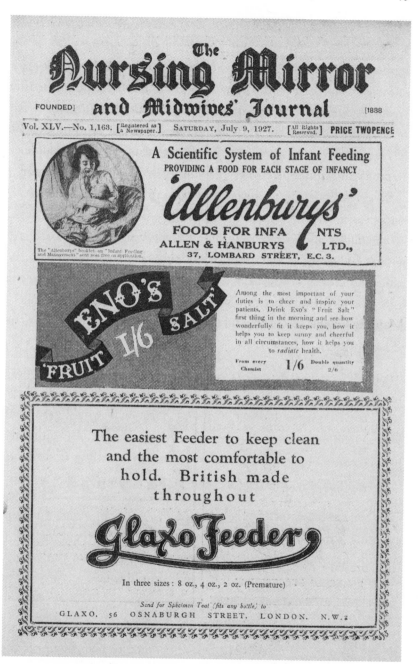

*The Nursing Mirror* continued to generate the profits which allowed
Faber & Gwyer to make losses on its nascent book business.

I come in conclusion to the subject of the letter which you wrote me a few days ago. I do not think that I can entertain the offer at the figure you mention, nor indeed could I afford to do so at the present time. I think too that it is substantially less than the shares are worth, because you must remember that *The Nursing Mirror* profit making capacity has been absolutely unaffected by anything which has occurred; indeed it has, if anything, increased. The business consists of two distinct parts, *The Nursing Mirror* and the books; and it seems scarcely fair to depreciate the value of *The Nursing Mirror* by setting against it the losses and liabilities which have been incurred on the books, and to value the shares accordingly. Clearly too if my wife and I agreed to sell all our shares we could sell them plus the right to discontinue the books altogether, and thereby increase the income which the shares might bring in by not less than 50%. In estimating their intrinsic value I do not think this could be left out of account.

> *That is only a short extract from Gwyer's letter. Although its tone appears quite mild now, it came at the culmination of an increasingly fractious year, and for Geoffrey it was the last straw.*

### Geoffrey Faber to Maurice Gwyer, 26 January 1928

The long letter which I received yesterday afternoon dispels the illusion that agreement between us is possible; and that conclusion is confirmed in my mind by the conversation I had with Mrs Gwyer this morning. After our recent conversation I had allowed myself to think that you were nearer to an understanding of the nature of the problem. I call it a problem, though to my mind there is no problem at all, but a perfectly obvious policy. I have put that policy in the simplest and most definite form possible, into my memorandum – a document to which you apparently attach no value whatever. The problem, which for me has assumed by now almost terrifying proportions, is the problem of keeping the vessel on the only safe course, under your powerful efforts to deflect it. [. . .]

The idea of the book-publishing development was yours; you set it in motion, and now you must go through with it, or go out, or throw me out and make what you can of the consequences. As for the figure I have named as a minimum, which you regard with such amazed horror, I agree that it is larger than the figure I should prob- ably have named (if I had had to name one) three years ago. But I had no fore-knowledge then of the long series of strikes, and the still-continuing trade-depression which lay ahead of us, and which have profoundly affected the publishing trade. Yet the figure I have named, spread over a period of nine years, is neither unreasonable, nor beyond our resources; I may point out to you that it is identical with the capital of Victor Gollancz's new company, of which £40,000 has already been paid up. Gollancz was, of course, Benn's Managing Director; and you will not forget that it was Benn's example which you quoted to me when we first met. [. . .]

I have no hope whatever of persuading you that I am right. From first to last I cannot recollect a single recommendation of mine which you have not opposed, or a single expression of approval of any- thing I have done. You have taken no trouble to acquaint yourself, at first hand, with the problems of the business of which you are the uncrowned king. Your criticism of the appointment of Stewart and de la Mare to be Managing Directors is a case in point and is, in effect, a criticism of yourself. They were not so appointed with the primary object of 'strengthening the Board', but in order to increase their powers of obtaining business. From that point of view their appointment has been abundantly justified. But I strongly repudiate your suggestion that I do not now myself think that their presence on the Board adds to its strength. It is true that they have not, as yet, taken effective part in the decision of financial questions; I do not see how they could have acted otherwise than they have, in view of the obvious fact that what I have called the centre of gravity lay outside the Board altogether. As for your suggestion that they should retire from the Board, and be given a rise in salary in compensation, it is so grotesque that I can scarcely believe you intended it seriously.

My views about the 'chartered accountant' remain unchanged. It is kind of you to devise this method of easing my burden; but if the new director happened to be of your way of thinking it would merely add to them, and if he were not, I do not suppose you would be satisfied. Nevertheless, if the right man is found, and if he has a knowledge of publishing, I should be prepared to give way on this point. But I must add that I have no intention, so long as I remain Chairman, of subordinating my judgment to that of any financial expert. [. . .]

I am quite aware that you can vote me off the Board; and I have made up my mind to face that contingency, rather than submit myself and the Company to an uninformed dictatorship, however agreeably disguised; and rather than remain to see the work of the last three years robbed of its fruition. But if that happens mine will not be the only departure. This is no personal matter nor am I taking this position on personal grounds. The interests of others besides myself are bound up in the future of the business and I have their authority for saying that if the policy for which I stand is abandoned, their positions will be vacant, as well as mine.

## Maurice Gwyer to Geoffrey Faber, 23 March 1928

You must of course have realised (and indeed I suppose so intended) that after your letter of January 26th things could no longer be on the same footing as in the past. The only possible plan for the future is to have what we ought to have had at the beginning, a definite agreement on strictly business lines. [. . .]

Of the £20,000 expended up to the end of last year, £15,000 has already, on your own figures, disappeared beyond recall; and the inducement therefore for the shareholders to subscribe another £30,000 is not a strong one. A comparison between the balance sheets of the first half of 1925 and the second half of 1927 makes melancholy reading. You quote against me the example of Mr. Victor Gollancz. This leaves me cold; though I agree that if at the end of three or four years Mr. Gollancz were to find his capital of £40,000 represented by stock worth £10,000, and the remaining £30,000 no longer in existence, his case would be an exact analogy.

## Geoffrey Faber, diary entry, Monday, 26 March 1928

This rather clinches matters. Either Gwyer or I must win, and if he does I shall have to find a new job!

> *Discussions between Faber and Gwyer were then suspended while Geoffrey and Enid went on holiday. When they returned, both Geoffrey and the Gwyers found it easiest to talk using T. S. Eliot as a go-between.*

## T. S. Eliot to Alsina Gwyer, 10 May 1928

I had a long talk with Faber this afternoon, with Stewart and De la Mare present for a part of the time. It seems to me that there is every possibility of an agreement, and Faber's modified demands seem to me possible of acceptance. Particularly as I cannot see any alternative to further negotiation than a General Meeting which could hardly result in anything but a complete revolution. As I told your husband and yourself, I should deprecate a Board Meeting on this matter; if it is so complete a difference of policy, it would satisfy neither Faber nor yourselves, and could only lead to a General Meeting.

My own opinion is quite simple: the pursuit of Faber's memorandum has to be contingent (1) on the continuance of the present dividend (2) on the ability to reduce the overdraft by £2,000 annually (3) of course upon the continuance during that period of the present prosperity of the *Mirror*. [. . .]

I speak with great diffidence, either to you or to Faber, as my position is an anomalous one. I hope you will not consider it impertinent.

## Geoffrey Faber to Maurice Gwyer, 16 May 1928

I want to do whatever is in my power to make a rapprochement easier. I realize that my letter of Jan 26 is a stumbling block between us: I wish to express my regret at having written it. You won't understand me to mean that I have changed my opinion about matters of business. But I do mean that I regret the tone and temper of the letter's allusions to yourself.

> *Maurice Gwyer accepted Geoffrey's apology and relations between them improved, but not to the extent that they came to any common viewpoint.*

## Richard de la Mare to Siegfried Sassoon, 17 May 1928

I have had a talk with my fellow directors about the terms for *The Memoirs* and I find that they consider a hundred pounds advance a little heavy for a book that is to come out anonymously.

> *Dick knew Sassoon through his father. He later remembered him saying, at a weekend spent with the de la Mares, 'I have been writing a book on foxhunting, would you like to see it?' 'Yes, for heaven's sake, YES,' was Dick's reply, and the book came to him chapter by chapter as Sassoon wrote it.*

## Geoffrey Faber to T. S. Eliot, 19 May 1928

I was sorry to hear from you yesterday that Gwyer saw little hope at present of 'bridging the gulf'; and I am also very sorry that in your own crowded life you should find yourself to any extent in the uncomfortable position of the third party. However, there seems no help for that. [. . .]

There is one point, however, in particular which I should be grateful if you could stress with Gwyer – and that is the extreme importance of settling the matter <u>soon</u>. I really can't go on in the present state very much longer. It's difficult to exaggerate the ill effects of this paralysing uncertainty. It affects me in the way of making it impossible for me to give my mind to any proper work; it affects all our plans for the future; and it inevitably communicates a feeling of malaise and discouragement to the whole staff – indefinite so far as they are concerned, but real enough.

### Geoffrey Faber to T. S. Eliot, 31 May 1928

The early book lists were not very good ones, as you say. (Though I have a very clear recollection of being complimented by Gwyer on the first seed list.) But one has to make a start. A new firm has only a choice of material offered to it, or sought by it; and until it has established its reputation with authors, agents, and reading-public, that choice is necessarily limited. Is that an argument for a small-scale start? I think <u>not</u>; unless the firm is accepted as a substantial one it will never get anything offered to it but the crumbs off the bigger publishers' tables. To get a footing is the real battle: and it is at this stage that money must inevitably be – as Gwyer would say 'lost', as I would say 'invested'. [. . .]

Simpkins complimented us the other day on being the <u>only</u> London publishing house from whom they have never refused to take a book.

I say these things not because I want you to repeat them to the Gwyers; but because I do feel <u>awfully sore</u> about the whole thing, and I must justify myself a little to somebody. It is hard to know that my portion is blame in every detail, when I am conscious that in general I have not merely done the best that it is in me to do, but that I <u>have</u> laid the foundations well and truly.

*To add to his troubles, Geoffrey's own finances were close to spiralling out of control.*

## Geoffrey Faber to Alsina Gwyer, 1928

There are two personal and financial matters which I want to put to the Board at the next meeting, but which as Chairman I feel some difficulty in raising for open discussion. I have asked Eliot and Stewart privately what they think, and they both think that the proposals are of a nature to be favourably considered by the Board. It seems to me that the best thing to do is to find out your view in the same way.

The first relates to the legal costs which I shall have incurred by consulting Cohen, of Linklater & Paine, solicitors, in connection with the matters under discussion between your husband and myself. I went to Cohen on my own responsibility; but as the matters in question concern the future of the Company, and as the desirability of legal advice arose out of my position as Chairman, I feel that it would be in order for me to ask the Company to pay the costs. I should suppose that the Directors would be likely, if they took the view that the Company should pay the costs, to take the same view of your husband's costs.

The second matter relates to *Elnovia*. There was never any written agreement between myself and the Company, but I said at a Board Meeting that I would stand any loss, or take half the profits. It was suggested at the time (I think by Taylor) that half-profits and half-losses would be a more equitable arrangement; and I very much regret that I did not adopt the suggestion. The book was very well received and reviewed, and though I say it I think it helped to do the Company some credit at the outset. But, owing to the strikes at the end of 1925, it never had a proper chance. I have paid to the Company out of my pocket £89 14s 11d – a good deal more than I would have been prepared to risk knowingly, and a good deal more than I could conveniently afford! There still remains a debit of about £100 – which may be possibly a little reduced by remaindering. I don't at all like doing it, but I feel constrained to ask if the Company will release me from the obligation to make any further payment.

Although I feel that a concession of this kind would, in the circumstances, not be inequitable, I should have preferred to pay and say nothing; but frankly I can very ill afford to do so. Will you forgive me if I say a word or two about my private affairs? My present income, from all sources, is only just enough to enable me to pay off my loan-charges, income and super tax, and insurance premiums, and to keep a very simple establishment. In order to pay for my wife's three operations, and for our holiday this spring, I have had to use up my reserves; and I have, at the moment, no capital resources at all. My family expenses are increasing, and I do not think after this year I shall be able to afford to keep a car. As it is, we find it impossible to do more than a very limited amount of modest entertaining, though in the interests of the business we ought to be doing very much more.

I thought it best to write and tell you all this, for of course I couldn't do it *coram publico*. I propose to come a quarter of an hour late to the Board Meeting, so that the matter can be discussed without embarrassment in my absence, and to ask Eliot to take the Chair until I come.

### Geoffrey Faber, diary entry, Thursday, 28 June 1928

Board Meeting. Retired at end to allow directors to debate *Elnovia*. Lady Gwyer[13] came in to my room afterwards, very friendly, and said

---

13  Maurice Gwyer had recently been knighted.

the Board were unanimous as to halving loss on book with me. Eliot
told me afterwards that she herself moved resolution.

## FABER & GWYER AUTUMN ANNOUNCEMENTS, 1928

*Selected Poems of Ezra Pound*
With an Introduction and Notes by T. S. Eliot

At Mr. Pound's request, Mr. Eliot has made this selection, with an introduction and notes. For those who do not yet know the poetry of Ezra
Pound, and for many of those who know it well, this critical selection by
another poet and critic, who has been in closer touch with the author than
anybody, should have great value.

[. . .]

*Memoirs of a Fox-Hunting Man*
Anonymous

*The Memoirs of a Fox-Hunting Man* will be enjoyed equally by the man or
woman who has never sat a horse, as it will be by the hardened rider to
hounds. To the one it will bring a new and intensely real and exciting experience, to the other it will surely recall many of his happiest experiences.
Finally, a book such as this reminds us how easy it is to forget the immeas-
urable changes that have taken place in England during the last twenty
years – there has been a social revolution, yet we forget it!

> *In Dick de la Mare's words, Sassoon had been 'quite shy' about
> the book as he had only published verse before. This was why he
> initially wanted the book to be published anonymously.*

> *Over the summer, Geoffrey and the Gwyers agreed to ask an
> accountant to examine the book-publishing business to see
> whether it had a future. Although he had concerns about this,
> Geoffrey initially thought that the man appointed, Kenneth
> Layton-Bennett, was sympathetic to his point of view.*

# THE WASTE LAND

1922

"NAM Sibyllam quidem Cumis ego ipse oculis meis
vidi in ampulla pendere, et cum illi pueri dicerent:
Σίβυλλα τί θέλεις ; respondebat illa: ἀποθανεῖν θέλω."

For Ezra Pound
*il miglior fabbro.*

63

In his *Collected Poems 1909–1925*, Eliot called Ezra Pound 'the greater craftsman'. A future Faber poet would suggest, however, that '*il miglior fabbro*' really meant 'it's better with Faber' (see p. 337).

## Geoffrey Faber to Kenneth Layton-Bennett, 17 September 1928

The reason why the Board have asked you to report is not that they have any doubt themselves about the policy they are following, but because they see no other way of effecting a reconciliation between the directorate and management on the one hand, and the majority shareholding interest on the other. We (i.e. the Board) do not doubt that we shall, in a reasonably short time, achieve success with the Faber and Gwyer books; nor do we doubt the capacity of the Company to finance our policy with due provision for the maintenance of the 100 per cent dividend. [. . .]

This solidarity is not due to any personal ascendancy of my own over the others, or to any hold which I have over them of a mere material kind. It is due to the fact that, in order to make a business of this sort work and succeed, it is essential to have the maximum of co-operation and joint responsibility. We <u>have</u> got that to a remarkable degree. [. . .]

Really the common-sense solution is – here is a board of able and intelligent men, working as hard as they know how to make the thing a success, and full of keenness and confidence; for goodness sake leave it to them.

## Richard de la Mare to Siegfried Sassoon, 27 September 1928

Things are beginning to get very exciting, for the *Memoir* is due to be published tomorrow and the subterranean excitement about it in London seems to me to be pretty considerable. The first impression has been sold out before publication date, and the second will be on sale on the actual date of publication. What I have done about the second impression is to keep the first 500 copies of it anonymous, but to print your name upon the rest. That, I think, will give time enough for the book to be reviewed anonymously, although, so far as I can judge, by far the majority of those who will be reviewing the book know of your authorship of it! The information hasn't come from me, or from us, but you know how once anybody hears a secret of this kind he hastens to pass it on.

I have read most of the book again since it was printed, and it becomes more and more of a joy to me – and as publisher of it I feel very proud.

## Geoffrey Faber, diary entry, Sunday, 30 September 1928, while on a visit to the Gwyers' country house

A glorious day. Really a very pretty place, and the Gwyers very friendly. But the whole day was practically spent in listening to Philip Guedalla.[14] *The Observer* had Squire's splendid review of *The Fox Hunting Man*.[15] I was glad this came at the time it did, to impress Gwyer with the solidity of Faber & Gwyer.

*Reviews did not, however, impress the accountant.*

## Kenneth Layton-Bennett to the Chairman, Faber and Gwyer Ltd, 22 November 1928

It is my opinion that Faber and Gwyer books should now be on a profit-earning basis. In view of the losses already incurred and the uncertainty in regard to the next two or three years I cannot find any real justification for continuing this branch of the Company's business. [. . .]

I am bound to say, therefore, that in my opinion the Company's activities should be mainly devoted to strengthening *The Nursing Mirror*, at the same time continuing the publication of Scientific works as in the past.

---

14 Philip Guedalla was a barrister and popular writer who had been a school friend of Geoffrey Faber's.
15 J. C. Squire, *Observer*: 'I cannot hope this year to see another book as good as this . . . We are given here the "reactions" of a keen mind and a tender heart.'

Immediate savings could be effected if this policy were adopted, and as, in addition, there would be no losses on Faber and Gwyer books to set against the profits earned by *The Nursing Mirror* and the Scientific Press publications, the discontinuance of the Faber and Gwyer Book-publishing business is clearly in the interests of the Shareholders.

> *In the face of such an unequivocal judgement, but quite certain that he and the rest of the Board were right, Geoffrey desperately cast about for a way to carry on. Over the last few years he had been gradually paying back his loan from the Arthur Faber Estate. If he could top up the loan once more, it might give him enough capital to buy out the books business. For that, however, he would once again need the support of Arthur's widow Ishti, and of his mother.*

### Geoffrey Faber to his mother Florence Faber, 4 December 1928

The last two years have involved me in a series of terrible difficulties with the Gwyers, who are perpetually trying to strangle the finances of the Book Publishing side of the business in order to get larger dividends from *The Nursing Mirror*. If they had their way the book-publishing could <u>never</u> prosper; and as I have given my whole energies and time for four years to the creation of the book-publishing side of the business, you can easily imagine how difficult a time I have been having. It has finally come to this, that I cannot go on in the present condition of things, and the separation of the two businesses is the only practicable solution.

Enid would tell you something of the harassing consequences of the Gwyers' attitude during these two years. He is a lawyer and a civil servant, of distinguished abilities but a nervous, distrustful temperament; she is a woman of the hysterical type, never of the same mind for two weeks together. Last year they were on the point of

Geoffrey Faber's author photograph for *Elnovia*.

separating, and both used me as an intermediary for interminable negotiations and squabbles; in the result they decided to go on living together, and I don't think either of them has forgiven me for the part I was compelled – most reluctantly! – to play in their affairs.

Neither of them has the faintest understanding of business – which further complicates the situation – and as between them they hold more than half the shares in the Company, they are in a position to make matters extremely difficult.

### Geoffrey Faber to Florence Faber, 6 December 1928

I should like to say that after three years of hard spadework we have definitely got our feet on the ladder and are quietly ascending it. We have had this season our first big success – in the *Memoirs of a Fox-Hunting Man*. We have now sold 10,000 copies of this book; and it is going better than ever, and is bound to sell for a long time to come. The importance of a success like that can't be over-valued; in publishing, more even than in other businesses, 'success breeds success'. Then we have several other solid books on our list; we have a good programme for next year; the whole of the book-trade is friendly towards us and interested in us; and we have a first class staff. These are, at any rate, encouraging facts. [. . .]

I am very much touched by all that you say towards the end of your letter; and I will only add that I have <u>not</u> neglected to ask God's help and blessing in this, as in other, periods of doubt and anxiety. I hope and believe that these are with me, in the decision which will shortly have to be made.

I have taken, too, the more worldly precaution of seeking advice and criticism from others, whose opinion confirms my own.

> On this occasion, however, Ishti Faber did not support the idea of a further loan. That avenue was closed. In the New Year, Kenneth Layton-Bennett (certainly exceeding his original brief) dropped a further bombshell.

### Kenneth Layton-Bennett to Harry Cohen, Geoffrey's solicitor, 8 January 1929

In the best interests of the shareholders, including Faber himself, I am of the decided opinion that he should resign the Managing Director-ship of the present Company in favour of Stewart. Faber's retention as Managing Director would necessitate the appointment of a Gen-eral Manager at a salary of not less than £600 a year, which would in effect nearly double the cost of the Managing Directorship as such.

### T. S. Eliot to his friend and adviser, the art historian and poet Herbert Read, 11 January 1929

I am bothering you again with a few manuscripts that I think are worth looking at. One is a short play by a boy named Auden whom I have seen and talked to several times. I think he has some merit and he really wants seriously to do something with some form of verse play.

### Kenneth Layton-Bennett to Harry Cohen, 15 January 1929

It has occurred to me that a solution of the present difficulties might be the sale outright of *The Nursing Mirror*.

I do not consider that there would be great difficulty in effecting a sale, provided all parties were agreeable. I think too that quite a rea-sonable purchase price might be obtainable.

> *Once again, Mr Layton-Bennett was exceeding his brief, only this time with a suggestion that would lead to a solution.*

### Alsina Gwyer to Geoffrey Faber, 31 January 1929

Many thanks for your letter giving me the approximate figures for the last half year. I could wish that those for the books were more cheerful. On the basis of roughly £100 profit for every 1,000 copies sold after the first 1,300 which paid the expenses of production I think that the

*Fox Hunting Man* must have brought in about £1,000 up to the end of the year. If the total loss still shows at about £2,380 how heavy it would have been except for that one stroke of luck. It is most disappointing that results should be no better after nearly four years' trading and I think that you must share this feeling. If only we could have made a success of the venture that was started with so much hope.

### Kenneth Layton-Bennett to Harry Cohen, 15 February 1929

I am authorized to offer the sum of £190,000, payable in cash, for the Goodwill and Copyright of *The Nursing Mirror*.

### Geoffrey Faber to Florence Faber, 20 February 1929

We are selling *The Nursing Mirror* for a very large sum; and I am to form a new Company to take over the books and other assets of Faber & Gwyer Ltd. The present Company will go into a voluntary liquidation, and the proceeds of both sales will be shared out among the shareholders. It is estimated that the ordinary shareholders will receive in the neighbourhood of £189 for each share – that is to say three times the amount that you gave for your holding.

I shall get, in this way, about £50,000. Of that I shall take £10,000 to pay off the amount that I owe to the Faber Trust Estate; and of the rest I shall have to put back about £20,000 into the new Company, which I am morally bound to provide for, and from which I don't mean to reclaim on any returns on my capital for a time.

*Florence's letter back does not survive, but we can guess its tone from Geoffrey's rejoinder.*

### Geoffrey Faber to Florence Faber, 22 February 1929

Well, well, well! I suppose, if you dug up a fortune in your garden you would find something to be depressed about.

Here are you and Dorothy getting back your original investment trebled; myself paying off the whole of my loan, becoming master of my own business, with some £20,000 over into the bargain; and all you can do is to write a letter which anyone would suppose to refer to a terrible financial calamity.

# 2: 1929–1935
# 'The Russell Square Twins'

Enid later remembered that Geoffrey had seriously considered giving up publishing and retiring with his £40,000 profit from the liquidation of Faber & Gwyer. The interest alone on that sum would have earned him £2,000 a year – more than three times his salary as All Souls' bursar. Given his experiences over the previous few years, retirement must have been an attractive proposition. He did not consider it for long, however, because of the sense of duty he felt to his fellow directors. He could not leave them high and dry. So Geoffrey spent about £20,000 of those profits buying back Faber & Gwyer's books business (including the old Scientific Press medical list) from its liquidator, giving him the overwhelming majority of the shares in the new company. The only question was what to call it. According to de la Mare family legend, it was Walter de la Mare himself who found the solution: 'You can't have too much of a good thing! Why not call it Faber & Faber?'

Although he couldn't know it, Geoffrey was launching his new firm just as the world was about to enter the Great Depression. The stock market collapse would certainly affect Geoffrey's own fortune, but its impact on his young firm was masked by the more general risks that accompany any start-up. The Appendix to this book shows how, without the protection of income from *The Nursing Mirror*, the firm lurched between profit and loss each year, and paid no dividend for its first decade. Yet it survived; more than that, it quickly began to develop a reputation that brought it and Geoffrey to the forefront of publishing.

This chapter charts Faber & Faber's transformation into a literary powerhouse. With one exception, the team remained the same as that which had overseen Faber and Gwyer. Charles Stewart managed much of the firm's day-to-day business, and ran the profitable medical list with quiet efficiency. Dick de la Mare was a publishing dynamo, full of ideas, creating arts and farming lists to add to his other interests, and, as Production Director, giving the firm a reputation for good design. T. S. Eliot used his growing fame and literary judgement to identify and publish the writers and young poets whose excellence means that they remain on the Faber list to this day. Freed from the need to answer to (as they saw it) ignorant external shareholders, and with the experience they already had from four years at Faber & Gwyer, these men became better publishers.

The catalyst to this transformation was the new member of the team: Frank Morley. Having arrived in England from the USA on a Rhodes Scholarship to Oxford, he had originally followed his distinguished father, also Frank, into mathematics; the two collaborated on a book of geometry as late as 1933. The Morley family, however, also had a strong foothold in the humanities. One of Frank's brothers, Christopher, was a novelist; the other, Felix, was to become editor of the Washington Post (both brothers would be published by Faber). So by the late 1920s Frank was earning his living as the London manager of the Century Company (Publishers) of New York. He was also an old friend of Dick de la Mare and a longstanding fan of T. S. Eliot. Geoffrey had already identified him in 1928 as the missing element: 'what the commercialist in his vulgar but pointed tongue calls a "contact man"'. Few of the books on the Faber list today can be ascribed to Morley, but he encouraged the others (T. S. Eliot in particular) and brought in very necessary moneymakers.

And what about Geoffrey? It is hard to describe him as a great publisher with a brilliant editorial eye, but he had an instinctive understanding of finance and, even more important, knew how to get the best from his fellow directors. This is how Frank Morley was to put it, in Geoffrey's obituary, many years later:

'For the Faber & Faber business, when it was set up on April 1, 1929, was more than an ordinary publishing house, and what was more than ordinary about it was the character of Geoffrey Faber. He had collected a very good team about him, and there quickly developed a distinctive 'Faber' character about the books he published. It would not be accurate to say that all of the books which exhibited the 'Faber' character gave Geoffrey Faber equal satisfaction as an individual. His was a complicated, sensitive, excitable and tolerant genius to which his love for music is really a clue. Faber's style was his team, and he made his team organic. Then he gave it his full trust. He had his work cut out as charioteer, but he guided his chariot.'

### Geoffrey Faber to Frank Morley, 15 February 1929

I want the Board of the new company to consist of myself as chairman, you, de la Mare, Stewart, Eliot. I shall not require any return on my capital until the Company can comfortably afford to make it; but I shall need a salary of (say) £1,200. I propose a salary of £600 each to you, de la Mare, and Stewart, and some interest on profits of a nature to be determined later – whether through shares or through commission.

Your own particular functions would be to advise on Manuscripts, to ingeminate policy, and to bring grist to the mill. I don't mean that you would be <u>limited</u> to these functions; only that they are what we specially want you for.

One of the most important points we have to settle, and may have to settle very quickly, is the name of the new company. There are four principal suggestions in the field.

1. Geoffrey Faber Ltd.,
2. Faber & Co., Ltd.,
3. Faber & Faber Ltd.,
4. Faber & Morley Ltd.

Of these I prefer the last, and so does Stewart; and I want to know if you would agree to it, supposing it commends itself to the others. It sounds well, and has a real basis in your accession to the firm. Stewart's name is not of value; de la Mare's is impossible.

*In a short memoir edited by Allen Tate,[1] Frank Morley recounted how 'his shrewdest consultants in New York', the publishers Alfred Harcourt and Donald Brace, took him 'to lunch on the question, strongly advised against. They would not put any of their money into it. They knew their London. "Faber is a gambler," said Don. "A bunch of Oxford amateurs," said Alfred; "won't last."'*

## Frank Morley, cable to Geoffrey Faber, 21 March 1929

ANXIOUS TO DEFER DECISION TILL MAY FIRST PLEASE CABLE WHETHER THAT POSSIBLE STOP COULD PROBABLY BRING IMPORTANT GRIST AND MAYBE READY CAPITAL BUT SUGGEST DELAY STOP SAILING MARCH NINE LAURENTIC

## Geoffrey Faber, cable to Frank Morley in reply

Delay impossible must register company immediately name Faber and Faber stop shall be away April third to thirtieth hope see you before then stop please cable date arrival England and write fully stop will keep berth open

*Frank Morley's children learned that an investment of only £200 would have enabled their father to add his name. Faber & Faber Ltd was formally incorporated on 28 March 1929.*

---

1  See *T. S. Eliot, The Man and His Work*, edited by Allen Tate (Chatto & Windus, 1967).

*Six days later, as Geoffrey's cable to Frank implied, he and Enid went on a four-week holiday.*

*Because of its previous history, the new firm was able to hit the ground running. Dick de la Mare, for example, was already in contact with some of the era's most original artists.*

### Richard de la Mare to artist Paul Nash, 8 May 1929

You were kind enough about two years ago to do two drawings for a poem by Mr Siegfried Sassoon that we published in our series of *Ariel Poems*. I am wondering if you would consider doing a second one for us. [. . .]

Would the fee of ten guineas, which we paid you before and which is our normal one for the series, be acceptable to you?

### Paul Nash to Richard de la Mare, 9 May 1929

I will say that if you really want designs by me I should be happier about taking them on if I was given a free hand as to the colours I used and if it were possible for the publishers to pay a little more for the designs. I do not wish to seem to be making a favour of it all. I am merely rather tentatively presenting my reaction!

### Geoffrey Faber, diary entry, Friday, 7 June 1929

Interview with Higham, aided by Morley: got the Reitz diary for straight 15% and an 'accrued' advance, + Canada; and let Higham see we were not to be stampeded into high advances. Morley very good at this – much better than I am – big and genial and convincing.

*David Higham was a literary agent, negotiating terms on behalf of his author, Deneys Reitz, whose journal about the Boer War, Commando, would be one of the new firm's greatest successes. The reference to Canada is a reminder that Faber & Faber was only seeking to publish books in the British Empire. Whether Faber or the US publisher got the rights to publish a book in Canada would always be a matter for negotiation.*

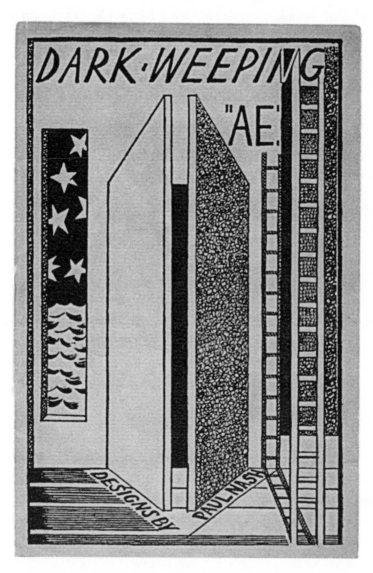

The illustration Paul Nash provided for the front of the *Ariel Poem* 'Dark Weeping' by A.E. (a pseudonym for the Irish writer and nationalist, George Russell).

### Geoffrey Faber, diary entry, Thursday, 27 June 1929

Turkish Bath. Office by 3, for Book Committee. Feeling extremely feeble! However, I perked up for the great 'Faber & Faber' dinner, which was attended by Stewart and Mrs Stewart, Tom Eliot, Dick de la Mare, and Frank Morley and Mrs. Morley. Champagne flowed; and afterwards we all played 'Red Dog' under F. M.'s tuition, for 1d points. To bed about midnight.

### A. J. B. Paterson, sales manager, to Geoffrey Faber, 23 July 1929

Reactions of the booksellers indicate that the <u>Autumn list is good</u>! And the *Criterion Miscellany* is getting a good showing.

> *The* Criterion Miscellany *was a new publishing venture, based on the* Criterion *magazine, which T. S. Eliot continued to edit. The series consisted of pieces that would be too short for a normal book, often by very well-known authors, including James Joyce whose* Anna Livia Plurabelle *first appeared in that form, along with several other fragments of the book that until the end of the 1930s would be known as 'Work in Progress'.*

### T. S. Eliot to James Joyce, 30 July 1929

I am sorry that I have not had an opportunity of answering your letter before. *Anna Livia Plurabelle* has arrived from Paris and I have read it with real enjoyment. Personally I should very much like to carry out the project I suggested to you but I shall have to wait a week or so until I can even take the matter up as two out of the five Directors are away on holiday.

### T. S. Eliot to James Joyce, 22 August 1929

I also enclose a specimen page in a type which should allow the whole book to be printed in 32 pages. 32 pages is a convenient form and would certainly allow us to publish the book at a shilling. We quite agree with you on the question of price and are anxious to keep it down to a shilling if possible but I do not know whether you will think this page too closely crowded. I shall get the opinion of the other directors on that point anyway but if you have any doubt yourself about this page I should suggest that you look in on Monday about noon and we will talk it over with de la Mare who is the Manager responsible for the printing.

## Geoffrey Faber, diary entry, Tuesday, 5 November 1929

To dinner with Morleys, where we met George Blake and his wife (editor of *The Strand* – how my heart would have throbbed to meet such a magnate when I was a boy!! – a nice little man, and very good at his job: also he is a novelist, and may come our way).

## T. S. Eliot to James Joyce, 30 November 1929

The Chairman (of Faber & Faber) suggested to me the other day that he thought that there was a remote possibility now that if *Ulysses* were published in England, it might be allowed to circulate. Of course we should have to make discreet enquiries about this; the point at the moment is that if it can be done we should like to do it. But we should like to know first whether you would have any objection, or whether it would conflict with your present arrangements for its publication.

*While both T. S. Eliot and Geoffrey continued to examine the possibility of publishing* Ulysses *– if the censor would allow it – the firm's catalogue for the next season was able to promise the next best thing.*

FABER & FABER CATALOGUE, SPRING 1930

*James Joyce's Ulysses*
by Stuart Gilbert

The situation of James Joyce's masterpiece *Ulysses* is unique in literary history. Of all modern novels it is undoubtedly the most famous and the most influential. Yet it is not permitted to enter this country; and even those who are able to read it are not always able to understand it. [. . .]

*Ulysses* is enormously long; it embodies an immense erudition, and employs a profound and difficult method of allegorical symbolism. Even therefore if the original were published in England, Mr. Gilbert's exposition would be valuable. As things are, it is invaluable.

## Geoffrey Faber, Memorandum on Finance, November 1929

Two principles should guide us: (1) to aim at building up a permanent list, so that the sales of our back-lists will go on increasing year by year (2) to aim at margin of income over expenditure. [. . .]

There is a certain conflict between the two principles defined above. We can neither afford to aim exclusively at a permanent list which will not show immediate returns, or at immediate returns on books of a popular and ephemeral character. A balance has to be maintained. But we must bear this in mind in constructing every list; and we must, I think, be very shy of doing books which offer little chance of immediate returns, unless (a) they are of classic, or something like classic, quality; or (b) they are a means to something else; or (c) they show promise. With regard to the latter consideration, I feel that our chief hope of building up a good fiction list lies in taking early work of distinctive character.

## T. S. Eliot, report to the Book Committee on *Who Moved the Stone?* by Frank Morison, December 1929

I began reading this book with every prejudice against it, but was very quickly interested. I should like to publish this book. I suggest of course no advance and modest royalties.

> *A considered and well-written discussion of the Gospels'*
> *description of the Resurrection,* Who Moved the Stone? *would*
> *be the first bestseller acquired for Faber & Faber by T. S. Eliot.*

## Frank Morley on Stephen Spender to T. S. Eliot, 12 January 1930

This is too unsure and tentative: doesn't seem to me to come off. But the lad needs and deserves encouragement.

> *I like these occasional reminders of how even T. S. Eliot*
> *appreciated the advice of his fellow directors.*

## T. S. Eliot to Stephen Spender, 24 January 1930

But I want particularly to urge you to send me more of your work from time to time; I liked this enough to have a great curiosity in your future writing.

## Geoffrey Faber, diary entry, Thursday, 6 February 1930

A profit of £1,000 all in on half year – not so bad.

## T. S. Eliot to Stephen Spender, 17 May 1930

Thank you for your letter and for sending me your poems. I like them, and I hope you will let me keep them for a time to show to one or two friends.

*Frank Morley had introduced George Blake (previously editor*
*of* The Strand Magazine) *to Geoffrey Faber in November 1929*
*and Geoffrey asked him to join the Board the following year.*
*Blake was to take particular responsibility for fiction, and*
*brought a link to the Glasgow-based Porpoise Press, whose*
*stable of authors included Neil Gunn. His novel* The Silver
Darlings *is still published by Faber.*

## Geoffrey Faber to George Blake, 20 June 1930

Morley will have told you what happened yesterday. I write formally
to say that I am authorized by the unanimous vote of the Board to
offer you a Principal Directorship in Faber & Faber Ltd.[. . .]

The office of Principal Director is more or less my own invention,
made with the deliberate purpose of securing continuity of policy
and control of the business by those engaged in it, independent of
the majority shareholding interest if that (being less than four fifths
majority) should pass into other hands in the course of time. My
experience of the disastrous consequences of unintelligent interven-
tion by shareholders ignorant of the nature of their business made
me determined to prevent, so far as I could, anything of the sort
happening in Faber & Faber. [. . .]

You will note that the issued capital is £24,700. Your £500 will bring
this up to £25,200. Four-fifths of this is £20,160. My own holding is
£20,000. So that when you come in I shall no longer be in the position of being able to remove a Principal Director by my unsupported
fiat! a power which I surrender without any regret!

*Dick de la Mare, Frank Morley and Charles Stewart were all*
*Principal Directors. T. S. Eliot, being part-time and therefore an*
*'Ordinary Director', was now developing the confidence to bring*
*younger poets onto the Faber list.*

## FABER & FABER BOOK CATALOGUE, AUTUMN 1930

When the history of English poetry in the first third of the twentieth century comes to be written, it will be found to fall into three periods. There are the poets whose technique was perfected and whose reputation was established before the war. There are the poets who perfected their weapons and who became established during and immediately after the war. And there are finally the poets who come long enough after the second type to have profited by their rebellion without being directly derivative.

It is only within the last few years that it has been possible to distinguish the existence of true growth among the third class, and the youngest of our poets. It is still a matter of adventure to publish and establish them. But believing that it is a matter of importance to make their work available not to collectors only but to as wide a public as may be found, we have devised a format which is both convenient and cheap. We do not regard this as a series to which titles will be added with regularity or frequency; but such titles as are chosen will, it is hoped, prove to be representative of the best work of coming men.

The first three titles are:

*Poems* by W. H. Auden
*The Pursuit* by P. P. Graves
*The Ecliptic* by Joseph Gordon MacLeod

> *Only one of these poets remains in print with Faber – but what a one! A hit rate of one in three is hardly bad.*

## T. S. Eliot to Geoffrey Faber, 23 August 1930

I have agreed verbally with James Joyce to publish another fragment[2] in the *Miscellany* next spring on the same terms as *Anna Livia*. This only after discussion with Morley, Paterson and De la Mare; but I wanted to let you know before the contract was drawn

---

2  Faber published *Haveth Childers Everywhere* in May 1931.

up. Joyce professed himself very pleased with the form, the price and results of the previous.

> *Joyce's satisfaction with the firm had expressed itself in the following ditty, which he offered to Eliot for use by Faber's sales department. The staff's bemusement may have been a factor in Joyce's subsequent dissatisfaction.*

### James Joyce to T. S. Eliot, 18 August 1930

Buy a book in brown paper
From Faber and Faber
To see Annie Liffey trip, tumble and caper.
Sevensinus in her ringthings,
Plurabells on her prose,
Sheashell ebb music wayriver she flows.

### T. S. Eliot, report to the Book Committee on the poems of 'Mrs Mackay', September 1930

This is sound, earnest and educated verse. Mrs M deserves publication better than most. For this reason, all the more, I think she had better go elsewhere. I think it would be better policy for F. & F. to make a bad blunder in publishing the wrong poet, than to blur their reputation by publishing too many respectable ones [. . .]

With the eyes of adolescent Oxford and Cambridge fixed hopefully upon us, I do not think we could afford to do this, on any terms.

### Barnett Freedman to Richard de la Mare, September 1930

I hope you won't mind this rather speedy account. I would consider it a great favour if I could have a cheque as soon as possible. I am sorry to trouble you over this, but perhaps you could expedite this for me, as I rather want the money – please forgive me.

*The artist Barnett Freedman is a name to conjure with these days. I do like the reminder from this correspondence that Faber & Faber was pretty much his first employer. He was to become one of the most prolific illustrators of Faber's book jackets.*

## Richard de la Mare to Barnett Freedman, 23 September 1930

Of course I don't mind in the least. You will find your cheque for ten guineas enclosed. I am simply delighted with your drawing, and I think myself it is quite the most successful we have ever had in the series.

## Barnett Freedman to Richard de la Mare, 26 September 1930

I am indeed pleased to hear that you like my drawings. I do hope it will make up for the bad ones I did for Mr. Bunyan's poem. Please allow me to ask, that if ever there is a job you think I can do, perhaps you will try me. I require work.

*Geoffrey's diary entry below is a reminder of the uncertainties surrounding the new firm, despite its public air of confidence. The income from acting as the London agent of Century & Co. had been part of Geoffrey's calculations when deciding to employ Frank Morley.*

## Geoffrey Faber, diary entry, Friday, 28 November 1930

Morley broke the ill news of his ending with the Century Co.; & T.S.E. talked gloomily about the *Criterion*. Am nervous about trade conditions next year: <u>this</u> season we are doing wonderfully well.

## T. S. Eliot to Tom Faber (aged three), 20 January 1931

I am glad you have a Case only if you come to see Me we Must be
careful not to get them mixed up, because Mine has Tom on it Too.
I am glad you have a Cat, but I do not believe it is So remarkable a
cat as My cat. My Cat is a Lilliecat Hubvously. What a lilliecat it is.
There never was such a Lilliecat.

 ITS NAME IS JELLYLORUM

And its one Idea is to be

USEFUL!!

THE

# CRITERION

A QUARTERLY REVIEW
EDITED BY T. S. ELIOT

TELEPHONE: MUSEUM 9543                        24 RUSSELL SQUARE,
TELEGRAMS: FABBAF, WESTCENT, LONDON                    LONDON, W.C. 1

20 January 1931.

Dear Tom,

Thank you Very much for your Letter To-day, which I should
have answered Before but could not Until after you had Written it,
as I have been Ill with Influentia and Milk-Toast; so there will
be a Smalstonnerproovle soon.

I am glad you have a Case only if you come to see Me we
Must be careful not to get them mixed up, because Mine has Tom on
it Too.  I am glad you have a Cat, but I do not believe it is So
remarkable a cat as My cat.  My Cat is a Lilliecat Hubvously.  What
a lilliecat it is.   There never was such a Lilliecat.

                    ITS NAME IS

                    J E L L Y L O R U M

and its one Idea is to be
                         USEFUL!!

FOR Instance

IT STRAIGHTENS THE PICTURES -

IT DOES THE GRATES -

## Geoffrey Faber, diary entry, Monday, 16 February 1931

Told T.S.E. of Tom's pleasant casual observation:- 'I think Uncle Tom's a very good writer' – a propos of Uncle T's really brilliant letter to his godson.

## T. S. Eliot to Tom Faber, 7 May 1931

Thank you for your Letters. I hope you like the Book, because it is a Poetry Book and I like it. I was very much Interested to hear about Ty Glyn Aeron, and the Island, and the Trout, and the Bees. I told the Practical Cat all about it, and the Practical Cat was so Excited that we finally said we would . . . Go in for COUNTRY LIFE.

> *Ty Glyn was a house in Cardiganshire that Geoffrey and Enid had bought in the summer of 1930, and to which they retreated as often, and for as long as they could. Otherwise, they lived in a rented house in Hampstead.*

## Geoffrey Faber, diary entry, Wednesday, 10 June 1931

Made some purchases for our dinner – the 2nd Faber & Faber anniversary dinner. A full house, all the directors and their wives or sisters – incl. mirabile dictu Mrs Eliot, who arrived ½ hour late, and very nervous: but she apparently enjoyed herself. The rest of the party didn't break up till 1.30 a.m.!

## Geoffrey Faber, diary entry, Thursday, 25 June 1931

Dined with the Eliots, and met James Joyce and Mrs. Joyce and Osbert Sitwell. An interesting party, and Mrs Eliot amazingly much better. Osbert very much the adequate man of the world – likeable. Joyce, a little tired-looking man, wearing glasses, evidently physically under the weather, talking little and quietly, perfect manners. One couldn't but like him, and feel his quality.

## Geoffrey Faber, diary entry, Wednesday, 15 July 1931

As for my own affairs, it is a sad and bitter story. Of the £21,000 odd which I invested originally I have drawn a little over £5,000, which has gone on Ty Glyn and furniture. Of the remaining £16,000, my assets are at this moment worth a little over £2,000. I have thus lost at least £14,000.

> *Geoffrey's stock market losses meant he had to make a success of Faber & Faber, and that was by no means guaranteed.*

## Geoffrey Faber, diary entry, Tuesday, 24 November 1931

Figures all morning – very depressing. We look like being £2,000 down on the ½ year. Such is life! Lunched at the club, and wrote, with little hope, to T. E. Shaw,[3] asking to let me put *Revolt in the Desert* into our new 3/6 library.

## Geoffrey Faber, diary entry, Monday, 30 November 1931

Heard from T.E.S. who was sympathetic, but couldn't let us have *Revolt in Desert*.

## T. S. Eliot, Confidential Memorandum to Geoffrey Faber, 9 December 1931

I feel that the committee system has been a little overdone, in that it tends to relax individual responsibility. In such an atmosphere, and especially in a committee which has to deal rapidly with a great variety of business and of books in an afternoon, any one person may now and then wake up to find that something has been done against which he would have protested had he been alert.

---

3   T. E. Shaw was the current pseudonym of T. E. Lawrence. He was a friend of Geoffrey but published by Jonathan Cape.

## T. S. Eliot to Eric Blair (George Orwell), 19 February 1932

I am sorry to have kept your manuscript. We did find it of very great interest, but I regret to say that it does not appear to me possible as a publishing venture. It is decidedly too short, and particularly for a book of such length it seems to me too loosely constructed, as the French and English episodes fall into two parts with very little to connect them.

> *T. S. Eliot turned down* Down and Out in Paris and London
> *(Victor Gollancz eventually published it in 1933) and thereby
> lost the chance to take on George Orwell at the beginning of his
> career. He was to get another opportunity.*

## T. S. Eliot to James Joyce, 20 April 1932

We have gone into the question of the publication of *Ulysses* in England as thoroughly as possible, and have taken every opinion available on the prospects. [. . .]

We are advised that we should certainly be liable to prosecution and heavy penalties, with the possibility of the chairman's having to spend six months in gaol, which in itself would be disastrous for the business. The opinion further is that such prosecution would certainly take place.

> *It is hard to believe now the extent to which publishers
> were circumscribed by censorship right up until the 1960s.
> Controversial material could still slip through, however, as
> Geoffrey's letter below makes clear.* The White Flame *was
> a translation from the German of Max René Hesse's book*
> Partenau. *Some of the robustness of Geoffrey's response to the
> customer's complaint can be ascribed to a fact not mentioned on
> the book jacket: he was responsible for the translation.*

## Geoffrey Faber to Sydney Comfort, bookshop owner, 11 May 1932

My Sales Manager has shown me your note of May 1st about *The White Flame*, and your customer's letter of April 15th. [. . .]

I don't think your customer's complaint is justified. If he had read the notice on the jacket when he bought the book he could hardly have missed the phrase 'a passion which society does not tolerate'. There could scarcely be a clearer danger-signal than that, for those who share your customer's views.

If I had the pleasure of your customer's acquaintance, I should like to suggest to him that the chief function of novels, as of poetry, is criticism of life; that criticism of life is not of much value unless it takes account of facts; and the facts, however repugnant, don't cease to exist, or to cause trouble and even misery in the world, because you refuse to think about them. *The White Flame*, in my opinion, as in that of every reputable critic who has reviewed the book (for example in the *Times* and the *Times Literary Supplement*), handles a difficult, delicate, and not unimportant theme in a way which ought not to give offence to anyone. However, if your customer really thinks the book ought to be burned, he is not likely to be within reach of these arguments.

## Richard de la Mare to David Jones, 3 May 1932

I have heard a rumour that you have nearly finished writing a book – to wit a book about the War – which is to be published first of all in a limited edition. I wonder if you have made any plans yet about publishing an ordinary trade edition of the book? Because, if you haven't, you can take it from me that we should be *exceedingly* interested, and I am *sure* we are the publishers for you, if I may be so bold as to pat myself on the back!

*Dick de la Mare knew David Jones for his art, and was never shy*
*of pursuing new leads for a book. In this case, however, he was*
*about four years too early.*

### T. S. Eliot to Louis MacNeice, 18 May 1932

I must apologize for having kept your poems for such a very long
time, but as you have since learnt they arrived in an envelope without
any letter from you, and without any indication of an address. I have
found them very interesting work. It does not seem to me that this lot
quite forms the justification for a volume, but I think I could choose a
few for publication in the *Criterion* if that interested you.

### P. G. Wodehouse introducing *Louder and Funnier*, 1932

When Faber and Faber, the Russell Square twins, wanted a book of
light essays and asked me if I had anything of the kind in my cellars,
my immediate reply was 'Boys, I've got a trunkful'.

*I just love the idea that someone like P. G. Wodehouse is already*
*making a joke of the firm's name.*

### Geoffrey Faber, diary entry, Monday, 13 June 1932

Nothing very special, except that my new forms for keeping abstract
records of the history of every book arrived – all the relevant par-
ticulars, sales, expenditure, profit and loss, etc. A long job I shall have
writing them all up – several hundreds! It'll take months, but will be
worth doing.

### Geoffrey Faber, diary entry, Thursday, 16 June 1932

We inaugurated a new Book Committee method to-day, by having
lunch together of sandwiches and beer in the board-room – with a great
resulting saving of time. In fact we got through by 4 or soon after.

*Edward Bawden was another artist with a huge reputation who would become a stalwart of the Faber list. In the correspondence below, Dick de la Mare is asking him to illustrate* Good Food *by Ambrose Heath, which remains in print.*

## Richard de la Mare to Edward Bawden, 27 May 1932

I want to find someone to illustrate for us a short and rather original book on Cookery that we are going to publish in the Autumn.

## Edward Bawden to Richard de la Mare, 21 June 1932

I send you with this letter four drawings for consideration for the cookery book you intend publishing. [. . .]

To do a finished drawing seemed to me a waste of time, instead, my concern has been to suggest the effect of a series, & towards this end I have planned each one in a similar manner. In the foreground I have placed a harvest of fish, fowl, fruit & vegetables appropriate for a certain month, combined with some incident from my own personal experience that had caused pleasure or remembrance – work in the garden, a picnic under the walnut tree, a scene from last year's Flower Show, & a memory of Scarborough.

I think I have a certain capacity to illustrate this book in the fact that I am a keen gardener, & by no means indifferent to good cooking, & what is perhaps more useful, I have access to the kitchen of a large hotel where I could easily make studies of cooks & cooking apparatus.

## Geoffrey Faber, diary entry, Friday, 30 September 1932

Very depressed this evening about things in general – business included. Am uneasy about next season's programme. It looks rotten. Feel I have made a dreadful mess of everything.

*It took three years from the first time Stephen Spender submitted his poems to Faber & Faber, but Eliot eventually decided he was ready to join the firm's list.*

## FABER & FABER BOOK CATALOGUE, SPRING 1933

*Poems* – Stephen Spender
These thirty-three poems introduce to the general public a young poet whose work has already created unusual interest in a small circle. [. . .]

If Auden is the satirist of this poetical renascence Spender is its lyric poet. In his work the experimentalism of the last two decades is beginning to find its reward.

*April 1933 saw Geoffrey back at Ty Glyn writing a history of Cardinal Newman and Anglo-Catholicism,* Oxford Apostles, *which Faber & Faber would publish later that year.*

## Geoffrey Faber, diary entry, Saturday, 29 April 1933

Ty Glyn was delicious, in spite of my forced labours – I had to get the book finished. I wrote the last sentence on the 22nd & then spent the last week revising and cutting and rewriting. I won't endure such labour again – it's not good for health or sanity. But I think the book has been worth writing, on the whole.

## Geoffrey Faber, diary entry, Friday, 5 May 1933

Stephen Spender all the afternoon – says he has planned his literary life, and means to be a writer first, communist second. After tea listened to Wyndham Lewis reading his *One Way Song* – a forcible affair – not over-nice. Grappled blindly in the spate, and saw light once and again. Finished my preface to *Oxford Apostles*.

All published by Faber: W. H. Auden, Stephen Spender and
Christopher Isherwood in 1935.

*The confidence with which Faber was now publishing poetry
that had previously been considered difficult can be judged from
the catalogue entry below.*

## FABER & FABER BOOK CATALOGUE, AUTUMN 1933

*A Draft of XXX Cantos*
Ezra Pound

Ernest Hemingway – 'Any poet born in this century or the last ten years
of the preceding century who can honestly say that he has not been influenced by or learned greatly from the work of Ezra Pound deserves to be
pitied rather than rebuked.'

*Two more people would join Geoffrey's team in these early
years. The first was Morley Kennerley, a young American
friend of Frank Morley's, the coincidence between their first*

*and last names causing a confusion similar to that between*
*Maurice Gwyer and Colonel Maurice nearly a decade earlier.*
*Kennerley and his wife had been cruising with her best friend,*
*the Woolworth heiress Barbara Hutton, when he wrote to Frank,*
*asking if there was any chance of a job at Faber. He was in*
*Saigon when the following reply arrived.*

## Frank Morley to Morley Kennerley, 7 June 1933

We discussed problems of personnel at a very hot Board Meeting, and the result is, to some extent, favourable. The first part of the Meeting was taken up with the gloomy business of going over the figures for the past half year and with examining the steady decline in returns from the bookshops. [. . .]

I made a respectable case and the Board agreed to offer you the job of General Utility man; but the economy gloom persisted to the extent of cutting down the salary I asked for to £5 a week. I think it would be fair to suggest that this arrangement hold for a year's trial after which we can review the situation.

*So Morley Kennerley came to the firm, initially as a kind*
*of assistant to Frank Morley, although he was soon taking*
*particular responsibility for publicity. The second new recruit*
*was a sales manager more in tune with Faber's developing*
*ethos than 'Pat' Paterson. A necessary precursor to this, of*
*course, was Pat's departure. The story of how this came about is*
*preserved in correspondence because Geoffrey was by now back*
*at Ty Glyn for the summer. It begins with Pat having broken*
*a promise to buy shares from George Blake, who had resigned*
*from the Board. Pat blamed his own father for refusing to*
*release the money.*

## A. J. B. Paterson to Geoffrey Faber, 2 August 1933

It has now been decided for me that I shall not take up the £250 of Blake's shares I originally agreed upon. The whole thing has been particularly disconcerting and I feel that some explanation is due to you. Incidentally I should like you to accept this explanation in strict confidence as I am sensitive of airing the family 'dirty washing' in public. [. . .]

I have probably hinted to you of my Father's weaknesses, the curing of which made me somewhat unpopular. He married a barmaid of questionable standing and that, plus his age has placed his ethics on a plane that is distinctly beyond any decent man's custom. [. . .]

Under the circumstances I feel that it is only right that I should offer my resignation.

*Geoffrey replied particularly carefully to Pat's offer.*

## Geoffrey Faber to A. J. B. Paterson, 3 August 1933

Whether you are or are not able to fulfil your bargain with Blake is your affair and not mine. I shall do what I can to find another purchaser, or purchasers, for his shares.

More serious is the offer of resignation which your letter contains. How much are you in earnest over this? I am in an uncertainty how to reply to it. You know, without the necessity of my saying so, that it would be a blow to me to lose you. We have worked together now for several years, and you have contributed a great deal towards our present position. But I have felt, increasingly, that your loyalty to me was standing in the way of bettering your own position; and that it was not fair, and in the end perhaps not to the good of all parties, that this should be so.

The present incident is, consequently, an occasion for looking this consideration squarely in the face. It comes to this: if you wish to repeat your offer to resign, after further consideration, I will accept it. [. . .]

You have <u>quite</u> exceptional gifts as a salesman. But it is only seldom that Faber & Faber have been able to give you an opportunity for really exercising those gifts. I am afraid of a certain opposition developing between (what I may call) the big business and the quiet business elements in the firm. [. . .]

Well, Pat, I think that is all that I can usefully say at present. I should advise you not to decide in a hurry. Wait, and have it out thoroughly with Frank Morley. If you <u>do</u> decide to make a change, it would of course be at six months' notice, unless by mutual arrangement; and you would carry with you my own warmest wishes for the future.

*The letter Geoffrey sent to Frank Morley the same day explained his view of the situation.*

## Geoffrey Faber to Frank Morley, 3 August 1933

Pat's resignation is the important matter. In a way I would have liked to accept it without more ado. I did not feel that was possible. My letter is, however, designed to make it easy for him to go; and I am rather hoping that you will know just how to carry its implications nearer home.

Pat is too expensive for us, and he is bad over the books we most want to, and must, publish. [. . .]

The point is, that Pat has done a lot to put us on the map. Therefore I (we) owe him loyal action. But, if he went, I should be more relieved than sorry.

*Geoffrey also needed to find an alternative purchaser for Blake's*
*shares. T. S. Eliot had just returned from a year at Harvard and*
*his next book was to be a collection of the lectures he had given*
*there. Determined on a formal separation from his wife Vivien,*
*he was living in the country with the Morleys.*

## T. S. Eliot to Geoffrey Faber, 4 August 1933

It seems to me that I could safely buy £200 worth of the stock from
George now, on one condition; which is, that you would guarantee
me £100 advance on my book <u>if and when</u> I found I needed it. In the
ordinary way I should not of course think of taking any advance on
the book; but in these circumstances I should like to know that the
money was there for me if I did find I needed it. And in the ordinary
way this sum would seem to me an excessive advance on this book. I
could also, perhaps, provide a book of semi- or quasi- children's verse
if it were judged that I had the talent for it.

*T. S. Eliot did end up buying Blake's stake, although I think that*
*today it would be illegal for a firm to offer financial assistance*
*in the purchase of its shares in the way Eliot is suggesting. Of*
*course the real significance of this extract is that it contains one*
*of the earliest hints that Eliot is thinking of writing children's*
*verse. I like to think he had been encouraged by the reception*
*Tom Faber had given to his letters.*

## A. J. B. Paterson to Geoffrey Faber, 8 August 1933

During the week-end I have given a good deal of thought to this
question of my resignation and the outcome is that I should prefer it
to remain. In offering this decision I ought to add that it is influenced
more by the very solid arguments in your letter, which epitomises
my own feelings, rather than as a result of the other humiliating
contretemps.

*So Geoffrey's piece of reverse diplomacy had worked. Pat still*
*had to work out his notice, but Frank had already suggested*
*the best replacement – William Crawley, then at Methuen.*
*He would soon become Sales Director and take particular*
*responsibility for Faber's children's list, which flourished under*
*his stewardship.*

## Geoffrey Faber to Frank Morley, 9 August 1933

There's one point I want to get right, entre nous and the other gangsters. In writing to Pat I have emphasised the 'quiet' character of the firm's policy. It was the only word I could think of, when I wrote, and it is right enough in its context. But I don't want you and the others to think that I meant by the word quiet what it looks to mean on the surface. I want more attention given to the solider books, in the selling of them; but I don't at all want to move back from good popular stuff into the highbrow region! On the contrary, I think we have still a longish way to go before we hit the desired 'popular' point! And I'm all for sensation and enterprise. I know you think as I do about this – and I only want to prevent a possible misconception arising out of my letter to Pat.

*Geoffrey was still on holiday, and had invited T. S. Eliot to spend*
*some days at Ty Glyn with the family.*

## Geoffrey Faber to Frank Morley, 10 August 1933

Tell T.S.E. we hope to have a proposal of dates from him soon.

## Frank Morley to Geoffrey Faber, 11 August 1933

I will give the Rural Dean your message; his dates are getting clearer to him. He is very perturbed about what costumes are suitable for Wales, and is being much tempted by Gamage's assortment of tropical outfits.

## Geoffrey Faber to Frank Morley, 12 August 1933

I have sealed my letter to TSE. Tell him clothes are of no importance. Flannels (gray) and a white pair if he plays tennis and a
bathing suit, if hot; anything he fancies if it's cold. Old clothes preferred. No rules or expectations! But let him be prepared for wet
as well as fine, and for struggling with a gun after a rabbit through
a briar-bush.

*Eliot became a regular visitor to Ty Glyn. Tom Faber later
remembered how he would always arrive 'carefully dressed for
the role of country gentleman in immaculate plus-fours, and
bringing some marvellous present for his fortunate godson,
chosen with enormous care to nourish my ambition to become
a scientist. He would accompany us on seaside picnics, where
my father would insist on walking miles to find a completely
deserted cove and Uncle Tom would be overcome by vertigo on
the climb down necessary if sand was to be reached. He would
help my mother entertain local spinsters to tea and be gently
teased for the effect that he produced upon them. After whisky
for the men behind the closed door of my father's study, he
would play his part in argumentative conversation over dinner.
And after dinner he could be persuaded, without difficulty, to
read aloud from* Pickwick, *which he did with deep relish and to
maximum comic effect.'*

*Faber published Geoffrey's book* Oxford Apostles *that autumn,
to a generally good response. It is just as well that Geoffrey
was (presumably) not aware of Virginia Woolf's reaction. I
suspect she had never forgiven him for poaching Eliot from the
Hogarth Press. By contrast, Faber quoted Hugh Walpole's praise
(prompted by* Oxford Apostles *and Ezra Pound's* Selected Poems)
*in its Christmas Catalogue for the year.*

### Virginia Woolf to Francis Birrell, 3 September 1933

I've been reading a stuck-up humbug called Faber on Newman with fury. How my gorge rises at the new generation of virtuous young men (but I suspect Faber of being bald) who have learnt all their tricks from Lytton, and then accuse him of not loving mankind! Lytton had more love in his little finger than that castrated cat in the whole of his mangy stringy partless gutless tailless body.

### Hugh Walpole, London Letter to the *New York Herald Tribune*, 17 September 1933

I owe Messrs. Faber a fine debt this month. It seems to me that they are almost the noblest publishers in England. This, indeed, is publishing, to produce finely works in which you believe, courageously hoping for the best.

### Geoffrey Faber, diary entry, Thursday, 16 November 1933

Cocktail party with the Marstons – everyone aware of fact that Faber & Faber are ahead at the exhibition, in sales. A good bit of advertisement for us!

> *The* Sunday Times *Book Exhibition started in 1933 at Sunderland House. It eventually grew to be a national book fair at Earls Court. The Faber stand had been largely run by Geoffrey's wife Enid.*

### T. S. Eliot to Marianne Moore, 5 January 1934

We have discussed the matter, and would very much like to have the honour of publishing your poems. I very much hope that this suggestion will not be unwelcome to you, and that you will accept in principle. There is not, of course, very much money in poetry for anybody, but we should like to add your name to our small and, I think, fairly select list of poets.

Faber & Faber was perfectly happy to poke fun at its name on
the cover of this catalogue from 1933.

D's for the de before the la Mare. *(Real
Name must be Prospero, master of Ariel.)*

Books by WALTER DE LA MARE

The Lord Fish. *Illustrated by Rex Whistler.* 10/6
A new collection of short stories.
'It's a treat.'—H. E. Bates in the *New Statesman.*

*Other Collections of Stories by Mr. de la Mare are:*

On the Edge
*In two editions: Library Edition, with wood-engravings,*10/6
*Pocket Edition in the Faber Library* 3/6

The Riddle  And other Stories           3/6

Seven Short Stories
*Illustrated in colour by John Nash.*        15/-

Memoirs of a Midget
*Pocket Edition in the Faber Library.*        3/6

Desert Islands
*Jacket, end-papers and decorations by Rex Whistler.* 7/6

Lewis Carroll                              3/6

Ding Dong Bell                            5/-
*Two children's books by Mr. de la Mare are described on p. 31.*
6

E is for Eliot, *a very stern man.
His prose is severe, and his poems don't scan.*

'Mr. T. S. Eliot is unquestionably the most influential
man of letters writing in English to-day.'—*Scottish
Educational Journal.*

Books by T. S. ELIOT

The Use of Poetry and the Use of
Criticism
Studies in the Relation of Criticism to Poetry in
England. A series of eight lectures delivered in 1932-33
by Mr. Eliot as Charles Eliot Norton Professor of Poetry
at Harvard.                               7/6

Selected Essays
The best of Mr. Eliot's prose writings from 1917 to
1932.                                     12/6

Dante
*Second Impression.*                        3/6
'He is not uttering the last word about Dante from
the heights; but humbly and reverently leading the
novice by the hand.'—*Manchester Guardian.*

For Lancelot Andrewes
*Second Impression.*                        6/-

Thoughts after Lambeth
*Second Impression.*                        1/-
*Mr. Eliot's Poems are described on page 20.*
7

The spirit of fun prevails inside the catalogue as well, with every
letter being given its own rhyming couplet.

## Geoffrey Faber, diary entry, Friday, 5 January 1934

A crisis over James Joyce's *Ulysses* – someone else has offered to publish it here.

> *Given a five-day deadline by Joyce, and paralysed by the fear of prosecution for obscenity, the firm had to watch as* Ulysses *went to the Bodley Head.*

> *Until the Second World War, T. S. Eliot and Ezra Pound enjoyed a relationship full of banter and deliberate misspellings. I am only including this short – and appropriate – extract (anything longer is likely to lead to headaches).*

## T. S. Eliot to Ezra Pound, 12 January 1934

If you were the sort of guy what ever admitted anything you would admit that Faber & Faber are good publishers.

> *There was to be one final interaction between Geoffrey and Paterson, Faber's former Sales Manager who had quickly moved on to Routledge, then run by Cecil Franklin.*

## Midland Bank to Geoffrey Faber, 6 February 1934

With reference to the guarantee you signed in June 1933 for £25 to secure the account of Mr. A. J. B. Paterson: We have to inform you that Mr. Paterson has not repaid the overdraft which stands at £22.17.2.

## Geoffrey Faber to A. J. B. Paterson, 8 February 1934

It can hardly have escaped your memory that I guaranteed your overdraft for three months to the extent of £25 for a particular purpose, at your special request. The purpose was to enable you to purchase Blake's shares in this Company, to the value of £250, pending the release of the purchase-money by your 'trustees'. I understood that the £25 was required as deposit on the purchase-price of £250.

Subsequently this transaction fell through, owing to the refusal of your parents to let you have the money. I assumed, therefore, that my guarantee would not be required. [. . .]

Unless I have a satisfactory reply from you by to-morrow morning (February 9th), I shall put the matter into the hand of my solicitors.

*According to Andrew Franklin (Cecil Franklin's grandson and founder of Profile Books), Paterson was sacked from Routledge 'for idleness' in 1934.*

### T. S. Eliot to Louis MacNeice, 5 April 1934

Of course you will understand that I can't in advance give any positive assurance of publication. It depends upon a number of business factors, as well as upon the merit of the book. I can only say that I am confident that I shall be able to recommend your poems to my firm.

*Faber continued to publish fragments from Joyce's 'Work in Progress'. The last of them,* The Mime of Mick, Nick and the Maggies, *had been printed in a limited edition of 1,000 copies by the Servire Press in The Hague. Faber distributed 250 of these, and perhaps understandably did not eat into this valuable stock by sending out review copies. The result of this was that they did not publicise the cover by Joyce's daughter Lucia.*

### James Joyce to George and Helen Joyce, 21 August 1934

Unfortunately no press notice of her cover etc for my fragment appeared in the English press because all the available copies were sold out before its publication and Faber and Faber or Feebler and

Fumbler did not circulate the 35 press copies because they did not want to be bothered by requests for copies they could not supply.

*One of the first publications in* The Criterion Miscellany *had been an essay by D. H. Lawrence, 'Pornography and Obscenity'. Given his reputation, it was perhaps inevitable that a title like that would eventually catch the attention of the authorities.*

## Geoffrey Faber to the Secretary of State for Home Affairs, 7 September 1934

I have just been informed by one of our customers, Sequana Limited, of 16 Buckingham Palace Road, S.W.1., that their premises have recently been visited by the police, and a number of publications seized and removed. Among these publications was a pamphlet entitled *Pornography and Obscenity* published by my firm. This pamphlet was first published in 1929, in a series called the *Criterion Miscellany*, simultaneously with a pamphlet in the same series entitled *Do We Need A Censor?* by the then Home Secretary, the late Viscount Brentford. The two pamphlets represented opposite points of view upon a question of no little importance.

It is not, however, upon this fact that we base our protest against the seizure of this particular pamphlet by the police, so much as upon more general grounds. It appears to us so astonishing as to be almost incredible that the police should conceive it proper to seize a copy of a publication, bearing the imprint of a reputable firm of English publishers, upon the premises of one of that firm's customers, without any previous or even subsequent communication with the publishers themselves.

I shall be glad to learn what explanation of this incident can possibly be forthcoming. In the meanwhile I am notifying the occurrence to

the Publishers' Association of Great Britain and Ireland, and I am
sending a copy of this letter to the President of the Association.

### Geoffrey Faber to William Watt, literary agent at A. P. Watt, 13 November 1934

I want to raise with you the general question of your 5 year clauses.
[. . .]

My reason for disliking it is not simply because one runs the risk
of losing a profitable book, through some whim or prejudice of
an author, or through the author being tempted into a rival fold.
This is one of my reasons, of course; for, although I know that
your firm exercises its influence wisely and justly, the risk does
and must remain a real one. It is perhaps a more serious risk to
me than to some other publishers, because the whole of my policy,
since I founded Faber & Gwyer, has been directed towards building up a solid list, and increasing the ratio of old turnover to new
turnover by means of a higher proportion of books which go on
selling year after year. There are already several books on my list,
making good annual profits, which have been published for more
than five years.

The second, and main, objection I have to the clause is this. A business, in the end, must be valued by its assets. Now I have no intention whatever of selling my business, either now or at any future
time. But that doesn't remove the possibility that it might some day
be sold; nor does it alter the fact that, like every other business man,
I must direct my efforts towards increasing its ultimate realizable
value as well as its immediate profits. Actually I put the first of these
two objections in front of the second. If, as the result of an increasing
business with you, a larger and larger proportion of the books in
my list come to be books in respect of which my rights expire after
5 years, I am obviously undermining my own main objective; for

the expectation of continued profit upon these books could not be a saleable asset.

## Geoffrey Faber to Allen Lane, Managing Director of publisher Bodley Head, 12 December 1934

We have had our attention called to *The Authors Handbook* for 1935, edited by Mr Kilham Roberts, and published by your firm.

I am sorry to have to say that we take the strongest possible exception to the description given of our firm in the book, and to the absence of all reference to our firm under various headings.

On page 191 it is said that 'The firms (sic) aims rather at <u>succès d'estime</u> than at commercial success, but it not infrequently achieves both'. The first part of this statement is not true (for we definitely aim at commercial success, as well as at <u>succès d'estime)</u>, and it is liable to do us great damage with present and prospective authors.

The account given on this page of the books we publish is extremely inadequate, and misleading. It does not include, for example, history, religion, science and sport – to name only four categories in which we publish. The impression produced on the mind of a reader must be that we publish books in a strictly limited field; whereas we publish books of all kinds. Furthermore I object most strongly to the suggestion that 'belles-lettres' (a phrase which I detest, describing a form of book which I dislike) form an important, not to say the most important part of our publications.

*This was the beginning of a long correspondence, in course of which Allen Lane mentions in passing that 'I wouldn't mind at all exchanging the note about your firm for the one about us', but this did little to satisfy Geoffrey.*

## FABER & FABER BOOK CATALOGUE,
## SPRING & SUMMER 1935

*Selected Poems*
Marianne Moore

In that poetic renaissance with which the names of Eliot and Pound are associated there is at least one other name the place of which is assured. The work of Miss Marianne Moore is already known to those who provide the opinions that are later accepted by all; she herself has been indifferent to wider appreciation.

*The same could be said at the time of Faber's own attitude to much of its poetry list.*

## T. S. Eliot to Michael Roberts, 21 February 1935

Miss Adam Smith has very kindly invited me to dinner on the 9th or 10th of March, and I look forward to seeing you then. I have a proposal which I should like to discuss with you when we meet. My firm has conceived the idea that there is room for another anthology of modern verse, and we wonder whether you would consider editing a collection for us.

*This is the first mention of* The Faber Book of Modern Verse, *which became a standard-bearer for Modernism and a signal of the firm's growing reputation.*

## T. S. Eliot to Michael Roberts, 14 March 1935

Your outline for an anthology has been accepted unanimously by the Committee. The only comment I am asked to put forward is that we should be glad if Yeats could be included, even if you decide not to include Hopkins. I hear, however, that Yeats is inclined to ask rather high fees for anthology rights.

## Frank Morley to Donald Brace, 7 June 1935

The best thing I have read recently is a quite unpublishable book called *Tropic of Cancer* by an American named Henry Miller. [. . .]

*Tropic of Cancer*, I repeat, is unprintable under Anglo Saxon laws, but I think the boy writes like a ball of fire.

### FABER & FABER BOOK CATALOGUE, AUTUMN 1935

*Poems*
Louis MacNeice

The most original Irish poet of his generation, dour without sentimentality, intensely serious without political enthusiasm, his work is intelligible but unpopular, and has the pride and modesty of things that endure.

*It is hard to imagine a publisher writing catalogue copy like that today, but it is wonderful.*

## T. S. Eliot to his friend John Hayward, 19 September 1935

We can confidently recommend the new giant crackers on sale at Hamley's at prices ranging from eighteen pence to half-a-crown. One of these petards was hoisted at Messrs. Faber & Faber's Book Committee yesterday, on the occasion of the return of the Chairman from the grouse moors. While the attention of the Committee was distracted, at the tea interval, by the presentation of a large chocolate cake bearing an inscription WELCOME, CHIEF!, the cracker was produced from under the table and successfully fired. It exploded with a loud report, and scattered about the room multi-coloured festoons, some of which draped themselves on the chandelier, others on the head of the Chairman. At this point another novelty, called 'Snake-in-the-grass', was introduced: one of them escaped and set fire to the festoons. After the conflagration had been extinguished the business of the committee was resumed, and an enjoyable time was had by all.

*According to a later memoir from Frank Morley, the cracker had been concealed in a coal-scuttle: 'Eliot and Kennerley and I spent most of the morning rigging up pulleys under the big table, and rehearsing how the scuttle could be pulled, unseen, across the floor to appear between the Chairman's legs.'*

*Among the business to which the Committee eventually returned must have been the forthcoming* Faber Book of Modern Verse.

## T. S. Eliot to Michael Roberts, 19 September 1935

According to the estimate the book will run to 384 pages. Some of the Committee were inclined to think that this was too long, but on second thoughts it was decided not to ask you to omit anything. We were guided partly by the stimulus of competition. Ian Parsons' book[4] is to be sold at 5s., and I rather infer from the advertisement in Chatto's catalogue that it will be a much slighter book than yours. We expect to bring your book out early, so the sooner it goes to press the better. It should precede Yeats's Oxford Book[5], and I do not fear serious competition from the latter. The existence of these two other anthologies, however, makes it desirable that our book should be a bulky one, and I think we are giving very good value for the money. Of course it will take us a considerable time to get our money back, but we are counting on a long run. Incidentally, I have all confidence that your book will succeed because it will be the best.

### FABER & FABER'S CHRISTMAS LIST FOR 1935

Wars and rumours of war cannot prevent us from looking back on 1935 with considerable satisfaction. It has been, for us, a year of notable suc-

---

4  I. M. Parsons (ed.), *The Progress of Poetry: An Anthology of Verse from Hardy to the Present Day* (Chatto & Windus, 1936).
5  W. B. Yeats (ed.), *The Oxford Book of Modern Verse 1892–1935* (Oxford University Press, 1936).

cesses in every field. Space and modesty alike prevent us from blowing our own trumpet, but the London correspondent of the *New York Sun*, John Hayward, has obligingly executed this brief preliminary flourish for us: 'In my opinion, by far the most interesting list of new books to be published this fall comes from the firm of Faber & Faber.'

*Somehow this piece of puffery fails to mention that John Hayward was a close friend of T. S. Eliot, Geoffrey Faber and Frank Morley. The four of them would meet at Hayward's flat in Bina Gardens and eventually collaborated on a book of poems,* Noctes Binanianae, *produced in a limited edition of twenty-five copies. This reveals the nicknames they had for each other. Geoffrey, whose baldness has already been noted, was the 'Coot'; T. S. Eliot was the 'Elephant', presumably because he never forgot; Frank Morley, whose geniality expressed itself in his girth and who had earned money during his Oxford vacations on a whaling ship, was the 'Whale'; and Hayward, who prided himself on his networking skills and was known for his ability to wound with a word, was the 'Tarantula'.*

# 3: 1936–1939
## 'With a very real danger of war'

By the middle of the 1930s, Faber & Faber was firmly established as one of the leading publishers in London. Regular profitability might still be an aspiration rather than an actuality, but turnover had doubled and would approach £100,000 in 1936. The year before, the company had expanded into one floor of the building next door at 23 Russell Square. One of Frank Morley's little jokes in 1931 had been to produce 'Dr Morley's Parabolic Prediction or Futurity Revealed' in a limited edition of seven copies. It showed how book sales since 1926 had followed a curve which implied they would be over £1m by the middle of the century (see Appendix for more details). The firm might be falling behind that particular prediction (which closed with an advertisement for Dr Morley's next limited edition: 'Breakers Ahead! Or Beaten by a Parabola') but it could still view its growth with some satisfaction.

What set Faber apart from all the other publishers who had started in the post-war period was, of course, the presence of T. S. Eliot on the Board. By 1936 his star was firmly in the ascendant. The surprising success of the play *Murder in the Cathedral* the previous year meant that he was becoming a household name. As we shall see, that made him a target for occasional ribbing, especially as he was still a mere 'ordinary director' (the only one). It also meant, of course, that the stamp of acceptance by Eliot came to have more and more significance. His reputation fed those of the poets he took on, and theirs fed his as a publisher, so that Faber became the home of literary Modernism.

It would be wrong, however, to think of Faber – even of Faber poetry – as a one-man show. The Book Committee remained the focal point of the firm's decision-making, and even encouraged risk-taking. Editors would be supported in their decisions by colleagues who had also read the manuscript. An author was not taken on by one man (such were the times that the gender-specificity is all too appropriate) but by the firm.

As the decade drew to a close, the increasing likelihood of war would inevitably cast its shadow over the firm's activities. The chapter begins, however, with Geoffrey writing a catalogue entry for a book that had been gestating ever since Tom Faber announced to his father that he thought Uncle Tom was a very good writer.

### FABER & FABER BOOK CATALOGUE, SPRING 1936

*Mr Eliot's book of Pollicle Dogs and Jellicle Cats*
*As Recited to Him by the Man in White Spats*

Mr. Eliot informs the Publishers that his book of Children's Verses should be completed by Easter, 1936. If this statement (for which the Publishers accept no responsibility) proves to be true, the book will certainly be published this year with the least possible delay.

There is no doubt that Mr. Eliot is writing it; for several of the poems, illustrated by the author, have been in private circulation in the Publishers' various families for a considerable time, and at least one of them has been recorded on the gramophone. (N.B. There is only one record in this country, and there is believed to be another in America. Applications for duplicates will be thrown into the waste-paper basket.)

### Geoffrey Faber, diary entry, Monday, 27 January 1936

Dined in office, and went round to City Literary Institute, where I took the chair for a paper read by Cecil Day Lewis. I liked Day Lewis very much. Drove back in taxi with him and dropped him at Auden's.

## Allen Lane to Geoffrey Faber, 17 February 1936

As you may have heard, I have formed a separate company called Penguin Books Ltd of which I am the sole director, to undertake the publication and distribution of Penguin Books.

> *Allen Lane's founding of Penguin Books, famously to sell 'books cheap enough to buy at the railway station bookstall', would have an enormous effect on the British publishing industry. Initially, however, hardback publishers were entirely happy to make a little more money by selling the rights to publish their books in paperback to Lane's new company.*

> *Meanwhile, in a memorandum headed 'Take your time over it', Eliot was betraying to Geoffrey his uncertainty over the book of children's verse already announced in the spring catalogue.*

## T. S. Eliot to Geoffrey Faber, 6 March 1936

I am more and more doubtful of my ability to write a successful book of this kind, and I had rather find out early that I can't do it, than waste a lot of time for nothing. And this sort of thing is flatter if it is flat, than serious verse can be. Nobody wants to make a fool of himself when he might be better employed. [. . .]

At the end they all go up in a balloon, self, Spats, and dogs and cats.

'Up up up past the Russell Hotel,
Up up up to the Heaviside Layer.'

There are several ways in which this might be a failure. The various Poems (how many should there be?) might not be good enough. The matter such as here attached may be not at all amusing: a book simply of collected animal poems might be better. Finally, the contents and general treatment may be too mixed: there might be a part that children wouldn't like and part that adults wouldn't like and part that nobody would like. The *mise-en-scène* may not please. There seem to be many more ways of going wrong than of going right.

> *It would be a few years before Eliot could overcome his uncertainty.*

John Hayward, a 'bearded stranger', visiting the Book Committee in 1939, with Frank Morley to his right.

> *Djuna Barnes's novel* Nightwood *provoked a fascinating correspondence between Geoffrey Faber on the one hand, who didn't see the point of it, and Frank Morley and T. S. Eliot, who were passionately in favour.*

### Frank Morley to Geoffrey Faber, 4 April 1936

I have now read *Nightwood* and want to go on record. It is much more remarkable than I knew at first glance. You may think that I say it wildly rather than clearly; but I have no doubt TSE can express it better, and I hope he will.

I don't see how anyone who has any appreciation of TSE's work can fail to see something in *Nightwood*. It can hardly be called a novel, any more than *The Waste Land* a detective story. [. . .]

Now being certain of all this (though very eager to see TSE translate the recognition of the book and lay it out all neat along the toothbrush), my main point, which is really serious to me, is that if I am right we <u>must</u> study to publish it. I think you know very well how my general activity, and general value to the list, depends on feeling that there are some good things in it. If I know of a lump of leaven I will work like a bottlebrush to make all the doughnuts pay for it; but I really can't work on a list with enthusiasm unless there is something which seems to me to have the chance to be literature. I know perfectly the necessity of making money; but I also know that the best stimulus, for me, is not merely that necessity, but the pride of publishing a few books which I really cherish. That pride sustains a host of other effort; and ~~honestly~~ is the only real sustainer. I feel that here is a book that I recognize and am proud of; to do it is to give me energy; to turn it down, for any insufficient reason, would make me apathetic.

## T. S. Eliot to Geoffrey Faber, 15 April 1936

Frank showed me a letter which he had written to you after a second reading of *Nightwood*, and which he said he would hold up until I had had an opportunity to read the book again. I have read it over the holidays, and I am more strongly in favour of the book than ever. [. . .]

But what is important to me is that I believe that this may be our last chance to do something remarkable in the way of imaginative literature. As for our literary reputation, remember that people like Joyce and myself may help to keep the temperature level, but we can't send it any higher. There is something an author does <u>once</u> (if at all) in his generation that he can't ever do again. We can go on writing stuff that nobody else would write, if you like, but *The Waste Land* and *Ulysses* remain the historic points. From a publishing point of view, there is a tremendous difference between getting a good author first, and rounding him in after his reputation is made; and if Joyce and I, for example, had up to now been published by some other firm, we should no longer be worth getting. To return to the first sentence of this paragraph – that is merely a prediction, for what it is worth: but my feeling is that this book is very likely the last big thing to be done in our time: (the rest of which will belong to the callow epigoni of the *Faber Book of Modern Verse*).

## Geoffrey Faber to T. S. Eliot and Frank Morley, 16 April 1936

The established rule applies to the case of Djuna Barnes:– if any director is all out over a book or an author, we must do it – him – her. And when <u>two</u> directors go all out in the same direction, still more so. And where they go so completely all out –

What distresses me is that I should have so hopelessly failed to see what you both see in *Nightwood*. After reading your two letters I cannot doubt that you are right, and that I am wrong – which is a discomforting, though perhaps salutary state of mind for a publisher, let alone an educated man, to be in. [. . .]

I still fail to see how it can sell. The technical difficulties of 'putting over' a book, which takes the form of a <u>novel</u> but will be unreadable by the novel-reading public, are great. If *Nightwood* is in the category of *The Waste Land*, yet there are no ready-made tracks for it to run on – FVM will have to lay them himself. He says he helped to do so for *The Waste Land*, and I don't doubt it: but the W.L. was 'poetry', and so there was a railway-system for it to move about upon! *Ulysses* shows, I suppose, that the difficulty isn't insuperable.

*In that autumn's catalogue T. S. Eliot did his best to explain*
*what* Nightwood *was all about. I rather suspect Frank Morley of*
*writing the later entry about the forthcoming book on Iceland*
*by W. H. Auden and Louis MacNeice.*

### FABER & FABER BOOK CATALOGUE, AUTUMN 1936

*Nightwood*
Djuna Barnes

This book, upon which Miss Barnes has been at work for a long time, is
extremely difficult to describe. It is in prose, but will appeal primarily to
readers of poetry; it has something of the form of a novel, but the characters suffer rather than act: and as with Dostoevski and George Chapman,
one feels that the action is hardly more than the shadow-play of something
taking place on another plane of reality. It is concerned with *le miserable au*
*centre de sa misère*, and has nothing to offer to readers whose temperament
attaches them to either an easy or a frightened optimism. [. . .]

*Iceland*
W. H. Auden and Louis MacNeice

We understand that the book will take the form of a series of letters, some
in verse, some in prose, written from Iceland in the summer of 1936. [. . .]

There may be a good many other books about Iceland and about other
expeditions, but this is the only book by Mr. Auden and Mr. MacNeice.

*Among the banter, the following letter from the American*
*publisher Ben Huebsch comes as a salutary reminder of what*
*was taking place under the Nazi regime. Geoffrey received*
*it because he was becoming a leading light in the Publishers*
*Association, and was already on course to start a two-year term*
*as its president in 1939.*

## Ben Huebsch to Geoffrey Faber, 15 June 1936

I can only hope that when the time comes you will fight against allowing your Association to participate in a Congress to be held in Germany as long as Germany restricts the expression and interchange of ideas. It shocks me to think that we might be blandly and smugly talking sweet nothings about ideals of publishing while one of Germany's most courageous editors, Ossietzki, languishes nearby in a concentration camp; and our conference will probably take place in the very building which contains the stock of Siegmund Freud's books that the German Government confiscated.

*America's Independence Day, the Fourth of July, was always an occasion for some joke to be played on or by the American directors of the firm. In 1936, T. S. Eliot was the target, following the appearance of a small advertisement in* The Times: *'GERHARD and his BAND have been engaged to play every night at ELIOT'S CLUB, 28 Charing Cross Road.' With 4 July landing on a Saturday that year, however, the joke had to wait for the following Monday.*

## Charles Stewart (writing as 'The Secretary') to T. S. Eliot, 6 July 1936

The enclosed advertisement, to which I understand that your attention has been already privately drawn, has been under the serious consideration of the Principal Directors of this Company. While it is true that there is no explicit written prohibition of a Director engaging in an activity of the kind referred to in the advertisement, the Principal Directors are unanimous in regarding it as very undesirable that a mere Ordinary Director should advertise himself in this way. Furthermore, they wish you to understand that, in their opinion, the nature of the occupation, in which you have engaged without their previous knowledge or consent, is open to the gravest objections. An Ordinary Director, they point out, who is expected to take part on equal terms in the deliberations of the Principal

Directors, can scarcely bring the necessary freshness of mind to a Board Meeting, if his nights are spent in the manner sufficiently indicated by the advertisement. A further highly unsatisfactory feature of this surprising disclosure is the evidence which it affords of the use of the connections acquired by you as a Director of this Company for the purposes of private profit.

I am, accordingly, instructed to invite you to make a statement, which should include an account of your profits as a Proprietor of the Club in question and a complete list of the members for submission to my Board.

*Eliot's rejoinder seems to me to be a comic masterpiece.*

## T. S. Eliot to Geoffrey Faber, '7th July, 1936: 1.30 a.m. of the 8th.'

My dear Geoffrey,

I have received this morning a letter from Stewart which has caused me considerable distress of mind. Having been engaged all day, and until 1 o'clock this morning, on business of the firm, I am now in a state of exhaustion, and therefore may not be able to deal with the matter as thoroughly as I should like to do. Still, I cannot let the imputation rest, even for a day; and I am writing to you privately and in confidence, before taking any further steps.

I am assuming that you have cognisance of the content of Stewart's letter; at least, I can hardly understand his having the effrontery to write to me as he did, without consulting you first. If he wrote without your knowledge, I ask your forgiveness for what I am about to say; but otherwise, I must say, Geoffrey, that I think that if such a letter was to be written at all, it should only have been written and signed by the Chairman. It has been said, I do not know when or where or by whom, that a man is entitled to be judged by his peers: in the firm of Faber & Faber Limited that is hardly possible for me; but the person who comes the nearest to being a peer is surely a Chairman. I do not feel that such a letter should have been addressed to me by Stewart: incidentally, he takes advantage of the occasion to provoke me with several cheap sneers. I feel that you, Geoffrey, would have put the accusation (for such in effect, it is) with much more grace and tact, even if just as cheaply.

The problem is exceedingly complex and must be regarded as having different angles and several facets. I will begin at the beginning – I mean, the nominal beginning, for I cannot help feeling that there must be a long history behind this, of intrigue of which I have been innocently unaware. I shall number my paragraphs, for your convenience and to hold your attention.

1. I do not consider it within the competence of three Directors, meeting informally in committee (which I was too busy to attend), to pass resolutions or make any strictures upon the conduct of an absent Director, in an official form. It is usual, of course, for any two or more Directors in informal conversation to make nasty remarks about absent Directors, but that is another matter. The breach to which I object is not a mere matter of bad taste – I am too accustomed to that to take notice of it – but of constitutional practice. Such matters should only be discussed by Directors meeting in quorum qua Board, and a full week's notice should be given by the Secretary (who is by the way very lax in procedure) and the Agenda circulated. Indeed, I think that a matter of such gravity as this should be brought before a General Shareholders' Meeting. I should like Miss Leigh[1] to be present.

---

1  Gertrude Leigh, a former employee of Sir Henry Burdett and thereby shareholder in the Scientific Press, had rolled over some of her eventual profit on Faber & Gwyer shares into Faber & Faber, making her one of only two external shareholders in the company (the other being Geoffrey's friend Stanley Robinson). Faber & Faber also published her books.

2. If there is to be any investigation of the conduct of one director, (and I for one should welcome a full investigation), then the activities of <u>all</u> directors should be passed in review. There are some directors, whom I will not name, who are obviously maintaining a scale of living (and I only refer to that side of their life which is quite open and regular) far beyond that which would be justified by the salaries they draw according to the books of the firm. I will say no more on this point.

3. I take serious exception to a phrase in Stewart's letter: 'a mere Ordinary Director'. I would point out that in this firm an ordinary director, so-called, is a good deal more extraordinary than a principal director: there are four of the latter, seemingly, and only one of the former. The term 'ordinary director' is therefore a risible misnomer. I suggest that the term 'extraordinary director' should be substituted. Stewart then goes on to say that as an 'ordinary director' I am expected 'to take part on equal terms in the deliberations of the Principal Directors'! There can be, of course, no fundamental equality between two kinds of person one of which is four times as rare as the other (I hope you follow this somewhat subtle reasoning); yet I challenge anyone to say that I have ever shown the slightest arrogance or <u>hauteur</u> in my dealings with ordinary Principal Directors. I pride myself on being as democratic as the next man, a good mixer, hail-fellow-well-met, always affable and tolerant. The innuendo is quite baseless.

4. The suggestion is made that it is improper for me to be connected in a business way with a Dance Club (for if there is a Band we may assume that dancing is one of the activities of the Club) – even when that Club has the guarantee of respectability afforded by the name of Eliot. (What sort of impression would the name 'Morley's Club' convey!!!) It is added that I 'can scarcely bring the necessary freshness of mind

to a Board Meeting, if my nights are spent . . .' etc. I should like
to bring to your attention another possible point of view which
is ignored. If the Directors of Faber & Faber Ltd. suppose that it
is improper for me to be associated with Eliot's Club, what do
they suppose the members of Eliot's Club think of my being
associated with Faber & Faber? Which is the more sordidly
corrupt activity – dancing or publishing? And would not the
members of Eliot's Club have the right to object, that if I am to
spend my days in Board Meetings, I can scarcely bring to the
Club in the evening the freshness of mind essential if one is to
carry on such a venture successfully?

5. I would point out that my emoluments from the publishing
   house of Faber are not only ridiculously inadequate in
   consideration of the burden of responsibility that I bear, but are
   only just sufficient to enable me to dress neatly and modestly
   and to entertain the innumerable bores at whom I should be
   able to snap my fingers were I not connected with a publishing
   house. In a dance club, if any individual fails to behave properly,
   you chuck him out; in a publishing house, you take him out to
   lunch. If the firm of Faber & Faber Ltd dislikes the thought of
   my having to earn a little money elsewhere (and the firm might
   well blush collectively, even though the Principal Directors,
   so-called, are unable to blush individually, at the thought of a
   situation so humiliating for the firm) then it has the remedy
   in its own hands: to provide me with an income on which I
   can live. Otherwise, I may find myself tempted to devote the
   whole of my attention to the legitimate entertainment industry,
   providing innocent and rhythmical pleasure for people's bodies,
   instead of conniving at providing so much trash for their minds.
   Anyway, I am glad to think that Senhor Ferro's next visit to
   London will be during one of my enforced absences, and that
   there is not a man among you who has the slightest notion of
   how to deal with a Portuguese diplomat.

6. Now about the name, 'Eliot's Club'. It does not seem to be realised that I can no more prevent my name being used while I am living, than I can prevent the people of London from erecting statues, memorial tablets, or hideous stained-glass windows in my honour after I am dead. This is one of the consequences of fame, which afflict anyone bearing on shoulders immense Atlantaean, the load Well nigh not to be borne Of the too-vast orb of his fate. Fame and infamy are divided only by the thinnest partition. I could not even prevent the Principal Directors from all taking, by deed-poll, the surname of Eliot. They could alter the name of the firm, if malice impelled them to go so far, to Eliot, Eliot, Eliot & Eliot Ltd. (T. S. Eliot, ordinary director, of U.S.A. Origin). Indeed, any organisation wishing to inspire confidence in the public, might easily be tempted to assume a name that is a synonym for probity, fastidiousness and impeccable behaviour.

7. What I think most heartless, in this most irregular inquisition, is that I am compelled to fling open a door revealing a family skeleton. I might cry 'This is unworthy of you, Holmes! I could not have believed that you would have descended to this. You have made inquiries into the history of my unhappy brother' ... Not that Arthur is my brother, far from it. Poor Arthur! Yet his affairs are no secret; he is known to all the magistrates of London and some in the provinces; and on more than one occasion he has been described from the Bench as 'a very bad case'. There is a strain of eccentricity in his family, deriving from the distaff side, which impels him to found clubs. I think his mother's people came from north of the Trent; anyway, there is something about him which is not English. Need I delve any more deeply into this painful wound?

LATER. 4 a.m. I dropped off into a sound sleep, from pure exhaustion, and now set to work to complete this document which has

already caused me so much anguish. This whole affair makes me
feel like a lonely Prometheus (the classical allusion will not escape
you) chained to a mountain crag, with his liver exposed to the beaks
of foul vultures. Yet it would be doing Stewart too much honour to
refer to him as a vulture. Morley's friend André Gide[2] once said <u>il
faut avoir un aigle</u>. He never said <u>il faut avoir un Stewart</u>.

8. This is really the last point. I have never had a penny, or the
   expectation of a penny, or the hope or intention of a penny,
   out of Eliot's Club. In everything that I have done, I have
   been completely disinterested, frequently at direct financial
   loss, with increasing anxieties and dwindling income. I will
   mention one incident, trivial maybe in itself, but suggestive
   and typical. Only last week I sacrificed my sense of dignity
   and reserve, to say nothing of a whole morning, to put
   myself into the hands of a number of coarse young men in an
   abandoned Baptist Chapel in the Marylebone Road, for the
   purpose of making a film which was supposed to be intended
   to persuade people to buy more books. I will pass over the
   humiliation and the physical discomfort, acute as they were.
   I performed this act at your request: you were careful, I
   thought, not to put it into so many words, but a nod is as good
   as a wink. I submitted myself to be made up, as the phrase
   is, by a villainous-looking and untidy young man of Jewish
   origin (I suspect); he was also supposed to un-make me. Later
   in the day, it was brought to my attention by a person whom I
   was entertaining at lunch at my own expense in the interests
   of the firm, that the young man in question had failed to
   unmake the back of my neck. When I changed my shirt in the
   evening I found the collar discoloured and probably ruined

---

2  This is a dig at Frank Morley, who had dined in Paris with Eliot, Joyce and
Gide, only to find himself completely tongue-tied because his polymathic
skills did not extend to French.

– 12s.6d. (all I can afford to pay for a shirt out of my modest income) thrown away, so to speak. Need I say more?

I remain, however, in a spirit of Christian charity,
Always your friend and well-wisher,
T. S. Eliot

*After Geoffrey's death, successive Chairmen of Faber & Faber kept this correspondence locked away, believing it to be evidence of a serious rift.*

*Dick de la Mare had originally enquired after David Jones's 'book about the War' in 1932; he continued to ask about it for the next four years. When the manuscript eventually came in, however, it was T. S. Eliot who reported on it.*

## T. S. Eliot, report to the Book Committee on *In Parenthesis* by David Jones, September 1936

The committee is not to think that it can escape the necessity for re-reading this book by relying on my opinion. That is to say that although I found this book quite fascinating, it is definitely not a one-man opinion book, whether mine or anyone else's. I should certainly recommend it if I thought it had any chance of paying for itself, but a book dealing with Flanders between December 1915 and July 1916 in a kind of prose which is frequently on the edge of verse is hardly likely to be popular at the present time.

*With the author uncontactable in Iceland, Eliot had to decide on a title for Auden's second volume of poems, choosing* Look, Stranger! *from one of the lines in it. As the poet wrote to his US publisher, he did not approve of Eliot's choice.*

## W. H. Auden to Bennett Cerf, November 1936

Faber invented a bloody title while I was away without telling me. It sounds like work of a vegetarian lady novelist. Will you please call the American edition *On this island*.

*An exchange in* The Bookseller, *the self-styled 'Organ of the Book Trade', prompted Geoffrey to write this revealing letter to its editor.*

## Geoffrey Faber to the Editor, *The Bookseller*, 11 March 1937

I should not like it to be thought that my own house has found it necessary to 'bring in enough capital to keep things going'. In point of fact, since its formation, I have not brought in any additional capital, whether by the issue of shares or debentures, or by any other means. The subsequent growth of the business has been financed entirely out of income. That, I believe, is the best way and, in the long run, the only way.

## T. S. Eliot, report to the Book Committee on *Guide to Kulchur* by Ezra Pound, June 1937

We asked for this and we have got it. It is only a damned kulchered person who will be able to find his way about this book, but for the perceptive there are a good many plums, and for the judicious who know how to trim the boat with their own intelligence there is a good deal of wisdom.

## T. S. Eliot, report to the Book Committee on *The Black Book* by Lawrence Durrell, June 1937

This man has some ability. [. . .]

The book as it is is unprintable, and it could not be printed merely by excisions: the author would have to rewrite it himself. I think that the book would be none the worse for being rewritten in a printable form. There are some good bits in the account of the commercial school and teaching the African lady to read Chaucer. In its present form, the book is a mess. Somebody else must look at it.

*Faber did not publish* The Black Book *until 1973. By then* The Alexandria Quartet *had made Durrell one of the mainstays of the Faber list.*

## Geoffrey Faber, diary entry, Thursday, 25 November 1937

To dine with the Morleys at Pike's Farm (Thanksgiving Day) – with TSE & Morley Kennerley. Played Frank's new Publishing game, and left – in fog and frost – about 1.30 a.m.

*I suspect this was the only occasion on which the game was played. The Faber archive contains its rules but not the cards or board. I will skate over the description of the role of booksellers – 'their money [. . .]is simply there to be plundered' – and note that 'the Game is won by the Publisher who survives longest'. From that point of view, this whole book is really about how Faber & Faber won Frank Morley's publishing game.*

## Geoffrey Faber, diary entry, Thursday, 9 December 1937

Lunched with Eliot and Auden at Tom's club. First time I've really met Auden – I liked him, and thought him obviously a man of real talent, and not mere surface stuff. We took him back to the office, so that he could work in the waiting-room. Black Book meeting[3]– the deuce of a long spring list – certainly 75 books, I hope it won't sink us!

---

3  The meeting to establish the next season's list.

## Geoffrey Faber, diary entry, Sunday, 12 December 1937

I now at 11.30 settle down to this melancholy job, with a number of gloomy reflections in my mind. Yet I don't feel as gloomy as I should, especially after the late nights and so forth recently. My reflections concern: (1) the state of Europe, the Far East, the world. Everything steadily seeming to grow darker and darker. With a very real danger of war, in my children's early lifetime. (2) My own persistent inability to cut my coat according to my cloth – here we are with a minimum gross income of about £3,150 a year.⁴ Income tax and surtax and insurance premiums reduce that to about £2,300. Education is costing me about £500 a year, and will cost me more. Keeping up Ty Glyn about £300. Household expenditure about £1,000. My own miscellaneous and personal expenditure not less than £400. Then there are drinks, cars and medical – some £250 a year, perhaps. Enid's own expenditure covering the children's clothes, uses up all her own income (about £260). So that I am spending some £2,450 a year on a net certain income of about £2,050. Share of profits in Faber & Faber reduces that gap, but is always uncertain. A dividend would put me right – but when the devil is a dividend going to come? The devil of it is that I can't cut down – except by giving up drinking and smoking (which might save me, personally, say £75 a year), or by selling Ty Glyn. But that's a difficult proposition, and would be stupid, until I'm forced to that. So I must go on hoping for better things next year.

*The following January, T. S. Eliot passed to Geoffrey a letter he had received from Paul Léon, Joyce's amanuensis, with the following handwritten addendum: 'Will you be dealing with this? You can control your temper better than I can.'*

---

4  In real terms, about £200,000 today.

### Geoffrey Faber to James Joyce, 26 January 1938

Eliot has given me his recent correspondence with M. Leon concerning the publication of *Work in Progress*, and has asked me to continue it, since he feels that M. Leon's last letter (of January 23rd) needs to be answered by the head of the firm. [. . .]

So far as we are concerned, we could publish on the date, which you so earnestly desire, July 4, provided that (1) we received the rest of the MS within the next two or three weeks (2) both you and we could be sure that the correction of the proofs would not take you too long a time. On the first point, we have no definite information. On the second point, is it not probable you will find the correction of the proofs a rather slow process? [. . .]

These being the facts of the situation, will you not ease the relations between yourself and your publishers by giving them fair recognition, instead of instructing M. Leon to write in the extraordinary terms of his letter of the 23rd? As it is, I propose to treat M. Leon's letter as if it had not been written, and to end simply with an appeal to you to reconcile yourself to publication in September, if publication in early July proves to be impracticable; and not to carry out the idea of breaking off your work now, just when its completion is in sight.

### Geoffrey Faber, diary entry, Sunday, 1 May 1938

Made friends with C. P. Snow – though he is taking his next books to Heinemann – away from Gollancz, anyhow.

> *C. P. Snow had already published three novels with Gollancz. On this occasion, according to a later letter, Geoffrey 'put some F&F groundbait in'. His work would bring its reward soon.*

> *For all this time, T. S. Eliot had continued to edit the* Criterion, *but with war increasingly likely, it was now time to call a halt.*

## T. S. Eliot to Geoffrey Faber, 1 October 1938

It occurs to me to suggest that nothing should be said about the termination of the *Criterion*, and that no rumour should reach even the secretaries, until we have decided exactly how and when. [. . .]

I wanted to say something more than this. It occurs to me that the thought may lurk in your mind that I may feel a good deal of regret. But you ought to know that for several years I have had doubts. These doubts do not merely stand for a conscientious thought that it is a waste of money for the firm. It is impossible to run a one-man show like this for fifteen years without feeling that it is going stale. I have run it without conviction for several years; only I felt that so long as you and Frank felt that it was of some advertising value to the firm – or that my chief value to the firm was running the *Criterion* – I couldn't well give it up. [. . .]

Incidentally, I am not at all happy about the position of the firm and its commitments. It seems to me that were we going to war now, the position would be highly critical: even as things are, it is delicate. And as I think that possibly war has merely been postponed to a still less favourable moment, I should like to see the decks kept a bit clearer.

P.S. [. . .] certainly the happiest editorial years have been those when the review belonged exclusively to Faber & Faber. For this, as for many things, I am grateful to you. Incidentally, I do not forget that it was on the pretext of the *Criterion* that I was insinuated – with some difficulty – into Faber & Gwyer's.

Mr Eliot's Book of Pollicle Dogs and Jellicle Cats as Recited to Him by the Man in White Spats *might have been announced in Faber's catalogue for spring 1936, but it had still not appeared. The diary entry below shows, however, that it had not been forgotten. Ralph Hodgson's poems still appear in anthologies.*

*I realise that the suggestion that he was the 'Man in White*
*Spats' may displease those who give that honour to John*
*Hayward.*

### Geoffrey Faber, diary entry, Friday, 7 October 1938

Met Ralph Hodgson for 1st time in Tom's room – and liked him
greatly. Introduced to me, cryptically, by T. as the Man in White
Spats & illustrator of Pollicle Dogs – which didn't help me to guess
who he was. But I tumbled to it.

The attentive godfather looks on as Tom Faber tries
out his most recent present.

*When Frank Morley went to New York to drum up business in October 1938, Geoffrey wrote him a long letter which gives a nice idea of the breadth of the firm's publishing by the end of the 1930s. The 'Bill' referred to in the letter is the literary agent William Watt at A. P. Watt. Geoffrey had developed a good relationship with him and his son Alan.*

## Geoffrey Faber to Frank Morley, 14 October 1938

The year's figures up to the end of August, from the monthly returns, aren't too bad. Total expenditure £53,415: income £54,148. The margin is certainly small. [. . .]

Gunn.[5] You'll have to blarney him on your return. He wrote to you saying that he wants to do another cruise round the Outer Hebrides and Orkneys next year; that we shouldn't be enthusiastic about that; and he was at work on a sort of a thriller which he would rather give to those who handle such things commercially; and in short that he wanted to clear out. (The hand of Collins – or, rather, the cloven hoof is evident here.) I have written to him, as well as I could; saying that we hadn't built on *Off in a Boat* (upon which, in spite of his £175, we haven't really lost money), but had wanted to ease his transition from a career in which writing had to be a side-line, to one to which it could take first place; that his kind of thriller couldn't be the sort of mediocre pattern stuff that the 'commercials' are good at; that his *Morning Tide* strain was much better handled by us than them; that we should certainly be ready to do the Hebrides book; and that at any rate I hoped he wouldn't commit himself till you came back.

Spender[6] is also trying to defect, by giving his poems to the Hogarth Press, and accusing us of robbing him. TSE has written an admirable

---

5  Faber hung on to Neil Gunn and published several more books by him, including *The Silver Darlings* (1941).
6  Stephen Spender did not defect.

letter; and we (Tom and I) have nailed him for lunch on Friday and will do our damndest to nail him down for good. [. . .]

Pearl Buck.[7] There's just a chance here. Bill says she's not keen on staying with Methuens, and he's afraid of losing her to another agent. Would we make an offer – or rather, equip him with one to make, if he can? She gets 25% from word go, & 6d on colonials! No use trying to scale that down. Her last novel had earned over £1,000 on 1st royalty. Methuens have done 14 books in all. I'd no idea there were so many. Crawley's hunting it all up, of course.

Liddell-Hart.[8] Utter silence!

Filchner.[9] Tom says a good book. Typical weighty Tomian report, delivered in apparent ignorance of the fact that we were committed, unless book was rotten. Everybody, in consequence now rather frightened of the £150 advance. [. . .]

Life is about to be hell with blurbs; and I don't feel very happy about the spring list – but that's how I nearly always feel. But we <u>do</u> want some good bright lighteners, or something that will sell by its own weight. By the way, I forgot to say that we have just got firm *Evening Standard* promise of 1st offer of their *Mein Kampf* articles, which are good and have been widely read. A rush job if it comes off. And maybe copyright obstacles, though the articles are descriptive not quotative.

---

7   Pearl Buck won the Nobel Prize in Literature in 1938, but was never published by Faber. Her royalties of 25 per cent of published price on UK sales, and 6d a copy on sales elsewhere in the Empire, reflect her status as a star author.
8   Captain B. H. Liddell Hart was a military historian and theorist, quite influential in the 1930s, published by Faber.
9   The Spring 1939 Catalogue includes this description of *A Scientist in Tartary from the Hoang-Ho to the Indus* by Wilhelm Filchner: 'This book is the diary of an exploring scientist: the hardships, the escapes, imprisonments and strange meetings are all the more impressive because incidental to the author's patient and indomitable scientific purposes.'

Harcourt[10] cabled yesterday about Duff Cooper's 'articles on crisis' in the *Standard*. What about them as a book? We've passed that on to Watt. It's a weekly article, and the first was just his answer to Hitler's 'men in England who want war – Eden, Duff Cooper, Churchill'.[11] Not exciting, and topical. I doubt the book, rather. But we'll see. [...]

Under Bill's benign approval I have been very thick with Alan, who doesn't lose anything on closer acquaintance. Nobody could have looked less like a future literary agent a few months ago, but I believe he will be running that show, and running it well, before he's finished. He is all set to go to New York. I suppose you couldn't somehow wangle an invitation for him?

Tidier writing indicates that I have resumed this epistle after lunching with Uncle Tom and wrestling with the Crossword – F&F's I mean.

*Throughout the 1930s, Faber included a crossword in its Christmas catalogue. My reading of that last paragraph is that Geoffrey took responsibility for setting it.*

## Alison Uttley to Charles Stewart, 25 October 1938

I am sending you an out-of-the-ordinary story for children, which a young child might find difficult to understand as the heroine moves through time from one century to another, but I think girls of twelve would grasp the plots, interwoven as they are.

*At the beginning of 1939, Faber was finally able to announce the book by James Joyce from which the firm had been publishing fragments since 1930. T. S. Eliot, of course, had to write the catalogue description.*

---

10 Alfred Harcourt, founder of New York publisher Harcourt, Brace and Howe.
11 This is a reference to a speech made by Adolf Hitler on 9 October 1938, saying that these men wished to start a war.

FABER & FABER BOOK CATALOGUE, SPRING 1939

James Joyce
*Finnegans Wake*
(hitherto known as 'Work in Progress')

When one of the very greatest of modern authors completes a work to
which he has devoted sixteen years of labour – and which has been more
talked about and written about during the period of its composition than
any previous work of English literature – then the publishers feel that
they should waste no words in describing the book, which would be the
most important event of any season in which it appeared.

A historic moment captured on a slightly out-of focus camera:
the junior editor Alan Pringle hands over proofs of the first part of
*Finnegans Wake* to T. S. Eliot.

## Charles Stewart to Alison Uttley, 10 January 1939

I am sorry we have been so long over *The Secret of Thackers*. We
read the manuscript and liked it, but as a book for older girls is outside our usual field, we decided to take another opinion as well.

The reader shares our liking for the book but thinks it might be improved in some ways. The reader's report and the suggestions seem to us so sound that I am sending a copy to you. I shall be very much interested to hear your views. We hope you will agree that the book needs some revision: when that is done, we should very much like to see the manuscript again.

*Marie Stopes, the celebrated campaigner for women's rights and birth control, was also a poet. Her submission to the firm of* Love Songs for Young Lovers *prompted a rejection letter from Geoffrey, which seems to summarise perfectly how his publishing business had developed.*

## Geoffrey Faber to Dr Marie Stopes, 20 January 1939

When I began to build up this business, my ambition was to give it a universal character. It happened that my principal personal contacts were what are called (often very unfairly!) 'highbrow'; and it followed naturally that our development at first tended in that direction. It is extraordinary how quickly that sort of thing becomes a label – one of those sticky labels which it takes a lot of time and effort to scrape off. Well, I have scraped most of it off by now; and all that is left of it, over the range of our <u>prose</u> publications, is simply a general sense that we set a <u>high</u> standard – as distinct from a <u>high-brow</u> standard. (Two utterly different things, you will agree!)

But in <u>poetry</u> it is different. There we have been confronted by a dichotomy in the world of poetry itself, a phenomenon which belongs to this uneasy transitional post-war age, that is perhaps at the same time a pre-war age. After the war, the publication of poetry became almost impossible. Then by degrees the distinctively modern school began to gain ground; and through my friendship with T. S. Eliot I and my firm became very specially and closely associated with it, as the publishers of Eliot, Spender, Auden, and others. I confessed to you when we met, that my own earlier ambitions had been in the direction of poetry. But after the war, for whatever reason, my talent – such as it was – began to wither; and the reason for that, I think, was not so much a change in me as a change in the world, and in the outlook of the younger generations by whose approval poetry must always live when it is first written and published. The direction taken by the representative modern writers was very different from the direction I would have taken. Nevertheless, I have grown to approve it – not absolutely, but in relation to the period; and I suppose publishing it has not only helped me to understand it, but has in some queer way satisfied my own frustrated ambition.

That was how our character as the publishers of this modern poetry began. But of course it very soon took on a commercial aspect. It became an important, and is indeed now a very important, part of our business. And it wasn't long before I discovered that <u>this</u> label was sticking for good. I have made occasional efforts to give our poetical list a more comprehensive character – but never with success. <u>Our</u> public will follow us in the one direction; it will not follow us in the other. And – another danger – our own authors (the poets I mean) watch what we do very closely.

## Air Raid Precaution organiser, Borough of Holborn, to Charles Stewart, 24 February 1939

With reference to my visit yesterday and the selection of the best refuge in your building, I think an architect's opinion on the various parts of the basement ceiling is necessary.

In order to withstand the collapse of the building due to blast, the room or rooms with the strongest ceilings should be shored up. More than one of the exits should be accessible and it might be advisable to fix detachable steel shutters to the large basement windows.

## Alison Uttley to Charles Stewart, 8 March 1939

I have rewritten a great part of this book and altered it according to the sound advice of your critic. I hope it will be satisfactory now. I have improved it I am sure and changed the 'modern period' to about 1900, with a Prologue and Epilogue added.

I like it much better myself. I am sorry I have been so long, but there was a lot of work to be done with it. [. . .]

I suggest 'A traveller in time', if that has not already been used, for the title.

Charles Stewart, one of the four principal directors,
nicknamed 'The Goblin'.

Geoffrey Faber, diary entry, written at Ty Glyn, Thursday,
13 April 1939

It's the thirteenth – the right day for a telegram to come from
Frank, while I was shaving, to say 'totally unexpected offer from
Harcourt Brace must consult you immediately' . . . I knew what
that meant, and confirmed it over the 'phone. Frank came down
by an afternoon train; arriving while I was sawing branches off
the fir tree pervading the lawn. In my study, I learned the par-
ticulars. He goes to New York, at a salary of 12,500 dollars plus
expenses, as a minimum, to run their editorial side, with certainty
of directorship. Probably in July. I couldn't say NO, or advise him
NO. But how the hell I am going to take on the Presidency of the
P.A., plus the Bursarship, plus my usual job, plus what I must do
in Frank's place – that's something that, for the moment, leaves me
shattered. Still, one learns to pick up one's pieces and start again.
As for Frank, of course, as he says, it's the plum to be had in publishing now anywhere. And he's been getting stale; he and I both
needed shaking up. Well – his dose has strychnine in it, but mine
seems all bromide!

Geoffrey Faber, diary entry, Friday, 14 April 1939

Talked with Frank in the morning, who warmly approved my idea
of having a private secretary, and of Alan[12] in particular. Thought
that Bill would jump at it, as a means of giving Alan a break outside in the open air. This morning – perhaps aided by this pleasant
thought of Alan's companionship – I began to feel I could still face
all I have got to do. Enid thought it a mistake to have Alan – it
would spoil play, she said – but in the end came round. Drove Frank
into Lampeter.

---

12  Alan Watt, son of the agent William ('Bill') Watt.

But, even with this solution, there's no getting away from the fact that Frank's going is a blow of the biggest kind. It may do me good, perhaps; but it's a smasher. It doesn't merely make everything more difficult; it means the final discovery that no anchor is an anchor to be relied on. I couldn't say that, or anything like it, to Frank. But after this, though I would behave as he does, if I were in his place and had his guts, I feel that no tie of any sort means what it seems to mean. Look at the bright side though! I have got to tackle things more in earnest, run my own show, beat the fates into giving me what they have half withheld. But I could wish that I wasn't nearly 50, and hadn't taken on so much.

### Geoffrey Faber, diary entry, Monday, 17 April 1939

A board meeting, at which we resolved to offer Morley Kennerley a directorship, if he would put £5,000 into the show. Then Publicity Committee. Then, an evening with Alan, which began by him telling me that the answer to my enquiry was in the negative – i.e. he wouldn't or couldn't come as my secretary. We dined briefly and not too well at the club. Then to Tom's play – the *Family Reunion* – which I was stirred by, though I had many objections to take to the production and casting. It was certainly fitted to my mood. And so, after a bit of mutual explanation between Alan and myself, home to bed, a sadder – and I don't think a wiser – man.

### Geoffrey Faber, diary entry, Thursday, 20 April 1939

Morley Kennerley says No: he can't try to raise the boodle. So that's that. We think again.

*A solution of sorts was found. Frank Morley remained a director, while Morley Kennerley was appointed as his 'deputy', entitled to vote at those meetings Frank could not attend (i.e. all of them, given Frank's move to America).*

*Geoffrey employed a series of secretaries, notably, from 1940*
*to 1951, Constance Sheldon, and awarded himself and the*
*rest of the Board a total increase in salary that would absorb*
*what had previously been paid to Frank. The truth, however,*
*as Geoffrey had acknowledged in his diary, was that he would*
*now have to take charge in earnest.*

## T. S. Eliot to Geoffrey Faber, 11 May 1939

Some time ago, I think I hinted to you that I thought the committee
system had gone a little too far. I shall welcome the new arrangement all the more if it leads to your adopting – what I think you are
more fitted for than you realise – a more Rhadamanthine persona.
However disagreeable you may find it at first, it will become easier
with practice, and I am sure that everyone in the end will be the
happier.

*In the meantime, Geoffrey's political connections were leading*
*him in new directions. He had never let go of his old ambition to*
*be a Conservative MP, and now he had the added bonus of links*
*through individuals like fellow publisher Harold Macmillan and*
*Enid's first cousin, Rab Butler. He was even starting to broach the*
*possibility of Faber publishing books on behalf of Conservative*
*Central Office. These – and the approach of another war with*
*Germany – led to the firm making what appears to have been a*
*brief foray into espionage.*

## Geoffrey Faber, diary entry, 4 May 1939

Rickman called in the afternoon, with £150 in notes, to square the
cost of publishing his book on Swedish Iron Ore – This is an elaborate Secret Service business – An intelligent fellow, and an amusing
game.

*According to the internet, Alfred Rickman, a British MI6 agent, was arrested in (neutral) Sweden in 1940 with large amounts of explosive and subsequently sentenced to eight years' hard labour. He probably intended to sabotage the cranes used to load iron ore bound for Germany. The book may have enabled him to enter Sweden in the first place, and pose as a journalist undertaking research. Faber's role seems to have been limited to publishing it. The only other reference I have found in the Faber archives is a letter from Dick de la Mare to Geoffrey on 27 November 1958 (see below).*

*The Faber catalogue for Autumn 1939 would carry suitably anodyne copy for Rickman's book. Before that, it could finally advertise – for certain – something much more exciting.*

## FABER & FABER BOOK CATALOGUE, AUTUMN 1939

*Old Possum's Book of Practical Cats*
T. S. Eliot

It is more than three years since we announced a book of children's verses by Mr. Eliot under the title of *Pollicle Dogs and Jellicle Cats*.

We have sometimes been accused, by members of the public who have complained that this book was not obtainable through their booksellers, of having invented it out of our own heads. [. . .]

Connoisseurs of fine points will observe that the volume now definitely announced for publication is not only devoted to cats, but that its title – when compared with the titles of the unpublished volume – makes a very significant advance of sentiment. These cats are not dear little cats; they are practical cats. [. . .]

*Swedish Iron Ore*
A. F. Rickman

Mr. Rickman's book on the Swedish Iron Ore industry is a new addition to our list of monographs on modern economic subjects . . . The best technical advice indicated that there was a gap to be filled by this book, and that Mr. Rickman was the writer to fill it.

### T. S. Eliot to Enid Faber, 12 July 1939

Now about the dedication of *Cats*. I had thought of putting something like the following:

> The Author wishes to thank several friends for their suggestions, criticisms and encouragement: particularly Mr. T. E. Faber, Miss Alison Tandy, Miss Susan Wolcott, and the Man in White Spats.

(Some two or three were composed for the second, and the third is a small American cousin who <u>thinks</u> that they were written for her.) Then it occurred to me that Tom has arrived at years of maturity at which he might not be pleased by having his name associated with anything so juvenile.

### T. S. Eliot to Geoffrey Faber, 27 July 1939

I was so anxious that the Cats should flourish, if at all, on their own merits, and not as a TSE curio, that I would have asked that it be published anonymously had I thought that fair to the publishers; it is <u>intended</u> for a NEW public, but I am afraid cannot dispense with the old one.

> *He did not need to worry. Although* Old Possum's Book of Practical Cats *was published on 5 October, with a modest initial print run of 3,005 copies, William Crawley could soon report that 'Cats are giving general satisfaction'.*

### Geoffrey Faber in *The Publishers' Circular and Booksellers' Record*, 12 August 1939

The big firms say that they intend to retain the imprints of the small publishers they absorb. But I doubt if that ever works for long. You might retain the imprint, but you must inevitably lose the elusive character of the individual firm, compounded by its proprietor's personality and taste.

*It seems appropriate to end this chapter, not with the announcement of war, but with Geoffrey's assertion that independence is crucial to individuality.*

# 4: 1939–1945
## 'Riding high on the crest of the highest wave'

The declaration of war on 3 September 1939 had been long expected.
Physical preparations had been going on for some time, and it is
quite possible that the undated memorandum with which this chapter begins really belongs earlier in the book. The initial months of
'Phoney War' were therefore something of an anti-climax, for Faber
& Faber as much as for the rest of the country. There is a sense, even
in the extracts below, of the company bracing itself for what was to
come.

When the war did start in earnest, in the spring of 1940, it brought
its share of tragedy, although I am not aware of any member of
Faber's staff being killed on active service. It caused enormous difficulties too – the conscription of younger employees, paper rationing,
additional taxes and insurance, the risk of bombs – but the rather
surprising overall effect on Faber & Faber was that business boomed.
The public still needed entertainment, and reading was one of the few
pastimes compatible with the blackout. Demand for books increased
hugely. At the same time, paper rationing meant that books were
inevitably rationed too. This turned upside down the economics of
book production. Usually, when publishing a book, Geoffrey and the
Board would have to guess how many copies to print. Over-printed
stock might take years to sell, if it ever did – but not when books
were rationed: almost every book produced by the firm during the
war found a market.

In all of this, Faber was in the same position as every other publisher, but it benefited even more than most. As a relatively young
firm, set up for growth, it still had the entrepreneurial spirit to take
advantage of wartime conditions. It was lucky enough to avoid the

bombs. And it published the right sort of books too. The farming list that Dick de la Mare had started before the war found a ready market in a country now seeking to grow its own food. Readers desperate for information fell upon the firm's war-related titles.

The frustration, for Faber & Faber, was that all this success did not translate into cash. Quite rightly, companies could not be seen to profit from wartime conditions, and the government naturally needed all possible sources of funds to fight the total war that was in progress. The Finance Act of 1940 dictated that 100 per cent of 'excess profits' should go to the Treasury. 'Excess' was defined by reference to profits in normal pre-war conditions; since Faber had not made much of a profit in the 1930s, almost all its profits went in tax; as Geoffrey effectively owned the business, he could not even take a higher salary.

So, like most other people in wartime Britain, Geoffrey was working harder than he had ever done before for no extra income. The reason for his hard work, however, lay not only in the fact that he was overseeing vastly increased activity at just the time when Frank Morley had left for the USA, but he had also taken on the role of President of the Publishers Association. During the first year of the war he found himself fighting a series of battles with government departments on behalf of the British publishing industry. The culmination was his great victory – if he had just this one achievement to his name, everybody working in the book trade and every reader would still have cause to thank him – in achieving the exemption of books from the wartime purchase tax, which lives on as VAT.

## Memorandum to all staff on New Permanent Air Raid Shelters

The new permanent air raid shelters in the basement are now ready for use and the coal cellars will no longer be used.

You now have entirely new shelter stations and should find your places on the list below and familiarise yourself with the location of your shelter. An air raid practice will be held shortly.

*Arthur, or 'A. G.', Street, a farmer who turned to writing to*
*supplement his income, was one of Faber's most important*
*authors at this time:* Farmer's Glory *(1932) was his most*
*successful book.*

## Geoffrey Faber to Arthur Street, 12 September 1939

Few of us have any doubt that, provided the technical difficulties are
not made too great for us, publishing will do progressively better as
the war goes on. In the immediate future, that is to say for the rest of
this year, it is extremely difficult to see what will happen. At present
the whole bookselling side of the trade is in a jittery and frightened
state, and is taking no sort of risks. It is only natural, with the disper-
sal of their customers all over the place, and the disorganisation of
the ordinary distributive system. But these are temporary difficulties, which will right themselves. Another thing we are all afraid of,
if Air Raid Precautions remain what they are at present, is the way
in which shopping hours will suffer as the afternoons shorten. If you
have been in London since the black-out began, you will realize that
it is something of an adventure to go about the streets after dark.
As for me, I have bought a bicycle, and rode about last night on it in
peril of my life. It was the first time I had sat on a bicycle since 1914.

## Geoffrey Faber to George Blake, 20 September 1939

I have been having the hell of a time as president of the Publishers Association over many war matters, more particularly over the
War Risks Insurance Act,[1] with which I seem to spend my entire

---

1   The War Risks Insurance Act 1939 decreed that all traders carrying stock
valued at £1,000 or more must insure against war risks at an initial premium
for the first three months of 1.5 per cent of the value of the stock. Publishers
were particularly hard hit because their stock was relatively slow-moving and
there was no consensus among members of the Publishers Association that they
wanted to insure in this way. See R. J. L. Kingsford, *The Publishers Association*
*1896–1946* (Cambridge University Press, 1970).

time, waking and sleeping! Fabbaf[2] is plugging steadily along. Everybody's trade went pretty well west for a time. There has been a certain recovery during the last few days, but nobody knows how long it will go on for, and we all dread the horrible effects of A.R.P. upon shopping, as the winter closes in. Rises in costs are also going to make things difficult for us all, unless the government starts taking more sensible action.

## T. S. Eliot to Frank Morley, 14 October 1939

At the moment, Geoffrey himself is staggering under the burden of the P.A. which in these circumstances seems to be a really serious affair for the first time: and nobody can take any of that off him. However, he is bicycling to the office every day – <u>and</u> back – and seems to be thriving on it.

## Geoffrey Faber, diary entry, Thursday, 9 November 1939

Lunched with TSE chez Maynard Keynes – whom I had never met before. Lying-up on sofa before and after lunch. I liked him and his wife Lopokova – little, shrewd, rather weatherbeaten, simple, protective to him. Keynes suggested Roy Harrod for our war commentary. Book rather than magazine. Keynes said millions had been spent on trying to blackout blast-furnaces!

## C. P. Snow to Geoffrey Faber, 15 November 1939

As I have threatened, I have written some comments on my roman fleuve.

Period: as I conceived it, this was to be 1919 to whenever the breakdown came. Events have comfortably settled it as 1919–1939.

---

2  Faber & Faber's telegraphic address and hence an internal nickname for the firm.

*The 'groundbait' that Geoffrey had laid for Snow in 1938 had done the trick. In this letter, the writer was offering him four novels (including* The Masters, *although it would be published fifth) of the eleven-novel series that came to be called* Strangers and Brothers. *He was probably the most significant novelist that Geoffrey persuaded to come to Faber.*

*After Frank Morley moved to New York, he and Geoffrey maintained a regular correspondence. Not only had they become close friends, but Morley remained a director of Faber & Faber. Geoffrey's letters to him therefore contain a terrific mix of both personal and professional news and reflections. The letter below includes Geoffrey's perspective on the growing romance between his daughter Ann, who was hoping to go to Oxford University, and Alan Watt.*

## Geoffrey Faber to Frank Morley, 8 January 1940

I won't write much about the war as such, except to reiterate my ever-increasing certainty that there will be something of a Governmental upheaval before very long. [. . .]

One continues to meet with every kind of instance of bureaucratic muddle – Doris Stapledon[3] who was here yesterday was illuminating and depressing about the lack of cooperation between the Ministry of Agriculture and the Ministry of Food; but I had better remember the censor and refrain from detail! As Maynard Keynes said to Tom and me: the trouble is that the civil service has had a year in which to get ready!

As for the general temper, it is very hard to say anything at all interesting or significant. There is a sort of steady acceptance of the war as

---

3  Doris Stapledon was married to the agricultural scientist Sir George Stapledon, author of *The Way of the Land*, published by Faber in 1943.

a background to ordinary life, without any excitement. People have got used to the blackout, and to the evacuation, and to the lack of petrol (I mean, for private use; for the truth is that the country is brimming with petrol; so much so that Greek tankers are held up at the ports through the fact that all storage is full to capacity). We had (F&F) an extremely good autumn, after a bad September, and must have done fairly well on the year. Morley [Kennerley] writes me this morning that January has opened badly – with a 7/- income tax, we could hardly hope for anything else! [. . .]

The Alan affair seems to be serious – at least Alan is serious, but we find Ann's mind impenetrable, and it isn't easy to know if she knows what being in love is, or whether Alan is going to beat Oxford or Oxford going to beat Alan! Alan is due for a commission this month, and spent most of his Christmas leave here.

*W. H. Auden's departure for New York with Christopher Isherwood in January 1939 was seen by many of those left behind as a betrayal. Hence the tone of T. S. Eliot's letter below.*

## T. S. Eliot to Frank Morley, 12 March 1940

First, it is rumoured here that Auden has got a job with Harcourt Brace as a reader. I should be interested to have your confirmation of this rumour. In any case, it is to be assumed that as New York is a small place, you must be in touch with Auden from time to time. As you may imagine, the Auden situation here is at present rather unsettled, and I don't know whether or how soon there will be any effect on his sales. We have just received from Random House copy of his new volume, which I have gone through with a censorious eye, and find to be quite publishable Auden, so we shall go ahead with that.

# SISSY BOOKS

This series is an innovation in the publishing of poetry.
The volumes are comprehensive enough to satisfy those
who have not the impulse to explore further; but
most of all they are meant as an introduction to the
work of contemporary poets.

*THE WASTE LAND & Other Poems by* T.S.Eliot

*SELECTED POEMS by* Stephen Spender

*SOME POEMS by* W.H. Auden

*SELECTED POEMS by* Louis MacNeice

*Faber & Faber Limited*
24 RUSSELL SQUARE, LONDON WC1

This spoof cover may well show the response of someone in the firm to
Auden's decision to see out the war in the United States.

## Geoffrey Faber to Frank Morley, writing from All Souls, 17 March 1940

Well, Frank, it's quite difficult to realise that the war is in its seventh month. For me, at least, it has gone quickly – I suppose because I have had so much to do. Tomorrow is the Annual General Meeting of the P.A. and I am halfway through my 2-year term of office. My 2-year term as Subwarden here ended yesterday – thank God! for I can now sit where I choose at dinner, and cultivate the conversation of such younger men as there may be, instead of spending the whole evening beside the dear old warden. [...]

The College, which was pushed at the beginning of the war by the Warden and one or two other puritans into giving up evening dress and gaudys, has now been pulled round – partly, I am pleased to say, by some adroit manoeuvring on my part. The Bursar's Dinner was celebrated last night, as of old, with champagne and the rest, though of course with a shortened menu; and we now change for dinner on Saturdays and Sundays.

*Since 1930, Geoffrey had kept his two external shareholders up to date with an annual letter.*

## Geoffrey Faber to Stanley Robinson, 19 April 1940

I am very sorry to be so late this year in reporting the F & F results for 1939, owing to the effect of the war upon our auditors' staff. But the delay may be tempered by the fact that we are proposing to declare a small, 2½% dividend. [...]

I wish I could assure you that this was the beginning of prosperity. But for the war it would have been; but now, with costs rising and incomes reduced, and with an appalling shortage of paper, I think we cannot expect to do more than keep afloat. However, people are still buying books. It is the paper situation, which is our greatest menace.

*The Phoney War ended on 10 May with the German invasion of France and the Low Countries. That was also the day Winston Churchill became Prime Minister, Neville Chamberlain having been forced to resign after the failure of the Norwegian campaign. One week later, when Geoffrey began writing to Frank, the Germans ('Boches' in his letter) had already broken through the Allied lines. By 20 May, when he finished writing, he had heard the text of French General Maurice Gamelin's notorious 'order of the day' for 17 May: 'Each defender must resist to the end and be killed rather than back away.' The encircled British Expeditionary Force was falling back towards Dunkirk.*

### Geoffrey Faber to Frank Morley, 17 May 1940

It's hard to imagine what's going on some 150 miles away. Here am I in the same old room (only that it's now a bright primrose yellow, instead of the familiar dirty green), with the sun coming round at the back, and the new wing of the University building making the usual building noises all day, and only the shining barrage balloons and my Air Raid Precaution curtains to hint at anything wrong. Are we going to hold the Boches or not? I'll tell you the answer next time. [. . .]

I believe we (F&F) shall be all right, unless everything begins to slide; the way trade has kept up is wonderful. Of course we are a long way behind last year – especially with new books (the back list has sold well) – and the whole trade is threatened by several very great dangers. Don't write facetiously about shortage of paper – it's one of those subjects that won't bear joking about unless you are taking the strain yourself! However, after endless and terrific exertions we do now seem to be getting the authorities to understand that there is some difference between books and paper bags. Another horror is the new purchase tax – no rate fixed yet, but it isn't going to be the sorta tax one doesn't notice. It looks like it would kill the book trade stone dead, and we've got to explain everything all over again from the beginning to the Treasury and the Board of Customs & Excise and a few more. In the last 3 or 4 weeks I have written 3 small books about publishing (in memorandum form) – one for the Ministry of Labour, and one for the Export Council, and one for the Treasury. Seriously, being President of the PA in <u>this</u> war is a wholetime job and a bit more. However, most people behave very nicely and are appreciative and loyal, and that makes a hell of a difference. Actually we now know how much trade is done at home and overseas by 231 book-publishers – almost everybody in fact except Blackie's who refused to play. Nearly £11 million all in, of which nearly £4 million is overseas. I'm not giving secrets away, because the figures are in the *Bookseller*. [. . .]

As time went on and the old gang stayed immovably where they had been at the date of Munich, one did begin to experience something like despair. The Norwegian fiasco was the best stroke of luck we've had so far – if not for the unfortunate Norwegians – because it brought about the change of Government just in the nick of time. By God, it was a close thing. Do you remember my saying at the beginning that the Government would fall before last Christmas? That was a bit out, but then we all expected bombs to fall too and they didn't. The forecast was right enough essentially – it was impossible for that lot to survive the first real piece of nastiness, and there was <u>just</u> enough time between Norway and Holland.

I suppose we'll have the bombs before very long now. [. . .]

As for other everyday matters – Tom is as usual, and is <u>not</u> going to Italy, God be praised. The Kennerleys are as usual, and dine with us tonight. Stew is doing 2 men's work, and seems to flourish on a semi-bachelor existence (Agnes and the kids evacuated somewhere, he joins them for weekends). John Hayward is chez Rothschild for the duration, and I have lost all touch with him.

And Mrs. Millington[4] remains my strength and stay.
Love to you all
Geoffrey Faber

Postscriptum, Mon. May 20.

I wrote the foregoing Friday evening, and left it unposted at No. 24; returning this morning, Monday, it already seems a bit behind the times. We had a dinner party on Friday. [. . .]

George Malcolm[5] retailed the worst of Friday's unpublished Fleet Street alarms; (he was also, incidentally, extremely interesting and amusing about the cyclonic impact of Beaverbrook on the Aircraft Production industry and the Civil Service). When all had gone, I switched on the midnight news, to hear, abruptly, in the BBC's remarkable PA's dead manner that the British Expeditionary Force had withdrawn behind Brussels and the text of Gamelin's Order of the Day. I went to bed contemplating the worst – both immediately and for all time. Well, it's only 2½ days later, and the worst seems not to have happened; but the weekend has done a lot to most of us, and I expect it's done something to the USA too. Did you hear Winston's broadcast last night? That was the right stuff – or so it seemed to me and Enid.

Surprising to be at Oxford on Saturday and Sunday, bathing at Parson's Pleasure,[6] and plenty of undergraduates about – quite rightly, of course, as the conscription scheme is planned to give them their (curtailed) time out.

---

4  Mrs Millington, 'Milly' in a later letter, was a blind masseuse in whom Geoffrey had enormous faith.
5  George Malcolm Thomson was a Scottish author who had helped establish the Porpoise Press but was by now a journalist in London.
6  Parson's Pleasure is a secluded area for male-only nude bathing on the River Cherwell in Oxford.

## Geoffrey Faber to Frank Morley, 24 May 1940

No reference to the war will appear in this letter.

I am sending you duplicates of two novels by C. P. Snow – *Strangers and Brothers* and *Mr March Loses His World* – which I hope you will consider for Harbrace. [. . .]

In my opinion Snow is definitely a coming novelist, and I shall be disappointed if these novels don't put him into the star class.

> *Both these novels would be published in the UK under different titles; Harcourt Brace, however, turned them down.*

## Geoffrey Faber to Frank Morley, 9 June 1940

Very glad to get your letter of May 22. I have been carrying it about for half a week or so, until I might find time to answer it: and now it is serving me in very good stead, as an excuse for withdrawing into a cool room in my mother-in-law's house, after a substantial lunch of cold chicken and ham and asparagus and lettuce and 2 kinds of potatoes and blackcurrant tart and cream and icecream and cider. I <u>may</u> go to sleep in a page or two. It is awfully hot and feels like thunder. Dear me! I suppose I oughtn't to have said that, and trust the Censor won't hold the letter up in consequence. I am writing at the end of an All Souls weekend – our June meeting yesterday morning – and before driving back to Hampstead after tea. [. . .]

No good writing about the battle in France. I suppose we shall know the worst, if that is going to happen, in another week or probably in another 2 or 3 days. [. . .]

Trade remains fair. May was definitely good; June, after staggering a little, is behaving well. Many new books aren't selling at all – one wonders if they will go on slowly but for longer than used to be the case. The old books sell well. Expensive books, of course, don't travel very far. I have been fighting a very long and hard battle as President . . . We have got special treatment for books as far as paper goes – 60% of pre-war consumption, plus possible extra allowances for educational reprints. Which is really a great triumph. Also, exemption in the schedule of Reserved Occupations at 35 for editorial and production staff of Book Publishers. Another achievement – result of months of memoranda, questionnaires, letters, and interviews. The 3rd great objective is escape for books from the purchase tax – that hangs in the balance. [. . .]

I thought I had filled this page. Not having done so, here's a short story from Gwynedd;7 whose Bermondsey girls all said to her, when the Belgians ratted: 'For Gawd's sake Miss don't lets have no more days of national prayer.'

## FABER & FABER BOOK CATALOGUE, AUTUMN 1940

*East Coker*
T. S. Eliot

This is a poem of the same length and in the same form – described by the author as a 'quartet' – as *Burnt Norton*, which was published in his *Collected Poems 1909–1935*. These two poems, and at least one as yet unwritten, are intended to form a kind of sequence. With the exception of a play (*The Family Reunion*) this is the first poem that Mr. Eliot has published for four years.

---

7  Gwynedd Richards, Enid Faber's eldest sister, had joined the 'Time and Talents' settlement in Bermondsey some years earlier. This was a project which transplanted educated women to some of the poorest parts of London in the hope that they would have a beneficial impact on their neighbours. She was a remarkable and lovely woman.

First published in June Mcmxlii
by Faber and Faber Limited
24 Russell Square London W.C.1
Second impression July Mcmxlii
Third impression October Mcmxlii
Fourth impression February Mcmxliii
Fifth impression July Mcmxliv
Printed in Great Britain by
Western Printing Services Ltd. Bristol
All rights reserved

BOOK
PRODUCTION
WAR ECONOMY
STANDARD

THE TYPOGRAPHY AND BINDING
OF THIS BOOK CONFORM
TO THE AUTHORIZED ECONOMY STANDARD

*Illustrations*

THE SQUADRON'S CREST
( *British official photograph No. QH 3959. Crown copyright reserved.*)
on the back of the frontispiece

A PORTRAIT OF THE AUTHOR                                    *frontispiece*
*Reproduced by kind permission of the artist, Captain
Cuthbert Orde.*

1ST JULY 1940: JOHNNY, MICHAEL, PIP, AND GORDON
facing page      20

AUGUST 1940: JOHNNY, MAC, MICHAEL, GEOFF, THE
C.O., NOEL. *In front:* D.M.C. AND SHORTY            20

13TH AUGUST 1940: MY SPITFIRE BEING REARMED
AFTER THE FIGHT ABOVE WEYMOUTH                       21

13TH AUGUST 1940: SOME OF THE SQUADRON JUST
AFTER THE WEYMOUTH FIGHT. *Standing:* RED, OSTI,
G., E., MICHAEL, FRANK, THE C.O., MAC, SERGEANT
F., NOVI, AND TEENY. *In front:* MIKE, D.M.C., AND
MICK                                                 21
( *Photograph by Wing Commander F. J. Howell, D.F.C.,
lent by his father, Mr. H. Howell*)

SEPTEMBER 1940: D.M.C. AND GEOFF                     56

15TH SEPTEMBER 1940: THE WRECKAGE OF THE
DORNIER AT VICTORIA STATION                          56
( *Planet News Ltd. photograph*)

SEPTEMBER 1940: JUST ABOUT TO TAKE OFF FOR ONE
OF THE LONDON BATTLES                                57
5

Paper rationing meant that wartime stock was printed on very thin
paper (so thin that the image on the other side of this sheet is visible),
with very tight typography.

## Geoffrey Faber to Frank Morley, 21 August 1940, writing from Ty Glyn

Are you surprised to see the address? You shouldn't be. What did
I buy T.G. for, 10 years ago, but as a safish sort of place for the
family in the next war! It did look as if invasion and a standstill
order might prevent us from getting here. But we did, at the end of
July, and have Dick and Tom under the parental wing. Ann is doing
duty by evacuee babies in Yorkshire, but joins us at the end of the
month. [. . .]

Enid is as she always is; and bids me say she will make a date with
you at any London terminus you like to name. My own life just
now is at a bit of a pause, after a really exacting summer. Your allusions to my success over the book-tax were distressingly premature.

The original purchase tax bill was, it is true, withdrawn; but reintro-
duced as part of the Finance Bill. As such it proposed to tax books
at 16 2/3% on wholesale prices. That would have sent most of us
down like ninepins. As no doubt you know, at the eleventh hour we
have been reprieved. Behind that lies a history of meetings, speech-
es, letters, lobbyings, which I can't begin to describe. My own last
effort was addressing a meeting of about 100 MPs in 'Committee
Room No. 10', along with the Archbishop of Canterbury and Jack
Priestley. [. . .]

I am . . . naturally very much bucked about the Book Tax success;
which is regarded generally, in the trade, as a personal triumph for
me and has put me in a pretty strong position as President. All very
nice; but my God, Frank, after a whole year of struggling with the
Civil Service, I doubt if I have enough energy left to take advantage
of my opportunities.

As to business – we (F&F) might be doing much worse than we
are, and I think we are doing a good deal better than most. But
the trade position is very bad generally. London bookselling, and
bookselling in the coastal areas, have been terribly hit; and the
commercial libraries are playing for safety all the time. Costs up,
overheads up in spite of fewer staff, and nobody with any money
left to spend. All as foreseen by me, when most publishers thought
they were in for a good time. The economics of this war are the
reverse of last time. Where this will end, God knows. If the war
lasts long, there will have to be something like socialisation of
industry. You can't put the whole burden upon private enterprise
without killing it. [. . .]

Bill comes here for ten days on Friday; and TSE afterwards. They'll
overlap for 3 days – but Uncle Tom says he don't mind. He has been
really pulling hard and well at his oar in Russell Square. Like the
rest; but Tom's best is rather special. It's possible that we may send

Dick to New York this autumn – object, to sell sheets.[8] We want all the money we can get that way – and so does the British Government. Morley spent a long weekend here, and was most charming. He needed his 4 days rest pretty badly. I have been very glad of him at Russell Square and he's worked hard and well. If possible I shall stay here now till September 14 – I want all the rest I can get, before the next battle whatever it may be.

*Anne Ridler was a poet who had been T. S. Eliot's secretary at Faber & Faber in the 1930s. Although she moved to Oxford after her marriage to Vivien Ridler, Eliot continued to publish her poetry and employ her in various ways, frequently asking her advice on manuscripts.*

## Anne Ridler to T. S. Eliot, 29 August 1940

I was especially glad, too, of what you said about aliens. What is going to be done, for instance, about those anti-Nazi refugees like my friend Berthold Wolpe (one of the best and the best-known type designers we have, who had lived here for five years), who was whipped off to Australia in June and had been gone a fortnight before his relations knew anything of it? Will the Government ever bring him back? And what are his mother and sister to live on?

## Geoffrey Faber, diary entry, Thursday, 26 September 1940

Early call from Stew. to say that a time bomb had fallen just outside office. Drove up to his house, where we had a council of war. Got temporary use of 41 Great Russell Street; dictated a letter or two there to Miss Sheldon in empty room. Started moving stuff out of 24 Russell Square. Back to Oxford.

---

8  The plan was to send Richard de la Mare to New York to try to sell unbound printed sheets of Faber books to New York publishers.

Morley Kennerley's photograph of the hole caused by the
unexploded bomb in Russell Square.

## Geoffrey Faber, diary entry, Sunday, 29 September 1940

Urgent telephone enquiries about the Hampstead bombs. Warned
not to return tomorrow, but safe on Tuesday.

## Geoffrey Faber, diary entry, Tuesday, 1 October 1940

Drove back to Hampstead with Enid and Ann, maids by train. Only
to find the bomb not removed. Huge pit, and derrick over it. Refused
to leave house, after slight scene with R. E. sergeant.

Went down to London to buy camp beds etc. While I was away, effort
made to remove bomb, by driving lorry up garden to haul at a rope
over derrick. Derrick collapsed, and bomb fell back to bottom of pit.
General alarm! But nothing happened, and bomb left in situ till
tomorrow.

First night in London, in the 'Blitz'. Slept in maids sitting room.
Enid, Ann, and maids in shelter. Noisy.

## Geoffrey Faber, diary entry, Wednesday, 2 October 1940

Office. Book Committee. Back in Russell Square, the time bomb having been removed.

A stick of bombs, which burst this time, fell over Oak Hill Park in the afternoon – one in the garden of No. 7, our old home.

## Geoffrey, diary entry, Sunday, 6 October 1940

Morley Kennerley came to lunch; and we got him to show us over the French-neo-Georgian house, built by Barbara Hutton (the Countess Reventlow) in Regents Park, where he is living alone, with his own furniture, in the magnificent room designed as Count R's bedroom, with one of those incredible bathrooms attached. His wife, Jean, and daughter, Diana, being now in California. The place is really superb – sort of Versailles fragment. From his windows he saw London apparently on fire when the Blitz began. The oddest possible way of living. The edge of complete luxury. Complete solitude. Bombs.

## Geoffrey Faber, diary entry, Saturday 19 October 1940

At home, Gwynedd to spend a quiet night (a respite from the horrors of Bermondsey). After dinner bombs fell – one at bottom of garden, destroying lodge and shaking but not in any way damaging our house, though only some 20 yards away. Water ran down like a river from the just restored main, making curious sound. Hurrying up road to see if Unwin's maids were OK, I fell into the crater headlong and had an extraordinarily narrow escape from putting out my right eye.

## Geoffrey Faber, diary entry, Sunday, 20 October 1940

Spent almost the whole day digging débris to clear the drive, so as to be able to get the car out tomorrow. Gwynedd and even Lily helped and so did members of the demolition squad.

### Handwritten note to 'Mr Kennerley' (undated)

Mrs Faber rang & left this message:–
A bomb has fallen in her garden & they cannot get the car out. If you
would care to go and help them dig, she can give you lunch.

### Geoffrey Faber, diary entry, Monday, 21 October 1940

The maids gave notice, with tears!! They went at the end of the week,
to Cambridge, where all three sisters got daily work and boarded
together. And Enid and I took possession of the shelter! The shelter, by the way, is our garage, protected on 2 sides by being beneath
ground level, on the 3rd side by the house, which it adjoins and with
which it communicates by a door to the semi-basement maids' sitting room, and on the 4th side by an elaborate construction of sleep-
ers, several feet thick. This was done at the beginning of the War . . .
Later, just before our return to London in September, I had the maids
sitting room strutted and made into a secondary shelter: and that is
where TSE sleeps on Wednesdays.

> *Without domestic help, for the first time in her life Enid had to*
> *cook. She rather enjoyed it.*

### Geoffrey Faber, diary entry, Wednesday, 23 October 1940

Enid had a bath at the office, where we have just got water again,
after a long absence of it.

### Geoffrey Faber, diary entry, Wednesday, 30 October 1940

TSE to stay for night. He is now living with the Mirrlees family
(3 ladies, including Hope[9]) in the country, and coming to town on
Wednesday morning, and returning Thursday afternoon. An excellent

---

9  The poet Hope Mirrlees was an old friend of T. S. Eliot, as well as of
Virginia Woolf.

life for him – breakfast by himself; no contacts till lunch; privacy for writing; and domestic comfort and peace from Air Raid Precautions. It was doing him no good, being an ARP warden in Kensington.

## Geoffrey Faber to Frank Morley, 13 January 1941

It's a long time – too long – since I last wrote. And your last letter, to which an answer is some 3 weeks overdue, is down at the office where I parked it on my desk this morning. I took it down to Wales with me before Christmas, and brought it back again. So you can't say I haven't treated it honourably. But – you know how it is. Moreover, of the 3 weeks in Wales we had Morley as our guest for a fortnight. And you couldn't wish for, still less find, a nicer one. But I set myself, with some success, the problem of finding Morley something, preferably strange to him, to shoot every day, and when one has a matter of that sort on hand, other jobs have to go by the board. In my presence, Morley has now shot his first partridge, grouse, snipe, woodcock, pigeon (I believe), and green plover. I'm not sure he didn't get a hare in the summer. He <u>may</u> even have killed his first rabbit under my nose; but if so, he didn't let on. He <u>tried</u> to kill his first buzzard – but . . . I knocked up the barrel of his gun – metaphorically speaking, with a hasty cry, since the Buzzard is a protected bird. Though the locals say he didn't ought to be; and we have the august authority of the Lord Mallard for the belief that the Buzzard should be represented at every lesser feast – does not his Lordship open our festivities at All Souls with the pregnant & sonorous words 'Griffin, Bustard, Turkey, Capon'? to disparage these birds, it is true, in favour of the one & only Mallard.

If all this sounds a bit inconsequential it is so because (a) I am rather tired (b) a series of dull thuds has been going on which sounded like rather distant anti-aircraft fire – and that bothered me because, as yet (6.23 p.m. precisely), no Alert has sounded. But I have just realised that it was merely Sally gnawing a very large bone on the floor of my dressing-room, which – as you may remember – is immediately above my study, in which I am writing! The thudding has now given place to unmistakable gnawing. [. . .]

You will have heard, of course, about the raid in the City and the extinction of Paternoster Row. There's no sense in filling letters with stuff you have read about in the papers – at least I assume that the annihilation of the 'historic centre of the English book trade' will have been reported in New York. We only came back from Ty Glyn on Saturday, and today's Monday, and I haven't had a chance of going to see the damage. But Enid and Tom (small Tom) went sightseeing there this afternoon; and Enid says it's a sad, yet impressive sight to see. St. Paul's barely touched – a bit of window gone, no more – and standing magnificent, majestic, in a scene of almost utter desolation. She says, it takes your breath away. The building in which I learned the rudiments of my still rudimentary knowledge of publishing – Amen Corner – is no more. And just as I felt a strange sense of personal resentment when I saw the wreckage in the garden of our old home across the road here – No. 7 Oak Hill Park[10] – where we spent several so very happy domestic years and the kids played and the roses bloomed along the ramshackle pergola, so I felt an equal surge of resentment at the destruction of the place where I was, to be truthful, extremely <u>un</u>happy as a young man. This is a personal, an intimate sort of war. It's everything that matters against everything that mustn't be allowed to matter. No bad thing, perhaps, to have the issue so naked and absolute – provided we win through. You'll notice I don't say 'win' all by itself. [. . .]

Apart from this shattering attack – which will have been for the good of the book trade here as a whole, though a horrible disaster for people like Longmans, who must have lost all or nearly all their old and famous stock – the booktrade hasn't done too badly in 1940. Not

---

10 The Fabers had moved within Oak Hill Park in Hampstead from no. 7 to no. 1, a few years earlier.

whoppingly, but tolerably. But for *Sex and Life*,[11] Frank, (and forgive me for pushing that one at you!) we should be ending up very nicely. But S. & L. will knock more than 'a couple of thou' off the profit which the Chancellor of the Exchequer will be taxing to the extent of nearly fifty per cent. Unless, of course, Brer Huebsch is lying low with loads and wads of coveted dollars. If you ever see him, tell him that <u>our</u> personal need of dollars grows greater and greater day by day, whatever happens to Roosevelt's new Bill!

## Geoffrey Faber to Frank Morley, 15 May 1941

Russell Square survived last Saturday's raid, though the 2 houses opposite us on the other side of Thornhaugh Street were burned out, and a [. . .][12] upset the disposition of door-frames and the like. You might begin to notice the damage to London now. My own chief private griefs are the smash-up of Westminster School – the big school and the famous dormitory – and the obliteration of the Hammam Turkish Bath, where about £2 worth of baths was still owing to me, and I don't think I can ask for my money back! We had been paying a hurried visit to my mother at Cheltenham, and helping my sister sort out things at the Cheltenham house, which is to be let unfurnished, and got back home, very tired, about 9.30 pm. I think the Blitz began in earnest about 11.15 or so. At any rate Enid and I were just going off to sleep upstairs when I painfully decided we had better go down to our shelter (which occupies what used to be the garage). But for some time I watched from the top floor windows, which give a pretty wide view over London. It was an absolute spectacle – a sort of sea of fire beyond the trees and the

---

11  Not as racy as its title might imply (they rarely are), *Sex and Life* was a book by two German doctors which clearly did not sell as well as expected. I understand this paragraph to mean that it was Frank Morley who originally proposed the book to Faber & Faber.

12  Excision by the censor.

church spire, with a gigantic cloud of smoke billowing up into the clear sky in brilliant moonlight. And somehow so beautiful that it was quite hard to realize what it meant or to feel unhappy. [. . .]

Trade is very good, though we are a bit slacker at the moment owing to the enforced postponement of several new books, because of Trend[13] being put out of action temporarily. There will be a profit of about £4,500 in 1940. Tom is in very good form, and so is everybody else. Crawley is now a director. The Goblin[14] has a son – so, of course, has Crawley – a new one I mean. Dick (this is a true story) after having said to Katta 'I'm expecting Göring to drop in tonight' (which is the latest London joke[15]) on Tuesday night, five minutes later found an airman and a parachute descending into his garden. But it was a British airman, unfortunately, unhurt. My mother is, incredibly, recovering, but will never be able to do so much again, and will probably spend the rest of her life in a nursing home. These are, I know, incongruous pieces of news, but what would you?

Amongst F&F books this summer or autumn there will, I hope, be a fattish volume of verse called 'Between Two Worlds'[16] (vide Matthew Arnold, 'Grande Chartreuse') containing the collected poems of one Geoffrey Faber. Sorry to break the news to you so crudely, but I think it's best that way. Tom has passed them, in spite of being given two or three chances of saying it would be a mistake, and the preface. There's a longish preface, which will, I think, interest you; though the poems aren't your meat I know. Still, they do combine into a whole which has some 'relevance' now, I think – to use one of your favourite words.

---

13  Latimer Trend, the printing firm in which Faber & Faber would eventually buy a shareholding.
14  The Goblin was the office nickname for Charles Stewart.
15  A propos of Rudolf Hess's solo flight to Scotland on 10 May 1941.
16  'Between Two Worlds' changed its title before publication to *The Buried Stream: Collected Poems, 1908 to 1941*. Both these titles come from poems by Matthew Arnold ('Stanzas from the Grande Chartreuse' and 'The Buried Life', respectively).

### Geoffrey Faber to Stanley Robinson, 2 July 1941

So far this year trade has been exceedingly good, almost embarrassingly so, since the difficulty by which publishers are likely to be more and more bothered as the war goes on is that of replenishing stocks. The paper problem is becoming increasingly serious. Fortunately we appear to be well placed, so far at any rate as the immediate future is concerned. It is a bit hard that the war, with its heavy burden of taxation, should have come just at the moment when we were beginning to reap the reward for the hard work of the last fifteen years, since it prevents us from accumulating the substantial reserves which it has always been my hope to build up. Still, we have a very great deal to be thankful for in comparison with many other trades.

### Geoffrey Faber, diary entry, Saturday, 23 August 1941

Agreed this morning to Ann's engagement to Alan.

### T. Brown, Paper Control, Ministry of Supply, to Geoffrey Faber, 22 September 1941

I thought it was very decent of you to write an apology for our somewhat heated argument over the telephone and I feel that I also must apologise for being very unpleasant. Actually, I had a slight regret after getting off the telephone that I had not been more unpleasant but I am thankful now that I was not as I do appreciate that you have quite enough to put up with in the commercial world nowadays without us adding to your trials more than we have to.

I also feel that I have some excuse for being irritable at times, however. The work of my Department has been increased enormously in the last twelve months and I am overwhelmed with work which I can never catch up with. The telephone goes all day long and I feel that I have to bear the brunt of the continual cutting down of supplies which is now so necessary. I sometimes think I shall go completely crazy and in fact, I sometimes wonder whether I have not already gone that way.

I agree with you that in the early days of rationing a year and a half ago, life was much pleasanter, it was certainly easier for me. Supplies were comparatively plentiful and if a publisher or any other user of paper wanted a little extra paper, there was not much difficulty in licensing it. As the restrictions and the licensing have been gradually tightened up from period to period and percentages cut down, however, the protests and arguments with regard to quotas have of course increased enormously. I can understand a man fighting for the existence of his business and I can sympathise with him but you will realise it is very tiring dealing with protests all day long.

I might mention that bagmakers who are down to 15% of their pre-War consumption and periodicals publishers who are licensed with 20% of their pre-War consumption are two particular sections of the community with which I have to deal who are admittedly hard hit and needless to say, as they are gradually cut down in their supplies, protests and appeals pour in. So far I have not had a lot of protests from book publishers compared with other sections but with these further restrictions, I have no doubt these will increase.

I feel sure as a result of this, if we again have a difference of opinion, we shall understand a little better the point of view of the other side and conduct our argument more calmly.

With kindest regards and again many thanks for your letter.

### Geoffrey Faber to agent William Watt, 17 October 1941

I am very sorry, but I am afraid that we don't feel able to offer to publish Mrs. Millin's *The Glass House*. I don't really quite know what to say about it, except that it seemed to us the sort of wishful thinking that is rather inappropriate at the present time. Have you read it? It assumes that the war is over and has been won by the Allies, and Hitler and his gang are deprived of their clothes and imprisoned naked in a glass house in Berlin. The result of which is that the Germans cease to regard them with veneration.

### Charles Stewart to the Exchange Manager, Ministry of Labour and National Service, 30 October 1941

We wish to employ Mr. Berthold Wolpe of 31 Linden Gardens, W.2., as a typographer and designer on account of his special qualifications. Mr. Wolpe has asked us to notify you since his permit is for free-lance work.

> *And so the question Anne Ridler had posed in her letter to T. S. Eliot in August 1940 was answered. After spending about a year in Australia as an enemy alien, Berthold Wolpe had been allowed to return to London in 1941. His elegant typographical designs were perfect at a time when wartime exigencies made it difficult to employ artists, and would continue to dominate Faber's covers for the next thirty years. In particular, he used his own 'Albertus' typeface so often that people came to call it the 'Faber' typeface.*

### Geoffrey Faber, diary entry, Wednesday, 10 December 1941

Spenders to dinner, with TSE. Natasha[17] played *Les Adieux*.

### Geoffrey Faber, diary entry, Saturday, 3 January 1942

Fetched Enid's ½ pig in the unlicensed and uninsured Vauxhall on a comprehensively criminal transaction!

---

17   Natasha Spender (née Litvin) was a distinguished pianist.

Berthold Wolpe posing outside the offices of his new employer.

## Geoffrey Faber, diary entry, Friday, 23 January 1942

Long discussion with TSE up to past midnight on first and last things.

## Geoffrey Faber to Frank Morley, 26 March 1942

Thank you for your letter about *The Buried Stream*, and thank you very much for letting it mean something to you. It ain't your idiom, I know; as Anne Ridler says it isn't hers. Which is perhaps truer of the older verses than the last ones. Myself, I felt I had done summat in 'Dark River';[18] but the stream has gone underground again, through sheer accumulation of day labour. I've had a lot of appreciative letters, some from people I never expected to see anything in the book. It has sold about 1,200, and will dribble on. Reviews, though, disappointing; and nobody has taken up the opportunity offered by the preface. [. . .]

I suppose there'll be a profit of over £20,000 for 1941, of which nearly half will go as Excess Profit Tax to the Treasury, and half of the rest as Ordinary Income Tax. If 1942 keeps on as it has begun, it will make 1941 look silly. This isn't happiness; it's a sort of nightmare, with stocks running out, and paper getting less and beautifully less; though we have been fortunate in getting the part use of another firm's quota (with the Controller's assent) and therefore have suffered less than we might have done. Labour is becoming a worse difficulty than paper. At the moment it looks as if all our young women were going to be taken. Uncle Tom and the rest are all much as you would remember them: except that Uncle T. has 2 dentures now, and imitates the speaking tube whistle from the kitchen at Oak Hill Park (signal that dinner is ready) with exasperating efficiency and practical jocosity, & Morley Kennerley isn't quite as young as he was and has had to go to Milly to get his back ironed out after drilling in his Home Guard unit.

---

18  Written in 1940, 'Dark River' was the last poem in the book, Geoffrey's *Collected Poems, 1908 to 1941*.

Morley Kennerley to Geoffrey Faber (then at Ty Glyn), 16 April
1942

Tar-rar-a! Tar-rar-a! Tar-rar-a! Here I am at play on my Dictaphone.
It is unfortunate that you cannot hear these melodious notes, as Miss
Melton will, but I am demonstrating before Uncle Tom who has hit
the headlines in today's summary of Home News in the *Times*, and
is here reading through a report of his speech[19] just to make sure that
he said what he wanted to. He has a message for you and I will put
him through:

'I do not appear to have much. Very many thanks to you and the
family for your telegram and I shall hope to reciprocate on my
return.'

Uncle Tom showed very little signs of stage fright but his wide
experience in the theatre world has no doubt prepared him for
dictaphoning. [. . .]

The Budget does not seem to have affected the firm's position in any
way, although I suppose it is nice to know that the 20% refund is
guaranteed[20]. Anyway, it's a tremendous relief to know that Income
Tax is not going up. [. . .]

Nearly all of us miss you very much. I say 'nearly' for some people evidently do not know you are away for they turn your electric
fire on every morning despite all I can do to prevent it. I first tried
disconnecting it and putting it in a corner, but that was no good so I
have now locked it up in your cupboard.

---

19  From *The Times* article: 'Mr. T. S. Eliot, speaking on "The Classics and
the Man of Letters", in his presidential address to the Classical Association
yesterday, held that the maintenance of classical education is essential to the
maintenance of the continuity of English literature.'
20  There was to be a 20 per cent rebate of Excess Profits Tax after the war to
finance reconstruction.

## Geoffrey Faber to Frank Morley, 14 May 1942

My real news is that I have sold – or am engaged in selling – Ty Glyn to Rear Admiral the Honourable George Fraser D.S.O., younger brother of Lord Saltoun. An uncommonly nice chap, with 2 small sons. So we feel at ease in our minds about Oaten[21] and our neighbours and shall be able to think of T.G. as in the right hands and all that. Which makes a lot of difference. But it's sad to think you'll never again sprain your ankle chasing rabbits out of the garden, and that we'll never be caught by the tide at Llangranog, or have to chisel away the rocks to release your Ford, or inspire Oliver with ancient castles.

The replacement of Ty Glyn is uncertain. I <u>hope</u> that the College may buy an estate in Sussex called Minsted – near Midhurst – about 670 acres, with a superb farm and some shooting and the Downs 3 miles off. If so, I shall become lessee of the house, and take over the flat at No. 23 for the insides of weeks. In fact I hope it so much, that I daren't say more. The Warden and Done are on their way there by road at this very moment, and my fate will hang on the Warden's impressions. (Fortunately the sun is coming out, and the bailiff is a Perthshireman.)

Uncle Tom (did you know?) has been in Sweden, as an emissary of British culture. From the little I have heard his visit has been a great success, and his lectures crowded. He does see life, doesn't he? I hope they haven't overfed him, as they did in Portugal! I expect he'll be here next week, and I'll find out about *Little Gidding* then.

## Geoffrey Faber, diary entry, Saturday, 13 June 1942

The Minsted scheme went through, though against some opposition.

---

21  Oaten was the name of the gardener at Ty Glyn.

*Wartime restrictions had made it impossible to maintain Ty
Glyn, so it was lucky that All Souls came up trumps for its
estates bursar. For as long as he continued to come into the
office, Geoffrey kept to the scheme he had outlined in his
letter to Frank, staying in a flat at the top of 23 Russell Square
during the week and returning to Minsted at weekends. Here he
indulged in the expensive hobby of breeding pedigree cattle.*

## FABER & FABER BOOK CATALOGUE, AUTUMN 1942

Little Gidding
T. S. Eliot

Little Gidding is the fourth and concluding poem of the series in which
Burnt Norton, East Coker and The Dry Salvages have already been published.

## Geoffrey Faber, diary entry, Thursday, 13 August 1942

Dined + TSE with Spenders, meeting Julian Huxley and EM Forster
('upsadaisy' – he and I were in a deputation about free journalism
to Home Secretary Sam Hoare 2 or 3 years back, and crossing in
the snow I slipped and he hoicked me up, and wrote an article in the
*New Stateman* or such about it).

## Geoffrey Faber to Frank Morley, 26 October 1942

Huge rolls of packing paper narrow the entrance to No. 24. Things
below stairs are an untidy chaos one can't bear to inspect. But now
we are taking over the whole of No. 23. Controversy rages as to
who shall go where; and plans for using the extra space are, of
course, hampered by the fact that it is now very difficult to get the
necessary alterations either permitted or made. For some time past
Crawley has been housed, with some of his minions, next door;
access, on this floor, provided by a new passage way through from
one house to the other, past the lift, a slice for the purpose taken
out of Morley's (formerly F.V. Morley's) room. We are doing an

incredible amount of business (incredible, that is, by <u>our</u> pre-war standards), and work now in a chronic state of being some weeks behind with invoices. But I mustn't go on with that sort of news or I'll never stop.

### Geoffrey Faber to Frank Morley, 19 November 1942

'Personally' (as Dick d.l.M. delights in saying) I should have found this war more difficult than I have, if Tom (S.E.) hadn't been on hand. (N.B. I put in the identifying final initials because I cannot allow the names Dick & Tom, when unqualified, to belong to anybody else than Dick & Tom Faber!)

I write light-heartedly; but the Faber clanlet has taken a hard knock in Alan Watt's death. He was killed in Egypt on the 2nd. We got this – I got it – from Bill by telephone last Thursday night. Enid got it through to Ann the same evening, via a friend – a very good and tight little friend – of Ann's at Somerville; and she (Enid) went next morning to Oxford, and she and Ann cried a good deal together. Which was helpful to them both. I haven't seen Ann myself, since this happened to her. From her and others' letters, she has taken it as one would want one's daughter to take it. But, but, <u>but</u> . . . it's just hell to have that sort of thing happen to one's children – I write that sentence, and instantly I should like to cross it out. Let it stand: it's as near the truth as deceitful words can get, even though I know well that Ann has another life, and very possibly a better one, given to her in exchange for the life she has lost. I <u>know</u> that; but for two pins I could be crying on to this bit of paper myself.

### Geoffrey Faber, diary entry, Thursday, 18 March 1943

F&F have had extra paper from the Sheed & Ward quota these last 2 years. Now S&W are under fire from the paper control, and likely to lose their quota. Which means, for us, if it happens, the collapse of our war-time economy. No cause of tears to any other publisher. For we have had our 'luck'. So be it: so must it be, if it must be. But F&F is caught all ways – by Excess Profits Tax and by the sudden withdrawal of 'help from the gods' – as the old established firms, even Cape, are none of them caught. It is not easy to philosophise on this; especially for anybody who has always been pulling against the stream and is then prevented from profiting when the stream flows with him.

The fire-watchers' register for December 1942. As long as bombs continued to fall, every member of staff not otherwise on war service had to watch for incendiary bombs from the roof of Russell Square. Generally Geoffrey and T. S. Eliot took their watch together.

*Later that year, the possibility arose of Geoffrey becoming warden of All Souls. He could not take the position and continue to run Faber & Faber, so wrote to Frank Morley, by now involved in the National War Labor Board for President Roosevelt, to*

*see if he could tempt him back to London. The letter also makes*
*clear that despite Geoffrey's uncertainty earlier in the year, the*
*firm continued to flourish.*

## Geoffrey Faber to Frank Morley, 18 August 1943

Anyway, may I ask you this question – this very hypothetical question? Suppose I said: 'Will you, at the earliest possible moment, come
back to F. & F. as (say) its Executive Vice-Chairman (whatever phrase
has to be used) with the definitely effective say-so at every point of
ultimate decision?' – would your answer be yes or no (according to
terms!), & (if yes) what would that earliest moment be?

I am setting you the thesis for an extremely elaborate essay! But I'd
be grateful for as round an answer as you can give.

Unlike Harcourt Brace I don't state any terms. I can't. While Excess
Profits Tax is with us I don't know what we should be allowed to
offer. We could get at that, if matters became serious. I should say,
drawing a bow at a venture, that it could be at least £2,500 a year
(including share of profits) – since that is what Dick and Stew have
been allowed by the Commissioners of Inland Revenue to take for
1941. In 1942 they will be allowed more, but we don't yet know
what, and our accounts are therefore still held in suspense.

But the war-time remuneration is an artificially-limited thing. What
will be possible after the war depends upon unknown factors. What
will happen to the demand for books here – now soaring far above all
conceivable and satisfiable levels? God knows. But one thing is clear:
F. & F. are riding high on the crest of the highest wave, and unless we
make a most awful mess of our chances, they are as good as one can
dare to imagine. Your old turnover, for example, is now running at
least 200 per cent higher. With more paper, it could be easily doubled.
I don't exaggerate.

*Geoffrey's reply to Frank's refusal of his offer makes clear that*
*in that case he saw Dick de la Mare as his successor. The only*
*person likely to have difficulty with that was Charles Stewart,*
*who had once been de la Mare's manager. It was also probably*
*time now for Frank to give up his directorship.*

## Geoffrey Faber to Frank Morley, 22 October 1943

Now about F. & F. I was 99 per cent certain that your answer to
my letter would run the way it did – and could run no other way.
After I had written to you, I had a sort of prowling talk with Dick,
and saw clearly enough that he considered himself the right successor to the seat of authority. I gave no indication to him of what
I thought – or, if I did give any indication, it was probably rather
discouraging than otherwise. Which wasn't quite fair, since actually I had made up my mind that, if you were out of the picture, it
must certainly be Dick and not anybody brought in from outside
(in spite of anything to the contrary in my letter to you). Later, I
had separate talks with TSE & Morley Kennerley – not, as yet, with
Charles Stewart. This was, in point of date, before I had your cable
or letter – both of which came to confirm a decision of my own.
Rather fortunate, and convincing. Both Tom and Morley agreed.

As regards Morley, I feel – and have said so to him – that the time
has come when he ought to be a director in his own right, and not
your alternate director. We missed him seriously when he was in the
States, and should miss him still more seriously if publicity began
to go back to pre-war scale. (At present, of course, it's almost completely dead.) This suggests the further question: do you not think,
perhaps, that you had better now cut the formal tie? It was a very
useful silencer, at the time, of the rumours and doubts to which your
departure might otherwise have given rise. But now it is apt to make
people think that there is a connection deeper than friendship (save
the mark!) between Harcourt Brace and F. & F., and it may possibly

seem to you as well as to me that rumoured connections of this kind are a bit dangerous. [. . .]

We have only just got our audited accounts for 1942! Profit (or rather what we should have called profit in the old days) £56,600. Excess Profits Tax takes at least £48,000 of that – and probably more, according to what the Inland Revenue allows Dick and Stew out of their covenanted share of profit. I can take no share of profit. And after a 15% dividend and income tax, the reserve is increased by the princely sum of £300. Meanwhile Cape rides through the war on his profits out of *Seven Pillars of Wisdom* – his 'standard' for E.P.T. purposes.[22] Can you beat that, for sheer inequity? For 1943 our 'profit' will, I imagine, be much nearer £100,000 than £50,000. But the ultimate result will be just about the same.

It's a good school of patience, anyway. [. . .]

There's a bit of wild blitzing going on in London at nights now. No damage to speak, of, except for the few nightly unfortunates. It's odd how one now feels 'this is bloody cheek of the Hun'! –

## Geoffrey Faber to Frank Morley, 29 February 1944

You wouldn't recognise Russell Square now. There's no grass left in the gardens, which (the railings went long ago) are half a complex thoroughfare for everybody going in every direction, half burrowed under by shelters (never, so far as I know, used by anyone) and half a football ground for the Gibraltese. The latter are a picturesque element in the Square's permanent population. But they are outnumbered by American soldiers who swarm here, as everywhere else in London (and in Oxford too). Nice lads, but with a great deal too

---

22  Excess Profits Tax was calculated by reference to a pre-war 'standard' profit. This was high for Jonathan Cape because of the success of *Seven Pillars of Wisdom*, which meant that its liability to pay EPT was reduced.

much money. Last week's raids haven't done us any harm, I'm glad to say, and were most spectacular to watch.

## Geoffrey Faber, diary entry, Friday, 16 June 1944

During the night I heard some odd sounding planes, and realized that the pilotless plane had arrived over London. One came very low over the top of no. 24. I saw one flying about 1,000 feet up. Didn't see any explode. Lots of wild shooting. Enid slept imperturbably through it all. Must confess I was worried, though not actually frightened.

## Geoffrey Faber, diary entry, Tuesday, 20 June 1944

A flying bomb fell yesterday (Monday) about midday – shortly before one – just off Tottenham Court Road, south of Goodge Street. Everybody thought it was coming down on No. 24! Did a good deal of damage.

## Geoffrey Faber, diary entry, Wednesday, 21 June 1944

A poor night. Alert went just before 12, just as I was going to sleep. Tom and I got up and 'firewatched' till after 3, when we decided to go back to bed again. Saw 2 flying bombs explode in sky. Coming over all the time at intervals of a few minutes. No shooting. None very near us. Not much sleep. All clear about 9. Other alerts during day.

## Geoffrey Faber, diary entry, Friday, 23 June 1944

Stewart rang up about 10.30 to say that a flying bomb landed in the night in Russell Square, so we went up by the 12.2 from Haslemere. The thing fell bang in the exact middle of the square, about 3 a.m. The square covered with green leaves, the trees stripped and no doubt killed. All the houses stripped of doors and windows, but no really serious damage at 23 & 24. Ceilings down in many rooms and a bad mess. If I had stayed up and been asleep I should have been more or less badly hurt. Since the ceiling came down on my bed. Flat uninhabitable, at least for some weeks. No one hurt; but Mrs. Lister[23] unable to stand any more. So brought her and the twins back to Minsted, at any rate for the week-end. Louise Cochrane (Morley)[24] came back with us for the weekend. Our train just escaped being hit by another of the 'doodlebugs'.

## T. S. Eliot to George Orwell Esq., 13 July 1944

I know that you wanted a quick decision about *Animal Farm*; but the minimum is two directors' opinions, and that can't be done under a week. But for the importance of speed, I should have asked the Chairman to look at it as well. But the other director is in agreement with me on the main points. We agree that it is a distinguished piece of writing; that the fable is very skilfully handled, and that the narrative keeps one's interest on its own plane – and that is something very few authors have achieved since Gulliver.

On the other hand, we have no conviction (and I am sure none of the other directors would have) that this is the right point of view from which to criticise the political situation at the present time.[. . .]

I am very sorry, because whoever publishes this, will naturally have the opportunity of publishing your future work: and I have a regard for your work, because it is good writing of fundamental integrity.

*It is that last paragraph that particularly strikes me: in turning down* Animal Farm *– essentially because it was being rude about our Soviet allies – Eliot was also turning down the unwritten* 1984.

---

23  The Listers were the caretakers of 23–24 Russell Square and lived on the premises.
24  Louise Cochrane was Frank Morley's niece, creator of the early children's television programme, *Rag, Tag and Bobtail*.

*In common with many of the firm's younger employees, David
Bland, Faber & Faber's Head of Production, had joined the
services, becoming a navigator in RAF Bomber Command.
When his plane was shot down over Germany, everyone feared
the worst, but the letter below, which his father sent on to Dick
de la Mare, showed that he was at least alive.*

## David Bland to his father, 9 September 1944

I'm afraid this must have been a very anxious time for you but I am all
right & perfectly well. My address will be Stalag Luft 3, Germany. [...]

Please tell everyone I am OK. We were shot down [...][25] & all got
out, only are slightly wounded. We are treated very well here, &
food is amazingly good (Red Cross).

---

25  Deletion by the censor.

The Book Committee in 1944, shown in *Picture Post* in March 1944 with the caption: 'The Meeting That Decides How to Use the Paper Ration.'

Clockwise around table from left: T. S. Eliot, Morley Kennerley, Geoffrey Faber, William Crawley, Richard de la Mare (with his head down), Charles Stewart and Geoffrey's secretary Constance Sheldon (with her back to camera).

*Frank might have already said to Geoffrey that he could not return to London, but T. S. Eliot persisted in trying to persuade him, showing remarkable clarity of thought in his analysis of the firm's future.*

## T. S. Eliot to Frank Morley, 19 September 1944

I don't need to tell you how warmly Geoffrey and I would welcome your return: but, quite apart from personal feeling, which can be taken as read, we both feel that somebody like yourself is needed, and will be more needed in the future; and we feel that nobody else likely to fill the same place is at all likely to appear. These last five years do happen to have been the time which we could best get on without you. The business went on, in a way, of itself: I mean, that the policy of expansion which suited the F. & F. temperament proved the right one; the bombs missed us; Dick has been brilliant in making the paper supply go further than anyone else could have made it go; and the kinds of book which we severally wanted to publish, happened to be the right books for the market, and for putting us in a favoured position for certain lines in the future. But now I am concerned about two things. Two of us have got to the age at which we are aware that the arteries eventually harden – the fact that the others are not yet aware of that prospect, is even more to the point. If you learn to obey the doctor's orders, you ought to have ten or twelve years more than Geoffrey or I, in which to adapt yourself to a changing world and keep in touch with the younger generation of readers as well as writers. A <u>young</u> man wouldn't fit in here: that would be skipping a necessary link. Dick, I fear, will go on thinking that what he wants to publish is what the public wants and needs, and that his friends can provide it, for twenty years after he and they are out of date. And I should like to think too, that the business will go on occupying the same place of importance (socially and culturally, as well as commercially) that it does now, for at least one or two generations.

My other concern is, that (especially as we are publishing on such a large scale) we need somebody like yourself who can consistently see our list as a whole (as no departmentalist can do), notice defects and weaknesses in some lines, and (what is almost more important) when we are producing too many of one type of book – and exercise watch and influence over the <u>pattern</u> of our publication. Both the Production and Distribution Departments need tactful handling. At one moment we seem to be putting everything into juveniles, at another to be sunk in Manures. I always feel that I am thought to be (or rather, unconsciously assumed to be) too much the high-brow specialist with over-fastidious tastes; and as for Geoffrey, that is not really the Chairman's job – it is not the job of a final arbiter, but of somebody on equal terms with the rest who will do it by persuasion. (And incidentally, I want Geoffrey to have enough time to attend to what I may call the political side of publishing – apart from any really outside interests – I mean the representative of Publishing in general, to both the State and the public, which he is better qualified to be than anyone in London.)

*Frank remained unpersuadable. In the meantime, the firm's thoughts were turning to expansion. After an ill-tempered meeting with Bedford Estates, Geoffrey felt the firm would have to move from Russell Square. Advised by All Souls surveyor John Done, he foresaw a shortage of London premises in the post-war years and decided to take the initiative.*

## Geoffrey Faber to Richard de la Mare, 15 December 1944

I went over No. 10 Grosvenor Place yesterday, and if Done's report is satisfactory, and you and the others concur – I should like to make an immediate offer.

## Geoffrey Faber to Frank Morley, 14 February 1945

F. & F. are in treaty for 10 & 11 Grosvenor Place, the late Lord Moyne's London place – palace, I meant. It seems pretty certain that we shall have it, and be moving there in a year or two – as soon as we can get the necessary alterations carried out. That, of course, may be more than a year or two away.

*The short extract below from a long letter Geoffrey wrote to Frank Morley late one night, while drinking Perrier-Jouët, shows T. S. Eliot's continuing interest in cats.*

## Geoffrey Faber to Frank Morley, 20 March 1945

Interruption at this point by Morgan. You don't know anything about Morgan. He is a very large, black, heavy, and affectionate CAT, who fastened himself on this establishment about 2 years ago. Uncle

Tom, who has just come in, maliciously introduced him into my room; and I have spent about ¼ hour in nicely getting rid of him!

## Geoffrey Faber to Frank Morley, 29 April 1945

I came back from Edinburgh by the Flying Scotsman on Tuesday, April 17. C.W.S. [Charles Stewart] was killed next morning. I didn't get the news till after one o'clock, and it wasn't known in the office till after that.

It was an undoubted accident. He had only just got his family all back again together in Glenloch Road, and left them in the gayest of his goblin moods on Wednesday morning, to come to the office. His sight, you know, had been getting worse, and he was wearing new spectacles for the first time. It was his habit to lean forward and peer at the incoming tube train to see if it was the right one. The platform, in Belsize Park Tube Station, where the accident occurred, has been rather dangerously narrowed by a wartime construction (I think, a urinal for tube-shelterers). He must have failed to see the edge of the platform distinctly and peering and leaning forward, just have toppled over as the train came in. I am told he was killed instantaneously.

His death has come as a really violent shock to us all; and you can well imagine how difficult we, at 24 Russell Square, will find it to fill up the resulting gap. He was one of those chaps who don't stand in any limelight, while they're alive; but, as soon as they're dead and gone, you'd give anything to have them back again. I go on and on, finding out how he counted, in his quiet unassuming way, with the staff at Russell Square, with authors of all sorts, and with outside people. A very great part of my time, these last 2 weeks, has been filled with answering letters whose burden is always the same – 'It was a pleasure to do business with him – or to come up to London and go to see him – he was always so nice and nothing was too much trouble.' And I have noted in many letters this expression: 'I/we have done business with Mr. Stewart for many years, and have formed a great regard for him'. Neil Gunn is one of those to whom he meant a lot more than I – and maybe you – ever realised. [. . .]

I wish you could have been of the party when TSE & dlM & I lunched last Thursday with Sir Charles Lidbury, general manager of the Westminster Bank, at the Head Office in Lothbury. We had asked for the Bank's backing in our move to Grosvenor Place and in sundry other modes of expansion; and went, at Sir Charles' bidding, to be looked over carefully. It was a great occasion. Not only did we pass muster, but we were delighted with Sir C. himself, who is one of the liveliest and wittiest talkers I have come across for a long time – the best, indeed, since I lunched with Captain Geering of the U.S. navy at San Diego.[26] Very different men, but full-size personalities and autocrats.

*Charles Stewart's tragic death meant that Geoffrey had to recruit a new general manager to take his place. He fixed 8 May 1945 as the day to interview the most promising candidate, Peter du Sautoy, who wrote about it in a letter to Tom Faber four decades later: 'Our appointment on that day was at 3.00 p.m, the very hour that Churchill was due to broadcast to the nation announcing the end of the War in Europe.' Geoffrey telephoned to say that Peter was to come in any case at the agreed time; the office would be closed, but he would come down and let him in. So they sat in Geoffrey's office and listened together to Churchill's broadcast. It seemed a good omen for Peter's future with Faber: 'I feel that I have belonged to the firm for 40 years.'*

---

26  Geoffrey had been part of a Publishers Association delegation to the US in the spring of 1943.

# 5: 1945–1950
## 'It taught me a valuable lesson'

Faber & Faber greeted the end of the war with both relief and confidence. It had flourished despite all the problems of the wartime economy. Now it could look forward to the return of skilled employees, to a world without excess profits tax, and to the end of paper rationing.

It was in this optimistic spirit that the company had bought a controlling interest in the printers Latimer Trend even before the war had ended. It followed this up with further investments. Fine Art Engravers Ltd made the blocks whose quality was essential for the art books that were an important part of the Faber list. Fama Ltd was set up as a joint venture with Kurt Maschler, who had a large stock of the four-colour blocks which had been used by the art magazine *Apollo* in the 1930s. Faber bought a long lease on 10 and 11 Grosvenor Place for £33,000. The only obstacle to an immediate move from Russell Square was that the Ministry of Works would not give permission for the necessary alterations.

There was a similarly gung-ho approach to the company's publishing. Peter du Sautoy eventually joined on 1 January 1946, after being demobilised from the Air Ministry, to find publication plans being made with little thought given to the end of the wartime boom: for example, 50,000 copies of Phyllis Bottome's new novel were printed with the price 'more or less left to the Sales Director to fix with no apparent calculation of possible profit (or loss) on the likely rate of sale'.

Of course the good times for publishing had to end. Peace meant that books once again found themselves having to compete with alternative forms of entertainment. Wartime stock, printed in close type on thin paper, became unsaleable. Tastes had changed too: no one wanted to read the military books that had filled Faber's catalogues during the war, and the farming list had narrower appeal. The great wartime boom had left the company with few long-term sellers. Sales fell from £407,000 in 1946 to £311,000 the following year. The firm had to adjust to a new reality.

By now, Geoffrey himself was approaching sixty, looking to take things slightly more easily after the efforts of the wartime years, and prone to occasional lapses of judgement. The chapter closes with him failing to retain one of his most important authors. There is a sense of the firm losing pace, as a new generation of writers and agents comes to the fore.

## Richard de la Mare to David Bland, 30 July 1945

I was delighted to hear that you have now got your release – both for your own sake and for ours, because we all of us very much look forward to your return to the office. It's difficult to tell you how much I personally have missed your help. [. . .]

I should add that the other directors are in complete agreement with me about what your position will be. You left us to join the R.A.F. as head of the production department, and it is as head of the department that we expect you to return.

### FABER & FABER BOOK CATALOGUE, AUTUMN 1945

*Prospero's Cell*
Lawrence Durrell

This is a book about Corfu, partly a 'guide' (Mr. Durrell tells you, incidentally, what to eat and drink there, and how to ask for it) and partly a diary, extracted from the record of several years' residence. Mr. Durrell's knowledge of the island is intimate, extensive and peculiar; and besides giving a picture of town and country, he gives delightful glimpses of the life of a few foreign denizens and their native friends, in the years just before the war.

## Geoffrey Faber to the Rt Hon. J. B. Hynd MP, 31 October 1945

It was a very great pleasure to make your acquaintance last Saturday at Minsted – the visit was marred, from my point of view, only by the loss of my pocket book which is certainly now inside one of our cows!

## Frank Morley writing from New York to T. S. Eliot, 14 February 1946

You have possibly seen this already, or its equivalent. I snatched it from the *NY Times* this morning, but had no chance to mail it from there, because I was running to catch a (most exhausting) train for Richmond.

POUND'S MIND 'UNSOUND'
Verdict Saves Writer From Standing Trial

WASHINGTON, Feb. 13 (AP) – A Federal District Court jury today found Ezra Pound, 60-year-old expatriate poet, to be mentally unsound. The verdict saved Pound from standing trial on treason charges arising out of his wartime writings and broadcasts in Italy.

> *Alan Pringle had returned to Faber after war service. Although, to borrow a phrase from Geoffrey Faber, he was never seen as someone who might 'set the Thames on fire', he was clearly a talented editor and would eventually form a deep relationship with Lawrence Durrell. The correspondence that follows is a reminder that Faber first published Philip Larkin as a novelist.*

## Alan Pringle to Peter Watt, agent, 14 June 1946

I met Philip Larkin as arranged last week and talked over certain suggestions we had to make for the revision of *The Kingdom of Winter*.

He took the manuscript away with him and is going to think it over and meet our suggestions so far as he can.

## Alan Pringle to Philip Larkin, 29 August 1946

On the whole, we think that *A Girl in Winter* is a better title than *The Kingdom of Winter*.

> *In 1946, Robert (Bob) Giroux joined Harcourt Brace in New York, reporting to Frank Morley, who introduced him to T. S. Eliot. Within a year, Giroux had acquired Robert Lowell's second collection of poetry,* Lord Weary's Castle, *and was proposing to Eliot that Faber should become Lowell's British publisher.*

## T. S. Eliot to Bob Giroux, Harcourt Brace, 24 September 1946

I have now finally digested *Lord Weary's Castle*. I think that on the whole Robert Lowell is up to form but I don't think he is a poet whom we want to introduce in this country on one volume alone at this stage. Indeed, as a general principle for application both ways, I think that the thing is to watch a man through several volumes of poems and then present a rather substantial selection.

> *Lowell stuck to this advice, rejecting the offers from other British publishers that flooded in after* Lord Weary's Castle *won the Pulitzer Prize for Poetry. By the time Frank Morley left New York to return to London in 1947 (but not to Faber; that ship had sailed), Bob Giroux was firmly established as Eliot's US publisher and talent-spotter.*

## T. S. Eliot to Anne Ridler, 25 November 1946

Now that we have settled Norman Nicholson for the present, Lawrence Durrell has popped up again. This is obviously a very different case, because if I know anything about Durrell, he sends everything in the confident hope of immediate publication.

## FABER & FABER BOOK CATALOGUE, SPRING AND SUMMER 1947

*A Girl in Winter*
Philip Larkin

**Much is to be expected of this young writer who came down from Oxford in 1943 and has already published a volume of poems and another novel.**

## Alan Pringle to Philip Larkin, 7 August 1947

I have some good news for you, which may also be something of a disappointment. *A Girl in Winter* has sold well and fully justified the hopes we had for it; it has sold so well that out of our large edition of five thousand we are reduced to a stock of one copy. We are not proposing to reprint, however, not only because the production situation with regard to paper, binding and printing forces us to ration ourselves pretty severely over reprints, but also because in our judgement the demand does not now justify a reprint. I thought it best to tell you this straight away so that you should know and appreciate the position. The important thing is that the book has done well and provided a good ground for the future.

> *I can only admire Alan Pringle's chutzpah in his attempt to persuade Philip Larkin that it was a good thing that his book had gone out of print.*

## C. P. Snow to Peter du Sautoy, 17 October 1947

My copies of *The Light and the Dark* have just arrived. I am delighted with the appearance of the book – though my judgement in such things isn't worth much.

## Peter du Sautoy to C. P. Snow, 13 November 1947

We are delighted with the sales of the book. The first edition is now rapidly running out and we are going to reprint straight away. This is really unusual and specially so at this time when the market has not been as good as it was.

## C. P. Snow to Peter du Sautoy, 14 November 1947

I hope you'll have plenty of copies in the bookshops ready for Christmas shoppers. The book seems quite unpurchaseable at the moment; and literally the only copies I've seen myself are in parcels going out to members of the Times Book Club, where I'm told that I am markedly popular. Impress on your people that I am unusually readable for a serious novelist, + that quite simple people find it so; I shall be surprised if this one doesn't go on selling.

### FABER & FABER BOOK CATALOGUE, SPRING 1948

*The White Goddess*
Robert Graves

This is a prodigious, monstrous, stupefying, indescribable book: the outcome of vast reading and curious researches into strange territories of folk-lore, legend, religion and magic [. . .] Mr Graves [. . .] is a true follower of Aeneas into the nether world.

## Alan Pringle to Philip Larkin, 3 February 1948

I am sorry that we have decided against making an offer for your new collection of poems *In the Grip of Light* which I am now returning to Watt. May I say how much I enjoyed reading them myself and how much we are all looking forward to reading your new novel when it is ready.

> *It took Faber a long time to realise that Philip Larkin was not going to produce another novel.*

## Geoffrey Faber to Peter du Sautoy, 4 March 1948

WJC [William Crawley] is 'critically' ill. There is peritonitis and there are more ulcers than the one which burst on Tuesday and necessitated an immediate operation . . . there is no reason to suppose that he will not eventually be able to resume work, and it is quite possible that he might go for years without further trouble. [. . .]

If Crawley were to die, we should have to consider what to do. It would be hard on young Crawley and on his father's great services to us, if he were to find himself deprived of the opportunity of succeeding to his father's position in a reasonable period of time, through the importation of a new man. [. . .]

I am quite certain that young Crawley has it in him to be our man. His youth and inexperience are very serious handicaps; but they are not impossible handicaps. He will have to learn by doing the job – or as much of it as we can entrust to him. I am most anxious to give him all the opportunity we can to show his mettle.

> *In the event, William Crawley, or 'Papa Crawley' as he came to be known, survived and remained Sales Director until his retirement in 1961. This letter, however, and others over the course of the next few years, shows how Geoffrey saw Faber & Faber as the sort of place where children would succeed their fathers.*

### FABER & FABER BOOK CATALOGUE, AUTUMN 1948

*Notes towards the Definition of Culture*
T. S. Eliot

His chief aim is to persuade his readers to endeavour to decide upon a meaning for the word 'culture' (and equally for the word 'civilization') before they use it.

## Board minute, 5 October 1948

Mr Faber reported that following the decision of the Board at the last meeting, he had interviewed the Steward of the Bedford Estate. He considered our suggestion in a very helpful manner and offered to give the Company a new lease of 23 and 24 Russell Square for a period of 21 years at the scale now prevailing for Bedford Estate rents and allowing for the unexpired portion of the existing leases. The formal offer had not yet been received but was expected in the course of the next few days.

In view of this, he had instructed Messrs John D. Wood & Co to dispose of the lease of 10 and 11, Grosvenor Place. After negotiations, their client Mr. Wohl had offered to purchase the lease at a price of £95,000 subject to several technicalities to be agreed upon.

*The firm had made a very welcome profit of around £60,000 from its foray into property investment – essential at a time when the profits from book publishing had collapsed.*

## Swedish Academy, cable to 'Mrs T. A. Eliot', 4 November 1948

THE SWEDISH ACADEMY HAS AWARDED YOU THIS YEARS NOBEL PRIZE IN LITERATURE AND INVITES YOU TO THE NOVEL FESTIVITIES ON 10TH DECEMBER KINDLY ANSWER BY WIRE TO THE SECRETARY OF THE ACADEMY DR OESTERLING BOERSHUSET STOCKHOLM WHETHER WE MAY HAVE THE PLEASURE OF SEEING YOU

*Eliot received this telegram while visiting Princeton. The same visit had given him the opportunity to meet Robert Lowell, whose subsequent letter, addressed to 'Uncle Tom' and signed 'Cal', shows how it had been a meeting of minds. Faber brought out its first book by Lowell – Poems, 1938–1949 – two years later.*

## Robert Lowell to T. S. Eliot, Thanksgiving, 1948

I'll have a little more than I thought for the Faber volume – there are
two more poems which I have since re-written for the Kavanaughs,[1]
in all about 500 lines. I've thought of calling it 'Sharp the Conquer-
ing' from the prologue of the *Parliament of Fowls*; but maybe poems
would be better. One of the longer poems has never been published
and will take some overhauling – I haven't looked at it for almost a
year; but I'll get the manuscript off to you at Faber, as soon as I can.
Also I'd like to make a list of poems from *Lord Weary* that I think
you ought to include.

When we finally said Goodbye, I had a wonderful feeling that happens scarcely ever – as if a whole life-time had welled up and we
knew each other for ever, no matter what. I'll miss you very much.

T. S. Eliot receiving the Nobel Prize in Stockholm. It is possible that he
was rather prouder of the Order of Merit he received the same year.

---

1   *The Mills of the Kavanaughs* was Robert Lowell's third book of poems.

FABER & FABER BOOK CATALOGUE, AUTUMN 1949

*Finnegans Wake*
James Joyce

We shall not attempt to describe James Joyce's masterpiece: but we have pleasure in announcing that it is, once more, available.

> *While the firm remained as shy as it had ever been of explaining* Finnegans Wake, *the fact that it had been allowed to go out of print is an indication of the effect of paper rationing.*

## Peter du Sautoy to C. P. Snow, 12 July 1949

We have just heard that *Time of Hope* is being recommended by the Book Society, and I thought you would like to know this at once if you have not heard it from any other source. We are very pleased about this and I hope you will be too.

> *The Book Society was a very influential book club in the post-war years. To be recommended by it was undoubtedly an accolade which would boost sales, but the real goal was to be a 'Book Society Choice'.*

## C. P. Snow to Peter du Sautoy 14 July 1949

Thank you for your letter. I feel something like Aeschylus on being congratulated on receiving the third prize.[2] I shall be extremely cross if one of the next three, all of which are lighter in tone than the first three, does not get chosen without any nonsense about it.

---

2 According to Plutarch, the Greek tragedian Aeschylus was so appalled at having been defeated by his younger rival Sophocles in the annual Athenian playwriting contest that he quit Athens in disgust.

### Geoffrey Faber to Richard de la Mare, 24 August 1949

We (Enid and I, and also Peter & Allan) saw the last rehearsal of *The Cocktail Party* which seems to have had a good first night in Edinburgh. I think it is an incredible feat for a man over 60 (!) to exhibit such powers of invention and advance in the dramatic medium. I knew Tom was a remarkable fish 26 years ago, but I could never have guessed, then, <u>how</u> remarkable.

### Valerie Fletcher to Faber & Faber, 25 August 1949

I understand indirectly that Fabers require a personal secretary. Perhaps you will consider my application.

### Peter du Sautoy to Valerie Fletcher, 30 August 1949

I am pleased to offer you the post of Secretary to Mr. T. S. Eliot, as described to you yesterday, at a salary of six pounds, ten shillings a week. This post will include, as I told you, a certain amount of editorial work in connection with our general catalogues.

### T. S. Eliot to Anne Ridler, 31 August 1949

We have now taken on a Miss Valery Fletcher. She was secretary to Charles Morgan[3] for a year, but as she seemed to lack enthusiasm about this experience I was ready to overlook it!

> *Gwen Raverat's wood engravings appeared in* Farmer's Glory *by A. G. Street (1932) and in books by Walter de la Mare. So it was natural that when she started writing a memoir of her Cambridge childhood, she would turn to Dick de la Mare for advice.*

---

3  Charles Morgan was a novelist and playwright who was very successful in his lifetime but whose reputation has declined since his death in 1957.

## Gwen Raverat to Richard de la Mare, 6 October 1949

I have been playing with the idea of writing a sort of autobiography as a peg to hang illustrations on; and I am now taking the liberty of sending you a scrap out of it (not the beginning nor yet the end) to see if you would think it would do to publish some day, with lots of pictures. I simply <u>hate</u> writing, and I can't be bothered to write it, unless it's good enough to publish. I am afraid that what I have written may be too flippant and rather odious, and I would like to know what some outside Literary Person feels about it. The idea of the book is not to be a continuous autobiography, but a series of separate chapters called Sport, Religion, Art, Relations etc etc.

A single page from the staff photo album shows both T. S. Eliot's new secretary and the man who offered her the job. According to Morley Kennerley, Eliot first described the woman who would become his second wife as an 'aquiline blonde'.

*This was the sort of book about which Dick wanted his wife Katta's opinion, especially as she and Gwen Raverat were old friends.*

### Richard de la Mare to Gwen Raverat, 14 October 1949

Both Katta and I – for, needless to say, I have consulted her – are entranced by your suggestion that you should write a sort of auto-biography, and we both of us very much enjoyed reading your pre-liminary skirmish on Propriety. I have shown it also to Geoffrey Faber who also very much wedded to the idea and greatly enjoyed reading your first chapter.

*The book would become* Period Piece, *a bestseller on publication in 1952 which remains in print.*

## Alan Pringle to Philip Larkin, 20 February 1950

It seems such a long time since I heard from you, and I have been wondering if you have any news at all about your new novel, the more so because I so often receive enquiries as to how your work is getting on. Of course a few years is not a long time to wait for a novel by Philip Larkin; but it seems a long time to wait without any news!

## Philip Larkin to Alan Pringle, 26 February 1950

I am afraid that the answer is simply that I have been trying to write novels and failing either to finish them or make them worth finishing.

*At the beginning of 1950, Geoffrey and Enid travelled to South Africa on board the SS* Edinburgh Castle, *accompanied by T. S. Eliot. The holiday presumably provided Eliot with the ammunition he required for another joke at the Chairman's expense.*

## T. S. Eliot, writing as 'the Rev. John McHaigh LL.D., B.Sc.' to Geoffrey Faber, 28 February 1950

Dear Friend,

Perhaps you have heard of me and of my nation wide campaign in the cause of TEMPERANCE.

Each year for the past 15 years I have made a tour of England and delivered a series of lectures upon the evils of drinking. This year I have been invited to speak in New Zealand, and shall be covering most of that great country. I am sailing in the M.S. *Rangitata* on April 14th.

On these tours I have been accompanied by my assistant, Norman Fortescue. Norman was a pathetic case, a young man of good family and excellent background, whose life was ruined because of excessive indulgence in beer, whisky, gin, rum and other strong drink.

Norman would appear with me at my lectures and sit on the platform drooping at the mouth and staring at the audience with bleary and bloodshot eyes, whilst I would point him out as an example of what drinking would do.

Unfortunately last winter poor Norman died.

A fellow passenger of yours in the *Edinburgh Castle* has given me your name, and I wonder if you would care to accompany me on this tour and take poor Norman's place.

Yours very sincerely
John McHaigh

### Board minute, 11 May 1950

Mr Faber stated that he wished the Board to consider the future of his son, Mr Richard Faber. As the board already knew, his son had taken examinations with a view to entering the Foreign Office and the results would not be known until July. Meanwhile, he had been employed since January in several departments of the Company and he (Mr. Faber) had gathered that he had done reasonably well. Mr. Faber stated that he hoped his son would finally decide to continue in the business as he was naturally keen to see another member of his family actively engaged in publishing. The Board fully concurred with Mr. Faber's views and it was agreed that Mr Richard Faber be offered a position on the Editorial side of the business at a salary of £600 per annum if he came in now with the prospect of a Directorship in a year's time and a further consideration of salary.

## Board minute, 7 June 1950

The Chairman stated that his son, Mr. Richard Faber, had been noti-
fied of his success in the Foreign Office Examinations and in consequence, he considered it extremely unlikely that his son would enter
the business.

*C. P. Snow remained convinced that Faber & Faber should be
doing more to sell his books. He had also acquired an agent,
Spencer Curtis Brown.*

## Peter du Sautoy to Spencer Curtis Brown, 20 July 1950

As you know, we now have the typescript of *The Masters* by C. P.
Snow. It is being read at present by Geoffrey Faber.

You will also know that there is a proposal, which we warmly welcome, that there should be at some convenient time a conference
between yourself, Snow and representatives of our firm to discuss
the sales promotion and other relevant matters in connection with
the book.

## Geoffrey Faber to Peter du Sautoy, 10 September 1950

I still think, after all the arguments and protests and our own anxiety
to please Snow, that he is mistaken in wanting to force the pace. I
think that he misunderstands – and, in a way, under-estimates – his
own work. [. . .]

If he goes all out now for a stimulated popular success, I am doubtful
for him. (a) He might get it, and be affected by it – by, thereafter,
always feeling that he had got to write to a popular audience. (b) He
might not get it, and be affected by the failure to get it, so that he
began to write in an astringent, disappointed, way. (c) He might half
get it, and half not, and begin to wobble.

Actually, in my opinion, he ought not to be concerning himself with all this. He should be executing his design as well as he knows how; instead of mucking up relations with his publisher in the way he is. It's a great pity that Curtis Brown hasn't told him this, but played the Literary Agent's useless game of sitting quietly on the fence.

### Spencer Curtis Brown to Peter du Sautoy, 14 September 1950

I hope you didn't think that I was a nuisance at our talk with Snow on Monday. I am sure you will agree with me that there are two consecutive aims (1) to get your travellers enthusiastic about the book, and (2) to enable your travellers to get the booksellers enthusiastic about the book. For this purpose it seems to me helpful if your publicity plans can be made well in advance. [. . .]

Incidentally, your first printing of 10,000 seems to me slightly on the conservative side. I would have thought that a number of publishers would have been printing at least 20,000. For that reason arrangements for reprinting and rebinding are all the more essential. [. . .]

No-one knows better than you, obviously, that the great change between pre-war and post-war publishing lies in the fact that it is now the better authors who sell best. It is inconceivable, for instance, that before the war Collins could have sold over 45,000 of Rose Macaulay, or Cape have sold over 35,000 of Elizabeth Bowen. I believe that figures somewhere in that neighbourhood are possible for Snow and I am sure that you believe that too and that you will be full of exciting and enthusiastic ideas towards that end.

### Peter du Sautoy to Curtis Brown, 18 September 1950

Thank you very much for your letter of 14 September and for the trouble you took calling here with Snow to discuss plans for selling *The Masters*. I am glad to repeat that we shall do everything we can to sell this book and others by Snow, with enthusiasm and success, and we shall make very careful plans both for press publicity and for presenting the book to the trade.

*By 21 September, Faber had cancelled the publication of* The Masters *and returned the manuscript to Spencer Curtis Brown. He then sold the book to Macmillan, for whom it became a 'Book Society Fiction Choice' and the first of many bestsellers for C. P. Snow. The story goes that the break came with an angry letter Geoffrey dictated to go to Snow one Friday afternoon (presumably on 15 September). His secretary later admitted that she almost kept the letter over the weekend to see if Geoffrey still wanted to send it on the Monday morning. She did not; the letter was sent, and Snow left Faber. The correspondence, however, has been lost. All we have of the 'Squabble' is Geoffrey's own recollection from a letter he wrote a decade later: 'He accused me of being a bad and inefficient publisher and of refusing to back him adequately. It is true that I was wrong in thinking him a genuinely "superior" novelist who would find his true level in time without too much "best-selling". But if I was wrong, so was Snow – or so I think – in his estimate of his own talents. I have often deeply regretted my mistake over Snow; it taught me a valuable lesson about authors, and about the publisher's own limitations; but I don't want it to spoil the end of my days.'*

# 6: 1951–1960

## 'Flair rather than taste'

In the early years of the 1950s, Faber & Faber continued to drift. That is not to say that it acquired no interesting writers, but it is hard to shake off the impression that, lurching from one financial crisis to another, the company had no great sense of how it was going to carry on once its current leadership had retired. The knighthood awarded to Geoffrey in the 1954 New Year Honours list could be seen as confirmation of this, something that set the seal on his career, and by extension on his company.

By 1960, however, when Geoffrey finally handed over the Chairmanship to Dick de la Mare, the firm had made the two crucial decisions that would enable it to survive. One of these was the idea that it should begin producing its own paperbacks. In retrospect, it seems amazing that hardback publishers should have voluntarily surrendered so much of the profit on a successful title to the paperback publisher to whom they sold the rights. No doubt they found it hard to wean themselves off the slug of cash they could get for selling the rights; they seem also to have believed that paperback publishing was such a different business from hardback publishing that it required a totally different set of skills. Whatever the reason, when Faber decided to issue a few experimental paperbacks of its own in 1958, it was possibly the first general publisher in the UK to do so.

The other important move was the appointment of Charles Monteith. This took over a year from Monteith's first letter to Geoffrey in July 1952, but once Monteith joined he immediately brought a new sense of purpose to Faber's literary publishing, acquiring writers whose importance rivals those brought onto the list by Eliot in the 1930s. Monteith's arrival demonstrates how Geoffrey's real skill was as a recruiter rather than a publisher. T. S. Eliot comes out of this part of the story well too, not just for the selflessness with which he encouraged the appointment of Monteith, but also because of the way Monteith clearly benefited from Eliot's advice and support during his first years at Faber. To vary an earlier theme, Monteith found it easier to take risks on new writers when he had Eliot to confirm his judgement.

T. S. Eliot would drop his own bombshell later in the decade, but we begin with something that few other firms could match: promotional copy written by a Nobel prize-winner. Featuring Morgan, the cat Geoffrey mentioned in his letter to Frank Morley in 1945, the complete poem would be included in later editions of *Old Possum's Book of Practical Cats*. The first and last verses, repeated below, were designed to be used in marketing material.

## FABER BOOK NEWS, 1951

One of the firm's directors, having a special affection for Morgan, who comforted him during the trying nights of fire-watching, offered to approach Morgan personally about his lives, and Morgan, with some show of affected diffidence, handed him the following a few days ago.

## CAT MORGAN INTRODUCES HIMSELF

I once was a Pirate what sailed the 'igh seas –
But now I've retired as a com-mission-aire:
And that's how you find me a-takin' my ease
And keepin' the door in a Bloomsbury Square. [. . .]

So if you 'ave business with Faber – or Faber –
I'll give you this tip, and it's worth a lot more:
You'll save yourself time, and you'll save yourself labour
If jist you make friends with the Cat at the Door.

*If anyone was the second Faber, it could only have been Enid, Geoffrey's wife. Like all the directors' wives, she was involved in reading manuscripts. I was pleased to come across the assessment below, in her handwriting, of a book which remains in print today and shows Faber building a more international list.*

## Enid Faber, report on *The Palm-Wine Drinkard* by Amos Tutuola, 4 January 1951

I read this with a ghastly fascination – It is curiously reminiscent of some of the fairy stories collected by Andrew Lang[1] – though of course it is far more nightmarish – I should much like to know something of the author, and what he really thought he was writing – or wanted to write.

## T. S. Eliot report on '*The Palm-Wine Drinker and his dead Palm-Wine Tapster in the Deads-Town*', 20 February 1951

I should hardly consider this a 'work of real genius': it is too unusual to fit into any such category. It is a long and very rambling ghost, spook and juju story by a W. African native. The W. African imagination is certainly a very creepy crawly one; it operates in this story with the capricious freedom of a very bad nightmare. In fact, the author seems to have written in a state of ~~dream consciousness~~ conscious dreaming.

*In a letter accompanying his manuscript, Tutuola had expressed concern about his ungrammatical English: hence the reassurance in the letter below from Alan Pringle, who would continue to edit him for a quarter of a century.*

## Alan Pringle to Amos Tutuola, 21 June 1951

We have read with great interest your manuscript, *The Palm Wine Drinker*, which was forwarded to us by the Lutterworth Press, and we find ourselves very keen to publish it. [. . .]

---

1  Andrew Lang was a Scottish collector of folk tales.

About the text – we agree that your English is not always convention-al English as written in this country, but for that very reason we think it would be a great pity to make it conform to all the rules of grammar and spelling. Just as no one but a West African could have had such a strange tale to tell, so your manner of writing it has a charm of its own. We therefore propose that our reader should go through the manuscript before it is set up in type, correcting what are evident-ly copying errors, accidental omissions, confusions or inconsistencies, but leaving intact all those expressions which, though strictly speak-ing erroneous, are more graphic than the correct expressions would be. You can depend upon it that we have the success of the book at heart, and we hope you will be content to leave the matter to our judgement.

## Amos Tutuola to Alan Pringle, 27 June 1951

I am very glad to read in your letter that you will publish the M/S and also the letter points out about the correction of my wrong Eng-lish etc., in conclusion, I leave everything for you to do as how it will profit for both of us, and is no need of sending me the Printers Proofs for correction as you are an expert in this field.

## Alan Pringle to Lawrence Durrell, 31 August 1951

Many thanks for your card, and for persuading your brother to send the manuscript of his first book about the animal-catching exped-ition to the Cameroons when it is ready. I shall look forward to read-ing *The Overcrowded Ark* in due course.

## Alan Pringle to Gerald Durrell, 20 March 1952

I am very glad indeed to be able to tell you that we have much enjoyed reading *The Overloaded Ark*, and we are very keen to publish it. It is an amusing and winning book, although one hasn't even heard of some of the creatures which you spent all your time collecting.

## Gerald Durrell to Alan Pringle, 3 April 1952

I am very pleased that you have decided to offer me £100 advance on account of royalties, and the other terms seem to me to be very fair. The only thing that causes me some misgivings is the matter of the payment of the advance. As I pointed out to you, what I really want is the full amount on signature. In my present financial predicament this money would tide me over and allow me to concentrate solely on the South American book.

## Morley Kennerley to Gerald Durrell, 23 May 1952

I have made sure to include your Christian name in my opening, for the other day I had a long talk with the Production Department about the Durrell book – only to find in the end that I was talking about your brother's and they were talking about yours!

*Alan Pringle decided that* The Overloaded Ark *would benefit from illustrations of some of the more esoteric animals mentioned in its pages. He commissioned them from a meticulous Swiss artist called Sabine Baur, only to find himself having to wait a very long time for them.*

*That summer, Faber would suffer another financial shock. At home in bed with an infected foot and dysentery, Geoffrey first heard the worst of it in a letter from Dick de la Mare.*

## Richard de la Mare to Geoffrey Faber, 19 June 1952

I have been keeping a close eye on the cash position during these past weeks and I had felt worried about it myself, although at first Simmons[2] had remained optimistic about the position righting itself

---

2  Leslie Simmons was Faber's company secretary and chief accountant from 1937 to 1973.

before the autumn. But that certainly doesn't seem to be happening and I quite agree with you in thinking that it is essential to act at once. I am giving all the thought I can to the matter in preparation for our board meeting next Friday, if you are well enough then to be here, which I sincerely hope you may be. [...]

Then, this really crushing shock about our loss for last year. I could hardly believe it when Simmons told me about it and I think he found it difficult to believe it himself and thought at first that there might be some mistake. [...]

It is quite clear to me that we have been tying up our money on too many books that won't show a profit in the immediate future or the near future, and that applies to some reprints as well as new books. That I think is one direction in which we shall now have to change our policy, and I expect we shall all agree that we must reduce the number of new books to a more manageable figure.

*The emergency necessitated cash injections from Geoffrey Faber and T. S. Eliot, the former through a short-term loan, the latter through a share purchase. It was at this moment that Geoffrey received a letter from Charles Monteith, a young fellow of All Souls who had been injured fighting the Japanese in the Second World War and was now practising as a barrister.*

## Charles Monteith to Geoffrey Faber, 7 July 1952

I have wanted to write to you for some time; but I hesitated – and indeed I still feel very hesitant about it – because I feel that I may be trespassing quite unwarrantedly on your friendship and on the fact that you have been very kind to me. If I am doing that, please forgive me.

What I want, and would be very grateful for, is your advice about something which has been worrying me, on and off, for a considerable time. It is, in brief, the perennial problem of what to do – (I dislike that pompous word 'career'.)

Before I went to the Bar I was always very uncertain that it was the right profession for me & my eventual decision to go on with it was very much a 'faute de mieux' one. [. . .]

But when I try to decide what I really do want to do I find that I can't be any more precise about it than to say that I am, I fear, incurably 'literary'. By that, I suppose I mean that if I could write that is what I should like to do most of all. But I mean too, I think – forgive all this introspection – that I'm only really happy in a 'booky' atmosphere; buying books, reading books, talking about books – in doing all those things I feel 'at home' in a way I feel about nothing else.

Charles Monteith on the lawn of All Souls College, Oxford.

And all this – as no doubt you've guessed – has led my thoughts very much in the direction of publishing. And it's on that, specifically, that I'd be very grateful for your advice, and for information about prospects of getting in, what is likely to happen afterwards and so on. In addition to the general 'bookiness' which I've already written about too tediously, I have, I think, got a certain amount of common sense and administrative ability. I don't know enough about the publishing world to know whether this idea is worth pursuing any further or whether I ought simply to drop it, and either think about something else or resign myself, with some distaste, to the Bar. (I ought to explain that by 'publishing' I mean, of course, getting a job in a publishing firm. And the reason I hesitated so long about writing to you was that I know this letter would look like a request for a job. But quite honestly, it's not that – at the moment anyway. I do need to know a lot more about it than I do.)

*Geoffrey's reply was clearly kind but not immediately encouraging.*

## Charles Monteith to Geoffrey Faber, 18 July 1952

I can't tell you how grateful I am to you for your letter; not only for all the information about the chances of getting into the publishing world but also for – I hope this isn't a bit blush-making – your sympathy and understanding. I'm very much in your debt.

I knew, in a vague general sort of way, that publishing was difficult to get into; now I know about it much more definitely. And I needn't say how much I appreciate what you told me about your own firm. My first letter wasn't – as I think I said – a request for a job; but of course if it had been possible, and if I did decide to turn to publishing, there is no firm I would rather have worked for. I do appreciate that it's impossible; but could I ask you to let me know if you should by any chance hear of an opportunity somewhere else?

*That appeared to be that, but a few months later the aftermath of the financial crisis prompted T. S. Eliot to write Geoffrey a letter whose wisdom shines through – not that Geoffrey originally saw it in that light.*

## T. S. Eliot to Geoffrey Faber, 18 October 1952

I hope that the enclosed notes will not strike you as a piece of imper-
tinence. Take them, not as a matured statement, but as a summary of
what I might say in conversation on some one occasion, and subject
to qualification. [. . .]

I know that you are busy with arranging the distribution of the new
capital, between share-issue and loan, and also with trying to devise
some scheme of traffic lights. I am aware that improvements in the
machine are desirable, and that they will be helpful. With these I
shall not concern myself: what little skill at figures and system I
acquired in my bank-clerk days has now evaporated. I shall be concerned with what, in the end, I think most matters in a private limited company and one, especially, occupied in publishing: personalities.
That is why this note is intended for your eyes only. [. . .]

I remember saying to you (you may not remember) that you didn't
have a Board: that the Directors were Directors only in name. What
you have is a number of Departmental Managers, each seeing the
business from the point of view of his department. This must be somewhat qualified. I am not suggesting that they shouldn't be Directors.
It is quite right, for instance, that Crawley should be on the Board.
But he is, by training and experience, primarily a Sales Manager. It is
more than right that De la Mare should be on the Board. But he is, by
training and experience, primarily a Production Manager. It is right
also that Kennerley should be on the Board; but he is, by temperament and unsureness of himself, an employé. (I must say, in support
of Morley Kennerley, that I think he has for some time shared my
misgivings, or some of them. I have never discussed these matters
with him.) There is Du Sautoy, who has, I think, more of the potential
Director in him (I mean, the capacity for seeing the interests of the
business as a whole) than any of those named. And there is finally
myself, who, as a departmental Manager, count for little, as my func-

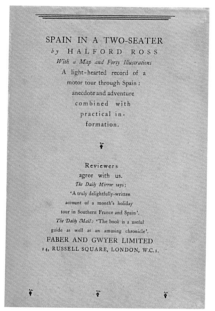

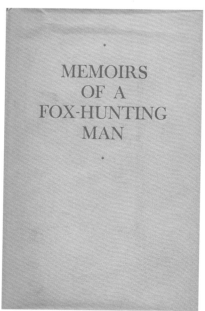

Spain in a Two Seater, 1925

The first book published by Faber &
Gwyer, of which Geoffrey Faber said,
'I do not think the binding is very
successful.'

Memoirs of a Fox-Hunting Man, 1928

The plain and anonymous jacket
of Faber & Gwyer's first bestseller,
written by Siegfried Sassoon.

Memoirs of an Infantry Officer, 1931

Barnett Freedman provided this cover
for his illustrated edition of Sassoon's
sequel, first published by Faber &
Faber in 1930. The commission
helped launch Freedman's career and
was also a sign of the new company's
confidence and creativity.

### Good Food, 1932

Having already illustrated an *Ariel* poem in 1928, Edward Bawden would still be appearing on Faber covers in the 1970s.

### Louder and Funnier, 1932

As far as I know, Rex Whistler included an image of the author in every cover he did for Faber, although most were rather more subtle than this one.

### Guide to Kulchur, 1938

As T. S. Eliot said, 'It is only a damned kulchered person who will be able to find his way about this book.' The cover incorporates Henri Gaudier-Brzeska's sketch of Ezra Pound's profile also used by Pound as a letterhead.

A Traveller in Time, 1939

One of the classics from Faber's growing children's list, illustrated by Phyllis Bray, a member of the East London group.

Finnegans Wake, 1939

'Buy a book in brown paper From Faber and Faber.'

Old Possum's Book of Practical Cats, 1939

T. S. Eliot's own illustration on the first edition of the book which would bankroll a revival in Faber's fortunes forty years later.

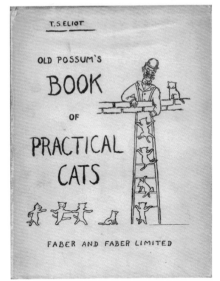

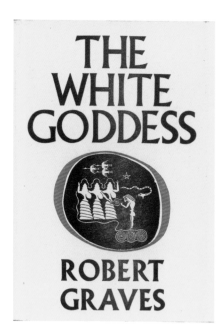

The White Goddess, 1948

In Eliot's words, written for the catalogue, 'prodigious, monstrous, stupefying, indescribable'.

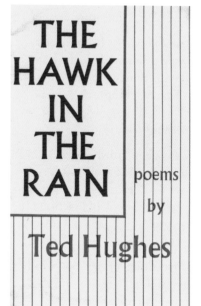

Justine, 1957

Although this was based on his own sketch, Durrell found Wolpe's version 'too artistic', but his suggestions for improvement arrived too late.

The Hawk in the Rain, 1957

A lovely Wolpe cover on the book that made T. S. Eliot write, 'I'm inclined to think we ought to take this man now.'

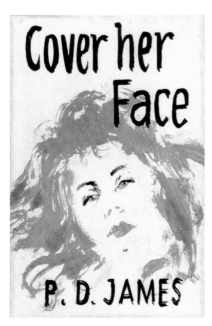

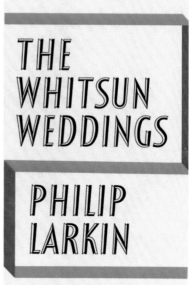

Cover Her Face, 1962

Charles Mozley, the illustrator of this beautiful cover, was a good friend of Berthold Wolpe.

The Whitsun Weddings, 1964

The core publication of Larkin's 'annus mirabilis'.

Ariel, 1965

Ted Hughes suggested that the cover should be 'red, the print either black or yellow, preferably black. That was what she imagined.' It is hardly surprising that the actual cover designed by Berthold Wolpe came 'as a bit of a shock'.

**Death of a Naturalist**

by Seamus Heaney

**ROSEN-CRANTZ** and **GUILDEN-STERN** are **DEAD**

by Tom Stoppard

The IRON MAN by TED HUGHES

Drawings by George Adamson

Death of a Naturalist, 1966

'If we are again going to publish poets before their name has been established elsewhere, I think we should take Mr Heaney on.'

Rosencrantz and Guildenstern are Dead, 1967

'Much to my relief – but not to my surprise – I find that *Rosencrantz and Guildenstern are Dead* does indeed delight me.'

The Iron Man, 1968

George Adamson's brooding cover for the book that began as a bedtime story for Frieda and Nicholas Hughes.

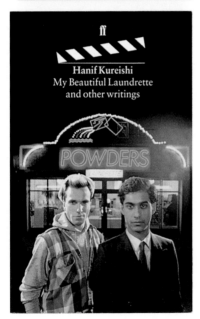

Slag, 1970

David Hare's first play, 'about women's rights, revolutionary feminism, girls' boarding schools, hysterical pregnancy, hockey and sex, in no particular order'.

The Unbearable Lightness of Being, 1984

The 'Pentagram Box' – seen here on artwork by Russell Mills – could go anywhere on a cover image, while making a Faber book instantly recognisable.

My Beautiful Laundrette, 1984

An early example of the clapperboard over the Pentagram box, identifying titles on Faber's growing screenplay list.

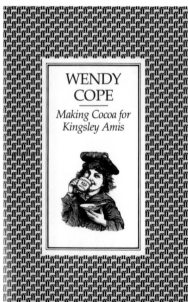

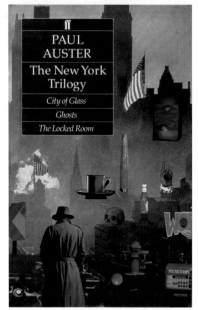

Spitting Image, 1984

The 'Appallingly Disrespectful' book that Robert McCrum knew Faber 'would love to publish'.

Making Cocoa for Kingsley Amis, 1986

Pentagram's ff wallpaper emphasised the power of the Faber name in poetry publishing.

The New York Trilogy, 1987

Irene von Treskow's jacket artwork for the book that established Paul Auster on the Faber list.

tion, with the type of book with which I am concerned, is not to make money, but to see that we lose as little as possible.

The Board qua Board, is in fact dominated by the Book Committee. [. . .]

I think it is chimerical to hope that, when another crisis occurs, we shall be able to attract outside capital, unless on such terms as involve complete outside control of the business. Certainly, I, had I been an outside investor but with my inside knowledge, would never have dreamt of putting a penny into the business.

Beyond relegating some new books to '1954 and after', is there any attempt made (or possible) to reduce our programme to our resources?

Now, if we survive the next two or three years, what of the future? You and I will both be ready to retire. When I say 'retire' for myself, I mean that, if my next play is reasonably successful, I should consider surrendering my salary, and asking (for a few further years) only for a room and a secretary. But what type of book shall we be able to get, in five years time?

So long as Dick is there, we ought to be able to keep at the top in gardening books and farming books (a much safer investment, to my mind, than expensive art books, because the bottom might fall out of <u>that</u> market, some day, quite suddenly). But we haven't any younger men in the firm with (1) the education (2) the social connections (3) the taste, to keep us in front, or put us in front, with general literature. I should be ready to retire, in due course, from the Board altogether in favour of some younger man (say in his forties) with these qualifications: but where is he to be found?

It is obvious, of course, that both Production and Sales have been working at such high pressure that neither can give close enough attention to any one book. And we are producing more books than we can afford to advertise properly.

My own feelings are, I have no doubt, partly attributable to age and decreasing energy and to the multitude of distracting claims upon my time. But my lack of zest is also partly due to the fact that when I contemplate our huge and amorphous list, I feel that the best service I can render is to add as little as possible to it.

## Geoffrey Faber to T. S. Eliot, 24 October 1952

Personalities. You know that I agree with much that you say (not quite all). But where does that get us? One cannot do other than use people as they are, or else sack them. I think that your remarks suffer from too clear a perception of defects, too grudging an awareness of merits. [. . .]

'Had I been an outside investor, but with my inside knowledge, I would never have dreamt of putting a penny into the business.'

This is a hard saying; especially when I consider what you have done so generously; and it is made harder still by your later reference to the huge and amorphous list, and your own unwillingness to add to it. Dare I suppose that they belong to the class of things one says rather for the purpose of shocking and hurting, than because they represent one's real view? For, otherwise, it must be that you have lost all faith and interest in what you and we have done and are doing. For myself, that would be a crowning disaster. You have your own great personal achievement to look back upon. I nothing but F. & F.

I won't elaborate that. But give me leave to say that I don't share your pessimism – perhaps partly because I cannot afford to do so, but also because I believe our position to be basically sound, and our cash position to be a misleading index. To justify this view to you, I would have to enter into an analysis of the whole war and post-war period. I can't face the labour of that. I admit that we have made some serious mistakes – for which we are not to be simply blamed – but we have all learned from them, and are all trying to put what we have learned

into practice. What has so greatly depressed me about your critique
is that you seem not to have seen any evidence of this at all.

The future. You are perfectly right in saying that we haven't any
younger man able to keep us in front, with general literature. I have
been worrying a lot about this. About 4 months ago Charles Monteith
(All Souls, very able, over 30-ish, N. Irish, at the Bar but disliking it,
passionately keen on our sort of stuff) asked if I could advise and help
him about getting a job in publishing. I believe he might be the right
man for us. (Do you recall his report on *Joyce's Dublin*,[3] or whatever
the book was called?) I discussed him with Dick (who is just as worried
about this aspect as you and I) and Dick thought it would be worth
considering him seriously. I took it no further: partly because I have
been waiting for the opportunity of a talk with him at All Souls, and
partly because of the money difficulty. Your letter brings the question
of some such appointment into the practical field.

## T. S. Eliot to Geoffrey Faber, 26 October 1952

I am sorry if, as your letter makes me feel, you have taken my remarks
in a personal way or as constituting a harsh censure upon the conduct
of the business. I regret now, that I coupled my expression of appre-
hension about future capital with any reference to my own cash contribution. The two things should not have been mentioned together. I
should be ashamed to exploit any advantage from making this investment (or investment + loan), as having any bearing on the question
of outside support. I was merely trying to make emphatically, a point
which is not discussed in your reply, namely, that we should be unduly optimistic if we hoped that, in a future crisis, we should be able to
attract outside capital. As for my own contribution, I should consider
it dishonourable on my part, and disloyal, to do less – and I might in

---

3 *Dublin's Joyce* by the Canadian literary scholar Hugh Kenner, which Faber
did not publish.

another emergency, be able to contribute a few thousand more, but nowhere near that amount. Considering how much I owe to you – more than you have ever known – I could not do less.

The gist of my comments, after all, is merely this: that as you are the one among the three forceful personalities on the Board who sees the business as a whole (the others being inhibited to some extent by the arduous preoccupations of their own departments) I have thought at times that you were too considerate and tolerant, and not quite autocratic enough.

If you feel reasonably assured that, as things are going, we can weather the next two years on the amount of capital at our disposal (and of course ignoring the impact of national disasters – if we tried to anticipate them we should be too paralysed to do business at all!) I am content. [. . .]

To return to an earlier point. I am inclined to infer that a Person has been wounded, when he responds with something that hurts in turn. It is perhaps not obvious why I should be hurt by your saying: 'you have your own great personal achievement to look back upon, I nothing but F. & F.' (Incidentally, it seems to me that you have several other achievements to look back upon.) There is an easy retort which I shall not make in a specific form: but only say that I have a great deal to look back upon, and to look inside at, which is anything but reassuring to a gloomy calvinistic temperament like mine.

But it also reaches another tender spot. I often feel that any usefulness I have had for F. & F. is a thing of the past. I am no longer in a position to undertake more work: the increasing pressure of outside burdens means a constant fight to get enough time either for F. & F. or for my own writing (when I say 'my own writing' I mean of course the writing I want to do). But I have been thinking for some time that I am probably being over-paid. I feel that my salary is in part a kind of retaining fee: that the only justification is that it is worth the firm's while to retain me from going to some other firm.

(Not that I have the slightest desire to do so, or that anybody else wants me: and not at all do I suppose that this notion has occurred to anyone but myself.) I certainly don't want any greater consideration than that I have always had. But I think I might feel happier if my salary were reduced to something like £750 or £600, as representing something nearer my true value.

That wouldn't make enough difference, of course, to go far towards making the addition of another director possible. (Here, incidentally, we run up against the Pringle problem.) I remember Monteith's admirable report on the Joyce book. I think it would be excellent if the All Souls' connection could be perpetuated. I'd like to know (1) what sort of people does he mix with socially (2) could he put any money into the business (I am not thinking of the need for capital, but of the benefit to him of having his own money at stake, and the status that would give him). The sort of man I had in mind would be a kind of Rupert Hart-Davis,[4] except that I don't like the Duff Cooper world, I am doubtful of R.H.D.'s business soundness of sense, and I suspect his temperament would be difficult: which doesn't leave much of Rupert!

*Every time I read that correspondence, I am more impressed by T. S. Eliot. The phrase 'the Pringle Problem' refers to the possible reaction of Alan Pringle if another editor was to be brought in above him.*

## Geoffrey Faber to T. S. Eliot, 28 October 1952

I am <u>very</u> grateful for your answer to my letter, and feel ashamed to have spilled so much querulous ink. Blame it on my cold, which has been making sleep difficult for nearly a week.

---

4  Rupert Hart-Davis was an English publisher who owned and ran his own imprint and was also nephew to the politician Duff Cooper.

*With Eliot's support, Geoffrey wrote back to Charles Monteith.*

## Charles Monteith to Geoffrey Faber, 10 November 1952

Yes. I did mean it completely seriously when I said to you that if I were offered a position in Faber & Faber I should take it, and take it very gratefully. As you know, I've been thinking about all this for a considerable time now; and the more I think about it the more certain I am that I should find publishing a much more congenial and satisfactory career than the Bar. And I think, too, that it's something which I could <u>do</u> – that I've got at any rate some of the qualities necessary – ; but that is something which you have to decide.

And I do of course understand that you're not in a position to make an offer yet, even of the most tentative sort; and I appreciate very much the fact that you told me so much not only about the general set-up at F. & F. but also about the exact nature of the possibility of a job there which exists at the moment. If nothing at all should come of it, I shall always be very grateful to you. [. . .]

If, therefore, T.S.E. would like to see me then I should be very pleased indeed to see him (though I would, I must confess, be slightly nervous and terrified – not that I imagine him to be a terrifying person; but it would be one of those Important Interviews).

## T. S. Eliot to Charles Monteith, 17 November 1952

I could arrange lunch during the following week – I am pretty well engaged up till then – but as I think dinner would be much more satisfactory and quieter for conversation, may I fix a week later, the evening of Thursday 11th December? I suggest the Athenaeum at any time after seven. The food is not very good but it is a better place for talking than the Garrick which is apt to be pretty full on Thursday evenings.

### Alan Pringle to Sabine Baur, 1 December 1952

We are becoming rather anxious over the delay in the production of *The Overloaded Ark*, which is now held up for your illustrations. I wonder if you have yet been able to finish them and send them off to me?

### Charles Monteith to Geoffrey Faber, 17 December 1952

It was very kind of you to write. My own impression was that the encounter had gone off well; it was a very enjoyable evening and I liked T.S.E. immensely. But then of course the inevitable doubts and misgivings set in and it was a very great relief and reassurance to hear from you.

### Gerald Durrell to Alan Pringle, 13 January 1953

By the way, I thought that you would like to know that I have asked Curtis Brown to act as my agent in the future, as I hope to be going abroad before the summer.

> *The time Sabine Baur took over her drawings had forced Faber to postpone* The Overloaded Ark. *This may have been a factor in Gerald Durrell's decision to appoint an agent; his choice of Spencer Curtis Brown should have rung alarm bells.*
>
> *In the meantime, the slow recruitment of Charles Monteith seemed to be progressing along its allotted tracks. Then John Sparrow, warden of All Souls, made an intervention in the form of this rather arch letter.*

### John Sparrow to Geoffrey Faber, 12 February 1953

Charles told me his hopes some time ago, & kept me <u>au courant</u>. I sat next to TSE at a dinner shortly before he and CM met for lunch, but did NOT then say ANYthing to TSE about Charles because he didn't ask me and it was not for me to interfere. Also because what

I would have said might have been a little damping. Then the other day I sat next to John Hayward[5] at dinner and gathered from him that the matter was settled, at any rate as far as TSE's view was concerned, and I felt myself justified then, in answer to actual inquiry by J.H., in saying what I felt. What exactly I did say I don't honestly remember, but it must have sincerely (if partially, I mean, 'only in part') expressed my views, which in confidence* are these: I think that C.M. is thoroughly competent, with plenty of (more than physical) weight (alas! expressing itself in pomposity) and with real keenness about present day literature and knowledge of it and flair for it (flair but not taste, I should say); and he is tremendously keen and would be absolutely in his element in publishing.

I don't think he'd let you down or that you'd ever regret having taken him on.

But (and this is the confidential part) I do think that he lacks distinction to an almost positive degree, and I probably expressed my surprise to J.H. that the coarseness** of his fibre or texture didn't grate on Tom E.'s great fastidiousness. [...]

*I mean to you and your partners in case you wish to tell them.
** That is not meant to be as strong as it sounds!

*Geoffrey showed the letter to T. S. Eliot.*

## T. S. Eliot to Geoffrey Faber, 14 February 1953

I am inclined to take seriously John S. remark that C.M. has flair rather than taste. So far as my observation went, this may be possible. I am not sure, however, that from the point of view of a firm's solvency flair is not a more valuable asset than taste. (I have a little flair, in limited areas, but I have found 'taste' to some extent a handicap.) I wonder

---

5   John Hayward shared a flat with T. S. Eliot from 1946 to 1957.

whether, if John S. knew the publishing world as well as we do, he would be quite so 'fastidious'. How many people are there in the business who have taste as well as flair? And how many men are there in the business whom a person of 'fastidiousness' would be wholly unjustified as criticising for 'coarseness of fibre'? I should have to rack my brains. C.M. is, no doubt, plebeian; but on one interview it would not occur to me to call him 'common'; and (what is the most important) I should be surprised to hear anyone designate him as 'vulgar'.

## Geoffrey Faber to Charles Monteith, 16 February 1953

I realised, when I saw you at Oxford, that you were somewhat disturbed by the slowness of events; and I want to assure you that there is no need for disturbance on that score. I cannot hurry matters – at least, it would be most unwise to do so; but I have asked de la Mare to get in touch with you sooner than he had been intending to do. Has he done so by now? I know only too well how irksome a prolonged period of uncertainty can be. But it can't be helped, I am afraid, unless I were to play the autocrat – and that, as I think you know, is a rôle I abhor.

The question of introducing a new member into a team, whose members are long accustomed to each other's idiosyncrasies, is full of snags. Moreover, if you join us, it will be an irrevocable step, both for you and for us. So do not be inclined to blame me for not putting my foot down on the accelerator. Especially as I am naturally prone to take quick decisions and am impatient of long delays. And do not think that inactivity, without, necessarily means inactivity within the hive!

## Geoffrey Faber to Giles de la Mare, his godson, 7 March 1953

May you have a very enjoyable last term at Eton, before you enter on your interim naval career (it is the navy, isn't it?) and may you follow that up with three happy & successful years at Oxford. After which, if you feel like it and F.&F. is still a going concern, I hope there will be room in Russell Square for a table and chair for your father's son.

*Giles de la Mare joined Faber in 1960 and became a director later in the decade. As a non-fiction editor with particular responsibility for art books, he published several important works and authors. My need to focus on titles which the firm continues to publish means that Giles will make only fleeting appearances in the rest of this history.*

## Alan Pringle, report on *Three Singles to Adventure* by Gerald Durrell

Gerald Durrell's story of his animal-collecting trip to British Guiana seems to me very good entertainment – full of humour, strange birds, beasts and fishes, and brilliant descriptions. And it seems to me that with practice his writing has improved, so that the book is shorter and better-shaped than his *Overloaded Ark*. [. . .]

Admirable though Sabine Baur's drawings are, I think we should try to find a more light-hearted and more accessible illustrator, who could do the work more promptly. Can V. H. Drummond draw animals?

Durrell now writes that he would like £350 advance on signature, as he is relying on the money from the second book to help finance his trip to Australia this summer, to collect ducks and geese for Peter Scott and the Severn Wildfowl Trust. One or two questions have a bearing on this matter of the advance. If I am right about the book, it is the kind of thing our list needs – American books excepted. On the other hand, even if it is better than *The Overloaded Ark*, as the second of a pair it may not go so well; and this time the British book rights are about all we should have.[6] As for the future, he mentioned over the telephone that he has another book, or part of another book, of a different kind in draft, and has asked Curtis Brown's advice on the presentation; that's all I know about it, but we could ask for an option.

---

6  Alan Pringle meant that now Gerald Durrell had an agent, Curtis Brown would be handling his American and other rights.

As an enthusiast for this book, I suggest that we might consider offering an advance of £250.

> *That was not enough. The story of what happened next is set out in the letter below from Geoffrey Faber to Stanley Unwin, whom Faber and Spencer Curtis Brown agreed to use as an arbiter in the dispute that had developed between them.*

## Geoffrey Faber to Sir Stanley Unwin, 2 April 1953

On March 12th we wrote to Spencer Curtis Brown making an offer of terms. In this offer we sought to provide the £350 advance for which the author had asked, partly by an advance of £200 on the second book, and partly by means of a further £150 advance on the previous book, both payable, after April 5th, on signature. We submit that the offer was a reasonable attempt to meet the author's wishes. [. . .]

This first offer was refused in S.C.B's letter of March 18th; and the negotiations continued. [. . .]

Meanwhile, without our knowledge, S.C.B. had offered the book to Rupert Hart-Davis, and for specific terms: 'a set 15% royalty throughout, and an advance of £400'. This approach to Hart-Davis was made after our first offer was refused by the author. S.C.B.'s conveyance of this refusal to us is dated March 18th. His announcement of Hart-Davis's acceptance was made in his letter of March 20th. Our second offer of the 19th was received and communicated to the author without our being told that the book had been offered to another publisher.

As soon as we were told (in S.C.B's letter of March 20th) that Hart-Davis had been approached and had agreed to the terms proposed to him, we said that we would pay those terms in order to settle the matter.

> *The next day, Geoffrey wrote on an entirely different matter to Charles Monteith.*

## Geoffrey Faber to Charles Monteith, 3 April 1953

We had a meeting on Wednesday; and, though we didn't come to a
<u>definite</u> conclusion, I can at least tell you that the idea of inviting
you to join us is being seriously and favourably entertained. It will
be necessary for you to meet the two other directors who haven't yet
seen you – W. J. Crawley our Sales Manager, and Morley Kennerley
who looks after publicity and routine editorial and takes care of certain authors – Peter du S. will arrange this as soon as may be. [. . .]

We should probably suggest to you that you should come to us for a
'probationary' year, and that you and we should make up our minds
during that year whether it was working out all right. If it did work
out all right – by which I do not mean that the year should exhibit
any <u>profitable</u> literary captures due to you, for that would be impossible! – if you wanted to stay with us, and we wanted you to stay,
our intention would be to give you the status of a director, with some
increment in salary, though not a very large one. We should I think,
feel it necessary to make Pringle a director; and might even take that
step at the time when you joined us, in order to prevent him from
feeling – as he would otherwise inevitably feel – that he was being
put aside, after a very long period of devoted and capable service, in
order to make room for a brilliant newcomer.

## Alan Pringle to Spencer Curtis Brown, 9 April 1953

Sir Stanley Unwin's verdict as arbiter has, of course, been communicated to us, and I am returning the typescript of *Three Singles to
Adventure*, with this letter.

*So Faber lost Gerald Durrell to what seems like some fairly
sharp practice by his agent. Apart from* The Overloaded Ark,
*which the firm still publishes, his huge bestsellers of the next
three decades all went elsewhere.*

*The losses of C. P. Snow and Gerald Durrell within a couple*
*of years give a definite impression of the firm starting to lose*
*its way, unable to cope with the more energetic approach to*
*negotiation pursued by agents like Curtis Brown. It was just*
*as well that, within a month, Geoffrey was finally writing to*
*Charles Monteith to invite him to join Faber in September.*
*That letter does not survive, but John Sparrow's and Charles*
*Monteith's reactions do.*

## John Sparrow to Geoffrey Faber, 9 May 1953

What am I to say? I don't think my view was quite as decided a
one as you supposed. I wouldn't – if asked to advise, have definitely
'advised against' taking C.M. Indeed, what I said to John Hayward –
and it was said post-prandially in every sense of that word – was said
on the assumption that you had already taken him, and was a sort of
relaxed reflection on the supposed <u>fait</u> <u>accompli</u>. [. . .]

But I should be insincere if I went back on the opinions which I
expressed – no doubt with excessive force and colour – to John Hayward, about the quality of his mind and personality, both of which
I think lack finesse and distinction to a degree which is remarkable.
And, his good nature is in danger, I think, of degenerating into a sort
of ponderous geniality; a middle-aged corpulence in which pomposity does duty for bone. I only say 'in danger of': keep him up to the
mark: keep him on his toes (if he still has any) and all will be well
– with his soul I mean; I have no fears for your firm. I'm sure he'll
do all right, and that neither you nor he will regret the steps you've
taken.

*John Sparrow's joke about Charles's toes – a reference to his war*
*wound – is in questionable taste, to say the least.*

## Charles Monteith to Geoffrey Faber, 11 May 1953

Very _very_ many thanks. I can't tell how delighted I am; and how grateful to you for all you've done.

> _That September, Geoffrey and T. S. Eliot prepared for Charles Monteith's arrival by agreeing, in a rather formal memorandum, the way in which Eliot (now almost sixty-five) would reduce his own involvement to make way for his younger colleague._

## Memorandum of Agreement between Geoffrey Faber and T. S. Eliot

T.S.E. further has in mind that he should, in a year's time, cease to be a 'working director' in the legal sense, and reduce his salary to a Director's Fee, say of £150 or £200 p.a. At whatever sum this fee was fixed, however, he would wish to retain a room and the services of a F. & F. secretary for part time (her responsibilities to him to have priority over her other duties, within reason).

T.S.E. proposes (subject to approval) to be somewhat in-and-out of Book Committees henceforward. He is prepared to attend as he has recently been doing until the return of Morley Kennerley. After that, he suggests that he should make a point of being in the building on Wednesday afternoons, so that he could be summoned for discussion of any problems on which his opinion might be thought worth having. It is not clear from the memorandum [sic] whether there would be room for him at the luncheon table or not. [. . .]

With these two successive alterations of status (apart from the possibility of his being later transformed from a Director into a Shareholder) T.S.E. expects that his services in the Department of Poetry and Belles Lettres will gradually diminish to zero; but he is aware (1) that authors like to remain in contact with the Director who has always served them, and some authors are more touchy on this point than others (2) that he will have to continue to take some responsibility about the Department of Theology. He would like also to keep a finger on Political Philosophy though not interfering in political topicalities.

*The formality of the memorandum was accompanied by a much more personal – and poignant – exchange of letters.*

## Geoffrey Faber to T. S. Eliot, 22 September 1953

Something must be said, and put into our Minutes. But it cannot possibly contain any real acknowledgment of the debt which I owe to you. Even if I live to write my own autobiography, I shall never be able to make that acknowledgement in terms that would satisfy my conscience without displeasing you. I believe that, in my offside way, I have been an instrument of use to you – I know, indeed, that you have never forgotten this, and that you have even been inclined to over-estimate the value of the contribution I have been privileged to make towards your achievement. Well, Tom, let us both praise the man who brought us together, and did better than even he could have foreseen – Charles Whibley.

We are both of us men of reserve. Neither of us finds it easy to down defences and speak our inmost feelings. So let me say, Tom, simply that, poetry and publishing and plays put aside, – and that is to put aside something! – nothing better has ever happened to me, short of my wonderful good fortune in marriage, than the meeting with you which Charles Whibley planned twenty-five years ago, or there-abouts. (It was more than that number of years, wasn't it? 1924, I think. At Ladbroke Grove. In the winter. Enid was at a nursing home, recovering from her illness when Dick was born. And we held a rather stilted conversation about 'Ballet'!)

P.S. Charles Monteith is coming to the B.C. tomorrow (to-day) to 'sit in'.

## T. S. Eliot to Geoffrey Faber, 23 September 1953

For the rest, I can only say that your letter has given me very great pride and pleasure – more than you could believe even if I endeavoured to find expression for it. As for my debt to yourself, it is beyond your knowledge simply for the reason that I could not give the terms of it without talking about matters so intimate to myself, and so painful at the time and in memory, that I have never been able to reveal them fully to anyone. One is none the less grateful to a man for having appeared at the right moment, to take a gamble on someone of whom he knew very little, and thus rescuing him from a desperate situation of which the benefactor was quite unaware.

I have a very definite memory – at least one clear snapshot preserved in the album of my memory – of our first meeting. We were both, I believe, ill at ease: I am sure that I was. I was also preoccupied by the effort to sell my services to somebody! My impressions were very pleasant indeed; but I little thought that the man I had gone to interview with such misgivings and trepidation would become one of my very few trusted – and, in our way, intimate – friends.

> *Charles Monteith would have been in the first few weeks of his probation, when, needing something to read on the train down to Oxford, he grabbed the top bundle from the 'slush pile' of unsolicited manuscripts. Its dog-eared nature was a testament to the number of publishers who had already seen and presumably rejected it, and it came with this rather unpromising covering letter.*

## William Golding to Faber & Faber, 14 September 1953

I send you the typescript of my novel *Strangers From Within* which might be defined as an allegorical interpretation of a stock situation. I hope you will feel able to publish it.

*The Faber reader had already taken a look. Her comments were handwritten across the top left-hand corner of the letter.*

'Time the Future. Absurd & uninteresting fantasy about the explosion of an atom bomb on the colonies. A group of children who land in jungle country near New Guinea. Rubbish & dull. Pointless. Reject.'

*With nothing else to read on the train, Monteith carried on beyond that 'rubbish and dull' first chapter, to find something much more interesting.*

### Charles Monteith to William Golding, 15 October 1953

I am afraid we've kept *Strangers from Within* rather a long time and I am writing simply to say that we are interested in it, but have not yet reached any decision about it. I hope to let you know something more definite before long.

### Board Minute, 29 October 1953

Mr Faber reported that Mr Eliot had regretfully decided to withdraw from the Book Committee and Mr Charles Monteith would now take his place, although Mr Eliot will be available should his opinion be required at any time.

### Charles Monteith to Philip Larkin, 5 November 1953

Henry Mackle[7] has doubtless told you why I was anxious to get in touch with you: simply because I was so enormously impressed by *A Girl in Winter* when I read it recently. Oddly enough I was lunching with J. D. Scott a day or two after I had finished it and he mentioned it quite spontaneously; said what a very good book it was, how vividly he remembered it, and wondered when there was going to be a successor.

When I got your card I spoke to Alan Pringle and he showed me the letter you referred to. I understand and sympathise; it must be utterly heartbreaking to go on trying when things either go dead or refuse to take any shape at all.

---

7 Henry Mackle was a distinguished chemist at Queen's University, Belfast who had been a post-graduate at Oxford and was a friend of both Charles Monteith and Philip Larkin.

May I make a suggestion? If you think it is silly or impertinent please forget and forgive it. It is simply this. You mentioned to Alan that you had in fact started novels and either failed to finish them or hadn't thought it worth finishing them. Could I, do you think, have a look at some of these attempts? It might be a help to have sympathetic comment.

## Philip Larkin to Charles Monteith, 8 November 1953

I think your suggestion that I should show you my failures a very kind and generous one, and if I don't accept it, it certainly isn't because I think it silly or impertinent. As a matter of fact, I took out the last and most promising failure after you wrote, and after reading it through could see plenty of ways to set it right, so you may have worked some sympathetic magic by remote control. [. . .]

By the way, I'll take the opportunity to ask a business question: I sometimes write poetry, and am submitting a selection (six or seven) to an undergraduate concern called The Fantasy Press, I should say almost certainly for no personal financial advantage. This doesn't worry you, does it? I think I am technically bound to show you any new book I write, but this is hardly a book.

I am glad you wrote; it did much to dispel my conception of Faber's as a reproachful father figure.

## Charles Monteith to Philip Larkin, 10 November 1953

So far as the poetry is concerned, we have no objection at all to your submitting a selection of poems to The Fantasy Press. Indeed we have no right to object even if we wanted to: I have had a look at the option clause in your contract and find that it refers only to novels.

## Charles Monteith to William Golding, 27 November 1953

As I mentioned in my letter of 15th October, we are interested in *Strangers from Within* and I should very much like to have a talk with you about it.

## Charles Monteith to Mrs James Morris, 3 December 1953

I am taking the liberty of writing to you, since I understand from the *Times* that your husband is at present in America and that you are joining him there shortly.

When you do so, I should be more than grateful if you would let him know that all of us here very much admired his despatches from Everest; and we wonder if there is any chance of persuading him to write for us his own personal account of the expedition.

## William Golding to Charles Monteith, 6 December 1953

Here are some bits of the emended version of my novel – the beginning, the middle and the end. I've done away with the separate bits, Prologue, Interlude, Epilogue, and as you'll see, merged them into the body of the text. Furthermore, chapter one, now begins with the meeting of Piggy and Ralph, and I'm allowing the story of how they got there – or all that is necessary of it – to come out in conversation.

Simon is the next job, and a more difficult one. [. . .]

What do you think of *A Cry of Children* as a title? It's got at least two levels, which is more than the other had.

## Geoffrey Faber to Richard de la Mare, 23 December 1953

For one reason or another I have had to take a few people into my confidence over the surprising fact that I am to be awarded a knighthood in the N.Y. Honours list; and I feel that I must, therefore, let you know about it before the list is published – in that respect behaving much less circumspectly than your father. But, of course, O.M.'s are fairy-tale stuff, compared to K'hoods! [. . .]

I went back to the flat to catch Enid, who was descending the staircase with a bag in each hand on her way to Waterloo to catch the 9.2 train. I gave her 3 guesses as to what had happened – no matter what she guessed, when I told her she collapsed on the staircase, dropping both bags, and said (I regret to report that in a moment of shock a respectable English matron now resorts to American idiom) 'You're kidding me'!

## Charles Monteith to William Golding, 11 February 1954

I am delighted to be able at last to write and say that we've definitely decided to accept your novel. And though I can't make any promises about this, I am quite hopeful that we shall be able to publish it this autumn.

## Charles Monteith to the Book Committee, 19 February 1954

William Golding's Novel

1) <u>Title</u>. Alan Pringle has suggested *Lord of the Flies*. I think this is very good myself and it refers to what is perhaps the central episode of the novel. Various other suggestions have been made and I have got a list of these which I'll bring to the Book Committee.

## Charles Monteith to James Morris, 26 February 1954

Your wife explained to me that *The Times* had imposed some sort of veto and I promised to see if we could do anything to make them relent. This letter, alas, is to say that we have made tactful enquiries and it very much looks as if there is no hope. I needn't say how sorry I am. All I can add is that if you plan to write any other book – possibly one about your present trip to the U.S. – we should be very grateful indeed if you would give us the opportunity to consider it.

*Geoffrey and Enid spent the first three months of 1954 on a*
*return visit to South Africa.*

## Note from Geoffrey Faber 'To the Staff of Faber & Faber, Tuesday evening, 6 April 1954'

When I arrived in my room this morning, after an absence of more than three months, I found on my table a folder, beautifully lettered with my initials, containing an inscription to 'Sir Geoffrey Faber, New Year 1954' and your individual signatures. Beneath it were two long-playing records – evidently a gift from you to me.

I do not know how to thank you. I cannot do so singly, and the only way of doing so collectively is to pin my thanks to the Notice Board. But what can I say adequately in a few lines? It is just thirty years since I took over the Chairmanship of the old 'Scientific Press', which changed its name to 'Faber and Gwyer'. It is just about twenty-five years since 'Faber & Faber' started a new existence upon these older foundations. I am often asked who is, or was, that other Faber. The answer I shall always give in future is that the name stands for all those, whether directors or members of the Staff, who have enabled me to realise the aim I set myself a quarter of a century ago.

The honour I have recently received belongs as much to you as to me. I am very happy to know that it has pleased you: and I have been very deeply touched by this gift you have made to me. May the spirit of comradeship remain with us always.

## Charles Monteith to William Golding, 20 May 1954

I have just finished reading the galleys of *Lord of the Flies* and this note is simply to let you know that I'm even more enthusiastic about it than I was before. Though I must have read it through four or five times by now and seen it at every stage, I still simply couldn't put the proofs down until I had finished them. And I'm delighted to find that it's had precisely the same effect on several other people here who hadn't read it before; indeed, in two cases I have had complaints that it resulted in nightmares! What a terrific book it is; I do congratulate you on it.

## Geoffrey Faber, Memorandum to the Board, 29 June 1954

It will be remembered that on April 3 1953 I indicated to Charles Monteith that, if we asked him to join us, it would be for a probationary year, and that if things went well we should then give him 'the status of a director, with some increment in salary, though not a very large one.' [...]

I have been rather careful not to have more than the minimum of conversation with CM since he joined us. But I have twice asked him how he liked the work – once when he had been with us for some six or eight weeks, and again quite recently. On each occasion he has used the same expression: 'I have never been so happy.'

My absence in Africa has, of course, meant that I have seen less of him than have the other members of the Board. But I have seen enough to enable me to form a clear opinion of my own and I would like to know how far this opinion is shared (or contradicted) by the other Directors. [...]

I have hesitated whether to express my own view in this memorandum, for fear of seeming to expect the Directors to attach too much weight to it. But, after much reflection, I think that it is part of my office to do so. My own view, then, is that CM is a first-rate acquisition; and that we should give him the status of a Director in September. [...]

I shall be 65 in August, and I don't wish to run in full harness till I drop. Ordinary 'retirement' doesn't seem to be open to me; and it wouldn't, I think, be to the advantage of the business, if I were to retire from the Chairmanship, as long as I remain <u>capax mentis</u>. The name, also, has a business value. So, given reasonable health of body and mind, I propose to go on much as I am now, and drawing the same substantial salary, for another 5 years. At 70, I propose to relax, in effect to retire, but to continue as the titular Chairman, at a reduced salary (say at half my existing salary). Precisely what part I would then take in the business must depend upon circumstances and my own capacity. Would I, for example, continue to attend Book Committee meetings? I don't know the answer to that, and to similar questions; and I shall be more than glad of candid advice – and by 'candid' I mean <u>really</u> candid, not merely kindly, advice.

## Morley Kennerley to Geoffrey Faber, 1 July 1954

Firstly CHARLES. I do not think there is any question whatsoever that he should be made a director at the end of his year – that is the right time. He has already shown himself a very valuable addition to the firm, full of enthusiasms for the work which he so obviously and thoroughly enjoys, and which comes naturally to him. Also important, he loves mixing with the literary folk, and some of us rather shy away from this as we grow older, quite aside from the time factor. In this connection alone he is just what is wanted, for he will develop this side of his life now he is in publishing and I foresee that interest growing rather than waning.

Above all, however, he has shown that he is outstanding in the job you hoped he would do – reading, editing, reporting, keeping in touch with literary developments – in fact he has taken to publishing like a duck to water and it is amazing how he has settled into the profession in such a short time.

It is not easy for someone to come in from outside without friction developing at times – I have not felt a shadow of this, which I think is a good omen for the future. I have been functioning on about two cylinders of late and would be the first to be conscious of it. [. . .]

As for your growing old and retiring, it just does not bear thinking about – except that it gives one pleasure to think of you having more leisure. You must have more leisure when you want it, even giving up coming to the Book Committee regularly in five years time – I do not think that so important. Dick did, I think, show that he felt the responsibility of the Chairmanship while you were away, and did not press his own foibles as he does at times when an ordinary member.

## Geoffrey Faber to Charles Monteith, 10 September 1954

You will be appointed a Director on October 6, which is the earliest practicable date for our next Board Meeting. [. . .]

I am very glad indeed that your 'probationary' year should end in this way; and I hope I shall live long enough to see you in full swing!

## Charles Monteith to Geoffrey Faber, 7 October 1954

Very many thanks for your note. I needn't try to say – for I think you know – how delighted I am; how very happy I am here, and how eternally grateful I am to you.

## James Morris to Charles Monteith, 21 October 1954

You may perhaps remember long, long ago – Feb 26th – writing to me about the failure of your kind assault on *The Times* in re an Everest book. I rudely didn't thank you for the letter, but my wife recently reminded me that at the end of it you mentioned the possibility of a book about the U.S.A. I don't know if you were really serious about the thing, but I am in fact planning to write a travel book about my American journey, and I wonder if you would be at all interested? I've motored through all 48 states, writing fairly regular turnovers for *The Times,* and I think I have established some kind of pattern for a book.

*Faber & Faber has now published Jan Morris for over sixty years — most recently, in 2018,* In My Mind's Eye.

## FABER & FABER BOOK CATALOGUE, SPRING AND SUMMER 1955

*The Usurpers*
Czeslaw Milosz

Translated from the Polish by Celina Wieniewska

Czeslaw Milosz's novel comes out of the agony of modern Europe. The story moves from the heroism and chaotic horror of the Warsaw rising – when the Red Army stood implacably idle on the Vistula – into the constricting gloom of the Russian occupation; into a poisoned and infected world, a world of equivocation and 'double think' where integrity and honesty have become dangerous eccentricities.

*This novel was the only book by Milosz that Faber published, but it meant the firm could claim him for its own when he won the Nobel Prize in Literature (largely for his poetry) in 1980.*

Lord of the Flies *was published on 17 September 1954. Although initially it sold slowly, its reviews included a notice from E. M. Forster, who called it the 'outstanding novel of the year'.*

## Charles Monteith to William Golding, 26 January 1955

It was tremendously good about E. M. Forster, wasn't it? And did I ever tell you, by the way, that T.S.E. read it some time ago and admired it very much.

## Robert Graves, speaking to the YMHA Centre, New York, 9 February 1955

I offered *The White Goddess* in turn to the only publishers I knew who claimed to be personally concerned with poetry and mythology.

The first regretted that he could not recommend this unusual book to his partners, because of the expense. He died of heart failure within the month. The second wrote very discourteously, to the effect that he could not make either head or tail of the book, and could not believe it would interest anyone. He died too, soon afterwards. But the third, who was T. S. Eliot, wrote that it must be published at all costs. So he did publish it, and not only got his money back, but pretty soon was rewarded with the Order of Merit, the Nobel Prize for Literature, and a smash hit on Broadway.[8]

*The retirement of Donald Brace in New York meant that the publisher which bore his name, Harcourt Brace, was becoming increasingly focused on textbooks, and an uncongenial employer for Bob Giroux, who wrote privately to T. S. Eliot expressing his concerns. Eliot's response was unequivocal.*

## T. S. Eliot to Robert Giroux, 24 February 1955

All that I want to say further about the matter at this moment is simply that if you make any changes for yourself, I shall want to follow you. If that statement has any value as a minor asset in bargaining or making a decision, there it is.

*Giroux submitted his resignation to Harcourt Brace on 24 March 1955 and was asked to leave the next day. On 1 April he joined the relatively new firm of Farrar, Straus and Young.*

---

8 A reference to the successful US run of T. S. Eliot's play *The Cocktail Party*.

*By the time he retired as chairman of what had become Farrar, Straus and Giroux, he had edited seven Nobel prize-winners, most shared with Faber & Faber in a close but non-exclusive relationship that benefited both firms.*

## Charles Monteith to Rosica Colin, Samuel Beckett's agent in the UK, 9 September 1955

You may remember we had a conversation on the telephone a few weeks ago about Samuel Beckett's *Waiting for Godot*; and that you told me you would find out if the British rights are still available. This is simply to say that I'm still interested in it and very much hope you will be able to let us have it on offer.

## Charles Monteith to Diana Pullein-Thompson, Rosica Colin agency, 11 October 1955

Thank you very much indeed for sending me a copy of *Waiting for Godot* amended to meet the Lord Chamberlain's requirements. We can now get on straight away with our production. As you know, we want to bring out the book as soon as possible next year.

*John Berryman had twice offered his poems to T. S. Eliot at Faber, to little effect, but the third time they came through Bob Giroux to Charles Monteith.*

## Charles Monteith to Robert Giroux, 2 November 1955

We have now read and had a chance to think about John Berryman's *Homage to Mistress Bradstreet* about which you talked to me last month, and we are certainly most impressed by it. At the same time we feel – as I know you anticipated we would – that this poem by itself wouldn't perhaps be the best way to introduce Berryman to the English poetry reading public; and we wonder if we could see some more of Berryman's work? What we would really like to consider – and about this we still haven't, of course, reached a final decision – is the possibility of doing here a selection from Berryman's poems with *Homage to Mistress Bradstreet* as the centrepiece.

*With his previous attempts at poetry rejected by Faber, Philip Larkin had turned to the Marvell Press, run by George Hartley, to publish* The Less Deceived, *the volume that would make his name. Charles Monteith was an early purchaser.*

## Charles Monteith to Philip Larkin, 21 November 1955

Just a brief note to say how enormously I enjoyed and admired 'Church Going' in the *Spectator*. Sincerest congratulations on it. I'm looking forward very much indeed to *The Less Deceived*. I imagine it should be arriving any day now. I noticed George Hartley's note about it in the current number of *Listen*.

*Monteith soon passed his copy of* The Less Deceived *on to T. S. Eliot, with a handwritten note on which Eliot wrote his own response.*

## Charles Monteith to T. S. Eliot

I thought you might perhaps like to look at this – rather good I think. Philip Larkin is an author of ours. We published his novel <u>'A Girl in Winter'</u> some years ago – but there's been nothing since.

*Yes – he often makes words do what he wants. Certainly worth encouraging.*

*Reassured, Monteith wrote back to Larkin. It is striking (and impressive) how often he uses the approbation of T. S. Eliot as part of his pitch to prospective authors.*

## Charles Monteith to Philip Larkin, 29 December 1955

Forgive me for yet another letter; but I thought that you might perhaps like to know that Eliot – to whom I lent *The Less Deceived*
– liked it very much indeed and has asked me to pass on to you his
sincerest congratulations on it.

When will you, I wonder, have another volume of poems ready for
publication? I very much hope that when you have you'll give us a
chance to consider it.

## Charles Monteith to Samuel Beckett, 16 February 1956

Do forgive me for writing again but I thought you would be interested to know that *Waiting for Godot* is being very successful indeed.
The book is selling fast and exciting much interest and discussion
everywhere.

By the way, may I mention to you an idea which came into my mind
the other day? It is simply that I wonder whether or not you have
ever thought of writing a book of personal memoirs and recollec-
tions: and to say that if you have we would be more than pleased if
you would give us the opportunity of considering it for publication.

## Samuel Beckett to Charles Monteith, 27 February 1956

It is good news your Godot is doing well. My only regret is that it
is not complete. Some passages are quite meaningless because of the
holes. They could have been bridged with a little rewriting. Well,
there it is.

Afraid my memoirs are unlikely. J'ai moins de souvenirs que si
j'avais six mois.

## Thom Gunn to Faber & Faber, 26 May 1956

I enclose the manuscript of a book of poems called *The Sense of Movement*. I hope you will be kind enough to consider it for publication. I enclose a cheque for five shillings, which ought to cover the cost of its return if you do not want to use it.

## Charles Monteith to John Osborne, 7 June 1956

I'm pretty certain that lots of publishers must have written to you already; but in case they haven't, may I say how very delighted I should be if I could have the opportunity of discussing with you the publication of your work? I saw *Look Back in Anger* last night; and I haven't enjoyed an evening in the theatre so much for a very long time indeed. My sincerest congratulations on it.

It struck me, too, that in addition to writing plays you might perhaps be thinking of trying a novel, either now or at some time in the future. If you are, need I say how very grateful I should be if you would let me know about it?

## Charles Monteith to Thom Gunn, 6 July 1956

We've now had an opportunity to consider *The Sense of Movement*; and I'm delighted to be able to let you know that we admire these poems very much indeed and that we do most certainly want to accept the book for publication. Mr. Eliot has asked me to send you his own personal congratulations on the poems; and to say how much he has enjoyed reading them. Thank you very much for sending them to us.

*The acceptance of the twenty-six-year-old Thom Gunn was an important signal that Faber was once again in the market for new young poets.*

### Lawrence Durrell to Berthold Wolpe about the cover for *Justine*, received 26 November 1956

Thank you for the pull of the cover. I feel rather conscience stricken as it is obviously the result of painstaking thought and effort – which was more than I wanted to put you to. My idea was something much cruder on a cancer livid Gollancz yellow. This is more artistic than I meant and I think it would be silly to start quibbling at this late stage. May I ask you however to drop the yellow and print on white . . . The title red is good visually but the blue is dismal – though factually accurate – it is exactly the livid hue of decomposing Islamic flesh they do use. But visually wouldn't it be stronger if the blue were black?

Then, couldn't we dispose of the words 'a novel by' and set the Lawrence Durrell a wee bit lower, just to let the hand ride free? I think these things would make it even stronger visually than it is. The scribbles on the spine don't make any sense to me. Why not a tiny black hand under the title again? Tiny. Or several. Thank you so much for the trouble you have so obviously taken.

Please don't swear at me. I want to establish a device for the cover which will last out a cycle of novels. Hence my fussing you so.

### Berthold Wolpe to Lawrence Durrell, 28 November 1956

Thank you for your letter which unfortunately did not reach me until Tuesday. The printer had started printing the jacket and I am sorry to say it was therefore impossible to make any alterations. I hope you will like the final jacket when you see it.

I am far from swearing at you and you can rest assured that all the details of the jacket are very carefully worked out and even the words 'A Novel by' were considered important by our Sales Department as your previous books we had published were not books of fiction. Also, as sometimes books on palmistry show a hand on the jacket, it is useful to counteract this idea by the explanatory words 'A Novel by'.

White paper is considered impractical as the wrappers become soiled too quickly in the book shops.

Please forgive us for sticking to your previous suggestions and for not being able to follow your too-flexible mind!

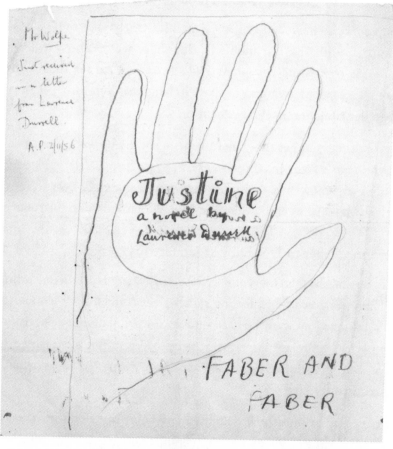

Lawrence Durrell had his own ideas about the cover for *Justine*, the first book of the bestselling *Alexandria Quartet*, which he communicated to Faber in this sketch. As the correspondence makes clear, he was not happy with how Berthold Wolpe interpreted it.

FABER & FABER BOOK CATALOGUE, SPRING 1957

*Justine*
Lawrence Durrell

We believe *Justine* fulfils the promise heralded by T. S. Eliot when he described *The Black Book* as 'the first piece of work by a new English writer to give me any hope for the future of prose fiction'.

### T. S. Eliot to Geoffrey Faber, 9 January 1957

I am sorry to have had to leave you, like nearly every one else, in the dark until the last moment. But there were three good reasons for concealing my plans from everyone except those who, like Higginson[9] to whom I propose to hand this letter for you, have been instrumental in their execution.

By the time you get this I and my wife should be well on our way to the Côte d'Azur for three weeks. I am marrying Valerie Fletcher, whom you know only as my secretary for nearly eight years. We are utterly devoted to each other, and I know that I am very fortunate.

### Geoffrey Faber to T. S. Eliot, 11 January 1957

Higginson brought me your letter along yesterday, looking rather solemn (he was, in fact, feeling rather sleepy, and I don't wonder). I couldn't imagine what he had come to see me about. *Paene cecidissem* – a Ciceronian phrase which my Mods. tutor was pleased to render 'You could have knocked me down with a feather' – when I opened your letter.

Let me say at once how delighted the news contained in it made me – as it has everybody here to whom I, later, imparted it, lest they should feel that they (the Directors & Ann & Simmons) had been kept in the dark until the announcement in *The Times* this morning.

---

9 Gordon Higginson had been T. S. Eliot's solicitor for several years.

My very warmest congratulations to you and to Valerie; and may you enjoy a very happy honeymoon, unfestered by newspaper men; and a long and very happy married life.

No doubt you will have heard from Higginson and John that the news of the wedding was given yesterday to the *Daily Express* – they think by one of the car-drivers. The only enquiry I have had was late last night by 'phone from the *Daily Mail*. Fortunately, I had already resolved to lie, and did so. When asked if I had been aware of what was happening and was I at the ceremony? I replied unhesitatingly that of course I knew of it, but was not in the habit of getting up at 5 o'clock a.m. to attend other people's weddings. I rang up H. this morning to tell him this; and was much relieved to find that he had read the report of my remarks in the *Daily Mail* and thought I had coped with the situation very well!

But, you know, Tom, the Recording Angel must make a cross entry between your account and mine. I don't think that fib should go down on the debit side of <u>my</u> account.

## Enid Faber to T. S. Eliot

What cunning old foxes you both are to be sure. It is the best news I have heard for a long time, and I want to congratulate you both most warmly, and most affectionately. [. . .]

In an excessively gloomy world, it is lovely to think of your happiness. Bless you both.

## Charles Monteith to Samuel Beckett, 29 January 1957

I would like to say, too, if I may, how unhappy I feel, in retrospect, about our decision last year to print the Lord Chamberlain's version of *Godot* rather than the full one. At the time it seemed, on balance, the most prudent course to take. We were in the middle of one of those periodic Home Office persecutions which blow up from time to time; there had been several criminal prosecutions of well-known and reputable firms and, as a result, we were all walking with great circumspection and had become infected with what seems – now that we can look back on it – perhaps an extreme and undue timidity. None of this is intended as an excuse; it is, at best, merely a faint plea in mitigation. I would like to assure you, though, of our very sincere regrets that it should ever have happened.

### Ted Hughes to 'Editor, Poetry Department', 20 March 1957

My first book of forty poems, *The Hawk in the Rain*, recently won the First Publication Award in an Anglo-American contest sponsored by the New York City Poetry Center and judged by W. H. Auden, Stephen Spender, and Marianne Moore. [. . .]

Since I have long admired Faber's poetry list, I thought I would contact you immediately and ask if you might be willing to publish my book in England. If you wish, I could have another copy of the book typed up for your perusal.

### Ann Faber to Ted Hughes, 21 March 1957

Thank you for your letter of March 20th. We were interested to hear of the publication of your first book of poems, but the fact is that though we have published the work of several American poets in England, we have not done so until they were relatively well known over here and we were able to publish a book consisting of selections from earlier books published in the United States. We should be interested to see your poems, however, if you would send us a copy of the manuscript to be published by Harper.

> *Following the tragedy of her fiancé's death in the war, Ann Faber had written an acclaimed first novel,* The Image. *A motorbike accident in 1952 paralysed her left arm. She then,*

*very much encouraged by her father, came to work at Faber*
*& Faber, but – possibly handicapped by prevailing gender*
*attitudes – never made her name as an editor in her own right.*

## Ted Hughes to Ann Faber, 24 March 1957

I am enclosing a copy of my manuscript of poems, *The Hawk in the Rain*, which is to be published by Harper's this coming August.

In my letter, I must have given you to believe that I am an American. I am, however, British. I graduated from Pembroke College, Cambridge University, in 1954. [. . .]

I made bold to presume Faber and Faber might be interested in publishing *The Hawk in the Rain* since W. H. Auden, Stephen Spender and Marianne Moore chose this volume unanimously as the winner of an open contest, and by the fact that you do promote the work of young English poets, such as Thom Gunn.

## Ann Faber to Ted Hughes, 28 March 1957

I am so sorry I got your nationality all wrong. Thank you for sending in your poems. We should be very glad to consider these for publication and you will be hearing from us again before very long.

*So Ted Hughes's poems made their way to Charles Monteith. He*
*at least thought them worth showing to T. S. Eliot, who wrote his*
*own reaction on the bottom of Monteith's memo.*

## Charles Monteith to 'MR. ELIOT', 9 April 1957

*The Hawk in the Rain:* Ted Hughes

I wonder if you'd like to look at this? I must confess that the name of Ted Hughes was unknown to me until these poems arrived; but – as you'll see from the correspondence – he's a young Englishman whose poems have been published chiefly in America. This book, his first, has won the First Publication Award in a contest sponsored by the New York Poetry Centre and judged by Auden, Spender and Marianne Moore. The quality seems to me very uneven; but I think there's some interesting poetry in the book. Though I don't feel we'd want to take him on yet, he might perhaps have a letter of encouragement. Would it, I wonder, be worth asking Spender informally for some more information about the Award; and about the judges' assessment of Mr. Hughes' work?

*I'm inclined to think we ought to take this man now.*
*Let's discuss him. T.S.E*

MR. ELIOT

THE HAWK IN THE RAIN: Ted Hughes

I wonder if you'd like to look at this? I must confess that the name of Ted Hughes was unknown to me until these poems arrived; but - as you'll see from the correspondence - he's a young Englishman whose poems have been published chiefly in America. This book, his first, has won the First Publication Award in a contest sponsored by the New York Poetry Centre and judged by Auden, Spender and Marianne Moore. The quality seems to me very uneven; but I think there's some interesting poetry in the book. Though I don't feel we'd want to take him on yet, he might perhaps have a letter of encouragement. Would it, I wonder, be worth while asking Spender informally for some more information about the Award; and about the judges' assessment of Mr. Hughes' work?

CM.
9.4.57.

*I'm inclined to think we ought to take this man now. Let's discuss him.*

TSE

### Charles Monteith to Ted Hughes, 9 May 1957

I am delighted to be able to let you know that we much admire *The Hawk in the Rain* and would like to publish it. Mr. Eliot has asked me to tell you how much he personally enjoyed the poems and to pass on to you his congratulations on them.

### Charles Monteith to Ted Hughes, 30 May 1957

One small point. Is it correct to describe you in the blurb as English? I only ask because it occurs to me that you might perhaps be Welsh and would prefer to be described as Welsh? Do please let me know.

### Ted Hughes to Charles Monteith, 1 June 1957

I am perfectly agreeable to being described as English since I come from Yorkshire.

I am, by the way, changing my address from now until June 18th to: The Beacon, Heptonstall Slack, Hebden Bridge, Yorkshire. After that date, I may be reached in America: c/o Plath, 26 Elmwood Road, Wellesley, Massachusetts.

> *Ted Hughes was, of course, already married to Sylvia Plath.*
> *She had encouraged him to submit his poems both for the First*
> *Publication Award in New York and to Faber & Faber. She even*
> *acted as his typist. Her own fame lay in the future.*

### Book report on *A Bear Called Paddington* by Michael Bond, 28 August 1957

I think the author has missed his mark in this story of a bear adopted by a middle class family called Brown. Unless I mistake him he means it to be funny but the jokes are all on the bear; the Browns treat him very much as I imagine they would treat a 'foreigner' and

as one's sympathies and affections are all with the bear it is difficult
to laugh with the author. Moreover the Brown family are perfect
fools, they leave him, who knows nothing of modern conveniences,
alone to bath and nearly to drown; they twice lose him, once on the
Underground and once in a large store simply through inattention
– the parents Brown that is. No – frankly the best of the book lies
in its title.

*Ah well.*

*The following year, Faber's Spring and Summer catalogue
contained an important announcement. Having observed the
success that Penguin was having with paperbacks and also that a
few hardback publishers in America were starting to produce their
own paperbacks rather than sell the rights, Faber had decided to
test the possibility of doing the same thing itself.*

## FABER & FABER BOOK CATALOGUE, SPRING & SUMMER 1958

Faber Paper Covered Editions are paper-backs with a difference. Here
is no series of books stream-lined to a uniform shape and type size to
sit pretty on the bookshelf. They are cheap editions in paper covers of
worth-while books and in most cases they are reprinted in the size and
style considered to be most suitable for the particular book when first
published.

The field covered by Faber Paper Covered Editions is a wide one. Given
the necessary encouragement the publishers intend to produce books of
every kind in the economical style, since it appears to offer the cheap
editions most suitable for present-day tastes and pockets. But a word
of warning must be given: at this time it is considered unlikely that the
publishers will wish or indeed be able to reprint any of these books in
paper-covered form when the necessarily large first printing is exhausted.
So, if you want to buy Mr. Eliot's *Collected Poems* in paper covers at 5/-,
do not delay. All but one of the books announced are available and will

William Golding
Lord of the
Flies

FABER

5s *net*

FABER paper covered EDITIONS

Peter du Sautoy found the term 'Faber Paper Covered Editions'
ridiculously long-winded, but it was undoubtedly strong branding in
Berthold Wolpe's own Albertus font, the 'Faber typeface'.

continue to be available – for many years, it is hoped – in cloth bindings but at considerably higher prices.

Below is given a list of the first twelve titles in Faber Paper Covered Editions . . .:

*The Ascent of F6 and On the Frontier*, W. H. Auden & Christopher Isherwood
*Best SF: Science Fiction Stories*, edited by Edmund Crispin
*Peacock Pie*, Walter de la Mare
*An Experiment with Time*, J. W. Dunne
*The Cocktail Party*, T. S. Eliot
*Collected Poems, 1909–1935*, T. S. Eliot
*Lord of the Flies*, William Golding
*The Riddle of the New Testament*, Sir Edwyn Hoskyns & F. Noel  Davey
*Archy and Mehitabel*, Don Marquis
*Who Moved the Stone?*, Frank Morison
*The Daring Young Man on the Flying Trapeze*, William Saroyan
*Verse and Worse*, edited by Arnold Silcock

> *The policy that a paperback would not be reprinted lasted as long as it took for the first printing of one title to be exhausted.*

> *On 20 September 1958, Geoffrey suffered a stroke. He was sixty-nine. Initially thought to have a reasonable chance of recovery, he spent most of the rest of his life at Minsted, making only one visit to Russell Square. There was no dispute about who should take charge in his absence: Dick de la Mare, the vice chairman.*

## Richard de la Mare to Geoffrey Faber, 27 November 1958

It was very nice to see Enid at the party last Thursday, and I only wish that you could have been there too – not that I expect you minded very much missing it! [. . .]

One of the people I met there was a certain General Grand, who was responsible in some way or other for the Swedish Iron Ore book,[10] and it was amusing and interesting to talk to him about it. He said that it achieved its purpose quite beyond hopes and expectations and he congratulated us on the part <u>we</u> played! He says the book is still referred to as a book of reference!

### Enid Faber to Richard de la Mare, 13 January 1959

This is just a progress report on Geoffrey.

He is getting on, but I must admit that at times the progress seems slow. I thought I ought to warn you, in confidence, that he is desperately anxious to do 2 days & 1 night a week in London. I do realise that as with Crawley you might prefer not, but it would remove all hope from him to tell him so now.

> *In an interview for the* Paris Review, *the American poet and critic Donald Hall asked T. S. Eliot if he had any more plans for poems like those in* Old Possum's Book of Practical Cats, *by now a staple of the Faber list. Eliot's reply referred to a scrap of a poem which was never written but would eventually achieve fame through a very different route.*

### T. S. Eliot in the *Paris Review*, Spring/Summer issue 1959

Those things do come from time to time! I keep a few notes of such verse, and there are one or two incomplete cats that probably will never be written. There's one about a glamour cat. It turned out too sad. This would never do. I can't make my children weep over a cat who's gone wrong. She had a very questionable career, did this cat.

---

10　See pp. 134–6.

## Charles Monteith to Ted Hughes, 3 July 1959

The last few times I've written, by the way, I've meant to say how much I've admired Sylvia's poems in *The London Magazine*. Do please congratulate her for me!

> *That September, Tom Faber, Geoffrey and Enid's youngest child, married my mother Penny. He would be the only one of Geoffrey's children to have children himself (Richard never married and Ann's marriage to John Corlett did not lead to any children).*

## Richard de la Mare to Geoffrey Faber, 15 October 1959

We had a meeting this morning to consider paperbacks for next year, but we didn't get any further than a full survey of what has happened to the 22 titles that we have published so far. The results are most encouraging and very instructive, but there isn't time to go into them in detail here now. We don't seem to have made any real mistake yet, except perhaps to include *Farmer's Glory*, but even that will pay its way and sell out in the end all right, Crawley thinks. What we must beware of is doing any book that now seems at all dated even if it is still selling fairly well in its cloth-bound form. One of the most successful recent ones is *Introduction to Astronomy*, but there are quite a number that are doing really well. Both *Verse and Worse* and *Lord of the Flies* have been reprinted and it won't be long before we shall need to reprint *Who Moved the Stone* also. Few of the books have suffered more than a little in the sale of their cloth-bound editions, and in some cases the cloth-bound sales have increased – *Lord of the Flies* and *Verse and Worse* for instance.

Eleven days after his godson's wedding, T. S. Eliot made sketches
of some his fellow members of the Book Committee, which Morley
Kennerley was quick to preserve and annotate.

## Wilson Harris to Messrs Faber & Faber Ltd, 24 October 1959

I have just finished the enclosed novel, *Palace of the Peacock*, which
I submit to you in the hope that you may consider it a work worthy
of publication. [. . .]

As my circumstances are rather extreme at the moment, I should appreciate it greatly if you would let me have an early reply with regard to this, in order that in the event of your not being interested, I could show it elsewhere. I hope this may not inconvenience you unduly.

### Charles Monteith to Ted Hughes, 30 October 1959

I wonder, too, if Sylvia has any stories? If she has, I'd very much like to see those as well. And I remember her telling me – when we all met in New York last year – that she was writing a novel. If by any chance that's finished, I very much hope she'll send it to me.

*Despite Charles's wooing, Heinemann was the first publisher of both Sylvia Plath's early poems and of her novel,* The Bell Jar *(initially published under a pseudonym).*

### Richard de la Mare to Geoffrey Faber, 27 November 1959

Peter and I went down to visit Harlow about a fortnight ago, as I told you we intended to do, and we paid a long visit to Longman's new warehouse there, lunching with them afterwards, and in the early afternoon we went to see the Manager of the Harlow Development Corporation. [. . .]

Well, we had a board meeting yesterday to discuss all this, when all the directors were present, including TSE I am glad to say, and the decision we came to then was that we should make the move to Harlow, if you agree, and let the Harlow Development Corporation know at once that we want them to retain the site for us.

*From 1961 until 1999, Faber & Faber distributed all its books from its own warehouse in Harlow. Its accounts department remains there today.*

## Charles Monteith to Wilson Harris, 10 December 1959

I'm sorry we are taking such an appallingly long time to give you a decision about *Palace of the Peacock*. Everybody who has read it – including myself – has been extremely interested and, indeed, impressed by it; but – as I think you'll realise – it's a difficult book, and one which we've got to think about pretty carefully. It may be that it will be another week or two before we finally make up our minds. This, I know, is rather unfair on you; so would you, I wonder, allow us to take an option on it for the next month? For this option we would pay you £15 now – which would be deductible from your advance on royalties if we do decide to accept your book and make a firm contract with you for it.

*Faber did publish* Palace of the Peacock *and all Wilson Harris's subsequent books.*

## Charles Monteith to Wilson Harris, 29 April 1960

In view of what you tell me, though, about your financial position, I think I really ought to write to you now in a more general way about the problems involved in publishing your work, and I do hope you'll forgive me if I sound a little avuncular! As you know, we are very impressed by the great literary and imaginative qualities of your writing; but there's no escaping the fact, I fear, that your books – compounded as they are of such elements as myth and images from the sub-conscious – are undoubtedly 'difficult' and though they will, I hope, attract attention among serious and discerning reviewers and readers and establish your reputation as a writer, I can't really – and I must be quite frank about this – hold out to you the prospect that they are likely to have very large sales – at any rate in the immediate future.

Left to right: Louis MacNeice, Ted Hughes, T. S. Eliot, W. H. Auden,
Stephen Spender. (© Mark Gerson)

## Sylvia Plath to her mother Aurelia Plath, 24 June 1960

Last night Ted & I went to a party at Fabers given for WH Auden. I
drank champagne with the appreciation of a housewife on an evening
off from the smell of sour milk and diapers. During the course of the
party Charles Monteith, one of the Faber board, beckoned me out
into the hall. And there Ted stood, flanked by T. S. Eliot, WH Auden,
Louis MacNeice on the one hand & Stephen Spender on the other, having his photograph taken. 'Three generations of Faber poets
there,' Charles observed, 'Wonderful!' Of course I was immensely
proud. Ted looked very at home among the great.

*By the summer of 1960, it was clear that Geoffrey would have
to give up the chairmanship.*

## T. S. Eliot to Richard de la Mare, 2 July 1960

I realise how delicate a matter this is for several reasons. But I should not like us to commit ourselves to continuing the same salary to Geoffrey whatever happens. As long as we can afford it, yes. But the publishing business has its ups and downs, and I am afraid of top-heavy expense. Strictly speaking, in justice, the President's salary should be reduced in proportion as the salaries of yourself and Peter should be adjusted appropriately to your new status. (I don't know what salaries any of you is getting but you can tell me this in private: I only know that I halved my own voluntarily – I now draw £500 p.a. – so that we could afford to take Charles Monteith on the Board, and he of course has taken over much of my work.)

## Board minute, 5 July 1960

The Vice Chairman told the Board of his recent talk with the Chairman at Minsted, when Sir Geoffrey expressed his intention to resign from the Chairmanship of the Company. His resignation is to take effect as from August 23rd 1960 (his 71st birthday). It is his wish to remain a Principal Director, since he has every intention of continuing his work for the Company. His resignation was accepted with great regret, and his desire to remain a director was welcomed. [. . .]

It was then proposed by Mr. Eliot and seconded by the Vice-chairman that a new office of President of the Company should be established and that Sir Geoffrey should be elected the Company's first President. [. . .]

Mr. Crawley then proposed that Mr de la Mare be elected Chairman of the Company upon Sir Geoffrey's retirement from the position. Mr. Eliot seconded the resolution which was carried. Mr de la Mare proposed that Mr du Sautoy be elected Vice Chairman of the Company at that time. Mr Eliot seconded the proposal which was carried.

## Geoffrey Faber to Richard de la Mare, 27 July 1960

Everything now seems in order, and I suppose that the announcement both of my retirement and of my election (or, rather, appointment) as President will soon be going out to the Press. Of course it is most important that it should be done in such a way as to exhibit the independence of the firm and the real authority of the Board and the Officers; regarding myself it is necessary only to say that I look forward to serving the Company in whatever manner that is open to the President and my health may permit.

So Amurath[11] to Amurath succeeds! And my very best wishes go with you – and with Peter, too. May Harlow, in particular, turn out all that you have hoped for and be free from harassing troubles! At least of the major kind!

---

11 Amurath was the name of several successive Turkish sultans, referenced by Shakespeare in *Henry IV, Part 2*.

# 7: 1960–1970
## 'People feel that we are smug'

The 1960s brought major developments. Sales nearly tripled. Each year Faber added new books to its paperback list. With the encouragement of Benjamin Britten, it moved into the entirely new business of music publishing. Having already constructed its own warehouse in Harlow, by the end of the decade the firm was ready to move into a new purpose-built office in Bloomsbury.

Faber's literary publishing flourished too. Established writers like William Golding, Lawrence Durrell and Ted Hughes continued to draw praise. Two more Faber authors won Nobel Prizes: St-John Perse in 1960 and Samuel Beckett in 1969. Although Charles Monteith was not as dynamic as he had been in the 1950s, he was now able to draw on the help and advice of several younger editors, including Frank Pike, Mary-Kay Wilmers and Rosemary Goad.

Yet all was not as rosy as it seemed. Publishing was changing. The *Lady Chatterley* trial in 1960 heralded a new era. Some sign of this can be seen in the correspondence below, as the firm gets braver about publishing words which once would not have got past the censor, but in other ways it remained remarkably old-fashioned. Faber appointed its first female director – Rosemary Goad – in 1970; there would not be another for almost twenty years. Attitudes within the firm meant that it was almost inevitable that Rosemary's responsibilities would include personnel and cookery books. In sales and marketing the firm seemed in danger of being left behind by its more entrepreneurial competitors.

The firm's growth was being fuelled by an amorphous and incoherent list. In 1964, Faber issued the following catalogues: Books on Music; Books for Schools and Colleges; Farming & Gardening; Books on the Arts; Poetry & Plays; Books for the Young; Books on Nursing, Hospital and Medical Subjects; and 'Theology, Philosophy and Religion'. There was little focus on the literary publishing which gave the firm its real distinction.

The sales growth also concealed increasingly precarious finances. Unable, for tax reasons, to offer many shares to his fellow directors, Geoffrey Faber had instead granted them bonuses based on percentages of profits (Dick de la Mare alone received 12.5 per cent). That may have contributed to a culture where the firm was unwilling to write off either dead stock or advances that were never going to be earned out by royalties. Each year the firm declared profits, but each year its overdraft grew. In 1970 the bank called a halt.

Overseeing all of this – both the expansion and the management failures – was Dick de la Mare. In the 1920s Dick had brought the firm its first bestseller, Siegfried Sassoon's *Memoirs of a Fox-Hunting Man*. Over the succeeding decades he had been responsible for the excellent production standards that were integral to Faber's success. Every season, he initiated more books on Faber's list than any other editor, although few of them remain in print today. Finally, in 1960, he got his chance to run the company. The tragedy is that he hung on too long. So I open this chapter with a letter from Geoffrey to Dick, presumably written in the 1950s, that gives an insight into his character.

## Geoffrey Faber to Richard de la Mare

None of us see ourselves as others see us, and I venture to draw a sketch of somebody whom you have evidently never seen. He is a man of strong will, and great physical and mental energy, very prolific of ideas, often of brilliant ideas, for which he argues with almost endless resourcefulness and tenacity and even (sometimes) a certain unscrupulousness. He is apt to attach himself with great ardour to particular subjects or causes. He is only just beginning to understand that neither he nor his business can take on everything, and is still not quite as familiar as he will become (of necessity) with the virtue of the word 'No'. If he got his own way every time, or even every other time, there would hardly be any room in the organization to which he belongs for any other really active person except himself. And since everything he brings forward is brought forward with similar energy and determination, it is inevitable that every time he starts on a fresh suggestion or scheme there should be a stiffening and tautening of everybody else's nerves. In other words the opposition he encounters is of his own making.

Not a complete sketch. Because he happens, also, to be one of the most loyal and affectionate of men – a fact that makes things, sometimes, even more difficult.

Richard de la Mare at his desk.

*Financial Times*, 27 October 1960

The Swedish Academy today awarded the Nobel Prize for Literature to the French poet and diplomatist St.-John Perse, 'for the soaring flight and the evocative imagery of his poetry which in visionary fashion reflects the conditions of our time'. [...]

St.-John Perse's reputation stands very high in literary circles and his work has been translated into many languages but is little known to the mass public. His fame rests largely on a long poem, *Anabase*, published in 1925, translated into English by T. S. Eliot.

*In the 1960s the firm published a number of important literary critics, including Helen Gardner, Richard Ellmann, Anthony Burgess and George Steiner. That is not to say, however, that every member of Faber's Board agreed with every word of what they published.*

### T. S. Eliot to Peter du Sautoy on *The Death of Tragedy* by George Steiner, November 1960

I thank you for showing me this book and I have read the passages which you have marked. I do not think I want you to alter a word of what the author says about me because I had rather be damned in the company of Yeats, Hofmannsthal, Claudel and Cocteau than praised by this extraordinary American who cannot write decent English and whose style is one of vulgar vehemence. What amount of lunacy moved the Committee to accept this manuscript is not a question which a non-medical layman can answer. As we have recently published a rather inferior book of scraps of theatrical criticism of the London stage, it is a pity that we should commit ourselves to this monster.

### Charles Monteith to R. P. McDouall, Travellers' Club, 4 January 1961

Thank you for your letter. I'm very sorry indeed that my guest's dress at luncheon yesterday should have caused complaints – complaints which I can entirely understand and sympathise with.

My guest was Mr. Thom Gunn, one of the most distinguished younger English poets, whose work is published by my firm. When I invited Mr. Gunn to luncheon with me at the Club I had no idea at all he would arrive so bizarrely attired. Since he was educated at Bedales and at Trinity College, Cambridge, I took it for granted that he would be aware of the ordinary social conventions in matters such as this; and he had, indeed, lunched with me at the Club last year when his dress was entirely orthodox. Mr. Gunn has, however, for the last few years lived in California and yesterday he had just returned from Germany, where he had been spending a few months on the proceeds of the Somerset Maugham Award, which he won for his poetry last year. So I can only suppose that the informality of his clothes is accounted for either by the general informality of Californians – to which perhaps he has become accustomed – or by the exigencies of travel.

When I first saw what Mr. Gunn was wearing, my immediate instinct was to take him somewhere else for luncheon, but unfortunately I had arranged for another guest to meet us; and he arrived so late that the opportunity for quick action was lost. I was in a dilemma; and decided – obviously wrongly – to brazen it out.

I can only apologise, which I do – most sincerely. I should be most grateful if you would convey this apology both to the Committee and to the members who complained. I should perhaps add that if on any future occasion I entertain Mr. Gunn at luncheon, it will not be at the Club.

*Apparently Thom had been wearing a leather jacket (possibly fringed) and cowboy boots.*

### Charles Monteith to Thom Gunn, 10 January 1961

Very nice indeed seeing you last week. Since I'm in bed with a cold at the moment, I'm dictating this over the telephone to my secretary and she is signing it for me!

> *A few weeks later, Charles Monteith was back in Oxford at a dinner at All Souls, bemoaning to his neighbour the death of author Cyril Hare: 'Now that he is dead, we will have to find another crime writer for the Faber list.' Monteith's dinner companion was an agent, Elaine Greene. 'Do you know,' she is said to have replied, 'I've had a manuscript posted through my door this morning which I think you might quite like.'*

### Elaine Greene to Charles Monteith, 27 February 1961

I have got a new detective story which I hope will appeal to you, *Cover Her Face* by P. D. James. The first four chapters need ruthless cutting but after a slow start I think it gets nicely into stride and characterizations seem to me particularly good. I hope you will agree.

### Rosemary Goad to Charles Monteith, 24 March 1961

I rang Elaine Greene of MCA 24th March 1961 and asked her if she could tell us a bit more about the author of *Cover Her Face*. She said that unfortunately she knew v. little about her – except that she worked in London and that her real name (E.G. <u>thought</u>) was White. I said that we would like to see author and have a talk with her about cutting, etc; and E.G. promised to get in touch with her on Monday and ask her to ring me up. I said that I thought – if author did cut it considerably – we would certainly be interested in making an offer.

### Rosemary Goad to Charles Monteith, 28 March 1961

Mrs. White (P. D. James) called here 28th March 1961.

I told her that, provided she cut her novel to a maximum of 80,000 words, we would like to publish it; and she took it away to work on it. She hopes to let us have it back within a few weeks; and if she gets stuck with the cutting, will get in touch before that. I told her that, if necessary, we would try and cut it here, but that we would much prefer her to do it.

She was bubbling over with ideas for new detective novels; and is at present at work on one set in a psychiatric outpatients' dept. She works at the North West Metropolitan Hospital Board . . . where she obviously has a fairly high-powered job. She is about 40, I should say, and has a daughter who is training to be a nurse at the Westminster. [. . .]

She seemed extremely nice, very easy to talk to, and I'm sure will do the cutting very competently.

## Charles Monteith to John McGahern, 14 March 1961

I was very interested indeed in the extracts from your novel which are published in the current number of X.[1] If by any chance you haven't yet made arrangements for its publication I would be absolutely delighted if you would give us an opportunity to consider it.

## Charles Monteith to John McGahern, 29 March 1961

The portion of *A Barrack Evening* which you sent to me has been read here by several people – including myself of course – and I am delighted to let you know that we have all been extremely impressed by it. So much so in fact that we would certainly be willing to make an agreement with you now for the publication of the novel when it's finished.

*Having suffered another major stroke, Geoffrey Faber died on Good Friday, 31 March 1961. While this could be seen as the*

---

1  X was a quarterly literary magazine which ran for seven issues between 1959 and 1962.

*end of an era, the truth is he had played little part in running the firm since 1958. I will leave it to the extracts to express the sorrow so many people felt, but there is surely symbolism in the fact that his first grandchild, my sister Henrietta, was born two days later on Easter Sunday, 2 April.*

### Board minute, 5 April 1961

The Chairman formally reported, with great regret, the death of Sir Geoffrey Faber, the President of the Company. It was resolved that suitable condolences be sent to Lady Faber on behalf of the Board.

The Chairman also reported that Mr. W. J. Crawley had decided to retire from active business and had tendered his resignation as a Director with effect from 1st April 1961. The Directors accepted his resignation with regret and were pleased to know that he will continue his association with the Company by continuing to advise the Company about Children's Books.

### Enid Faber to Tom and Valerie Eliot, 5 April 1961

First, Tom, I must tell you that Geoff did know that you were conscious of a debt, but as well as that he came back from the one visit he paid to 24 [Russell Square] after the 1st stroke most touched by the warmth of your greeting. I remember him saying 'Tom almost kissed me, and really did seem pleased to see me.' Indeed so much of our lives have been interwoven that one can't even begin to enumerate it all. I'm only sorry that his illness prevented him from knowing Valerie, as well as I am beginning to.

### T. S. Eliot, address at the Memorial Service for Geoffrey Faber, 10 May 1961

Any calling that Faber had accepted would have been, with him, the occupation of a gentleman; but for him that of Publisher most certainly was. He loved good books, and what he chiefly wanted as a publisher was to publish good books. If they were good enough, they were worth losing money on. [. . .]

Geoffrey Faber was endowed with many talents which he employed happily and well. He was fortunate in many ways, fortunate especially in his marriage. His wife, I know, was his wise counsellor, even in publishing, particularly in the early days when we were learning to be publishers: the partaker of all his interests and his strong rock and his bulwark in his last painful years of illness. [. . .]

I remember Geoffrey Faber in many situations, in peace and in war, in work and in play, on land and on sea, at home and abroad. I loved the man, and part of my own life is in the grave with him. May he rest in peace.

## Charles Monteith to Philip Larkin, 26 April 1961

News has reached me on the grapevine – the grapevine being Anthony Thwaite! – that you've probably got enough new poems now to make up a book; and that you are free at last of your commitment to the Marvell Press. If all this should be true – and I needn't say how much I hope it is – do please let us publish them. We really would be delighted to.

## Philip Larkin to Charles Monteith, 10 May 1961

The option clause in my contract with the Marvell Press has certainly now expired, so Anthony Thwaite is right as far as that goes. I am not sure about his second point, that of having enough poems for another collection. I should like a little more time to think this over and see what there actually is. Naturally I am most gratified that you should be interested in such a collection. My feeling is that anything published now would be no better than, if as good as, the last one – a point which would I think be widely canvassed by reviewers. I would really rather wait a little longer and offer something solider.

The menu for William Crawley's retirement dinner at the Ivy, 1 June 1961.
References to a number of famous books on the children's list include:
*The Pirate Twins, Sam Pig, The Little Red Engine* and *Filofus*.

## T. S. Eliot: Lines inscribed on W. J. Crawley's lawn mower, presented on his retirement

He who in ceaseless labours took delight,
And scarcely ate or slept, by day or night:
Let this obedient engine as it mows
Teach him with Grace[2] to enjoy well-earned repose.

---

2   Grace Crawley was William Crawley's wife.

## Faber & Faber: Press Release

Lady Faber has accepted an invitation to join the board of Faber and Faber Ltd with effect from 7 June 1961. Lady Faber is the widow of Sir Geoffrey Faber, the founder of the firm, who died in March of this year.

## Tom Faber to Enid Faber, 8 June 1961

First and foremost, we are both terribly pleased and excited about your grand Directorship. We can now confess that we were sad that you seemed to have resolved not to have much to do with the firm, not to take books any more and so on. I guess that this was mostly a wish on your part not to seem too eager or interfering – a misplaced bashfulness and I am really so glad that the other directors have of their own accord decided to draw you more into the firm. I am certain you will get a lot of pleasure from still doing things for them, and that what you do will be well worth the £500. From a purely selfish point of view it is nice to feel that <u>we</u> may still have an occasional excuse to go to Russell Square and greet Miss Swan³; we have been melancholy to think that our trips to the flat were at an end. But what is more important is the point Dugald⁴ has made to me, and I daresay to you, that we can't cut ourselves off from the firm if we still want to own it – as of course we all do; obviously the shareholders have got to have some responsibility for, and say in, major policy decisions, if not in the day to day running of the firm. At the moment we know all the people in the firm, but with the passage of time it would become harder to preserve any sort of link without a family representative amongst the Directors. All this has been plain to you I am sure. So three cheers. And the £500 won't come amiss either.

## FABER & FABER BOOK CATALOGUE, AUTUMN 1961

*A Grief Observed*
N. W. Clerk

*A Grief Observed* is a very unusual document. It consists of a series of reflections, forming a coherent whole, by a husband upon the death of his wife. A man of mature mind, a Christian, has seen a wife to whom he was deeply attached approach death by the way of slow, painful and incurable malady. Now that she is gone, he probes his own feelings and reveals his thoughts with relentless honesty.

---

3  Ethel Swan had started as a receptionist at Faber & Gwyer in 1925, and stayed until 1972.
4  Dugald Macpherson was Geoffrey Faber's solicitor and would play a vital role in 1970.

### Rosemary Goad to P. D. James ('Mrs White'), 4 July 1961

I think that Mrs Greene has already let you know that we should much like to publish *Cover Her Face*; but I felt that I must just write you a personal note to say how very glad I am about this. I must apologise, too, for the appallingly long delay in letting you have our final decision – I do hope you have forgiven us now!

### Frank Pike, book report on *The Vision of Gombold Proval* by 'John Orton', 7 July 1961

Mr. Orton's opus is certainly good for a number of individual laughs and is also not without its sardonic perceptions, but I must confess I found it generally somewhat incomprehensible and boring. If the author cut his work up into revue sketches I'm sure he'd have a *succès fou* on his hands, but I think the book as a whole is just a bit too eccentric to be a publishing proposition. It's definitely worth skimming through for amusement's sake, nevertheless.

> *'John Orton' later changed his writing name to 'Joe Orton'. Charles Monteith never took him on either as a novelist or a playwright, but he was sufficiently interested in him to pay a visit to the Islington bedsit he shared with Kenneth Halliwell, where Monteith was fed boiled rice with sardines.*
>
> *Frank Pike spent his entire career as an editor at Faber, from assisting Charles Monteith to taking responsibility for the play list, and finally as House Reader.*

### Board minute, 21 December 1961

Mr de la Mare moved and Mr Kennerley seconded a proposal that Mr P. D. Crawley be appointed a Director of the Company with effect from 1st January 1962. This was unanimously agreed upon.

*So, in accordance with Geoffrey's wishes, Peter Crawley did succeed his father as Sales Director of Faber & Faber.*

## John McGahern to Charles Monteith, 10 February 1962

I have just been awarded the AE Prize[5] for some chapters of an unpublished novel. It is the first time the Award has been made to an work of fiction.

Please accept my dear gratitude, for were it not for your insistence I wouldn't have dreamed of entering.

## John McGahern to Charles Monteith, 15 June 1962

I forward a copy of the completed novel with this letter and I am hoping very much that you will like it. I call it *The Barracks*, almost in despair of finding a true title. Is it any use, do you think? Or does any other come into your mind? [. . .]

Some of the words in the dialogue are doubtful, but I am hoping they may be publishable, because in no place has it sexual significance – it indicates a kind of social breakdown. The AE Award people passed it, they were given to page 140 (4 chapters).

## Charles Monteith to John McGahern, 6 July 1962

I have just finished reading *The Barracks* and I must write at once to tell you how enormously I admired and enjoyed it. It really is quite first class and I couldn't be more delighted. I do congratulate you on it. [. . .]

One other thing. We have no objection in principle to printing the word 'fucking' which is used occasionally in the dialogue and I don't

---

5   The A.E. prize was awarded in memory of the Irish writer and nationalist George Russell (1867–1935) who used the pseudonym 'AE', including on an *Ariel Poem* illustrated by Paul Nash (see correspondence for 8 May 1929).

think that nowadays there would be any legal risk in doing so in this country. I think I ought to point out to you, though, that if we do print this word it is likely to have two results which would to some extent impair the sales of the book. Some libraries and bookshops, particularly in the Provinces, do still have fairly strong objections to buying books which contain such words and expressions; and moreover – and this is probably more important than usual in the case of *The Barracks* – the retention of this word would of course almost certainly lead to your novel being banned in the Irish Republic. I am quite happy to leave the final decision about this to you and if you really do insist on the word going in it will go in. But it could have an appreciable effect on the sales of the book and I really would be grateful to you if you would bear this in mind when you make your decision about it.

## John McGahern to Charles Monteith, 19 July 1962

I have gone through the 'fuckings'! I could eliminate all Reegan's, indeed every one except three or four in chapter 3, the doctor's dialogue, used to shock Elizabeth's awareness into a harsh despairing world of a particular consciousness. I don't know how I can really leave out these without harming the work. I am indeed anxious not to harm the sales, and I would be pleased to try to find a satisfying compromise, if it is possible. Could we leave it till we meet?

## Charles Monteith to John McGahern, 20 September 1962

Only a brief letter, I'm afraid, since I am in a most fearful rush, trying to get everything straight before I go. But I am delighted to say that this is to let you know that everybody agreed at our editorial meeting yesterday that we would take our courage in both hands and print the word 'fucking' in full. Like you, I don't really think there should be any trouble; and certainly it strikes me as a much more rational and honest thing to do than to go on printing f—.

### Board minute, 12 October 1962

The Chairman reported on the difficult cash position caused by the additional expenditure incurred in the production of the series of Paper Covered Editions. It was agreed that further consideration be given to dates of publication of the new Paper Covered Editions to be issued in 1963.

*Tom Stoppard was a journalist in Bristol when Faber first made contact with him.*

### Frank Pike to Tom Stoppard, 23 November 1962

Some time ago we published a book called *Introduction*, which contained three stories each by six unpublished writers, the idea being to give them the opportunity of having a reasonable body of work presented to the public at one time. We are, at the moment, gathering material for a second volume of this kind and your name has been given to us as being a possible contributor by Anthony Smith of the *Western Daily Press*.

### Tom Stoppard to Frank Pike, 28 November 1962

Thank you so much for your letter and for the interest it conveyed. Of course I had fair warning from Anthony Smith, and of course it didn't do the slightest good: I am little prepared, having concentrated on playwrighting for the last couple of years. [. . .]

Thank you again – By the way, on the question of a novel, I have begun work on one but am now waiting for a play to go on, hoping that if it runs at all I can leave journalism and, for a few months anyway, devote all my time to it.

## John McGahern to Charles Monteith, 28 November 1962

The first part of the proofs came today and I was disturbed to see <u>fucking</u> printed <u>f--</u>. Is it that they were printed before the Board's decision, or some mistake?

## Charles Monteith to John McGahern, 30 November 1962

I am frightfully sorry about the printers' prurience! Do please, when you are correcting proofs, replace f— by fucking in full; and David Bland, our production manager, will get in touch with the printers personally to make sure that nothing goes wrong.

*Tom Faber spent his entire life as an academic physicist at Cambridge and was the only one of Geoffrey's children who had never worked in the firm. Nevertheless, he had a good head for business that saw him serve several years as Treasurer of his College. So, whether it was because he was the only one of his siblings to have children himself, or because he was at least based in the UK, he became the member of the family who took the most interest in the company's fortunes. In December 1962, he wrote to his mother agreeing that the firm should use the opportunity created by a share issue to increase the stakes held by working directors.*

## Tom Faber to Enid Faber, 15 December 1962

Obviously it is particularly desirable that the de la Mares and Crawley should have a greater stake. Perhaps we should realise that the more they identify themselves with the firm the harder it will become, morally, for us ever to sell our equity at the advantageous rate that I imagine is now theoretically possible (3 or 4 times the present price of the shares, I shouldn't wonder). Since we can none of us envisage the possibility of wanting to sell this doesn't worry me. There is quite enough in the family coffers already for your grandchildren to be brought up in as much luxury as will be <u>good</u> for them, I guess. They would be likely to resent the sale of the firm and the loss of the opportunity to work in it and develop it much more than they might resent our neglect of the opportunity to turn an extra £100,000 or two. Henrietta is destined for the stage of course, but perhaps she will have a brother or a cousin with literary leanings!

*Sylvia Plath died on 11 February 1963.*

## Charles Monteith to Ted Hughes, 15 February 1963

We've just heard the shattering news about Sylvia, and I wonder if we can help in any way at all? I've just been talking to Peter du Sautoy and we both hope that you won't hesitate to get in touch with us if you feel there's anything at all we can do.

## Frank Pike to Tom Stoppard, 6 March 1963

I don't know if you finished the story you said you wanted to write for us, but I am very glad to be able to tell you that, on the strength of the stories of yours we have already, we want to include your work in *Introduction II*.

## Charles Monteith, Memorandum, 22 March 1963

I lunched with Philip Larkin 22nd March 1963. The first point he raised was that he is very much inclined to break off his relations with A. P. Watt and to deal directly with us – and with any other publishers who might be interested – in future. As I pointed out to him it's always rather difficult for a publisher to advise in this sort of situation; but I got the impression that he's got a pretty shrewd idea of the pros and cons. His chief grievance against Peter Watt seems to be that P.W. didn't give him any practical assistance when he was making a contract with the Marvell Press for *The Less Deceived*; and that this has turned out in fact to be an extremely disadvantageous one from his point of view. [. . .]

*Jill* – new edition
He definitely said he would let us do this. He will go through the book again and may make a few very minor changes for editorial or stylistic reasons. And he will also write an introduction. [. . .]

New volume of Poems
Much to my pleasure, he then said, without any prodding, that he thought *Jill* should be buttressed by a new collection of poems coming out at about the same time – and I hastened to agree. He has got enough poems now to make up a book – between 30 and 40; and he has promised to let me have them by 30th June 1963 for spring 1964 publication. He very much wants advice as to which ones, if any, should be left out.

*A Girl in Winter* – F.P.C.E.
In principle, he is entirely in favour of this idea. Until the Watt situation is sorted out, though, we clearly can't make a firm contract. I have no doubt that everything will be all right.

1964 looks like being a Larkin annus mirabilis.

*He was only a year out.*

## Frank Pike to 'Mr Monteith (for Book Committee)', 24 September 1963

I met Ted Hughes socially the other night and he was talking to me about the prospects of bringing out a volume of Sylvia Plath's last poems (or he may possibly have meant a volume containing all of her poems, which is not unlikely). He is anxious to get a good royalty on any such edition because I gather the money will go into a trust fund for the children or something like that. Sylvia Plath's previous books were done by Heinemann but Ted says he doesn't feel any particular loyalty to them although they do offer him a royalty of 12½%. I got the strong impression that he would very much prefer us to do the book all else being equal even if we could not improve on that royalty. It seemed to me that he wanted to put this to us but wasn't quite sure how to bring it up and he obviously wanted me to pass his feelings on. I think it is now for us to make some kind of reciprocatory move.

### Charles Monteith to Ted Hughes, 26 September 1963

Frank Pike told me about the conversation he had with you the other evening; and this is simply to let you know that if you did feel like offering Sylvia's poems to us we would be absolutely delighted to publish them. To judge from the ones I have seen in various magazines they seem absolutely magnificent.

### Frank Pike to 'Mr du Sautoy and Mr. Monteith', 24 December 1963

I had a 'phone call from Tom Stoppard's agent, Kenneth Ewing of Fraser & Dunlop, telling me that as a result of publication of one of his stories in *Town* magazine, Stoppard has received overtures from another publisher which the agent thinks may culminate in the commission of a novel. He said he felt we should be kept informed about this because 'other things being equal' he would much rather Faber published such a novel, but he had to bear in mind that Tom was in difficult financial circumstances.

### Frank Pike to Kenneth Ewing, 24 December 1963

As regards the choice of another publisher commissioning a novel from him, it is good of you to say that 'other things being equal' you would rather Faber did the novel. When it comes to adding up things that are to be equal I hope that the fact that Tom mightn't have written a couple of stories at all if it hadn't been for *Introduction* and the fact that the interest of the *Gentlemen's Quarterly* was aroused by our sending them proofs will be laid in the balance!

Let me know how things turn out; in the meantime I will investigate the chances of our commissioning a novel from Tom. I feel I should say though that this is something we do very rarely indeed.

### Samuel Beckett to Charles Monteith, 13 January 1964

I am returning to you under separate cover the two Godots and corrected proofs of *Play*.

The final Godot text I propose is the Grove text as corrected by me (black corrections, ignore red), with spelling anglicized where necessary.

The Lord Chamberlain's objections, as well as I can remember, were to <u>button it</u>, <u>pubis</u>, <u>erection</u>, <u>clap</u>, <u>arse</u>, <u>piss</u>, <u>ballocksed</u> and <u>farted</u>, pp. 7, 8, 12, 15, 21, 38, 50 and 52 respectively of Grove edition.

### Charles Monteith to Ted Hughes, 14 February 1964

I realise that so far as Sylvia's poems are concerned, you have got to clear things with Heinemann; but certainly, if they can be cleared, there's nothing we would like more than to publish them ourselves.

### Benjamin Britten to Donald Mitchell, Faber music books editor, February 1964

I sometimes dream of Faber and Faber, music publishers!

### Richard de la Mare to Enid Faber, 3 April 1964

It seems to me the kind of opportunity that comes to one only once in a lifetime, and I think we would be very foolish to ignore it. If Britten goes on producing new music as he has in the past few years, I can see no risk in this at all, but very considerable profits, and a

useful hedge I would say against possible setbacks in other directions – not that I see any signs of this on the horizon at present.

## Enid Faber to Richard de la Mare, 5 April 1964

Thank you for your letter. I am very excited at the possibility. I feel
that it would renew the kind of cachet the publishing of T.S.E. &
others originally gave us. [. . .]

Publishing Britten would obviously be VERY profitable for 10–20
years, one does not know how long he would go on producing. But
during that time wouldn't an enormous amount of this profit have to
go on building up a real music branch, of composers who won't pay
nearly so well? [. . .]

I really wanted to say that I guess we are all a bit blind to the great
difficulties, but my imagination is fired, and frankly I would sooner
lose my money over this, than over something duller.

## Ted Hughes to Charles Monteith, 7 April 1964

I'm just arranging Sylvia's poems. There were <u>two</u> things I ought
to have mentioned before – could I have a say in the design of the
jacket, & in the print used? For instance, I'd like the cover to be red,
the print either black or yellow, preferably black. That was what she
imagined. Very simple, first the colour – the print. Another detail:
she prided herself on having a remote Mongolian ancestor. The
national emblem of Mongolia is a horseman riding into the sunrise.
Her title poem 'Ariel' is about riding on horseback into the sunrise,
and she played with the idea of having that emblem, small, on the
cover, though she couldn't decide whether she preferred a rose.

For the print, she wanted it large – she was pained by the small print
of the Heinemann *Colossus*. She liked the print of *The Hawk in the
Rain* – big and black.

I hope the designer will be willing to do something with this.

## Charles Monteith to Ted Hughes, 22 April 1964

What a magnificent volume *Ariel* is. I really have been enormously impressed by it. It's too late, alas, for our autumn list – but we'll certainly be able to bring it out in the spring of 1965. [. . .]

You mention a possible Collected edition for some time in the future – and that's something which we would certainly be very interested in publishing, when the time comes. But before that can be done it's essential, of course, to make sure that the rights in *The Colossus* have officially reverted to you from Heinemanns.

> *At just this time, when Faber was launching its own music publisher as well as publishing some of its most important writers for the first time, Dick de la Mare seems to have had some sort of short illness. The only evidence I have for it is this message from Peter du Sautoy, which while sympathetic still foreshadows the tensions that would mark the end of the decade.*

## Peter du Sautoy to Richard de la Mare, 26 April 1964

I am so distressed to think that you have reached this point by exhaustion, but I hope that perhaps a little enforced rest at this moment may be rather a good thing! I wish you could take things a little easier now. [. . .]

I feel that in general we are trying to do two somewhat incompatible things – expand enormously and at the same time retain the close personal touch. I am not sure how long we can combine these two!

## Press Release, Friday, 15 May 1964

### NEW WORKS BY BENJAMIN BRITTEN TO BE PUBLISHED BY FABER & FABER

Faber and Faber Limited announce that they are entering the field of music publishing and are forming a Music Department. It is their intention to build up a list of the highest quality comprising both old and new music. Among their first publications will be Benjamin Britten's *Curlew River*, a Parable for Church Performance, with a text by William Plomer based on a medieval Japanese No-play. [. . .]

The Head of the Faber and Faber Music Department will be Mr. Donald Mitchell, at present on the music staff of the *Daily Telegraph* and well known as an authority on Mahler and on the music of the twentieth century. Mr. Mitchell will assume full-time duties on September 1st, 1964.

## Richard de la Mare to Benjamin Britten, 24 May 1964

I am so very happy that all the preliminary arrangements between us have been completed, and that we are now able and ready to get on with the job! But before we go any further I do want to tell you how deeply we appreciated your coming to us with this what at first seemed to me astonishing proposal, and how much it means to us.

## Benjamin Britten to Richard de la Mare, 26 May 1964

I am very grateful to you for your kind letter, and was very touched by it. I am also much excited by the new and courageous venture which you are making, and I look forward to many years happy collaboration with Fabers. It is an honour for me to be associated with such a splendid publishing firm.

*Faber Music will play only a peripheral part in the rest of this story. It is now a flourishing independent music publisher, with*

*a strong reputation and still essentially owned by the Faber*
*family, but there is no doubt that the cash drain associated with*
*starting the new venture was one of the main causes of Faber's*
*financial problems later in the decade.*

*Thirty years on from its failure to publish* Ulysses, *the firm was*
*still having censorship problems with James Joyce. The lawyer's*
*letter on the subject gives some idea of the regime that was still*
*in place, despite the* Lady Chatterley *verdict.*

## Colin Wadie, solicitor, to Peter du Sautoy, 20 July 1964

Letters of James Joyce Volumes II and III

My opinion is, that in view of the description of sexual abnormalities and malpractices contained in the letters, they would clearly tend to corrupt and deprave those of a weak or immature nature. Descriptions of normal practices, in my view, cannot tend to corrupt or deprave but there are few of these in the letters. [. . .]

The risk is, of course, that in university libraries the book is likely to come into the hands of undergraduates who will be of immature years and for this reason I feel that the risk in publishing it too great and the Director of Public Prosecutions might well decide to try to prevent or curtail publication.

## Faber & Faber Book Catalogue, Autumn & Winter 1964

*A Grief Observed*
C. S. Lewis

When this book was submitted to us in 1961 the author's name was given as N. W. Clerk. It was made perfectly clear to us that this was a pseudonym: and it was made equally clear that 'Mr Clerk' did not want us to make any enquiries about his true identity. We had to judge the typescript purely on its merits. [. . .]

Though we had always suspected that 'N. W. Clerk' was in fact C. S. Lewis we took no steps to confirm this because of the understanding on which we accepted the book for publication. Shortly after Dr. Lewis's death in 1963, however, rumours about the book's true authorship began to circulate and even to appear in the Press. In the circumstances, we felt justified in approaching Dr. Lewis's executors and in asking their permission – if the rumour should turn out to be true – to reissue the book under its author's real name. Confirmation and permission were very readily and courteously given; and we are very pleased that *A Grief Observed* can be added to the list of C. S. Lewis's published works.

Marianne Moore looking at Jacob Epstein's bust of T. S. Eliot
in September 1964.

## Frank Pike to Tom Stoppard, 6 November 1964

This is just a note to re-establish contact if that is possible. We have been wondering here how things have been going with you and whether you have had any more thoughts about a novel.

### Tom Stoppard to Frank Pike (undated)

As to 'my thoughts about a novel', I'm afraid your memory has let you down; I think I told you last spring that Anthony Blond has commissioned a novel from me (due to be completed by April). I had sounded you out on the prospect of a commission from Faber but I gathered there was no chance of that. Then Blond approached me, and agreed to commission a book.

### Frank Pike to Tom Stoppard, 9 December 1964

I must have been having a brainstorm or something last spring, because I can't remember hearing that Blond had got as far as signing on the dotted line in his scheme to commission a novel from you. [. . .]

Anyway, it's all water under the bridge, and you can always be sure of a sympathetic reception here if your plans ever change.

*Frank was still thinking of a novel, of course, but it is just as well he kept the relationship with Tom Stoppard friendly.*

### Berthold Wolpe to Ted Hughes, 8 January 1965

I am sending you now a proof of the jacket for *Ariel*. Mr Monteith has passed on your suggestions about colour and the possible use of drawings on the cover. After careful consideration I have found it would not be possible to use the drawing of a horseman or a rose on the wrapper, but I have used some of the colours which you suggested.

May I have your comments? Ariel is such a provocative word that I have given emphasis to it.

### Ted Hughes to Charles Monteith, 13 January 1965

I've just received a copy of the dust-jacket of *Ariel* from Mr Wolpe. It was a bit of a shock: they always are. [. . .]

T. S. Eliot's office at Faber & Faber, photographed the day after
his death on 4 January 1965.

The news about T. S. Eliot was a great blow. It's left things feeling
extremely windswept. I for one lived very much under his eye,
inwardly. Please do send me a ticket for the service.

> *Ted Hughes summarises magnificently the way in which T. S.*
> *Eliot's death could be seen as a watershed for both Faber and the*
> *poetry world in general. Although he had been suffering from*
> *emphysema for some time, Eliot had remained an active and*
> *involved director. Nevertheless, a letter from Charles Monteith*
> *eleven days later shows how the firm's ability to spot new*
> *poetry talent remained undimmed.*

## Charles Monteith to Seamus Heaney, 15 January 1965

First let me explain how I come to have your poems in my possession. I was very struck by the three poems which appeared in the

*New Statesman* last month; and after making enquiries at the *New Statesman*, we got in touch with Mr Lucie-Smith[6] who was kind enough to send us this group of poems.

Several people here, including myself, read them and were very impressed by them. Our over-all feeling is that the collection is not quite strong enough for publication, but that it does indeed show definite promise. [. . .]

We will continue to look out for your work with the keenest possible interest and when you yourself feel that the time is really ripe for publication in book form, we would of course be very glad indeed if you would give us the opportunity to consider them. T S Eliot always took the view that it was advisable for a young poet to make his reputation first by regular appearances in literary periodicals such as, for instance the *New Statesman* or *Encounter*, before being published in book form. I myself would agree that this is the best course of action.

*Interviewed later in life, Seamus Heaney said of receiving this communication from Faber, 'I just couldn't believe it, it was like getting a letter from God the Father.'*

*Philip Larkin had always been a fan of the author Barbara Pym, who had recently been dropped by Jonathan Cape. He did his best to get Charles Monteith interested.*

## Philip Larkin to Charles Monteith, 8 February 1965

After consideration I'm sending herewith *Excellent Women*, and I shall be interested to know if you can read it with enjoyment. They aren't all 'like this', but a certain plangent astringent autumnal tone is common to them, which I like very much. Again I must emphasise that I've never met her, but we exchange letters occasionally.

---

6 The informal chairman of 'The Group' poets, Edward Lucie-Smith had been submitting Seamus Heaney's poems to magazines.

### Robert Lowell to Charles Monteith, 26 February 1965

It's so melancholy writing after Tom's death. So many friends of mine have died this year, and yet his though long on the verge seems the most impossible and intolerable of all.

### Charles Monteith to Philip Larkin, 10 March 1965

I read *Excellent Women* at the weekend and enjoyed it very much indeed. Do please ask Miss Pym to send me her new novel – the one you talked to me about – any time she likes.

Though this sort of novel isn't, I fear, very modish nowadays and therefore has to be very good indeed of its kind to stand much chance of success, we would, I promise you, take it seriously.

### Charles Monteith to Ted Hughes, 13 May 1965

I wrote to Heinemann's the other day asking if we could do *The Bell Jar* in our own paperback series; and I was delighted to get a letter from them this morning to say that we may – and that terms are agreed. I don't know, I confess, when it will be coming out – certainly not until some time in 1966 at the earliest. As soon as I know something more definite myself, of course, I'll let you know.

One point. I think it would help sales very much if we could describe the book as being 'by Sylvia Plath'; and I wondered if you might allow us to do so? There's no secret any more about the identity of 'Victoria Lucas'; and we could always put in some sort of little bibliographical note at the beginning to make it clear that the book was originally published in hard covers with that pseudonym on it.

### Ted Hughes to Charles Monteith, 15 May 1965

I'm glad to hear *The Bell Jar* is coming to you, and it's correct, I think, now, to publish it under her own name. It's an essential accompaniment to the poems, I think. I was talking to Alan Sillitoe the other week and he'd just re-read it. He called it one of the best things he'd ever read. When it's read as coming from the same place as the poems I think it does move out of the category it might just be left in otherwise.

Faber's edition of *The Bell Jar* (1966) bore a cover design by Shirley Tucker, a talented young designer who joined Faber in 1959 and worked alongside Berthold Wolpe.

## Seamus Heaney to Charles Monteith, 18 May 1965

I enclose a selection of poems for your consideration. You have already seen a few of these in the batch which you obtained in December. I hope this group is a bit stronger.

## Mary-Kay Wilmers, Memorandum, 26 May 1965

After reading through the new collection of Seamus Heaney poems, I had another look at the first lot of poems which Edward Lucie-Smith sent us five months ago and the improvement is indeed very noticeable. [...]

Mr Heaney's most powerful gift is still in the description of the Irish countryside, but there is strong evidence that his range is extending and his talent with it. Though he is a less sophisticated poet than Ted Hughes or Thom Gunn, like them he succeeds in combining power with control and his work is very much his own. Honest, direct and lucid. If we are again going to publish poets before their name has been established elsewhere, I think we should take Mr Heaney on.

## Charles Monteith to Seamus Heaney, 15 June 1965

I am delighted to let you know that we all like *Death of a Naturalist* very much; and that we would certainly be happy to publish it. No chance of getting it out this year – since publication of a book nowadays does seem to take at least twelve months. I hope that we'll be able to get it out in the spring of 1966 – but experience has taught me not to make absolutely firm promises about publication at this stage!

## Charles Monteith to author Barbara Pym, 13 August 1965

I did enjoy *An Unsuitable Attachment*; but I simply couldn't, I fear, convince myself that it would sell enough copies to justify us in making an offer to publish it. And I find that everyone else here who read it – and it was read by a considerable number of people – formed exact-

Charles Monteith talking to Seamus Heaney; Terence de Vere White,
literary editor of the *Irish Times*, looks on.

ly the same view. Novels are, I'm afraid, becoming increasingly difficult to sell nowadays; and I rather suspect that this is partly the result
of the so-called 'paperback revolution'. People who formerly would
have bought an occasional novel and ordered them regularly and in
reasonably large quantities from whatever library they normally used
now tend to buy quite a large number of novels – but buy them only
as paperbacks . . . Before this change from library borrowing to paperback buying took place I think that *An Unsuitable Attachment* would
probably have had a large enough basic library sale – so to speak – to
make its publication fairly safe from an economic point of view; but I
doubt very much if it would have that sort of basic library sale nowadays. And I don't think that it's the sort of novel which could very
easily be sold to a paperback firm since they tend, I fear, to go for
something rather more violent and sensational!

*So the death of the old subscription libraries such as that run*
*by Boots, as a result of the increasing popularity of paperbacks,*
*was making it difficult to publish 'ordinary' fiction. Faber was*
*still only feeling its way towards the obvious solution to the*
*problem: a single publisher being responsible for both hardback*
*and paperback.*

## Philip Larkin to Charles Monteith, 15 August 1965

I am not very good at expressing my thoughts on the spur of the moment, but in retrospect what I feel is this: by all means turn it down if you think it's a bad book of its kind, but please don't turn it down because it's the kind of book it is. I believe you said that in your view it was a Boots book which wouldn't sell now Boots was going. But surely, Charles, Boots public isn't going? A woman who can't borrow B. Pym from Boots isn't going to buy Grace Metalious[7] in paperback, she's going to borrow B. Pym from the public library. [. . .]

Personally, too, I feel it is a great shame if ordinary sane novels about ordinary sane people doing ordinary sane things can't find a publisher these days. This is the tradition of Jane Austen and Trollope, and I refuse to believe that no one wants its successors today. Why should I have to choose between spy rubbish, science fiction rubbish, Negro-homosexual rubbish, or dope taking nervous-breakdown rubbish? I like to read about people who have done nothing spectacular, who aren't beautiful or lucky, who try to behave well in the limited field of activity they command, but who can see, in little autumnal moments of vision, that the so called 'big' experiences of life are going to miss them; and I like to read about such things presented not with self pity or despair or romanticism, but with realistic firmness and even humour. That is in fact what the critics would call the moral tone of the book. It seems to me the kind of writing a

---

7  Grace Metalious was the author of the sensational bestseller *Peyton Place*.

responsible publisher ought to support (that's you, Charles!).

## Charles Monteith to Philip Larkin, 20 August 1965

I've got a feeling that when I talked to you about it I expressed myself very badly; and that, in particular, I put too much stress on the purely 'hard-headed' and 'business' reasons for our decision – whether they were right or wrong – and not enough on the fact that, though I did quite honestly enjoy the book, my enjoyment wasn't of that rather excited and dedicated kind which sometimes makes a publisher determined to publish something even though he's pretty certain that he's going to lose money over it.

*The son of Faber author George Ewart Evans, Matthew Evans had joined the firm aged twenty-three in 1964, initially as Peter du Sautoy's assistant. The following year, he and Mary-Kay Wilmers went to the Frankfurt Book Fair. They then took joint responsibility for the memo below, which was sent to all the executive directors.*

## Mary-Kay Wilmers and Matthew Evans: Memorandum, October 1965

I was surprised at Frankfurt to discover how little Fabers counted outside the circles of literary appreciation; and in this sense it was salutary to see us in relation to other publishers – American, European and English.

Our list of course is respected by everyone, but our publishing methods are not. People feel that we are smug and that in some ways we don't work to do our authors or our books justice.

## Tom Faber to Enid Faber, 'Monday', December 1965

I have written to Dick to suggest an appointment some time when we might discuss the accounts and related matters, and I hope he won't think this interference too tiresome. You seemed to regard it as strange that I should even contemplate going to the meeting on Wednesday, but I thought we agreed some months ago that I should do just this and that I should make some effort to get to understand the finances of the firm. Of course there is no question of <u>changing</u> the audited accounts, but in most public companies the annual general meeting at which the accounts are presented is treated as an occasion for scrutinising the conduct of the Company's affairs and I don't know that it <u>ought</u> to be treated as a complete formality.

### Rosemary Goad to Charles Monteith, 31 January 1966

Elaine Greene rang me on Monday morning to say that she had just heard that Scribners are taking both Mrs. White's books: *Cover Her Face* and *A Mind to Murder*. She is not going to send them the latest one until it is in final shape. Much excitement all round, needless to say; and she was particularly anxious I should tell you the good news.

*The interest from a US publisher meant that 'Mrs. White' was on her way to becoming the internationally bestselling author better known as P. D. James.*

### Frank Pike to Christopher Hampton, 12 April 1966

I and some of my colleagues have been reading your work and we are all most impressed with it in general and *When did you Last See my Mother?* in particular. We are wondering if it would be at all possible for you to call here for a chat.

### Charles Monteith to 'Mr Bland', 18 August 1966

*Wodwo*: Ted Hughes – Jacket

Though Ted Hughes liked the early jackets which Berthold Wolpe did for him he hasn't, I gather, been so happy about some of the later ones – in particular I think he was a bit upset by the jacket for *Ariel* – particularly after he'd made one or two specific suggestions which were treated a bit cavalierly, I suspect!

When he sent in his new book *Wodwo* he said quite specifically that he would like a chance to discuss the jacket with whoever designs it before any final design is settled on. We have actually made a note to that effect on the back of the editorial form; but I'd be very grateful indeed if you would keep a very careful personal eye on this and make sure that it's done – since I'm anxious not to upset Ted Hughes over it.

Ideally, of course, I'd like you to give the jacket to Shirley Tucker; but I realize that in practice this is probably impossible since Berthold Wolpe has done all the other Ted Hughes jackets – and, indeed, with one or two very minor exceptions – does all the poetry jackets.

Sorry about this cri de coeur.

*Many people found it much easier to deal with Shirley Tucker than Berthold Wolpe.*

*In 1966, Ted Hughes submitted to Faber a book that had begun as a bedtime story for Frieda and Nicholas, his children with Sylvia Plath. Faber had published his works for children in the past, but this one provoked some disquiet in the children's department.*

*Following William Crawley's retirement, the children's list had been taken over by Phyllis Hunt, who was its editor from 1961 to 1987, with authors including Lucy Boston, Rosemary Harris and Helen Cresswell (names I have chosen because I remember them as favourites from my own childhood). She was highly regarded and very successful, so this particular story should be seen as a rare aberration.*

## Charles Monteith, Note on 'The Iron Man Saga: Ted Hughes', 6 September 1966

I thought I had better circulate all this material – including the story itself which is very short and doesn't take long to read – since there's a sharp division of opinion between the juvenile department (PH & JA[8]) and the adult editorial department (CM, MKW, SG[9]). Reports by all the women readers are attached; and though there's no report by me, I've read the story and agree completely with SG and MKW. It seems to me an excellent little tale of very considerable imaginative force and no more frightening than many fairy tales. It could certainly be tidied up in detail in the ways suggested by MKW and SG; and I imagine that Ted Hughes would be amenable to such suggestions.

In an ordinary case, none of us would want to press our views against PH's and JA's so far as a children's book is concerned; but I do feel myself that it would be a great mistake to turn down anything by Ted Hughes – particularly something as good as this. He would be quite free if we did to offer it to some other publisher – who would thereby of course acquire an option on all his future writing for children. Moreover, I don't think I'd like to put to him JA's suggestion of waiting until he has accumulated a few more short pieces and then publish this as one of them. He lives entirely by his writing and isn't at all well-off – and such a course wouldn't, I think, be fair to him.

*It is lucky for Faber that the adult department got its way.* The Iron Man *continues to sell thousands of copies every year.*

*That summer, a play by Tom Stoppard was the sensation of the*

---

8  Jasmine Atterbury (née Cleaver) was a part-time reader in the Faber children's department from 1946 to 1976.

9  Sarah Goad (née Lambert) came to Faber in c.1960, introduced by the man who later became her husband, Tim Goad, Rosemary Goad's cousin.

*1966 Edinburgh Festival. Frank Pike's memo on the subject has*
*Charles Monteith's handwritten comment on the bottom.*

### Frank Pike to 'Mr Monteith', 20 September 1966

As I mentioned I had an oddly inconclusive conversation on Friday
with Kenneth Ewing, Tom Stoppard's agent. I assume he was playing it extremely cool; at any rate he affected extreme indifference
to the possibility of publication of the play in book form. Apparently Penguin have already made an offer, though no contract has
been signed. Anyway Ewing promised to let me have a copy of the
play as soon as they could be duplicated and he assured me that we
were perfectly free to make an offer and that he would think about
accepting it!

If we do make an offer our best chance of acceptance would I think lie
in making it as fully and firmly (i.e. including things like provisional
publication date) as possible and as soon as possible (after seeing the
text of course).

*Told FP he cd. offer 10% straight & £100 advance. CM*

### Frank Pike to Kenneth Ewing, 23 September 1966

We have been thinking about Tom Stoppard's play *Rosencrantz and
Guildenstern are Dead,* and we have decided we would like to make
a formal offer to publish it, sight unseen as it were. The terms we
suggest are a royalty of straight 10% of the published price, with an
advance on royalties of £100 payable half on signature of the agreement and half on publication.

### Frank Pike to Kenneth Ewing, 3 October 1966

This is just to confirm in writing what I said on the telephone on
Friday afternoon – namely, that we are willing to increase our offer

for *Rosencrantz and Guildenstern are Dead* to £150 advance against the same royalty of a straight 10% of the published price. We have always been interested in Tom's work since we published his stories in that anthology and we are very keen to do his play.

### Frank Pike to 'Miss Goad (for BC)', 18 October 1966

*Rosencrantz and Guildenstern are Dead* by Tom Stoppard

I have just heard from Kenneth Ewing that 'subject to contract' we have got this play in spite of Giles Gordon [at Penguin] (from whom it is still a secret).

It is almost certain that there will be a National Theatre production in May 1967, and I think it is important to try and get it out in time for that.

### Frank Pike to Kenneth Ewing, 9 November 1966

Much to my relief – but not to my surprise – I find that *Rosencrantz and Guildenstern are Dead* does indeed delight me. It is a brilliant idea, brilliantly and wittily carried out. And what a collaborator! We won't go to press until we have Tom's alterations.

### P. D. James to Rosemary Goad, 11 December 1966

You will agree that one's first avocado is an Experience and I couldn't have eaten mine in more agreeable company nor in pleasanter surroundings.

> *By now, the University of London owned the freehold of 23–24 Russell Square, which it planned to develop. Faber & Faber's lease saw them through to the end of the 1960s, but then the company would need to move. According to his own unpublished memoir, Peter Crawley volunteered to spend his lunchtimes walking around Bloomsbury to find a replacement office 'in*

*which our publishing could flourish'. He came across the perfect
set of buildings in Queen Square.*

## Board minute, 6 April 1967

The Chairman reported upon the position arising out of the purchase
of the freehold of 3, 4 & 5 Queen Square WC1 for the Company's
new offices and for which a 99-year lease has been completed with
the Norwich Union Assurance Co.

## Faber & Faber Press Release, 3 May 1967

The success of Tom Stoppard's play *Rosencrantz and Guildenstern
are Dead*, the text of which Fabers published on Thursday (cloth 18/-,
paper 6/6), has in a few weeks become part of post-war theatre history. When the play opened at the Old Vic on April 11th Stoppard
became the youngest living playwright to enter the repertory of the
National Theatre. The glowing unanimity of the first-night notices
left no doubt about his future. To Faber's chagrin, however, none of the
amusing interviews that followed the play's opening mentioned that
Stoppard's first appearance in a book was in *Introduction 2*, the Faber
anthology of new writing published in 1964. This collection contained
three of his short stories, and is still in print (21/-).

## Frank Pike to Tom Stoppard, 4 May 1967

If in any of your myriad interviews you could work in a tiny plug for
*Introduction Two*, we might shift a few more of that too. No money
in that for you, unfortunately.

## Charles Monteith to Alan Bennett, 1 September 1967

I was absolutely delighted to hear from Mary-Kay about *Forty Years
On*. I'm looking forward tremendously to reading it, to seeing it &
to publishing it.

*The same 'Introductions' concept which had brought Tom
Stoppard to Faber & Faber was also being used to identify young
poets.*

### Mary-Kay Wilmers to Douglas Dunn, 21 November 1967

Derwent May suggested that I should write to you in connection with
the poetry anthology which we are planning to publish. I am enclosing with this letter a description of the anthology, and we would be
delighted if you would give us the chance to consider your work.

### Douglas Dunn to Mary-Kay Wilmers, 24 November 1967

Thank you for writing to me about your anthology. Seldom does
someone actually <u>ask</u> to see my work, so I send you the enclosed
poems happily indeed.

### Charles Monteith to Alan Bennett, 17 January 1968

I've just realised that I've never written to you – as I meant to do
ages ago – to say how tremendously I enjoyed *Forty Years On*. It's
great fun to read; and it's going to be, I'm certain, great fun to watch.
I needn't say how much I hope you'll let us publish it – which, Mary-
Kay assures me, you will.

### Philip Larkin to Charles Monteith, 2 April 1968

You may be interested to know that the Eric Gregory Award Committee (on which I sit) is giving £400 to Douglas Dunn, who is a
small muttering bearded Scotsman of 26 studying at the University.
He and Brian Jones (who is getting an equal amount) were the only
two candidates recommended by all four judges; I believe that Dunn
has some poems in with you at present, though he mutters so that I
can never be quite sure what he is saying.

## Board minute, 7 June 1968

It was proposed that a holding company be formed to control the publishing company and the various subsidiary companies. The Principal Directors would be appointed to the holding company to control the financial side of the companies as well as holding office in the publishing company. New Editorial Directors would if necessary be appointed to the publishing company without their having to be involved in financial affairs.

*The restructuring meant that the old Faber & Faber with various shareholders (still, mainly, members of the Faber family) became a holding company. It did not trade, but instead had two wholly owned subsidiary companies – Faber & Faber Ltd and Faber Music Ltd – and stakes in Latimer Trend (printers), Fine Art Engravers (blockmakers) and the Fama Ltd joint venture with Kurt Maschler. Geoffrey's widow Enid remained on the Faber & Faber board. Tom Faber joined the board of the holding company.*

## Charles Monteith to Alan Bennett, 16 July 1968

I was delighted to see in Sunday's papers that *Forty Years On* is all set for November; and that Gielgud is taking the lead. I'm looking forward to it <u>immensely</u>.

Now that production plans are settled I'd be delighted if you felt you'd like to make a contract with us to publish it. If you would, should I settle details with you direct; or should I do it through an agent?

It <u>would</u> be nice to have you as a Faber author.

### Charles Monteith to Alan Bennett, 19 July 1968

I was delighted to hear from Mary-Kay that you would like a formal contract for *Forty Years On*. She's warned you, I believe, that there's virtually no money in it at all! [. . .]

I feel absolutely heart-broken that Mary-Kay is going to leave us.

> *Mary-Kay was going to be deputy editor of the* Listener *under Karl Miller, and later followed him to the* London Review of Books, *becoming deputy editor there.*

### Charles Monteith to Douglas Dunn 8 November 1968

After all these long months during which you've been very patient indeed with us I'm absolutely delighted to let you know that we have at last made a decision about the *Terry Street* poems and others and we would most certainly like to accept the volume for publication. We'd hope, all being well, to bring it out sometime next year, probably in the early autumn. I'm very pleased indeed about this – particularly as I've always admired your work very much since the time you first submitted poems for *Poetry Introduction 1*.

### Douglas Dunn to Charles Monteith, 20 April 1969

Incidentally, *Poetry Introduction* comes out the same day my final examinations start!

### Charles Monteith to Seamus Heaney, 9 September 1969

Any chance of seeing you before too long? I was over in the west of Ireland – staying with Richard Murphy[10] – for the bank holiday weekend; and I had a couple of very enjoyable days in Dublin.

---

10  Richard Murphy was an Anglo-Irish poet published by Faber from 1963 to 1989.

But I didn't get to the North. [. . .]

By another very happy coincidence, while he and I were drinking our pre-lunch gins on Monday, we were suddenly aware of a bespectacled figure peering through the window which turned out to be Philip Larkin! A happy time was had by all!

## Samuel Beckett wins Nobel Prize, *The Times*, 24 October 1969

Stockholm, October 23 – The Irish-born playwright, Samuel Beckett, acknowledged as one of the greatest living dramatists for his pioneering new modes of theatrical expression, was today awarded the 1969 Nobel Prize for literature.

*At the beginning of 1970, Peter du Sautoy wrote a memo to Dick de la Mare which shows the depth of the malaise from which the firm was now suffering, his own personal frustration and his increasing regard for his assistant, Matthew Evans, who had taken responsibility for sales to American publishers.*

## Peter du Sautoy to Richard de la Mare, 18 January 1970

The sad thing is that enjoyment in working for Faber and Faber has faded in recent years, initiative is often stifled and many new ideas don't see the light because of the necessity for long and exhausting arguments with Sales before they have even the slightest chance of being accepted. The atmosphere of caution and the lack of enthusiasm are very depressing to many of us. That has been the result internally. Externally the firm has undoubtedly declined in standing, among authors and agents and in the trade generally. We have no flashy appeal, and don't want it; and it is of course nothing new to be told 'Fabers cannot sell books' (it lost us C. P. Snow and Gerald Durrell on a famous occasion). But one would have hoped that in the last 10 years we might have been able to dispel the illusion. [. . .]

We have survived a number of difficulties, but it is depressing to find, after all the efforts of recent years, that we are now in a more serious situation than ever before. [. . .]

I have already argued the special importance of Matthew to us at this present moment when the American sales contribute so largely to our income and this has been recognised by the decision to make him a director at the end of the year. I think this appointment should now be brought forward to March 1st, before his next American trip. Matthew is immensely valuable to us in other ways – editorial and managerial, for example, as well as in 'public relations'. He is exceptionally (and I mean exceptionally) good with authors and gets on well with agents and American publishers. [. . .]

I wish I could offer you more help in this situation, but I am not sure of my role. This is why I have not signed my contract of service; a deliberate abstention and not due to negligence. In it I am described as 'joint Managing Director' (with you), but I do not really fulfil that function. Unless I am confident that the kind of changes I have indicated will be put into effect without delay I shall not be able to accept the present contract and I shall ask to be released in a year's time. The great strain and often unhappiness caused by the present state of affairs cannot be borne much longer.

## Charles Monteith to John Carey, 5 February 1970

Forgive me, please, for writing to you out of the blue about a publishing idea which occurred to me recently. Quite simply it is that there's probably room for a new book on Bunyan – a critical biography – and I found that Christopher Ricks with whom I discussed the idea agrees with some enthusiasm. When we discussed people who might possibly write it he at once suggested you; and certainly it would give me the greatest possible pleasure if I could persuade you to take it on.

### John Carey to Charles Monteith, 14 February 1970

Now that I have finished my work on Milton . . . I am turning my attention to the more modern period. This change is partly the result of the new Oxford syllabus, which pays a good deal of attention to the nineteenth and early twentieth centuries. I hope to be able to do enough work in the next couple of years to write something on Dickens.

### John Carey to Charles Monteith 29 March 1970

I should stress that the Dickens book isn't written yet, and may not be for a good while . . . I have not spoken of this to a publisher, and should be only too pleased to give Fabers first refusal. If you liked it, I should, of course, be honoured to have a book published by you – who wouldn't?

*Towards the end of 1969, Peter Crawley had been in Australia, visiting one of the writers on the firm's medical list, Derek Llewellyn-Jones. He handed Peter a manuscript entitled 'Woman', a departure from his previous work on obstetrics and gynaecology in that it was aimed at a general readership.*

### Peter Crawley to Professor Derek Llewellyn-Jones, 4 February 1970

Jean Cunningham, who is very much on the ball, has just spotted a review in the *Nursing Times* of a book by the Professor of Obstetrics and Gynaecology at St. Thomas's called *WOMAN*! This is a decided surprise but I don't think we should let it alarm us unduly!

*A new title was duly found.*

## Peter Crawley to Professor Derek Llewellyn-Jones, 26 March 1970

I am delighted to say that *Every Woman* has been received with acclaim and this is a formal letter to suggest terms to you.

## Charles Monteith, Memorandum, 16 April 1970

This collection of poems by Paul Muldoon was left with me by Shamus Heaney when he was last in London. He knows Muldoon, who is, I think, an undergraduate at Belfast – and thought that his work was at any rate worth serious consideration.

I was rather impressed by these poems myself, and I would be very interested to know what you think of them. I suspect that all we need to do at this stage is register positive interest in him and advise him to start placing his work in various magazines etc. which regularly publish poetry. He would obviously be worth bearing in mind too, for our next *Poetry Introduction*.

> *I can only assume that this memo was dictated by Charles, and typed by someone who did not know the correct spelling of 'Seamus'.*

## Charles Monteith to Seamus Heaney, 23 April 1970

I'm sorry I've been such a very long time in writing to you about Paul Muldoon's poems; but I'm more than glad to be able to say – now that I've read them – that I have been considerably impressed by them – as have the other people who have read them too. Do please tell Paul Muldoon that we will be extremely happy to see any future work; and I do hope that you or he himself will keep in touch and let us see more.

## Charles Monteith to Paul Muldoon, 30 June 1970

It's excellent news that some of your poems are going to appear in the *Listener* (you're right in suspecting that I steered them in that direction!)

## Faber & Faber Book Catalogue, Autumn and Winter 1970

*Slag*
David Hare

*Slag* is about women's rights, revolutionary feminism, girls' boarding schools, hysterical pregnancy, hockey and sex, in no particular order. Its author sets his three characters at each other's throats, mouths, and occasionally feet, in an attempt to play off middle-of-the-bat public school tradition against the new ethic of sexual anarchy and freedom.

## Rosemary Goad to Carol Heaton, Elaine Greene Ltd, 29 September 1970

I've just had a further word with our Production Department and gather that proofs of *Shroud for a Nightingale* should be in towards the end of the year or at the beginning of 1971. It's difficult to be more precise than that at this stage and I hope this will be enough for you to pass on to Scribners.

> *This is what Rosemary Goad sent to P. D. James's agent. The carbon copy of the letter, however, has the following typed addendum.*

TRUTH
RG rang Ray Thorne who said no such book existed and there was no card for it. After a hunt he found the manuscript on Brian Rooney's shelf, untouched. Promised faithfully to send it off to the printers today saying we wanted an estimate AS SOON AS POSSIBLE and telling them we would like page proofs before the end of the year (if possible).

*Shroud for a Nightingale* won P. D. James her first Crime Writers'
Association Silver Dagger award in 1972. There would be several
more. In this 1990 publicity shot, she poses with one of them and a
magnifying glass that lived on her writing desk
(© Lucinda Douglas-Menzies).

*Faber's Production Director, David Bland, had died suddenly in
January 1970, plunging his department into the sort of chaos
where it could lose a manuscript from the firm's bestselling
author. The resulting delays in production exacerbated Faber's
cash-flow problems.*

*When Enid Faber had both Dick de la Mare and Peter du Sautoy
to stay at the end of October 1970 cash was part of what they
talked about, but as the gossipy letter she sent to her son Tom
shows, another objective was to persuade Dick that, as he
approached his seventieth birthday, it was time to retire.*

## Enid Faber to Tom Faber

You may have noticed that Dick de la Mare very much favours Peter
Crawley, as against Peter du Sautoy. The 2 Peters are not soul bud-
dies – Dick has said to me before now that I ought to hear what Peter
Crawley says about the other one – Dick claims to get on well with
Peter du Sautoy, but does not like Molly who once made a wounding
remark to, or about Katta.[11] He suspects Molly of being ambitious for
Peter. These remarks, of course, highly confidential – Dick is also a
bit chilly when mentioning Dugald Macpherson, though, again, is at
pains to say how well he gets on with him. [. . .]

I forced myself to discuss money, and was told the Bank had had
instructions from Government to stop overdrafts – also EVERYONE
says we are undercapitalised for such a large firm – also nearly every
firm is in same trouble and only 4 are still on their own – I feel I
have failed both you and Peter. His (Peter du Sautoy's) last words
were 'well you won't be able to do anything – we must just get him
to resign' – I have not dared to mention this even. [. . .]

---

11 Molly and Katta were married to, respectively, Peter du Sautoy and
Richard de la Mare.

So I can't do more than dangle the charms of a catalogue of his collection[12] . . . in the hopes of making retirement more attractive.

Meanwhile Dick eats heartily at <u>every</u> meal – gets up for cooked breakfast and all – Peter has bread and coffee in bed, and only pecks the rest of the day! [. . .]

I should be very sad to sell out now. Geoffrey took so much trouble to try and preserve the firm – what happens after my death is another matter.

> As Geoffrey's solicitor, Dugald Macpherson was a trustee of a trust (the '1947 Settlement') into which Geoffrey had put most of his Faber shares in 1947. He is the perhaps unlikely hero of the story that follows. It begins with a summary from Tom Faber, who had recently returned from a nine-month sabbatical in California, of the firm's current financial situation.

## Tom Faber to Richard de la Mare, 7 November 1970

I must let my mother and Macpherson know what was said at the Board Meeting yesterday. The easiest way is for me to summarise the position in a letter to you, of which they can both have copies.

1  The immediate cash problem is more serious than I had fully appreciated and alleviation is not in sight until the end of February, when payment of some large U.S. orders is due. It has become urgently necessary to persuade the Bank to enlarge our overdraft limit from £75,000 (already exceeded) to £175,000, so that the firm may pay its royalties and other debts.

2  It is thought that the only terms on which the Bank will agree to accommodate us are:

---

12   Richard de la Mare was a great connoisseur and collector of Japanese porcelain.

That we renew our declaration of intent to sell Fine Art
Engravers. (This is already under discussion with a broker,
though she has not seen the most recent figures. We hope to get
a minimum of £30,000 for our share, and with reasonable luck
£40,000.)

That we declare our intention to raise £60,000 from the
shareholders of Faber & Faber within say 3 months, and provide
guarantees that at least £50,000 will be forthcoming.

[...]

8 We agreed that as soon as the immediate financial crisis is over
we should have a thorough discussion about future policy,
and especially about the wisdom of recruiting a director with
financial expertise.

I hope that this covers the ground with reasonable accuracy. I expect
that I seemed a bit petulant at our meeting, so I hope you appreciate
that, although I may not be as optimistic by temperament, I really
share your faith in the long term future of the firm.

### Enid Faber to Tom Faber, 9 November 1970

As to the Chairmanship – I wondered whether Dugald could ask if he
was planning to retire at 70, next June 4 – I failed so lamentably in
the past that I doubt if I am the right person to take it on – especially
as I am fond of Dick and hate to think of him hurt. [...]

My only hope is that after a lot of fuss at a party, Dick will feel it an
anti-climax not to become President.

*On 25 November the bank made it clear that, in effect, there
would be no increase in the overdraft facility. Faber & Faber
was about to run out of cash. Tom wrote a memo to his mother
and brother Richard (who was by then fully committed to the
Foreign Office) which appeared to accept that the firm would*

*have to be sold. The Pearson group, which owned the* Financial
Times *and one or two other papers, had recently diversified
into book publishing by taking over Longman and Penguin. It
seemed the obvious purchaser.*

## Tom Faber to Enid and Richard Faber, 2 December 1970

Peter du Sautoy and Charles Monteith are both absolutely clear
that this would be much the most satisfactory group for Faber to
join – it has enormous resources, the three publishing houses would
complement each other neatly, and the people concerned seem to be
respected. [. . .]

I must report that the directors struck me as a pretty demoralised lot
yesterday – Dick unincisive and obviously very tired. Peter Crawley
inclined to bluster for a bit and then relapse into silence. Simmons
thrown into a dither by the suggestion that figures about assets and
projected earnings should be produced in time to lay before Pearsons next Monday (figures which we should have had long ago). So
I am gloomily aware that among our assets a vigorous and efficient
management team is unlikely to figure as one. Of course Pearsons,
on taking control, would be more than likely to remove the present
chairman for us, but what a price to have to pay for this reform!

Looking through what I have written I am led to wonder whether
I have been infected by the despondency of others. Over the phone
Dugald sounds less willing than me to admit that we now have no
option, more inclined to fight. He had in mind, I think, that we might
go above the area manager level in the National Westminster to the
chairman – whom he knows – and see to what extent their tough
attitude is determined by the general credit squeeze and to what
extent by loss of faith in the firm's management. If the latter, we
might try a plea for mercy, coupled with an undertaking to replace
Dick at once, and to embark on a policy of ruthless economy.

*Indeed, on the same day that Tom wrote the memo to his family, Dugald Macpherson was writing a letter to him that would put steel in his spine.*

## Dugald Macpherson to Tom Faber, 2 December 1970

I am strongly opposed to all take-overs, mergers, umbrellas, etc. unless the Company taken over is so inefficient that it is bound to go bankrupt otherwise. It would be particularly distressing in the present case bearing in mind your father created the 1947 Settlement expressly to ensure that the control of F. & F. remained in family hands. There is no doubt it can provided (a) F. & F. can be managed efficiently and (b) things have not already gone too far downhill. [. . .]

It seems to me that in return for putting up £30,000 your family must impose conditions to ensure improved efficiency. One of these seems to be that there is a change in the chairmanship. And it seems clear that Faber & Faber need a finance efficiency expert. [. . .]

I could probably help over the Bank, but I could not do this unless it was absolutely certain that Faber & Faber will pull round fairly soon.

*And so Tom Faber brought himself to write the necessary letter to Dick de la Mare.*

## Tom Faber to Richard de la Mare, 8 December 1970

What with the power cuts last night, which almost immobilised traffic, we got to Cambridge too late and too exhausted for me to sit down and write to you straight away. Otherwise you would have had a letter from me this morning to amplify one thing I said at our meeting yesterday, which I am quite sure came as a brutal shock to you and no doubt to all the rest of the Board. I hated having to distress you by speaking so bluntly then, and I shall struggle through the rest of this letter with the greatest distaste for the task. But there is no time left for prevarication.

What I said at the meeting was that Macpherson was inclined to make it a condition of his providing £30,000 from the family trusts that the Board of the holding company should resign. When I got to his office afterwards I found that he had toned this down slightly, by adding the phrase 'if required to do so by the Trustees'. It does seem to me, however, that the resignation of all of us is called for. The Company is in a severe crisis that could and should have been foreseen and avoided, and we are all to blame. I certainly cannot except myself, for you began to put me in the picture as long ago as June 1969. I shall therefore resign as soon as the opportunity arises, certainly before the Annual General Meeting, and if my example is followed it will be one of the tasks of that meeting to elect a new Board.

I imagine that during the last few weeks, while you have had so many problems to worry about, you have been thinking a good deal about your own role in the firm. If I read the situation aright, you have been desperately anxious to get it back onto an even keel before handing over the Chairmanship to a successor, and perhaps you were planning, like my mother, that 70 would be the right sort of age for you to retire at. From what I have gathered during sporadic conversations with both Peters and with Charles since my return from America, that would have seemed right to the rest of the Board too. They have given me the impression, confirmed by my own observation, that you were beginning to find it a strain running the business, together with its subsidiaries, and that you would secretly welcome the chance to spend a bit more time in your garden. They have all of them, quite independently, spoken warmly of the work that Giles is now doing and have suggested that retirement would be easier and pleasanter for you with the knowledge that he was carrying the de la Mare torch so effectively.

The sad thing is that events have now overtaken us, for whatever may be said about leaving the personnel of the firm unchanged I am quite convinced that if we are obliged to sell control to someone outside, whether it is Pearson-Longman or Max Reinhardt, one of their first steps will be to replace you as Chairman, on grounds of age alone. [. . .] If, on the other hand, we are to struggle on by ourselves, we have got to put up a very convincing case to the Bank. One of the features of that case must be a guarantee that we are going to run our business on more efficient lines. With the Bank's two recent letters before me, in one of which Mr. Edridge draws attention to a warning he gave you in 1968, I cannot escape the conclusion that they have lost confidence in our management. It seems to me that we have no hope whatever in our plea for reprieve, unless we prom-ise to reorganise ourselves with a younger Chairman. So I fear that you will be obliged to hand over the reins prematurely, whichever way things work out. I hate to think of you being cast in the role of a scape-goat for a disaster for which all of us are partly to blame. But what other options are left to us, or to you?

So what it comes down to is that if the Board is to resign en bloc, as I have suggested, we cannot guarantee that you will be re-elected to it, at any rate in the capacity of Chairman. We shall have to turn to Peter du Sautoy instead, as the best substitute at hand. I am perfectly aware that he cannot expect to command the loyalty and devotion that you have done from all members of the firm, but perhaps his rather detached shrewdness is what we need to carry us through a period of economy and reform. At any rate he will need all the support we can give him and there could be no question of dividing the responsibility of day to day leadership. Frankly, I think it would strengthen our hand in the very complex negotiations that lie ahead if Peter were to be seen from the start to have undivided responsibil-ity for them. [. . .]

I would like you to know that this is a private letter. I have read it to my mother over the telephone and it has had her general approval, but no-one else has seen a copy or will see one. My mother wants me to add a word of sympathy from her, but no doubt she will write to you herself in due course.

*Tom had been in constant touch with his mother throughout this period, relying on her deep knowledge of the personalities involved.*

## Richard de la Mare to Tom Faber, 10 December 1970

I must make it clear that I am not at present prepared to offer my own resignation, and I have no idea what the reaction of the others will be, because I haven't yet spoken to them about it at all. But as Chairman – and I am still Chairman – I think I ought to say this: that it seems to me most unwise and unnecessary to humiliate the others in the way you have humiliated me, if it is your intention to go on working with them. If I was in their position I would resent it intensely, and it is no good pretending that your own resignation would be of the same kind as theirs, when you are in fact your own master and able to do as you like. I say this frankly because I still have the future of the firm very much at heart, and I think you might do it great damage, which gives me further cause for concern in our relationships with the minority shareholders, whose interests can so easily be forgotten in a situation like this. [. . .]

I can assure you that I don't want to stay on a minute longer than I am wanted by my colleagues; but there <u>are</u> things that I ought to look after for a little time longer before I go, and it is clear that I cannot do that if I have all my authority taken away from me – I am thinking of our production department, our relations with Latimer-Trend, where my sudden disappearance might cause a lot of trouble, and the many other matters that I have been looking after that will need to be tidied up. So I am suggesting that for the firm's sake as well as my own the obsequies should at least be decently carried out, and the last thing that I would want would be any kind of wrangle.

I would have no objection to handing over the Chairmanship to Peter du Sautoy, at a suitable moment, or to his taking over any further negotiations with the bank on that assumption, but there are many matters concerned with all this that will need discussion, and some of them before the meeting next Monday, I suppose, even if it is only an informal meeting of the shareholders then.

This is a private letter, written from home, but since your mother knows the contents of your own letter to me, and to my surprise approved of all that you said, if you did read the whole of it to her, I would like her to see it, and Macpherson as well, in the circumstances. [...]

I don't deny that I am overtired – one cannot work as hard as I have had to do during the past six months without that happening, but fundamentally my health is very good indeed, my doctor says, including my heart which he described as ten years younger than my age; but I have been suffering slightly from tachycardia lately – not a serious condition – which comes from overwork and stress and cannot be entirely ignored. I can't say that I feel better today in the circumstances than I did yesterday!

## Tom Faber to Richard de la Mare, 11 December 1970

My letter has evidently distressed you every bit as much as I feared. And it seems to have surprised you also to an extent that I had not quite expected. A copy of your answer will go at once to Macpherson and to my mother, and it will be up to them to decide – perhaps in the light of the way that other shareholders express themselves on Monday – whether or not my suggestions about resignation were ill-judged.

The less that I write at this stage the better, I imagine; I don't want to exacerbate the bitterness that could so easily arise on both sides. But I might just add that <u>of course</u> we shall need your help desperately in connection with the production department and with Latimer Trend and Fine Art Engravers, and that it was always in my mind that you would be in a good position to provide this if you would accept the office of President. Had I not wanted the initiative for that suggestion to come from inside the firm – as I think it may have done by now – I would have included it in my odious letter.

## Dugald Macpherson to Tom Faber, 15 December 1970

May I congratulate you on the way in which you managed a difficult meeting yesterday, and in particular getting the Chairman to agree to give up the chair.

I enclose copy of a letter which I have written to David Robarts today. I do not propose sending a copy to anyone else until I know what is his reaction.

> On 31 December 1970 Dick de la Mare formally resigned the chairmanship of both Faber & Faber and the Holding Company in favour of Peter du Sautoy. Matthew Evans joined the Board at the same time.
>
> Dugald Macpherson's letter to David Robarts, the chairman of the National Westminster Bank, seems to have done the trick. The bank relented enough to give Faber access to the cash it needed and the firm survived as an independent company, but it had been a close-run thing.

# 8: 1971–1979
## 'A reasonable hope of survival'

In March 1971, Faber & Faber moved into purpose-built offices in Queen Square, but it was going to have to behave very differently from the firm that had planned the move in the 1960s. Cost-cutting was a priority. The new chairman, Peter du Sautoy, already knew that the offices were going to be too large.

Soon, the necessary financial expert, Peter DuBuisson, was appointed to the Board. By the end of 1972, the stakes in Latimer Trend and Fine Art Engravers had been sold, bringing in much-needed cash. Shareholders contributed more capital, in the form of loan stock which was in due course converted to shares. The medical list generated a surprise bestseller – *Everywoman*. Gradually, the firm's finances stabilised. The economic outlook, however, remained grim. At the end of 1973 the miners' strike and associated power cuts brought the three-day week. Almost every year, inflation was well into double figures; there was a continual risk that costs would outrun income. Later in the decade, the government's policy to combat inflation was based on prices and income control: salaries and dividends were capped and any increase in the price of a book might be subject to challenge by the Price Commission.

So when, in 1975, the firm held a party at the National Book League to celebrate fifty years since the foundation of Faber & Gwyer and the tenth birthday of Faber Music, it seemed like bravado. Few present could have thought it likely that either firm would remain independent for much longer. There had been numerous approaches from potential suitors. Mergers with other publishers such as Cape-Chatto, Allen & Unwin and Edward Arnold received serious consideration.

With the focus simply on survival, the firm was stagnating

editorially. Faber continued to publish great poetry and plays, but its commitment to new fiction in particular appeared to have died. The firm's bestselling book of the decade – John Seymour's *The Complete Book of Self-Sufficiency* – was brought to it by a packager. It all speaks of a company lacking confidence and creativity.

If that sounds excessively gloomy, I am sorry. There is still amusement enough, I think, in the extracts that follow. Relief would come at the very end of the decade when Faber appointed a new young fiction editor: Robert McCrum. The firm's editorial spirit had not died. It was only resting.

### Charles Monteith to Paul Muldoon, 19 March 1971

On the whole I'd be inclined to advise you against putting a first collection together yet. My general view is that it's always advisable for a young poet to make some sort of reputation first, by fairly frequent appearances, not only in poetry anthologies like *Poetry Introduction 2* but also in the magazines and periodicals which regularly publish poetry. In that way, people who are interested in poetry get to know his name and begin – even if only subconsciously – to look forward to his first collection long before it appears. As you probably know, I first became aware of Seamus Heaney's work here through seeing some poems of his which were published in the *New Statesman*.

### Peter du Sautoy to Derek Stephenson, architect, 29 March 1971

We want to reduce our occupancy of nos. 3 to 5 Queen Square and let at least two floors. The reason for this is that it is no longer possible for any book publishing firm to retain in central London a staff of the size that we now have here. Book publishing has been very seriously affected by the reduction in local authority spending power (we are very much dependent on public libraries and on schools), by the enormous increase in production costs (printing and binding costs have gone up astronomically in the last 12 months or so) and

The architect's representation of Faber's new offices in Queen Square.
On the back of the same catalogue, a useful map showed how to walk
there from the old offices in Russell Square.

lastly by the recent postal strike which is going to leave behind a legacy of quite lasting financial loss.

## FABER & FABER BOOK CATALOGUE, SPRING 1971

*Everywoman*
Derek Llewellyn-Jones

*A Gynaecological Guide for Life*
Modern woman is considerably interested in herself. She is anxious to know about the changes which occur in her body each month. She participates more in her own care each pregnancy, and seems increasingly to desire to know what happens then and during childbirth. She is even more involved with her sexual role in marriage. *Everywoman* is the intelligent woman's guide to herself from the start of menstruation to the menopause.

> *Despite its rather unpromising catalogue copy,* Everywoman *became an international bestseller, particularly in paperback, selling over a million copies. In a way very traditional for publishing, it was the bestseller that gave Faber some very necessary financial breathing space.*

## John Seymour to 'F. C. Friend Esq, Messrs Faber & Faber', 1 May 1971

It is so long since we met or had any communication that I doubt if you will remember me, but I wrote a book for Faber that you looked after called *The Fat of the Land* and another (much worse one) called *On my own Terms*. I think the *Fat* sold one impression and a 'Country Book Club' edition but neither of them had any incendiary effect on the Thames. Since then I have been very much involved with Collins, having done a 'Companion Guide' for them (East Anglia), and two great big bumper guide books since which will come out, no doubt, in the ripeness of time. The mills of Collins are like those of the Deity.

I want to suggest writing an enlarged, extended, and improved *Fat of the Land*.

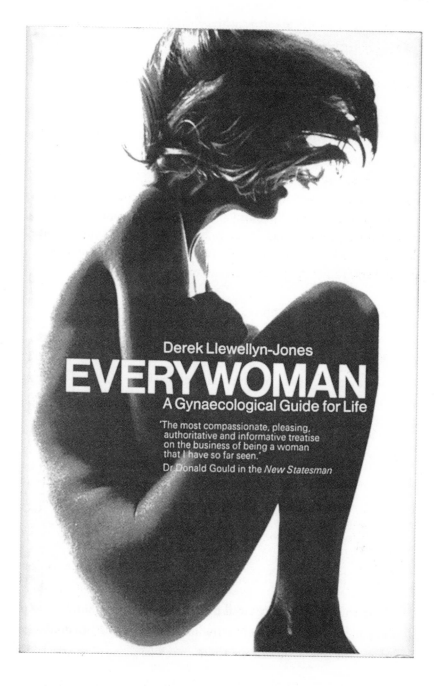

Derek Llewellyn-Jones

# EVERYWOMAN

A Gynaecological Guide for Life

'The most compassionate, pleasing, authoritative and informative treatise on the business of being a woman that I have so far seen.'
Dr Donald Gould in the *New Statesman*

I am now free to write about poaching, as I am no longer a tenant on a game-preserved estate.

### Kathleen Ash, Faber editor, to the Book Committee, 3 May 1971

A long letter, with a suggestion for a book, from the author of *The Fat of the Land*. Morley Kennerley looked after that book, and obviously Mr. Seymour has forgotten his name – but I'm sure MK was a friend to him anyway!

> *The true importance of John Seymour's return to Faber & Faber would become clear five years later.*

### Charles Monteith to Paul Muldoon, 5 May 1971

My very best wishes for the examinations!

### Paul Muldoon to Charles Monteith, 4 July 1971

Mr Crawley has been in touch about publicity for *Poetry Introduction 2* – I'm afraid that my autobiographical note is rather undistinguished, mostly in the future tense.

### Philip Larkin to Charles Monteith, 2 November 1971

I thought you might like to see an article on the novels of Barbara Pym which has just appeared in *Ariel: A Review of International English Literature* (October 1971). You will remember that some time ago I tried to persuade you to take her on when Cape dropped her, and I still think that it would be a good idea. [. . .]

I do think she would fit very well into the Anglican tradition of your House, which is why I am venturing to remind you of her existence . . . come early and avoid the crush.

*I applaud Philip Larkin for his persistence, but Charles Monteith could not be persuaded. He was to regret this when, championed by both Larkin and Lord David Cecil, Barbara Pym enjoyed a huge upsurge in popularity in 1977.*

## Faber & Faber Press Release, 10 January 1972

John Berryman, the American poet, jumped to his death from a bridge over the Mississippi last week. He was 57 and had been awarded a Pulitzer prize in 1965 and a National Book Award in 1969. The London poetry audience remembers him for an astonishing appearance at the International Poetry Festival in July 1967. Fabers are his English publishers and they have all his books available.

## John Carey to Charles Monteith, 22 February 1972

Seeing you on Saturday reminded me that I had promised – it must now be two years ago – to let you see anything I eventually wrote on Dickens, lest you should care to publish it.

## Paul Muldoon to Charles Monteith, 22 February 1972

I hope that the bulk of this parcel isn't too offputting. I've been thinking about this for a long time, as you know, and I've decided now on the poems that I've written over the past three or four years that I want to keep and read together. I'd be grateful if you would read them together, too, and more than grateful if you would keep them.

*Tom Faber was now vice-chairman of the Holding Company and a director of Faber & Faber. As he came to terms with the firm's way of doing things, he started applying his physicist's brain to some of its less logical policies, for example the way in which books were priced according to a multiple of cost, regardless of how long they would take to sell and how much revenue they were likely to generate.*

## Tom Faber, memo on Book Pricing Policy, 2 March 1972

My instinct when faced with a problem of this sort is to use mathematics and I hope to be forgiven for indulging it.

Let us suppose that $n_o$ copies having been printed they sell off at such a rate that the number left in stock after time $t$ is given by

$$n = n_o(1-f) + n_o f e^{-t/\tau}$$

This formula implies that a fraction $(1-f)$ of the edition fails to sell at all, and that the rest decays exponentially with a so-called time constant of $\tau$ years – selling fast to begin with and more and more slowly as time goes on. [. . . for several pages]

I attach no weight to details of my calculation or to the resultant graph, but I am sure the principle is correct – that because overhead costs are more or less independent of the size of the print order while production costs are not, the economic multiplier should be larger for books which justify only small editions than for those which justify large ones.

> *According to Peter Crawley, the Book Committee, 'which included two double first Fellows of All Souls, was completely floored and begged to be given time to digest the document'. The existing method of costing remained unchanged.*

## Charles Monteith to Paul Muldoon, 22 March 1972

I'm absolutely delighted to let you know that we do definitely want to publish 'The Electric Orchard'. I like and admire it immensely, and I'm very much looking forward to its appearance. [. . .]

I wonder if the title is right? [. . .]

One idea which occurred to me – and this is even more tentative – is that you might perhaps think of using the concluding two words of the first poem, 'New Weather'. (Might it be an idea, I wonder, to

consult Seamus Heaney about the title? It would be very interesting
to have his views.)

## Charles Monteith to Seamus Heaney, 22 March 1972

Just a line to let you know that I've written to Paul Muldoon today
to tell him that we definitely want to publish his first collection,
which he sent to me a month or so ago. I really am, as you know,
very impressed by his work, and I'm most grateful to you for having
steered him in my direction.

> *The following month, Peter du Sautoy, now aged sixty, sent a
> note to the other directors to kickstart a discussion about the
> firm's strategy.*

## Peter du Sautoy, note on Forward Planning, April 1972

I am not the best person to lead the firm towards the 1980s. Someone
much younger, more vigorous, more forward-looking yet still appreciative of the past, is needed. I wish there were a Faber. In the absence
of one, great thought must be given to the question . . . by the Fabers.
I should like to stay at least until April 1974 and if possible for my
full term which would be to February 1977, but I do not want to
stand in anyone's way or in the way of the firm.

## Tom Faber, response to Peter du Sautoy, 1972

If only the firm can maintain a good profit record for some years
running, then I think that we should be well advised to become a
public company. I see that as the best way to ensure independence
in the long term, i.e. when control of the Company passes to my
children. Whether they turn out to be publishers themselves or not,
they are bound to have literary inclinations and to relish their connection with the firm that bears their name. If it becomes a public
company they may be tempted to sell a few shares from time to

time, but I feel quite sure that they will retain for many years a large enough block to prevent an outsider from acquiring control.

*My father eventually changed his view that Faber would benefit from being a public company. Matthew Evans, meanwhile, was seizing the opportunity that Peter du Sautoy's note represented.*

## Matthew Evans on Forward Planning, April 1972

I don't think that there is much to be gained by spelling out precisely why our list is weak in the general trade area as most people who will see this note know precisely where this weakness lies. The list will always reflect the interests of the editors and we desperately need new blood in the editorial department [. . .]

The Chairman has suggested a budget for acquiring new books and I don't think that this would be a bad thing at all. I would also like the editorial department to become much more personal in the sense that an editor is seen to be responsible for his books and this would help us to judge the work of each editor. [. . .]

One of the areas that we are going to have to pay great attention to is that of marketing – how do we best publish the books we have to offer. This is a new appointment that will have to be made to the sales department and will be particularly important if we expand our paperback list. But generally speaking I see no alternative other than further re-consideration of everybody's function in the sales department to meet our new needs. What is missing now (as with the editorial department) is the flair and flexibility that perhaps an enlightened appointment on the marketing side might provide.

*Peter Crawley, as Faber's Sales and Marketing Director, interpreted Matthew's advocacy of individual editorial responsibility as an attack on the collective judgement of the*

*Book Committee, and his last comment as a personal attack on himself, as indeed it may have been.*

## Peter Crawley, 'response to ME attack', 12 April 1972

When we were asked to give our thoughts about the firm in five years time it seemed reasonable to approach the problem in as constructive and broadbased a manner as possible. We are a highly individual firm, different from many others through the enlightened policies of GCF, taking corporate responsibility through sub-committees to the Book Committee for the books we publish, through the Board for making management decisions, and working together as a team, with all our individual warts and blemishes. And surely, without sounding too pompous I hope, it can be only through working together and supporting each other in the fullest sense that Faber books still continue to mean something worthwhile to the outside world. Because the principle of corporate responsibility for our books and for the running of our affairs appears to be challenged in one particular report (by Matthew Evans) and because a number of statements are made in the same report which are not supported by the facts, I think some specific replies must be made to them. [. . .]

ME's comments on the Editorial Department will doubtless be answered appropriately by the Editorial directors, but as we all do some editorial work I would like confirmation that by saying 'an editor is seen to be responsible for his books' ME is in fact advocating a policy radically different from GCF's that we should sponsor our books collectively? [. . .]

I had not realised that ME's sales experience was such that he would be ready to criticise the Sales Department with so much freedom. What is meant by saying 'sales can be improved by improving systems'? I would like examples backed by firsthand experience please.

## Charles Monteith to John Carey, 14 April 1972

I've read your other Dickens lectures, and like them just as much as the first ones you sent me. We'd be more than happy to commission you to turn them into a book for us – and I don't imagine, in fact, that much additional work is necessary.

*The title of Carey's book remained an issue, however. Initially he was concerned that Faber might insist on sticking to Hart's Rules, endorsed by its own style guide, and call it 'Dickens's Imagination', i.e., with the "s" after "Dickens'".*

## Charles Monteith to John Carey, 24 August 1972

So far as the title is concerned, we certainly wouldn't insist on sticking to *Hart's Rules*; and we'd be perfectly happy to accept *Dickens' Imagination*.

At the same time, I must say that I'm not sure that this is absolutely the right title for the book though, as you say, it is brisk and business-like; but it sounds just a trifle flat to me. I haven't any bright alternative suggestions to offer, I confess.

## Frank Pike to Charles Monteith on John Carey's book, 14 November 1972

I think my ideas on this book have now more or less sorted themselves out: it's a brilliant and suggestive study by a very intelligent and perceptive if slightly arrogant and impatient man.

## John Carey to Charles Monteith, 6 December 1972

As for title. It strikes me (it's only an idea) that a more arresting title, and one that relates to the book's main theme, would be *The Violent Waxwork: A Study of Dickens' Imagination*. If we used this title we might place at the front of the book, as epigraph, the excerpt from *The Old Curiosity Shop* which I have typed out. You have more experience of titles than I, and if you don't like my new one I'm quite prepared to drop it, of course.

## John Carey to Charles Monteith, 15 December 1972

Sorry to bother you again about the title for the Dickens book which is much on my mind. It struck me that *The Violent Effigy: A Study of Dickens' Imagination* might refer a little more broadly to the book's theme than *The Violent Waxwork*. The epigraph from Mrs Jarley would then be unnecessary. But maybe you will feel that neither is right.

> *The title was confirmed as* The Violent Effigy: A Study of Dickens' Imagination, *becoming the first of many books written by John Carey for Faber.*

### FABER & FABER BOOK CATALOGUE, SPRING 1973

*The Black Book*
Lawrence Durrell

*The Black Book* was written in 1936. The author was talented, and 24 years old. [. . .]

It was published, however, under the midwifery of Henry Miller, in Paris, for at that time, in 1938, publication in Britain would have invited prosecution for obscenity. Thus *The Black Book* gained a reputation among works like James Joyce's *Ulysses* or like *Lady Chatterley's Lover* or like Miller's *Tropic of Cancer* and *Tropic of Capricorn*, which could not be issued this side of the Channel.

Here – at last – is *The Black Book*, the missing forerunner of *The Alexandria Quartet* and of *Tunc* and *Nunquam*.

## Philip Larkin to Charles Monteith, 10 May 1973

Many thanks for your letter of the 9th May and the good news it contained of a prospective paper-covered edition of my first, worst book. Welcome, at least, for base commercial reasons; I am not sure how pleased I am at the prospect of further dissemination of this drivel.

W. H. Auden's unexpected death on 29 September 1973 meant
that this event became a memorial for him.

### Tom Faber to Enid Faber, 28 July 1973

Cape-Chatto having approached us approached the Bodley Head too and some sort of marriage between them has already been agreed – highly confidential this. Meanwhile Peter has been approached by Rayner Unwin, and we three are to meet together sometime for an exploratory chat. Charles has met and talked to three potential editors who might be brought in to the firm – all good but none of them so obviously ideal that he must be landed immediately. Donald is full of enthusiasm about a possible tie-up with Stockhausen, who came and saw round F&F and found the 'vibes' good – he subsequently lunched with the Mitchells, where he ate 2 lb of cherries and drank 5 bottles of tonic and nothing else.

The large profit for 1972 is confirmed and is now attributed mainly to psychological factors in 1970, which led the Directors to write down their stock by more than they should have. This reduced the 1970 profit, but now that the stock has been sold off (at prices which have since increased) the money shows up in the accounts. It means that the absurdly large sum of £60,000[1] is payable to the Directors as their 'share of profits' and emphasises the fact that the details of the share scheme must be revised when their service contracts are renewed in 2–3 years' time. A dividend of 11% (the maximum payable) should be dished out to shareholders in about November.

*On 19 July 1973, Peter du Sautoy and Tom Faber met Peter Crawley. The subsequent events are described below.*

### Tom Faber, Memorandum to all directors of Faber & Faber, 19 October 1973

The object of that meeting was to acquaint Mr Crawley with the Chairman's intention to propose to the Board (a) that Mr Monteith

---

1 In real terms, this would be approximately £750,000 today.

be nominated as his successor as Chairman, and (b) that Mr Evans be promoted at an early date from Deputy Managing Director to Managing Director. Mr Crawley agreed readily to (a) but expressed himself as strongly opposed to (b).

Some two weeks prior to our meeting on 19 July Mr Crawley had suggested, at the end of a memorandum sent to the Chairman, a different plan for the future, namely that he and Mr Evans should be made joint Managing Directors. [. . .]

At the end of our meeting on 19 July it was agreed that I should seek the views of Mr Monteith and Mr Evans, and that I should then make a decision between the two schemes under discussion. [. . .]

Accordingly, I had a brief talk with Mr Evans the same afternoon and a longer one the following week with Mr Monteith. I also consulted members of my family, all of them shareholders in the Holding Company. I reached the decision that to have Mr Crawley and Mr Evans as Joint Managing Directors would not be in the best interest of the Company. [. . .]

After the Annual General Meeting on 27 September an informal meeting took place, attended by all the Directors of Faber & Faber Ltd with the exception of Mr Crawley, and by Mr Mitchell, in his capacity as Managing Director of Faber Music. [. . .]

During the discussion many tributes were paid to Mr Crawley's qualities as a publisher. There was general recognition of the contribution that he had made, over a period of 26 years, to the development of the Company and of all that resignation would mean to him personally. But as to whether it would in the long term be in the best interests of the Company to appoint him and Mr Evans as joint Managing Directors strongly divergent views were expressed. [. . .]

To avoid the need for further divisive argument, I was unanimously asked to make the decision myself. [. . .]

I decided that it was in the best interests of the Company as a whole for Mr Crawley's resignation to be accepted.

*So Matthew Evans became Managing Director, but given the economic situation at the time, it was hardly a sinecure.*

Matthew Evans, Faber's newly appointed Managing Director.

## Board minute, 20 December 1973

The latest information was that Queen Square would not be allowed to use electricity on Sundays, Mondays, Tuesdays or Wednesdays but these dates might be changed at short notice. [. . .]

During the emergency it was agreed that the Book Committee would meet on Thursdays.

## Philip Larkin to Charles Monteith, 7 January 1974

*High Windows*

Publication day reading. This flummoxes me rather. On the one hand, I am not keen on poetry readings, even those involving Jill Balcon;[2] I think they belong to the demi-monde of poetry. If you held one, it would be difficult for me not to attend it, and I am inclined to think that, unless one is extremely impressive in the flesh (like Bernard Shaw or Rupert Brooke), one gets more dividends from keeping out of sight, as people's imaginary picture of you is always so much more flattering than the reality. Nor do I think that new poems – unfamiliar poems – reap the full benefit of public reading, as people don't know them and find it hard to follow them. The only reason Jill Balcon read my poems at the Royal Society of Literature was because I funked doing it myself.

On the other hand, it is quite true that I did appear on such an occasion in connection with the Oxford Book, and I shouldn't like you to feel that I won't do for Faber's what I would do for Oxford.

There seems rather more on the one hand than the other, doesn't there? Can you give me a little more information on the credit side – do you think it would sell a lot of copies, or be valuable in some other tangible way? Personally I think it might provide an opportunity for what Oscar Wilde called scenes of violence in Grosvenor Square.

---

2  Jill Balcon was an actress and widow of the poet laureate Cecil Day-Lewis.

*They compromised on a publication day reading, but in Larkin's absence. Larkin did, however, attend a small launch party at the Garrick, at which he made the joke, 'I now know what Eliot meant when he put "Il miglior fabbro" on the dedication page of* The Waste Land: *"It's better with Faber."'*[3]

## Tom Faber to Enid Faber, 25 January 1974

Peter is very cock-a-hoop at having secured Tony Pocock to succeed Peter Crawley and is confident that we have an excellent team to look after the business for the next decade. Pocock is certainly a very nice man, who will do a lot to make everyone work happily together, and all members of the Board have expressed enthusiasm for the appointment. Peter Phillips, the efficient production manager, is to become a director too and he should be an asset. So now all we need is new blood on the editorial side to replace Alan Pringle (who is still in severe trouble with his eyes). It won't be the same firm as it was 20 years ago – how could it be, with a turnover of £2,000,000, separate premises at Harlow and a new computer (on order!) to handle all the invoices and royalties? – but I don't see why it shouldn't be a lively and happy and profitable one still. The state of the nation permitting, of course; 3-day weeks don't help.

## Board minute, 28 February 1974

All paper deliveries were at the moment 3–4 weeks late. Special makings now required 5 months notice. If coal production were not resumed 70–75% of our cartridge paper requirements would be unobtainable by the end of March.

## Board minute, 28 March 1974

Over the last year production costs for laminates, paper, cloth etc.

---

3  See Andrew Motion, *Philip Larkin: A Writer's Life,* p. 444.

had risen between 45% and 75%, and a similar increase was likely over the next twelve months. An average book price of over £4 could be envisaged by the end of 1975.

As the material content of total book production costs was now increasing to such an extent, it was thought that longer runs might not be the answer to keeping down the published price of a book.

### Board minute, 25 June 1974

An offer had been received from Penguins (based on our old agreement with them) to take over children's paperbacks. A 7½% royalty would be payable to the author with Faber and Faber Ltd. receiving 5% of gross receipts. Penguin would take 10 titles now which were not yet in paperback with a £400 advance on each and possibly some of our other titles. It was thought that Penguins would require an eight-year licence and would be printing about 50,000 copies of each title initially.

*Faber still did not have the confidence (or possibly the cash) to produce its own paperbacks of children's books.*

### Faber Production Director, Peter Phillips, Memorandum, 28 May 1975

We need a more active typographic adviser to succeed Berthold Wolpe when he retires at the end of this year: someone already qualified and capable of discussing, advising, teaching and supervising a co-ordinated approach to the future design of our books, jackets/covers and publicity material (including posters and exhibition material). The two main objectives would be improving the overall level of typography and establishing a coherent, distinctive contemporary Faber style.

*In the meantime Shirley Tucker took over as design manager.*

## Tom Faber to Nicholas Smith,[4] Currey & Co., 26 June 1975

There was a Board Meeting at Faber's last Tuesday when I reported some of what was said in your office the previous week. It was generally agreed that although further talks with representatives of Allen & Unwin should certainly take place, it would be a mistake to hurry a decision about whether the two firms should join up. [. . .]

The problem of financing next year's publishing programme (truncated though it is) remains a serious one and the firm would dearly like another £200,000 or so to see it through next year, while efforts are made to reduce the size of the company to a level at which it can operate more safely in future.

## Tom Faber to Peter du Sautoy, 26 June 1975

I think on reflection my ideal solution is for a merchant bank to buy a share (30%??) of the equity in Fabers, Unwins & Arnolds simultaneously, to agree to provide the interim financial support that we at least require, and for us all in some mysterious way to preserve our independent status until at some agreed date in the future we are floated simultaneously by the bank onto the open market.

But I can't easily see that happening.

I do hope you and Charles and Matthew are all clear that if a plan for contraction can be worked out that offers a reasonable hope of survival in 1976 there will be no question of a merger unless the advantages are clear to us all.

## Tom Faber to Rayner Unwin, Allen & Unwin, 26 June 1975

It is only fair to warn you, indeed, that during my discussions I have heard strong arguments against going ahead with the proposed mer-

---

4  Nicholas Smith succeeded Dugald Macpherson as the Faber family solicitor.

ger at all. The Trustees, for example, find very unattractive the prospect of exchanging their majority holding in one unquoted company
for a minority holding in another and would in many ways prefer to
sell their shares outright, for cash. So you may find at the end of the
day that we are not pressing our suit at all.

A joint meeting of the Faber & Faber and Holding Company boards in
July 1975; standing, from left: John Nichols (Company Secretary), Giles
de la Mare, Rosemary Goad, Tony Pocock, Matthew Evans, Donald
Mitchell and Peter Phillips; sitting, from left: Peter DuBuisson, Charles
Monteith, Tom Faber, Peter du Sautoy and
Richard de la Mare (President).

*Tom Paulin had followed the tried and tested route of appearing
in* Poetry Introduction 3 *before sending his first collection,* A
State of Justice, *to Faber.*

### Rosemary Goad to Tom Paulin, 8 August 1975

I'm just off on holiday but before I left thought I must drop you a
rapid note to say how delighted I am that we are going to publish

your collection. I wanted to write before – and to speak to you when we met at the Arts Council Bookshop reading – to say how much I like your poems and how really bowled over I felt by the collection – but obviously couldn't do so while we were still reaching a decision (during which time I was busy chewing my fingernails on your behalf).

*The Times* diary, 10 September 1975

Faber and Faber held a cosy little party at the National Book League on Monday night to celebrate the opening of an exhibition marking 50 years of Faber publishing. Lady Faber, wife of the firm's founder, was the senior guest and many members of the Faber dynasty – including some of the very youngest – were in attendance.

Three generations of the Faber family modelling some typical 1970s fashions; from left: Toby, Polly, Tom, Enid, Penny, Matthew and Henrietta.

## Faber & Faber Press Release, Wednesday, 1 October 1975

This year's John Llewellyn Rhys Memorial Prize has been awarded to David Hare, for his play *Knuckle* (Faber) and Tim Jeal, for his novel *Cushing's Crusade* (Heinemann).

This annual award is made to a young writer (under 30) who in the opinion of the judges will be recognised as a major creative talent in the future. [. . .]

The Prize, administered by the National Book League, was inaugurated in 1942 by the widow of John Llewellyn Rhys, a writer-airman killed in action, who was posthumously awarded the Hawthornden Prize. It is a happy coincidence that one Faber author should share an award founded in memory of another; and that this should also be the 50th anniversary of Faber & Faber.

## Amos Tutuola to Alan Pringle, 11 October 1975

I was greatly shocked when I read your letter saying that you are retiring as a director of the firm . . . in respect of eye trouble. This is a great pity to me and that I am going to miss you . . . Not only that but as well as you had helped greatly to make a wild publicity of my books to all over the world which in return, had put me in a class of the African writers. Furthermore, this publicity had promoted my poor job to a rich one. However I shall not forget you throughout my life time.

## Matthew Evans, Memorandum on 'ECONOMIES', 20 October 1975

Although inflation in its present form has been with us for a couple of years and measures were taken to combat its effect, it was quite clear in the middle of this year when we were looking at our cash flow through to mid-1976 that we were entering a period when the real effect of massive inflation on the firm was going to show. In its broadest terms what has happened is that our costs have risen in all areas while the revenue we obtain from our sales has not increased by enough to cover increased costs. For example, production costs have risen by about 45% in the last two years. We are, therefore, caught in the classic pincer effect of an inflationary spiral: costs rising with sales revenue rising, but at a much lower rate, with the firm bridging the gap between the two with an increasing overdraft from the bank.

## Board minute, 30 October 1975

Out of thirty-eight persons who had left the Company's employment in 1975 eighteen had not been replaced. A committee of Directors considered what further reductions in staff were required and had agreed that the copy/edit unit should be disbanded and that the Publicity and Promotion Department should be reduced by two persons and that one part-time editor should leave. In addition to these five redundancies three of the staff would be retiring at the end of the year and one other had been offered early retirement which she had accepted.

## Matthew Evans, Memorandum to All Staff on 'ECONOMIES', 12 November 1975

Telephones. All of you will have read about the quite staggering percentage increase in telephone costs. Unless extremely urgent, please make all Trunk calls after 1.0 p.m. and keep telephone calls as brief as possible.

We suggested to the Staff Association that all members of staff, including Directors, should not make personal calls at Faber's expense. It is really rather a bad joke that in the last quarter the rental of the coin-box in the reception area exceeded the amount of money paid into it.

### John Seymour to Peter du Sautoy, 12 September 1975

Have you heard from some firm which wishes me to participate in some grandiose compendium of Self-Sufficiency? I told them I would do it provided that you were willing to publish it, for I feel that it would be better to stick, in future, to one publisher if possible. I have felt for some time that *Self-Sufficiency* should be written again, much bigger and more complete, taking in artefacts as well as food, and energy sources as well.

> *The 'firm' to which John Seymour referred was Dorling Kindersley, then a book packager, i.e. a company that would have the idea for a book, put it together and sell finished copies to a publisher. It was very lucky for Faber that Seymour insisted it should be that publisher.*

### Christopher Dorling to Peter du Sautoy, 8 December 1975

*How Self-Sufficiency Works*
Or whatever we decide to call it!

It was a pleasure to meet you today. I said I would let you have a detailed proposal so that you can thoroughly consider the possibility of Faber publishing the book.

### Peter du Sautoy to the Book Committee

*How Self-Sufficiency Works* or *Everyman's Complete Book of Self-Sufficiency* by John Seymour [. . .]

We might consider taking 15,000, though it is really too big an investment, but even then £4.95 seems impossible. [. . .]

John Seymour wants us to publish the book; and clearly someone will publish it. I think it will be a good book and if we make a special point of adding it to our list in Autumn 1976, and making a fuss of it, we might sell it very well. [. . .]

If we want to go ahead we must formulate our own proposal to Dorling Kindersley Ltd.

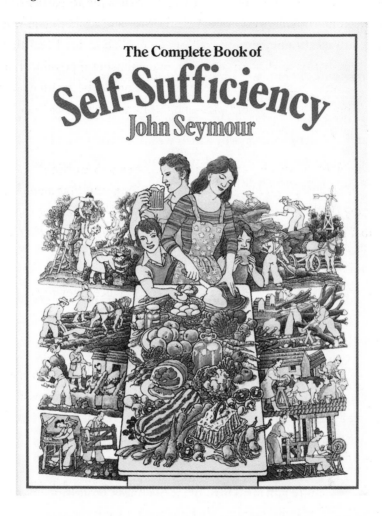

*If one book kept Faber & Faber going during the most difficult inflationary period in the 1970s, it was* The Complete Book of Self-Sufficiency. *Riding a wave generated by the TV sitcom* The Good Life, *it and its sequel sold over a million copies in various formats. As the correspondence shows, however, the book may have been published by Faber but it was essentially conceived and produced by Dorling Kindersley.*

## Eileen Brooksbank[5] to Peter du Sautoy, 13 February 1976

You asked me the other day to let you know what books I like to set against those I sometimes criticise and this is a perfectly fair challenge I must try to meet.

To start with, I confess I find it very difficult to rethink our publishing policy in the changed circumstances of 1976. To get a few things out of the way at the beginning, we must obviously continue to publish poetry and plays in which we are successful and for which we have become well-known. I would also say that we must hang on to fiction, however difficult it may be, because that is an area of creative writing in which we must continue to stake a claim. But we have never established 'Faber fiction' in the way we have established 'Faber poetry' and 'Faber plays', so thought must continue to be given to that. However, this is not really what you are asking, I think.

We must also, I believe, continue to stand by our writers of the modern movement, which is beginning to come to an end now, not only Eliot, Pound and Joyce but also David Jones and Djuna Barnes (though I don't mind *The Antiphon* going out of print). But again this is not your point. [. . .]

The really difficult thing to get used to is that we must no longer say that we will publish any good book on any subject, however limited. [. . .]

What we want to aim at all through is liveliness, professionalism and enthusiasm. It is no good publishing without enthusiasm and this must be shared by as many people as possible. The question of cost must be dealt with in an inflationary situation by producing books very much more quickly, which is why the preliminary work is so important, before the books goes to production. And this is also the

---

5  Formerly Richard de la Mare's assistant, Eileen Brooksbank was editor of the firm's gardening and farming list.

reason why we must get out of the way all the old books for which we have ancient contracts and for which we can't expect very extensive sales. This is a new concept for Faber & Faber but one that is very necessary for us to understand. [. . .]

A very good test, I always think, is to ask yourself how many books we publish you want to give to your friends for Christmas or birthdays. There are often paperbacks that are suitable for small presents, but otherwise it very often boils down to the very expensive books! What there very seldom appears to be is a book that everybody is talking about and would be glad to receive.

The children's books on the whole I like very much, and we do very often find them suitable for presents.

I don't know whether this begins to answer your question, but perhaps it is a start. I can't help remembering that on many an occasion when I have asked the travellers what is selling they simply reply 'the usual things, bridge books, cookery and gardening'. So we must try to keep them supplied.

> Peter du Sautoy retired in 1977. Tom Faber succeeded him as Chairman of the Holding Company and Charles Monteith as Chairman of Faber & Faber Ltd, where Matthew Evans was already Managing Director. Helped by Everywoman and The Complete Guide to Self-Sufficiency, Peter had kept the firm going, through cash-flow crises, three-day weeks and rampant inflation, but Faber was in desperate need of new editorial inspiration, and the Board Minute below is a reminder of the extent to which the firm was subject to government interference.

## Board minute, 26 January 1978

Following a complaint from a customer the Price Commission had enquired about the price increases on *Erica Wilson's Embroidery*

*Book.* A verbal reply explaining the reasons for the increases had been given to the Price Commission who appeared to be satisfied. They had asked for a copy of the 1976 accounts.

## Board minute, 25 May 1978

It was reported that the main flat sheet stock warehouse at Redwood Burn in Esher had been destroyed by fire. It was understood that no bound stock was affected but there were possibly two work-in-progress books lost. Burn held approximately 39% of the Company's sheets although 2/3rds of these had been written down to nil value. The full extent of the loss would not be known until a detailed report was received from Burn but at the moment it appeared that the cost of the sheets would be covered by the insurance policy.

> *This proved to be the gift that kept on giving. It took four years before the warehouse operator, Elmbridge Borough Council, admitted full liability, but in total Faber ended up receiving over £400,000 in compensation for stock that would almost certainly have eventually been pulped.*

## Matthew Evans to Andrew Lloyd Webber, 30 June 1978

Fortunately I was talking to Valerie when your letter arrived and I'm happy to say that she would have no objection to you setting one of Eliot's poems from *Old Possum's Book of Practical Cats* to music.

## Faber director John Bodley to Matthew Evans, 21 December 1978

I talked to Val Eliot about her meeting with Lloyd Webber. She agrees that they got on very well and is pleased that he thought so, too. He sat there like a schoolboy she says! [. . .]

Her last words to me were that she sees great possibilities in the idea.

## Board minute, 18 January 1979

It was agreed to advertise at once for an editor, probably in their twenties or early thirties, preferably with an academic degree and a literary bent. A University leaver would be acceptable although someone with publishing experience would be preferable. The person appointed would join the Company as a general editor and it was hoped that he would be a source of new ideas in the Editorial Department. [. . .]

The Managing Director said that there were certain areas of the list which were probably not producing the profit which they should. In particular, gardening, cookery and craft books probably fell into this category and possibly fiction, although certainly the Company would be very loth to cease publishing fiction.

## Board minute, 29 March 1979

Junior Editor. An advertisement had been placed in the newspapers approximately two weeks previously and had resulted in over 400 replies being received.

*The successful applicant was Robert McCrum. His father Michael was a former colleague of Tom Faber at Corpus Christi College Cambridge (to which Michael would soon return as Master). Robert recently told me about his application: 'It was Penny, your mum, who was instrumental in my move to Queen Square. I vividly remember her ringing me up, to ask if I'd seen the ad. in the Bookseller. Well, I hadn't, and of course, at the age of twenty-four, I was intrigued at this remarkable opportunity. Fabers were looking for an editor with an interest in fiction. In truth, I'd been an in-house reader for a year, and had only published about three books at that stage, with no track record in contemporary fiction, but I applied.*

'I was working for the then-independent house of Chatto
& Windus at the time, and had just been awarded the Tony
Godwin Prize, a fellowship for young editors which took me on
a work-placement to the immensely distinguished imprint of
Farrar, Straus & Giroux in New York, a firm that (by chance)
had very close ties to Faber. I'm fairly sure that Matthew
(Evans) asked Roger Straus to do some informal vetting.
Anyway, during my eight-week visit to the FSG offices in Union
Square, Matthew came to New York on business. And thus it
was that he interviewed me there, over a drink in the Algonquin
Hotel, and offered me the job on the spot. I believe that Roger
Straus, who'd been keeping an eye on me, told Matthew he
thought I'd be OK.

'In a slightly ridiculous coda, my redoubtable boss, Norah
Smallwood, at Chatto, then got very upset, tried to prevent me
leaving, and refused to pay for my New York expenses, asking
Faber to pick up the bill. I remember Matthew had some fun
with this, and ended up writing Norah quite a sarcastic letter.'

## Charles Monteith to Robert McCrum, 29 May 1979

I was absolutely delighted to hear from Matthew at the end of last
week that you are going to come to work for us when you get back
from America. All of us here who saw you very much hoped that
you would agree to take the position and we all look forward – I do
personally very much indeed – to working with you in the years
to come. I am sure Matthew has talked to you in some detail about
things here in Queen Square: I am certain that you will be able to
bring us new books, new ideas and new authors – which is what we
badly need. [. . .]

Could you please let me know . . . when there is no longer any need
for secrecy? For one thing, we have promised to let all the other

candidates know – the entire field of five hundred plus – when the appointment is actually made.

Welcome again to Faber and Faber.

## Board minute, 28 June 1979

It was reported that Mr. Robert McCrum had been appointed a Junior Editor and would commence with the Company on 1st August, 1979 (now amended to 30th July, 1979) at an initial salary of £4,500 per annum.

## Robert McCrum to Peter Carey, 8 November 1979

I wanted to write at once to say how delighted Faber and Faber are to have become your publishers. We are all of us here very excited about your work, and I can promise you that we will do all we can to ensure the best possible British launching.

## Peter Carey to Robert McCrum, 17 November 1979

I really don't know what to say except that I am, of course, delighted too. Being a pessimist my only concern is that the world will be totally destroyed before the book comes out. I don't give a damn if it happens afterwards, but it mustn't happen before. I am therefore taking a keener than average interest in the games being played in Iran and America.

## Robert McCrum to Peter Carey, 26 November 1979

Very many thanks for the Australian edition of *War Crimes* – a minority opinion within the building holds the opinion that you look like Woody Allen. I hope this will not discourage you from visiting us very soon. We are all very excited about your work.

## Kazuo Ishiguro to Robert McCrum, 31 December 1979

I was told recently by Malcolm Bradbury[6] that you had contacted him in connection with a new Faber collection in your 'New Writers' series, and he suggested I wrote to you. I am thus sending you these three short stories I have written over the last few months hoping they may be of some interest. [...]

P.S. I enclose stamped addressed envelope.

*I vote for these. R. McC.*

---

6   Malcom Bradbury was a novelist and Professor of Creative Writing at the University of East Anglia; Ishiguro was a student on his creative writing course.

# 9: 1980–1986
## 'Faber has been taken over by a different generation'

Robert McCrum had been appointed as a junior editor, but Faber still felt it needed someone more senior to lead the editorial department as Charles Monteith approached retirement. Simon Jenkins, who had been editor of the *Evening Standard* and was later editor of *The Times*, was a potential candidate, and in January 1980 Tom Faber asked him to write his impressions of the firm. It makes for salutary reading: 'All the agents with whom I have spoken remark on how little personal contact they have with Faber editors. They sit waiting for the world to beat a path to 3 Queen Square and fail to notice that it is mostly old-timers and rejects who are coming. Like an old and genteel hotel, Faber is relying heavily on overspill from more dynamic competitors.' It was a fair assessment. Although Simon never joined the firm full-time, he became a non-executive director of the Holding Company for some years.

The seeds of the firm's rebirth had already been sown with the appointment of Robert McCrum. In fact, he had already made contact with the two authors who would – by the end of the decade – exemplify the revival in Faber's fortunes: Peter Carey and Kazuo Ishiguro. Over the next few years, supported first by Frances Coady and then by Fiona McCrae, and often using the strong relationship between Faber and Farrar, Straus & Giroux in New York, Robert acquired writers who remain hugely important on the Faber fiction list today.

Robert was lucky, of course – the firm was lucky – in that his arrival more or less coincided with the phenomenal success of the musical *Cats*. As it was based on the poems in *Old Possums Book of Practical Cats*, T. S. Eliot was its lyricist. His widow Valerie therefore received the lyricist's share of the royalties from *Cats*, with Faber acting as her agent. Andrew Lloyd Webber has said many quotable things about the money to be made from a successful musical. My favourite is probably '*Cats* has been a pension fund for all concerned.' Faber's percentage of a percentage gave the firm enough financial headroom for an act of real rejuvenation: paying the advances that Robert's acquisitions demanded, transforming Faber's image through outsourcing design to Pentagram, building a proper sales and marketing operation for probably the first time, and – most crucially of all – finally committing the firm to being a 'vertically integrated' publisher which would never sell on its paperback rights.

In 1981, Matthew Evans became Chairman as well as Managing Director of Faber & Faber. Over the next few years, he and Robert would almost be a double act, and occasionally partners in crime. The management style had its failings – sales directors never lasted more than a couple of years; the culture remained male-dominated; despite the money from *Cats*, Faber still could not make consistent profits – nevertheless, there is no doubt that Matthew and the people in his favour had fun. When he persuaded Pete Townshend, lead guitarist of The Who, to join Faber's editorial team, the firm's transformation into 'Fabber and Fabber' (to quote the satirical magazine *Private Eye*) seemed complete.

## Robert McCrum to Professor Malcolm Bradbury, 29 February 1980

Thank you so much for advertising our *Introduction* anthology to your students, past and present. Although our selection committee has not yet made its final decision, Jody Klavans, Kazuo Ishiguro and Steven Kupfer are all holding strong contending positions on our shortlist.

Another recent find of mine is the Australian, Peter Carey, whose collection, *The Fat Man in History*, we are publishing in the Autumn.

I am enclosing a copy for your interest and would be glad to have your comments.

## Charles Monteith, Memorandum to Directors, February 1980

<u>Art</u>

This is an area where the investment involved is particularly heavy and the need for caution, in consequence, is of primary importance. A few relative successes, such as *Victorian Panorama* and *Correggio*; but some disasters. (The results of *Incised Effigial Slabs* and *Monumental Brasses* should render us forever on our guard against the funereal, however artistically satisfying.)

## Robert McCrum to Kazuo Ishiguro, 14 April 1980

I am delighted to say that we have chosen your work for *Prose Introduction 7*. If you could give me a call at your convenience, I should like to arrange a short meeting to discuss the details of publication which will be next January, 1981.

## Matthew Evans to Andrew Lloyd Webber, 26 June 1980

I saw Valerie the other day and asked her if there were any more cat poems or related material that you might see. She said there was one and I think she said that there was another that was not completed because it was so depressing. Anyway I encouraged her to show you everything she had and she seemed more than willing to do so.

> *This 'depressing' incomplete poem was 'Grizabella, the Glamour Cat', mentioned by T. S. Eliot in his interview with the* Paris Review *in 1959. When Andrew Lloyd Webber saw it the following month, he was ecstatic, telling Valerie that she had provided the key to the musical he was by then trying to write.*

### Robert McCrum to the Book Committee on Adam Mars-Jones, 17 July 1980

I'm attaching two stories by a young British writer whose work I very much admire and would like to bring on to the Faber list.

In addition to these two pieces ('Lantern Lecture' will appear in *Quarto* next month), he has written two short novels, one a Capote-esque account of the trial of the Black Panther and second a satire on the Royal Family. Taken together all this material, after revisions etc., would make one good volume.

> *Adam Mars-Jones duly joined the Faber list, although not before the firm took extensive legal advice about how to mitigate the danger of publishing the satire 'Hoosh-Mi', in which the Queen catches rabies from one of her corgis. One solicitor went so far as to say 'I can visualise that, if Fabers were to publish this book, it would be considered by many an outrage, harm Faber's high reputation and even possibly lead to one or two authors wishing to change their imprint.'*

### Valerie Eliot to Tom Faber, 29 July 1980

I expect Matthew has told you about our extraordinary weekend at Newbury as guests of Andrew Lloyd Webber, who has done – is doing – an exhilarating setting of *Practical Cats*. As he needs more material I am offering him the poems on Billy M'Caw, The Pollicle Dogs, Cows and Mr. Pugstyles. How it will all work out on the stage I cannot imagine!

### Robert McCrum to Andrea Rosen, US publisher at Alfred A. Knopf, 11 September 1980

Just back from holiday but have now re-read KUNDERA. Regret do not want to offer.

## Tom Faber, confidential letter to shareholders, 19 September 1980

From time to time during the last year or so Charles Monteith's health has given us cause for concern at Faber's, and I have felt obliged to put to Charles in consequence the idea that it might be in his best interests, and in the best interests of the Company, for him to surrender the responsibilities associated with the Chairmanship of Faber & Faber Ltd before reaching the normal retirement age of 65.[1] [. . .]

I have received conflicting advice from a number of sources as to who should succeed Charles. One school of thought has it that I should enter the firm on a full time basis and do the job myself. After deep reflection I have rejected this possibility, for personal reasons and because I believe the firm to need leadership of the sort that only someone with experience of the publishing trade could provide. I therefore recommend that Charles's successor should be Matthew Evans, who has filled the role of Managing Director and Chief Executive with success, and who, in my opinion, is better qualified than any other person to provide the necessary leadership inside Faber's, to represent the Company in the trade at large, and to recruit the talented young people who are badly needed if we are to flourish in the future.

## Kazuo Ishiguro to Robert McCrum [undated]

I'm sending you the first five chapters, and the start of the sixth, from the novel I'm working on. This is as far as I've got, but I have the rest planned out now.

Whatever your feelings about it, I'd be interested to hear what you have to say. As you can probably appreciate, it's very hard for me to get any critical distance on it at this stage.

---

1   Charles Monteith was born in 1921, so this implied retirement approximately five years early.

### Robert McCrum to Kazuo Ishiguro, 29 September 1980

It's been a great pleasure to read the first five and a half chapters of your novel which I've done in some haste before going to Germany this week. In general, I think it's developing in a most interesting way but I'd like to make a number of more detailed comments when I've had a chance to reread the text on my return. Meanwhile I'm going to pass your work round one or two of the other editors for their comments so that we can be as helpful as possible to you when we give you a finally considered opinion.

But anyway, the main thing is to congratulate you for getting on so well this Summer and to say that so far *A Pale View of Hills* seems to be extremely promising.

> *The note Robert sent about Ishiguro's novel to his colleagues in the Faber editorial department has a handwritten addition by Charles Monteith which is reminiscent of T. S. Eliot's on similar memos from Charles himself twenty-five years earlier.*

### Robert McCrum to Rosemary Goad, Frank Pike/Charles Monteith, Giles de la Mare, 29 September 1980

*A Pale View of Hills* by Kazuo Ishiguro
I'm attaching the first five and a half chapters of Kazuo Ishiguro's novel. I'd very much like to have a discussion about this as soon as possible.

*I enjoyed & admired this – CM 11/10/80*

### Literary agent Deborah Rogers to Robert McCrum, 15 October 1980

I very much hope that the contract for Ishiguro will come speeding through, since as you know, I am anxious to make time for him to write more. He is frightfully pleased about this and promises to deliver by February at the latest. All fingers are crossed.

## Letter from Robert McCrum to Robert Gottlieb, US publisher at Alfred A. Knopf, 21 October 1980

I know that Deborah Rogers is sending you a remarkable first novel, *A Pale View of Hills* by Kazuo Ishiguro. We are about to publish three short stories in our *Introduction* series: I found him last year and believe that he is a very important addition to our fiction list. So that, for what it's worth, is my five cents of enthusiasm.

## Robert McCrum to Charles Monteith, 12 November 1980

Ishiguro is coming in at 12.30 on Monday, 17. He and I are planning to have lunch but I think you said at the Book Committee that you would very much like to meet him. Perhaps we could all of us have a drink beforehand?

> *This 'drink' consisted of a carefully choreographed sherry, with Robert and Matthew seeming strangely solicitous. It later turned out that they had been (unnecessarily) concerned about how Charles Monteith might react to an author of Japanese descent, given his experiences in the Second World War. Robert remembers how 'Ish – of course – was oblivious to the whole thing. But he and I have often joked about it together.'*

## Robert McCrum to Charles Monteith, Thursday 13 November 1980

Milan Kundera: *The Book of Dreams and Forgetting*
Here are the salient pieces of correspondence. The position is that, after some discussion, we decided not to make an offer. On re-reading the text in English – at the time we could only consult the French – my view is that I made a mistake, and that I should have

recommended it more strongly. If you are interested I can bring the translation in tomorrow for you to look at.

I have spoken to Gallimard and they understand that we are now reconsidering our verdict.

### Robert McCrum to Milan Kundera, 10 February 1981

As you probably know, Faber and Faber, who admire your work profoundly, have made an offer to your publishers, Gallimard, for the British rights to *The Book of Laughter and Forgetting*. We very much hope that you will want to join the House that publishes, among many great writers, T. S. Eliot, James Joyce and William Golding.

In addition to an offer for your latest novel, I should like you to know that I have been in conversation with my friend Aaron Asher in New York, and I understand that a new edition of *The Joke/La Plaisanterie* is planned. For this, too, I should like to make you an offer, subject to your approval of the terms for *The Book of Laughter and Forgetting*.

Above all, Faber and Faber are anxious to be your publishers in London and to provide a home for your writing in England in the years to come.

### Board minute, 19 February 1981

*Cats*. Four units of £750 each were in the process of being purchased by the Holding Company. It might be possible to arrange the purchase of a block of tickets for one of the rehearsals for use by the staff.

*Andrew Lloyd Webber was desperately trying to finance the first production of* Cats. *This minor investment in the show, of which little was expected, was simply to show willing.*

Andrew Lloyd Webber, Valerie Eliot and Matthew Evans.

### Robert McCrum to Milan Kundera, 4 March 1981

All of us here at Faber and Faber are very delighted to have become your publishers.

### Milan Kundera to Robert McCrum, 9 March 1981

Thank you for your kind letter. I shall go in England to Oxford at the beginning of June. It will be quite easy for me to stay for a while in London and I am looking forward to meeting you.

### Matthew Evans to Charles Monteith, 16 March 1981

NOT THE NINE O'CLOCK NEWS 1982 CALENDAR

While I was in at the weekend just clearing a few things up I thought I would dictate a short note to you about this project. On Friday I made an offer to the agents looking after the team who we hope are going to do the calendar for us. [ . . .]

I just wish to say that I am strongly in favour of this thing if we can get it off the ground as not only is it likely to be extremely profitable but I think it will enhance our reputation in the marketplace as a publisher prepared to do new, good and interesting things.

### Board minute, 30 April 1981

The Chairman welcomed Messrs. J. R. McCrum and A. R. Wagstaff[2] on their appointment to the Board, Dr Mitchell whom he had invited to attend and the other Directors attending in their new roles.

On behalf of the Directors, Dr Faber welcomed Mr. Evans as their new Chairman. [. . .]

*Cats*. The Secretary was asked to contact the Really Useful Company Limited to try and obtain an assessment of the probable cash flow which would ensue were the production of *Cats* to prove successful.

> *Faber's reputation for excellent design had suffered in the years since Berthold Wolpe's retirement in 1975, with attempts to find a coherent look for the firm's books frustrated by the perceived need for consensus. So in 1981 Matthew Evans – advised by longstanding director John Bodley – took the bold decision to outsource design to the agency Pentagram.*

### John McConnell, Pentagram, to Matthew Evans, 1 May 1981

The first stage of our design work would be to tackle the basics, i.e. the colophon, and when we have approval for our proposals, to apply them initially in the less controversial area of stationery.

-----

2   A. R. Wagstaff was the new Distribution Director.

## Board minute, 28 May 1981

*Cats.* The Chairman reported that the show was now considered a 'hit' and options had been bought by eleven other countries. It was expected that gross receipts from the London production would be £8,000–10,000 per month. It was proposed to publish a book of the show in July and work on this was well advanced.

## Robert McCrum to Kazuo Ishiguro, 1 June 1981

*A Pale View of Hills*
This is just a quick note to say that I have now re-read your novel, and I think that you have solved all the problems triumphantly. It is a really marvellous first novel and one which we shall be very proud to publish next Spring.

## Milan Kundera to Robert McCrum, 22 June 1981

Vera has sent you, it seems to me, an absolute suitcase of my writings. [. . .]

I remember our meeting and Indian meal with great pleasure and I rejoice to have you as my English publisher.[3]

## Member of Faber staff to Matthew Evans, 10 July 1981

*NOT 1982*
You find herewith my 'free' copy of *NOT 1982*.
I have all along found the idea of this enterprise distinctly unappealing. [. . .]

---

3  Vera is Milan Kundera's wife. The original letter was written in French and read: 'Vera vous a envoyé, me seble-t-il [sic], toute une valise de mes texts . . . Je me souviens avec grand plaisir de notre rencontre, de notre dejeuner indien et je me rejouie de vous avoir comme mon editor anglais.'

I believe most strongly that Fabers is in business to produce books which can be considered important on a number of different criteria. Because we believe in the books we produce I think everyone here wants to see them edited, produced and sold to the best of all our abilities. *NOT 1982* is something else and energies which could have been employed on worthwhile projects have been dissipated. I am disappointed to have been associated with it.

I should also point out that I am distressed by the reference to myself on the inside front cover and shall take legal advice on this. You may or may not agree that it would have been courteous if those of us at Fabers whose names have been used in this way had been consulted before the copy went for press.

> *The writer of this rather po-faced note (whom I have deliberately kept anonymous) seems unaware of the role that humour has always played in Faber's history (the other possibility, of course, is that the note itself was a joke). The fact that the NOT 1982 calendar was both extremely funny and earned over £250,000 in gross profit should be answer enough, but it reminds me that many Faber employees never quite understood that the firm could only publish great literature if it also made a profit.*

## Matthew Evans to Charles Monteith, 21 August 1981

The point I want to discuss with you is this: ought we to be taking action to protect the future of the Faber poetry list over the next decade or more, now that your full retirement is only five years off and that you are in part retired already? [. . .]

Robert has now come up with an interesting proposal that we should start to employ Craig Raine on a part-time basis. [. . .]

The proposed arrangement would in no way affect your relationship with any of the poets you look after on the Faber list as I would imagine that Craig would be keeping an eye on those poets of his own generation and younger.

> *Craig Raine – leader of the 'Martian' poets (a group taking its name from Craig's famous poem 'A Martian Sends A Postcard Home') – duly became Faber's poetry editor, and brought his own poetry to Faber as well.*

## Tom Faber, Holding Company Chairman's Statement for 1981, 1 October 1981

On the design side, we have sought advice from Messrs. Pentagram Limited, and Mr. John McConnell of that Company is collaborating with the staff in our Production Department to raise standards. A new colophon designed by Mr. McConnell, based on a printer's double f, will start appearing shortly on most Faber books and stationery. [. . .]

Finally, I should draw attention to the success of the musical *Cats*. It is too early to make quantitative predictions of the revenue that this will generate for the group, directly and indirectly, but there is no doubt that it will be of significant assistance to both Faber & Faber Limited, and Faber Music Limited. We are particularly grateful to Valerie Eliot for her insistence that publication of the music for this show should be handled by our Music Company, and as one of the fortunate recipients of the poems when they were first written I await her projected *A Propos of Practical Cats* with some impatience.

## Memorandum on 'NEW STATIONERY' [undated]

In line with other changes to the company's image a new style has been designed for the office stationery. A complete set has been produced to replace all items currently in use, and is to be introduced throughout Queen Square from start of work on Monday January 4th 1982. [. . .]

It is emphasised that this is a complete changeover, and that the disposal order refers not only to letterheads and envelopes, but also to such less obvious items as labels, internal memos and continuation sheets.

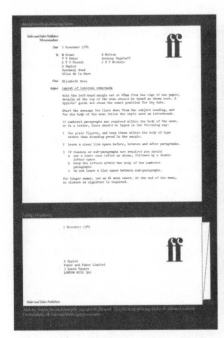

Suddenly, Faber had a house style based on rules.

*The next few extracts show Faber benefitting from its relationship with the US publisher Farrar, Straus and Giroux with the acquisition of two future Nobel Prize-winners: first, Mario Vargas Llosa and then Derek Walcott, who had previously been published by Cape in the UK, with FSG always being his main publisher.*

## Matthew Evans to Carmen Balcells, literary agent, 10 November 1981

Robert McCrum, our editorial director, is in New York at the moment and has just phoned after talking to Roger Straus, about

Mario Vargas Llosa. Would it be possible for you to give us an option on his British rights? If so, we would be very happy to see some reading material and if we take it on, we could co-operate with Farrar, Straus.

## Carmen Balcells to Matthew Evans, 29 January 1982

Thank you first of all for your telex January 19th and your offer for *La Guerra del Fin del Mundo* and *La Tia Julia y el Scribador*.

We have not yet received Robert McCrum's letter but this is to let you know that we spoke to Mario and he is frankly happy with the idea of being published by F&F.

## Robert McCrum to Carmen Balcells, 1 February 1982

You have recently received a telex message expressing our profound enthusiasm for the work of Mario Vargas Llosa. I would like now to write formally to say how impressed we have been with both *Aunt Julia and the Scriptwriter* and also, of course, *The War of the End of the World*, which is one of the most extraordinary novels it has ever been our privilege to consider. We very much hope that you will want Mario Vargas Llosa to join the House that publishes, among many great writers, T. S. Eliot, James Joyce, William Golding, Milan Kundera and Andre Brink.

## FABER & FABER BOOK CATALOGUE, SPRING & SUMMER 1982

*The Fortunate Traveller*
Derek Walcott

We are delighted to welcome this distinguished poet to the Faber list.

## Board minute, 14 January 1982

Mr. DuBuisson was presented with a toy pink pig by Miss Rosemary Goad on behalf of the female staff, occasioned by Mr. DuBuisson's remark at the Computer Meeting in the morning when he said a firm employed 'five people and three women'!

*By 1982, Pentagram was taking responsibility for all Faber's jacket designs. Poetry covers were wallpapered with the 'ff' colophon that had been rolled out the previous year. The play list had a uniform look based on diamond hatching. For more mainstream books, Pentagram used a box to contain the author and title information: strong branding because the box was instantly recognisable, but also flexible because it could be placed in the most appropriate place on the cover image.*

## Board Minute, 24 June 1982

In reply to a question from Mr McCrum about what effect Pentagram had had on sales, Mr Taylor[4] said it was difficult to give a clear-cut answer but that on the reprint side it meant that we could resubscribe established titles,[5] and there was no doubt that the new jackets had been noticed although not all comments had been favourable.

## Robert McCrum to Milan Kundera, 28 January 1982

Here's some good news: I hope you'll be delighted to hear that Penguin Books, the most important paperback company in Britain, have offered £5,000 for *The Book of Laughter and Forgetting* and for the re-issue of *The Joke*. This is marvellous news and Penguin executives have expressed a very keen commitment to your work for the future. I hope the combination of Faber and Faber and Penguin will ensure that your writing gains an ever wider circle of readers from now on.

---

4  George Taylor was Faber's sales director in the early 1980s.
5  That is, the new jackets provided a reason to re-introduce older titles into bookshops.

*Despite publishing its own paperbacks since the 1950s, Faber was still happily selling paperback rights in its new books to specialists like Penguin. Thankfully for Faber's long-term future, that was about to change.*

## Matthew Evans, note on Faber Paperbacks, August 1982

We have never had any fundamental discussions about what precisely is the nature of the beast or where it's going, and this brings us up to the present. [. . .]

We have a total of 2,160 titles in print, 945 of them in paperback and the paperback list is growing much faster than the hardback list. [. . .]

All this leads me to believe that Faber is on course to become a predominantly paperback house in the eighties and nineties, which is almost a complete reversal of our role twenty years ago and in the years before. The first problem I see, therefore, is that we now perceive ourselves as hardback publishers with a paperback imprint, a view that creates a structure and atmosphere of a hardback house, whereas many forces are rapidly making us become a predominantly paperback house. We have, first of all, to acknowledge this and then to say, well, if this is the case, what changes do we need to make within the firm to recognise the reality of our situation and to realise our ambitions? [. . .]

We cannot be at all complacent about the future, and we must make sure that after our discussions and any changes that emerge, we assert ourselves in the market-place as a major publisher of paperback books. We have experience and strength that perhaps no other British publisher has, and whatever we do we must make the most of these very considerable assets.

*The following month, Matthew decided it was time to resign from the 'Editors Dining Group'.*

### Matthew Evans to Liz Calder, Jonathan Cape, 22 September 1982

I thought that you were going to . . . recreate it with the same bunch of aging trendies that I love to spend time with, and keep out all the earnest prawns.

### Robert McCrum to Louise Cooper, literary agent at Judy Daish Associates Ltd, 14 October 1982

Caryl Phillips came in this afternoon and we had a good meeting. We've agreed that we'll be in touch again in April next year when I'll go through the text of his novel as it stands, making editorial suggestions. He said that he then planned to go away a la Agatha Christie to complete the novel. I'm optimistic that he will produce a manuscript in which Fabers would be more than interested, so I hope you'll encourage him to get back in touch when he's back in the country in April.

### Faber poetry editor, Craig Raine to Wendy Cope, 26 January 1983

If your job ever allows you time off for a lunch, give me a ring. How are your poems going? Have you thought any more about Strugnell?[6] I don't mean to badger you at all: just when you feel like it, as we agreed.

> At the beginning of 1983, Desmond Clarke at the Book Marketing Council had the idea of promoting books in general (which was his job) by persuading a panel of judges to nominate the twenty 'Best of Young British Novelists'. Promoted by Granta magazine, the list had an enormous impact and seemed to typify the revival in literary fiction that by now seemed well under way. Faber already published two of the writers listed (Adam Mars-Jones and Kazuo Ishiguro) and it soon acquired a third.

---

6 Several of Wendy Cope's poems are written in the persona of a fictional poet, Jason Strugnell.

## Robert McCrum, Memorandum to Sales and Publicity, 31 January 1983

I hope you will all be delighted to know that we shall be publishing Maggie Gee's second novel, as yet untitled, in September 1983. We won this after quite a fierce tussle with some tenacious rivals (probably because Maggie is one of the twenty Best of British) and I hope that we can do a good job to launch her on the Faber list in the Autumn. Copies of the text will be coming round shortly.

## Maggie Gee to Robert McCrum, 1 February 1983

I am just writing to say how pleased I am, in my turn, to be coming to Faber and Faber. In the sometimes dim and dark days that followed the (semi-)publication of *Dying, in Other Words* your letters and interest meant a very great deal to this particular author, and of course that affected my final decision (my only uncertainty was as to your and Faber's enthusiasm about <u>this particular book</u>, and what you said at lunch settled my mind on that point).

## Maggie Gee to Robert McCrum, 9 February 1983

Great that you like the new title – so do I, and a straw poll of my friends/acquaintances came up with a great majority for *The Burning Book* (as soon as I write that I realise that I do not really know what a 'straw poll' is or whether s. polls come up with majorities, but that's writing for you – full of pitfalls).

## Robert McCrum to Louise Cooper, Caryl Phillips's agent, 6 June 1983

I have now read the revised draft of Caz's novel and I am afraid to say that, although it has improved greatly since last year's draft, it still seems to me to fall a bit short of what I had hoped.

## Robert McCrum to Caryl Phillips, 15 July 1983

Thanks for coming in the other day: I hope what Frances and I had to say was helpful. That was the intention anyway.

## Milan Kundera to Robert McCrum, 7 October 1983

I am very pleased that you like my book! Very pleased! But the trans-lation is very very poor. We are still working hard with Aaron[7] to improve and clarify it. But all will be well because my stars are aligned from December 1983 to autumn 1984. In other words: May would be OK, but no later if we want to take advantage of the months follow-ing publication when the book's echo is resounding (it's because of the conjunction of Uranus with my star sign, it is a very slow transit, which takes a whole year; at the same time – through truly exception-al luck! – Mars is blocked in a neutral position for the entire time!).[8]

## Tom Faber, Holding Company Chairman's Statement for 1983, October 1983

In the opening paragraph of this Statement I referred to trading prospects for the current year as 'uncertain'. Principal uncertainty concerns the sales revenue of Faber & Faber Ltd. [. . .]

There is confidence within the Group, however, that the lively image which Fabers has re-established for itself in recent years will be

---

7 Aaron Asher, publisher at Farrar, Straus and Giroux in New York. See p. 360.
8  Again, Kundera's original letter was in French, as follows: 'Je suis très heureux que vous avez aimé mon livre! Très heureux! Mais la traduction est très très defectueuse. Nous travaillons encore beaucoup avec Aaron pour l'améliorer et preciser. Mais tout sera en ordre parce que les astres sont bonnes à partir de moi de décembre 83 jusqu'à l'automne 1984. Autrement dit: mai, c'est bien, mais pas plus tard pour profiter même des mois qui suivent la parution et pendant lequels l'echo du livre retentisse. (Il s'agit du trigon de l'Uranus avec mon Soleil, c'est un transit très lent qui occupe tout une année; en même temps – ce qui est une chance tout à fait exceptionel! – Mars est pendant toute cette époque bloqué dans une position neutre!)

matched by profits before too long. The Nobel prize for literature recently awarded to William Golding is naturally a great encouragement.

*There is little hint of this in my father's business correspondence, but for the previous few years he had been nursing my mother Penny. She died from cancer at the end of November 1983.*

William Golding in Stockholm to receive the Nobel Prize in Literature, 1983. From left to right: Charles Monteith, Ann Golding, HM Queen Silvia, HM King Carl XVI Gustaf of Sweden, William Golding.

## Robert McCrum to Milan Kundera, 6 June 1984

I thought I would write you a little bit of a personal letter to tell you what an extraordinary reception *The Unbearable Lightness of Being* has had in London these last few days. It is, simply, the novel of the year!! Wherever I go there are people talking about it, and people congratulating Fabers (quite undeserved, of course) for publishing such a remarkable work of fiction. The excitement is enormous – in fact, I don't think I've ever seen anything like it since we've been in the business. The latest event in the remarkable rise to prominence of your work is that in less than one week it has shot to the top of the best-seller lists (enclosed) and has been talked about on no less than five television programmes, any number of radio programmes, and reviewed in practically every newspaper in the land. The sales have been phenomenal. Our first printing has sold out almost overnight, and we are now reprinting to try to meet the demand. The excitement is extraordinary, and if you think normally this kind of fever is generated by the presence of a celebrity-author, not a real writer, then it's all the more remarkable. You must be very glad that you are safe and sound and secret in Paris.

> *Later that month Faber announced its first 'Minimum Terms Agreement' with the Society of Authors and the Writers' Guild (the two writers' unions). Its purpose was to enable authors without agents (for example poets) to negotiate directly with the company, in the knowledge that they would be signing a fair contract. What drew the most comment was the idea that the licence granted by a contract would expire after twenty years instead of when the author's own copyright expired (now generally seventy years after the death of the author).*

### The Bookseller, 7 July 1984

There is some surprise that Faber should have allowed itself to be boxed in by a 20-year licence. 'What . . . would be the implication for Faber without T. S. Eliot or Auden? Would Matthew Evans be suggesting a renegotiation of contracts with the two authors' estates? No renegotiation would allow Faber to derive a substantial income from *Cats*, though I imagine T. S. Eliot, as a publisher himself, would be proud of what Faber manages to do with those funds.'

## Publisher Christopher Hurst in *The Bookseller*, 21 July 1984

Neo-Faberism – or Matthew Evans-ism – is an aberration with recognisable historical roots. Those roots are in Faberism *tout court*, as
represented by the first and second generations of the firm's directors. Evans' excuse – that Faber numbers several authors among its
staff and is therefore particularly sensitive to the author's point of
view – gives some idea of how much he has lost touch with reality.

> *There was an air of flamboyance around Faber now. Fresh
> from his triumph with the 'Best of Young British Novelists'
> list, Desmond Clarke had joined Faber as Sales and Marketing
> Director, and soon drew attention for his suggestion that Ted
> Hughes and Seamus Heaney should tour the UK by helicopter
> (it never happened, but still acquired legendary status). When*
> The Guardian *interviewed Matthew Evans, Clarke and John
> McConnell, the Pentagram partner who was now also Faber's
> Art Director, it found the three men in an expansive mood,
> giving quotes that were a gift to a punning sub-editor.*

## *The Guardian*, 'Old Possum's Push in Boots', 23 July 1984

John McConnell – the selling of a novel by William Golding and the
selling of a box of tissues in Boots is 'absolutely identical – it's all
commodity'. [. . .]

Poetry was the first task, because of Faber's commanding position in
the field. McConnell, who had designed a new double-f logo for the
company, uses the repeated logo as a decorated band around a simple
title panel on all the new and repackaged poetry books. Different
colours can be used, and original illustration can be commissioned
for the panel, but the format remains fixed. He calls it 'formal, classic – a reflection of the quality of the writers and the strength of the
brand'. [. . .]

Desmond Clarke – 'Two out of every three books that are bought in a
bookshop by the general public are bought on impulse. If you're looking for a book in a particular category, you want to be able to identify
it quickly. If you take the example of the Faber poetry list, we're now
exploiting its collective visual image. In marketing terms, we're seeing
that we are to poetry what Mills and Boon are to romance.' [. . .]

Matthew Evans – 'Faber has been taken over by a different generation in a very short space of time. It's inevitable that when you have
a whole new group of people coming together, you get a different
attitude, a different atmosphere, and you start publishing different
books.'

Robert McCrum (left) and Matthew Evans (right) flank Sydney
Higgins and Tony Benn at a press conference to announce an
anthology of socialist writings, *Writings on the Wall*, that Benn had
(nominally) edited (© Caroline Forbes).

### Robert McCrum to John Lloyd, co-creator of *Not the Nine O'Clock News* and *Spitting Image*, 1 August 1984

I was very shocked to see the press report about a new series for *Spitting Image*. As you know, all of us at Fabers are sorry to think that you have become mixed up with such low-brow filth, especially after all we have done to introduce you to the cream of the British literary establishment. Just for the record, I have to say that your attacks on the British Prime Minister and the President of the United States (leader as he is of the Free World), are in the worst possible taste, and bring an already dreadful television channel down to new depths.

However, none of us here is afraid of putting personal and company gain before literary and cultural scruple. WE WOULD LOVE TO PUBLISH THE BOOK!

### Deborah Rogers, literary agent, to Robert McCrum, 4 October 1984

I thought that you would like to see a copy of Lorrie Moore's short stories *Self-Help*, which Frances phoned about last night. I am delighted that she has intercepted the book so to speak – I was just deliberating as to who to send it to first.

### Faber editor Frances Coady to Lorrie Moore, 8 November 1984

This is a letter to welcome you to Faber and Faber. I am sure that Melanie Jackson has already told you that I was recently in New York and read a proof of *Self-Help* during my stay. I was so excited by the book that I wanted to make an offer straight away. On my return to London I finalised negotiations with Melanie's other half here, Deborah Rogers.

### Robert McCrum to Mario Vargas Llosa, 6 November 1984

I take great pleasure in sending you a copy of the novel I told you about at lunch: *Illywhacker* by Peter Carey. I hope you enjoy.

### Wendy Cope to Craig Raine, 11 January 1985

I hope there are enough good ones here. I'd be grateful if you would get in touch when you've had a look at them and tell me what you think. [. . .]

I've always wanted to call my first book 'Lonely Hearts' – that seems to cover all the categories, including poor Strugnell. But there have been other books with that title – I don't know of any books or pamphlets of poems but I'd want to check. I have a few other ideas – about 50 actually – and could send you a list if you like. I am quite keen at the moment on 'Serious People'. Or 'Simple Wishes'. I know we don't have to decide this just yet but I thought I'd put my oar in before you get carried away with some idea of your own.

### Matthew Evans to Desmond Clarke, Sales Director, 29 March 1985

I have to tell you that I was dismayed to get your memo of 27 March showing a £90,000 variation on sales expenditure in the current financial year. When you assured me at at least three Board meetings that there would be a zero variation at the year end, I was not simply asking this as a pointless exercise.

> *Desmond Clarke had revived Faber's sales department, but at the cost of such over-spending that he had to leave the firm after less than three years. Few of his successors would last much longer.*

### Robert McCrum to Caradoc King, literary agent at A. P. Watt, 26 April 1985

Garrison Keillor: *Lake Wobegone Days*
Thank you so much for this remarkable book. I have not enjoyed a volume of American writing so much for a long time. In your letter you refer to it as 'a novel': I'm inclined to see it as living in

a unique category of its own, and being all the more appealing for that reason. [. . .]

Obviously we would like to do this book for you and the author here in Britain (and the Commonwealth excluding Canada). I think we could not only sell and promote it as well as anyone in the United Kingdom, and, by placing it alongside 'big' contemporary writers like Mario Vargas Llosa, Peter Carey, Jayne Anne Phillips, and Milan Kundera, draw special and favourable attention to something which, in this market, is a first novel by an American unknown – even allowing for what I hope will be favourable reviews from Viking [the book's US publisher].

## John Lloyd to Robert McCrum (end April 1985)

The Spitting Image Book will be fabbo on present form, though, as usual the deadline is frightfully tight . . .

## Peter du Sautoy to Tom Faber, 14 May 1985

It is a pity that there is now a sort of gulf between the Shareholders and the Directors but I don't see what can be done about it. It is a penalty of growth and the simple passage of time. Of course you are the only Shareholder who really matters and I feel a bit of an impostor when I open my mouth at the A.G.M.! I'm afraid I can't keep pace with all the changes at Queen Square but I feel quite optimistic about the future – in fact much more so than I did a year or so ago. It is a question of keeping one's nerve, which you manage so admirably to do.

## Wendy Cope to Craig Raine, 22 May 1985

The reasons I'm inclined to put 'Making Cocoa' at the beginning are so people don't think there has really been anything going on between me and Kingsley Amis or that any of the love poems are about him.

Dear Buyer,

We are delighted to inform you that you have been selected to receive this magnificent FREE GIFT – a miniature, trial-size edition of MAKING COCOA FOR KINGSLEY AMIS.

It is yours to enjoy and to treasure without any obligation whatsoever to order five dozen copies of the BUMPER FULL-SIZE EDITION. However, we are sure you will not want to miss the opportunity to sell Wendy Cope's remarkable book, with its 64 pages of fun-packed poems, tastefully bound in our Pentagram-designed jacket, and available to your customers for only £   . Another winner from Faber, the firm that puts the TRY in POETRY.

## Author Vikram Seth to Matthew Evans, 28 May 1985

After we had lunch yesterday, it struck me that you would be a good person to send my novel in verse to. If you like *The Golden Gate*, you might want to do a British edition – and even if that doesn't happen, reading it might somewhat increase your affection for a city that is – I promise – far from dreary and provincial.

I've told Anne Freedgood at Random House – who tells me that TGG is out at a few British houses – that I'd like to send it to you, and she says that's fine. (She showed it briefly to Robert McCrum, but when he offered to consider it only for the poetry list, she refused. The book is fiction, and to put it on a poetry list would be to kill it.) [. . .]

The book is due out in February 1986, and I can think of nothing more pleasurable than to appear simultaneously on the fiction lists of the British and American houses I most respect.

## Robert McCrum to Vikram Seth, 18 June 1985

I'm delighted that Fabers will be publishing *The Golden Gate*. When I've had a chance to discuss its future here with people in sales and publicity (you know the form) I'll be in touch in more detail about our plans. For the moment, let me say how entertaining I found it, and to welcome you on to this list.

## Vikram Seth to Robert McCrum, 26 June 1985

Thank you for your letter of last week. I'm very pleased that I'm with Faber, which I've admired for a long time, and I'm sure I'll enjoy working with you and Matthew. Matthew may have mentioned to you that I was at Tonbridge for a year after my high school in India, and that your father was my housemaster (and headmaster) – not a very meaningful coincidence, but certainly a curious one. I have been out of touch with him for many years now, and I hope things are well with him.

## Peter Simpson,[9] Memorandum, 14 August 1985

It would appear that there may well be a requirement for a micro computer to be based on, say, the third floor for use by all departments at Queen Square. This micro computer would be available for word processing and financial modelling.

## Robert McCrum, Memorandum, 16 August 1985

We must make a special note to ourselves that our author, Caryl Phillips, does not wish copies of either of his books – *The Final Passage* and *State of Independence* – to be sold in South Africa, at any price!

> *Faber's move into publishing screenplays was a natural extension of its play list, and would also bring it an author who has been one of the lead voices on Faber's fiction list ever since: Hanif Kureishi.*

---

9  Peter Simpson was Faber's finance director from 1985 to 2001.

## Robert McCrum to Sheila Lemon, literary agent, 1 October 1985

I've had an introduction to *My Beautiful Laundrette* together with
a long and very interesting prose piece from Hanif. I wonder if you
could let me see now a copy of the film script itself. I am, in principle,
very interested in the idea of a complete book.

## *The Wall Street Journal*, Tuesday, 1 October 1985

<u>Legendary Rock 'n' Roller Becomes a Man of Letters</u>
Matthew Evans – 'I was keen to change Faber's reputation, make it
more modern, get a more varied, unusual list . . . I grew up in the
1960s. I had all those early *Who* albums . . . Maybe that's my Achilles
heel. I'm a failed rock 'n' roll star. I'd sit in those first meetings and
think, 'That's *Pete Townshend* sitting over there.'

'Ah,' asked one elderly editor, 'is that the dashing Peter Townshend
who was almost engaged to Princess Margaret?'

John Bodley – 'He really writes good old-fashioned publishing
reports, very serious, very diligent reports on the books we're considering.'

## Matthew Evans to Ted Hughes, 17 January 1986

As you know Peter Townshend works at Faber and is also a friend. I
had lunch with Pete yesterday and he told me that he would like to
have a shot at turning *The Iron Man* into a musical.

I thought I would write to you at this early stage so that if you hate
the idea you can say so now. If you have no objection in principle he
would simply spend the next few months developing the idea before
there were further discussions. [. . .]

I have to say that I'm keen to encourage Pete. Not only has he got
a good track record with musicals but also since the development of
*Cats* has finished and it's now showing throughout the world, I do

miss the painful excitement of it and I'd love to be involved in another exploitation like that!

## Ted Hughes to Matthew Evans, 15 February 1986

If Pete Townshend can make even a rambling kitten of *The Iron Man*, I'll be more than delighted. Spur him on.

Pete Townshend and Ted Hughes, meeting outside the flat in Kensington that T. S. Eliot and Valerie moved into after their marriage.

*In early 1986, Tom Faber and Liesbeth van Houts, a Cambridge historian, decided to marry, telling only family and a few close friends. Liesbeth was therefore surprised to be approached in the University Library by a fellow of New Hall who congratulated her on the news. It turned out that Matthew Evans had told George Steiner, a man who had the reputation of being the greatest gossip in Cambridge, 'in strict confidence'.*

## Robert McCrum to Ellen Levine Literary Agency, 30 January 1986

I've come back from my trip to New York to find that Joanna Mackle in the Faber Publicity department has done a superb job on Garrison Keillor. In summary, and of course a much more detailed breakdown will be sent to both you and him very shortly, he is to appear at least three times on television, most notably on the top rating *Wogan* TV Show, no less than 8 times on radio, including the extremely prestigious *Kaleidoscope* and then in the *Sunday Times*, *The Times* (or perhaps *The Guardian*), the *Listener*, the *Radio Times*, and *Time Out* (all profiles). There is of course the *Book at Bedtime* for which we have to thank A. P. Watt. And that, of course, is to say nothing of the review coverage that we expect in the national and provincial press.

Joanna Mackle, in one of the hats that she made her trademark, had originally been introduced to Charles Monteith – and therefore Faber & Faber – by her father Henry. When she was appointed to the Board at the end of the decade, she became Faber's second female director.

### Robert McCrum to Garrison Keillor, 10 March 1986

I hope, by now, the news will have filtered back that *Lake Wobegon Days* is number one in the British bestseller list. That's an amazing achievement especially for a book and a writer who, until February 17, was virtually unknown here.

### Board minute, 15 May 1986

Mr Simpson made available revised estimates for the year to 31 March 1986, showing a net profit for the Group of only £541k before tax. This compared with the figure of £970k reported to the Board on 28 February 1986. [. . .]

The estimated pretax profit for Faber & Faber was £1,006k on 28 February, was £804k on 8 April and was currently £585k. The last figure was made up of £950k from *Cats*, perhaps £214k from *Spitting Image*, and a loss of say £579k on other activities. [. . .]

These results were noted without enthusiasm.

### Board minute, 25 July 1986

A schedule of the draft, unaudited, results for the year ending March 31, 1986 had been circulated by Mr Simpson before the meeting. It showed a further reduction in new pre-tax profit for the Group, from £541k according to the revised estimate dated 15 May 1986 to only £246k, despite net revenue from *Cats* amounting to £1,014k.

### Robert McCrum to Paul Auster, 30 October 1986

This is just an introductory note to say how delighted I am that Faber will be publishing your work in Britain. All at once, we seem to have contracts for five of your books! Our plan is to start with the marvellous *New York Trilogy* which, according to our present plan, we shall publish volume by volume to build up expectation and suspense. At the moment of writing I am virtually the only person at Fabers who has read everything, so the publishing plans for each volume are still fairly embryonic. As soon as there's more to report, I'll write again.

Once again, I'm so glad you are on this list, and I hope it will be a happy experience for you.

## Paul Auster to Robert McCrum, 4 November 1986

You have no idea how happy your letter made me – how happy I am that Fabers will be publishing my books. For as long as I can remember, that company has stood as a model for me: the image of publishing at its best. To think that my little books will be added to the Faber catalogue is nothing short of over-whelming. It's impossible to thank you enough.

## Sheila Lemon, Hanif Kureishi's agent, to Robert McCrum, 10 November 1986

Many apologies for the delay in confirming to you that, subject to agreement on terms, Hanif wishes to accept your offer to commission the new novel.

## Hanif Kureishi to Robert McCrum, 16 November 1986

I'm involved in so many things at the moment, but the thing I really want to do – write a novel – is no nearer starting. In fact when I think about it I get physical symptoms: acute anxiety and general fucked-upness. I have so much doubt about my own talent, which is usual in writers I suppose, but I find it terribly debilitating. But also it's difficult to get started because the enemies of promise are open to me: journalism, writing films and all the easier options that waste your time and life and keep you from doing what you should. I'm grateful that you and Faber have been so encouraging and supportive to me.

# 10: 1987–1990

# 'A week is a long time in publishing'

In many ways, the second half of the 1980s was a golden time for Faber & Faber. It won the Booker Prize two years in succession, with Peter Carey's *Oscar and Lucinda* in 1988 and Kazuo Ishiguro's *The Remains of the Day* in 1989. The following year, Faber was the first ever 'Publisher of the Year' (Matthew Evans never had much time for the sponsor of the award, *Publishing News*, and sent the trophy to the warehouse in Harlow, where he was, to say the least, an infrequent visitor). I find it mathematically interesting (it may even be significant) that in 1989 sales overtook Frank Morley's parabola for the first time since he had suggested it in 1931.

There is little hint of these triumphs in the short chapter that follows. For this was also a time of uncertainty. Every publisher in London seemed to be for sale, and Faber's very success only made it more attractive to potential bidders. Many of its authors were not yet convinced that the firm could be a good paperback publisher. Sales directors left the firm with alarming regularity. Every year the company was only making profits because of the money it received from *Cats*. Tom Faber, still Chairman of the Holding Company and essentially the owner of the firm, was frequently exasperated.

So this chapter really seeks to give a sense of the mood that led, in 1990, not to the sale of the company, but instead to a restructuring that made the company almost impossible to sell. Initially intended to enable employees to buy shares, this reorganisation brought in Valerie Eliot as a sympathetic shareholder in Faber & Faber on equal terms to the Holding Company. The move effectively meant that the Faber family gave up the ability to sell to a deep-pocketed competitor and has protected Faber's independence ever since. To my mind, it is the happy ending towards which this story has been building since 1924.

### Robert McCrum to author Maggie Gee, 23 January 1987

I have just torn up the long letter I wrote you immediately after our telephone conversation because I realised, as I was writing it, that there is really no publishing relationship between you and Fabers.

I like you, I admire your work, and I have done my best to promote it both within the company and outside and yet, to be frank, I feel you do not trust me, and that you have lost confidence in all of us. The more I think about it, the more I'm sure that you will be happier on another list, working with an editor you can trust and have confidence in. [...]

I shall always remain proud to have *The Burning Book* and *Light Years* in our backlist.

### Robert McCrum to Matthew Evans, February 1987

Finally, I've come back with the impression that apart from Eliot, Auden, Pound, Golding, Durrell and Larkin (and a few odds and ends), Faber and Faber 1987 is really a new company. That's fine, but I'm not willing to stay on the present terms. It's medieval to expect either you or me to spend years and years creating this list and have no stake in that beyond a comparatively small monthly pay-cheque. In the past, I've wanted to stick around to see what could be done. Well, that's over now. The ship is afloat. And I don't want to be on the bridge during the cruise, if I haven't got a stake in the ship itself.

*Robert's desire for a stake in the firm came at a time of frenetic takeover activity. Having taken over Routledge and Kegan Paul in 1985, Associated Book Publishers had then itself been bought by International Thomson in June 1987. Six months later,*

*Methuen, which had been part of ABP, was sold on to Octopus. Perhaps unsurprisingly, this was unsettling for one of Methuen's most prominent authors.*

## Matthew Evans to Judy Daish, literary agent, 22 February 1988

I don't quite know what's happening at Methuen since the take-over but I've heard one or two things on the grapevine that suggests that a number of authors may be a bit unhappy with the way things have developed. Without wishing to take advantage of any difficulties there may be, I thought I would drop you a line to say that if Harold Pinter might be looking for a more settled environment in which to publish his work, we would be absolutely delighted to have him at Fabers!

## Maggie Gee to Robert McCrum, 23 March 1987

Sorry to have taken so long replying to your letter but it left me feeling rather blank. I didn't, in fact, at any stage say that I had no confidence in Faber as a whole. My unhappiness was specifically related to the paperback of *Light Years* and the major changes which had taken place since the plans for it were drawn up – on the basis of which I originally made my decision to stay with Faber for the paperback.

*It is ironic that Nick Rankin, Maggie's husband, was having his first book published by Faber that summer. Since leaving Faber, Maggie Gee has published nine novels, a book of short stories and a memoir.*

## Antony Harwood, Caryl Phillips's new literary agent, to Robert McCrum, 5 May 1988

Here is Caz's novel, *Higher Ground*. We have strong views as to how it should be published. Looking forward to hearing from you.

### Antony Harwood to Robert McCrum, 13 May 1988

I thought it best to put something in writing even though we have talked; that is, that after much deliberation we do not feel able to accept your offer. As you know, our principal concern from the beginning has been <u>how</u> the novel will be published (rather than for how much, although this matters too) and we therefore feel compelled to look elsewhere.

### Robert McCrum to Roger Straus, 13 May 1988

You will not be surprised to hear that Caz has not accepted our offer and is going elsewhere. Do let me know what happens with you. We are of course sorry, but we feel he'd made up his mind before the book was delivered. However, Harold Pinter joining the list sort of makes up for this . . .

### Antony Harwood to Robert McCrum, 18 May 1988

I am writing to let you know that we have now accepted an offer for the novel from Viking Penguin. You know that we wanted a Penguin paperback at the start; I should also mention for the record that their offer is substantially better than Faber's.

*The departures of writers like Maggie Gee and Caz Phillips, together with Faber's disappointing financial performance, highlighted problems with the firm's strategy of 'vertical integration' (publishing both hardbacks and paperbacks).*

### Matthew Evans, Memorandum, 14 June 1988

<u>Need for Action</u>
It is quite clear that we have not achieved our objective of making a profit from publishing, and in addition the full benefit of *Cats* income is not having the impact it should on our cash flow . . . The time has

come to recognise that certain major changes instituted in the past are not working, and to address the problem to secure the future of Faber's as an independent firm. [. . .]

We must remember that in 1987/88 although we just missed our revised sales budget there was a shortfall from the original budget by nearly a million pounds. This, for a company of Faber's size, is a staggering shortfall. [. . .]

I continue to believe in vertical integration as the only way ahead for the firm. [. . .]

It is significant that most of Faber's competitors who have been taken over are firms that do not have strong paperback lists. The problem therefore was not with the idea of vertical integration, but in the implementation within Faber. [. . .]

We are still a hardback house, selling hardbacks in soft covers, rather than a genuine hardback publisher, and a genuine paperback publisher. [. . .]

This is a very serious problem, as it raises doubts both within and outside the firm, about Faber's credibility as a paperback publisher. The cracks are beginning to show. Three years ago we could have published Timothy Mo,[1] but Mo insisted on separating out hardback rights from paperback rights with Faber's doing a hardback, and a paperback being published by somebody else. [. . .]

Kazuo Ishiguro, with whom we've just signed a contract for his new novel, was concerned enough to have talked at length to Robert and to me about Faber's as a paperback publisher. [. . .]

We have just lost Caryl Phillips, a young black writer who Robert has nurtured through two novels and one non-fiction book.

---

1 Timothy Mo was a novelist who, at the time of Matthew's memorandum, had been twice shortlisted for the Booker Prize, and would be again.

Peter Carey won the 1988 Booker Prize for *Oscar and Lucinda*.
© Adam Butler/PA Archive/PA Images

## Tom Faber, Holding Company Chairman's Statement for 1988, September 1988

For some years now, since the full success of *Cats* became apparent, the budgets which are prepared each spring have shown pre-tax profits of over £1m and an overdraft declining towards zero, and the single most important reason why these expectations have never yet been fulfilled is that we do not sell enough books. [. . .]

Shareholders will remember the plans for Faber Music which I described in a confidential memorandum dated 27 November 1987. They involved the appointment of Mr Robin Boyle as Chairman in succession to Dr Mitchell, and the formation of a new Company, Faber Music Holdings. Mr Boyle duly joined Faber Music in December (together with his colleague Mr Tom Pasteur on a part-time basis). [. . .]

I expect to have much more to say about Faber Music Holdings in next year's Statement, but I can say at this point that Faber Music is prospering under its new leadership.

*Tom Pasteur's involvement in the management of Faber Music brought him to the attention of Matthew Evans, who, in 1989, asked Tom to prepare his own report on how to improve the profitability of Faber & Faber.*

## Tom Pasteur, review of Faber & Faber, April 1989

Management have not been successful . . . in adapting the business to the rapidly changing market and competitive environments and in the application of modern management techniques for this purpose. The most serious weakness is the absence of a strong and stable team of senior managers across all the functions of the Company. In particular the long saga of the appointments to the position of Sales Director and the current absence of both a Sales Director and a Distribution Director are potentially disastrous at a time when the Company faces a bookselling and publishing revolution.

Lower down the scale, at departmental level, management structures and discipline are extremely loose, and with one or two exceptions, there is no real profit consciousness.

The absence of effective management shows up in the financial results. . . . *Cats* income has helped to soften the blow, but it has also had the effect of delaying the corrective action needed.

*To meet Tom Pasteur's criticism that staff in Faber & Faber needed to be more profit-conscious, and to help retain key individuals like Robert McCrum, the company decided to set up an Employee Share Ownership Plan (ESOP). Such a scheme would have lost its tax advantages, however, if the Holding*

*Company retained a majority of Faber & Faber. The logic pointed towards finding a third shareholder, to sit alongside the Holding Company and the employees. That led to Valerie Eliot and 'SET Copyrights', which held T. S. Eliot's copyrights and therefore received the royalties from* Cats. *Negotiations commenced between Tom Faber and Valerie's advisers.*

Matthew Evans's talent as a cricketer undoubtedly helped his relationship with Harold Pinter, who tried to recruit him for his own team, 'Gaieties'.

## Matthew Evans to Harold Pinter, 20 April 1989

Caroline and I would love to come on Sunday 7 May at 7 o'clock to meet President Ortega,[2] and we will see you there.

## *Evening Standard*, 22 June 1989

A week is a long time in publishing. Two weeks ago brought news of the surprise takeover of Century Hutchinson by the American giant Random House, who almost two years ago stepped in to save the distinguished but ailing Chatto, Cape and Bodley Head combine. [. . .]

Meanwhile, who will buy Gollancz – the venerable company recently put on the market by Livia Gollancz, daughter of founder Victor? Simon and Schuster, who failed to nab Century Hutchinson and who badly need to beef up their British subsidiary, or perhaps Presses de la Cité of France? We'll know in a couple of months. By that time, the persistent rumours about Faber and Faber – whose only real income derives from *Cats*, the Lloyd Webber musical based on T. S. Eliot's poems – may have come to pass. Is it really to be sold over the head of Chairman Matthew Evans?

As they say, watch this space.

> *The short answer to that question was 'no'. Nevertheless, the speculation that Faber might go the same way as Methuen was worrying Harold Pinter.*

## Matthew Evans to Tom Faber, 27 June 1989

If you could write to Harold Pinter about the rumours I would be grateful.

I should warn you that he's quite paranoid so if you could make your letter totally unambiguous, I think this would be a great help!

---

2   Daniel Ortega, president of Nicaragua.

*My father wrote as definitively as he could, receiving an
enthusiastic reply from Harold Pinter which showed how
keen he was that his new books would be published by an
independent firm. He also expressed the hope that Faber might
eventually take over his backlist. A year later, following a legal
argument between Pinter and Methuen, orchestrated behind the
scenes by Matthew Evans, Faber were publishing all Pinter's
books and plays.*

### Faber Board minute, Thursday, 29 June 1989

Tom Faber assured the Board that the Company was not for sale. It
was also agreed that the Chairman would address members of staff of
the Company to assure them that contrary to rumours in the press
the Company was not up for sale.

Lorna Ishiguro congratulates her husband on winning the Booker prize
in 1989 for *The Remains of the Day*.

© Alex Lentati/Associated Newspapers/REX/Shutterstock

## Press Release: THE FUTURE OF FABER AND FABER, 17 November 1989

The shareholders of the Faber Group have recently approved a scheme which is designed to safeguard the prosperity and continued independence of the publishing house of Faber and Faber Ltd. [. . .]

The central feature of the scheme is the sale by the Group's Holding Company of over 50 per cent of the shares in Faber and Faber Ltd to Directors and other members of the staff, through an employee benefit trust, and to Mrs T. S. Eliot, through SET Copyrights Ltd.

Mrs Eliot already has shares in the Holding Company and will become, through SET, a major shareholder in Faber and Faber Ltd. She will also participate as a Director.

It is the intention of all those participating that Faber and Faber's commitment to editorial excellence across a wide range of books, especially in new fiction, poetry and plays, should be as strong as ever.

The scheme is designed to assure all Faber authors, and Faber's friends throughout the book trade generally, that the Company is determined to live up to the hopes and intentions of its founder, Sir Geoffrey Faber.

# Afterword

'Here ends the history of Faber & Faber'? Well no, of course not. Faber & Faber is still independent. It continues to publish exciting and important books. Since 1990, Faber authors have won eight more Nobel prizes: five for writers who were already on the list then (Derek Walcott, Seamus Heaney, Harold Pinter, Mario Vargas Llosa and Kazuo Ishiguro) and three for relative newcomers (Wisława Szymborska, Günter Grass and Orhan Pamuk). Booker (or, more recently, Man Booker) Prizes have gone to Peter Carey (again), DBC Pierre and, in 2018, Anna Burns. She thereby became Faber's first ever female winner of the prize, itself an indication of the firm having travelled a very necessary distance from the chauvinistic 1980s. The same could be said of Barbara Kingsolver's victory in the Orange Prize for Women's Fiction in 2010. Ted Hughes and Seamus Heaney each won the Whitbread Book of the Year twice in the 1990s; more recently, Sebastian Barry has done the same with its 'Costa' successor. There have been too many poetry prizes to mention.

So how did Faber & Faber hang on to that independence, when all its contemporaries and competitors were being swallowed by conglomerates? The standard answer is that it has been lucky. It's hard to portray *Cats*, in particular, as anything but a huge slice of luck. On that basis, of course, the firm has been frequently lucky – the weekend with Siegfried Sassoon that led to *Memoirs of a Fox-Hunting Man*, Charles Monteith happening to grab *Lord of the Flies* from the slush pile, John Seymour insisting to Dorling Kindersley that Faber should publish *The Complete Book of Self-Sufficiency*.

That repeated 'luck' points to something else: a publishing philosophy that, without ignoring commercial imperatives, has always focused on excellence and the long term, whether that applies to relationships with authors that last for decades, or to books that enter the literary canon. A philosophy like that can lead to books that continue selling; Faber's backlist has given it the income at the core of its financial stability.

Philosophy alone, however, is not enough. It needs to be allied to good editorial taste. One of the most striking aspects of this history, perhaps, is that the great publishing decisions were not made by my grandfather, although the firm carries his name. I think he can probably be given some credit for the genesis of *Old Possum*, by encouraging Eliot to turn his attention to children's verse, but other than that few of the books that he acquired are still generating income for the firm today. He was not, in the end, a brilliant editor. Instead, he was something much more important for the longevity of the company he founded: he was a brilliant recruiter, harnessing the talents of a remarkable set of individuals in the 1930s – Eliot, de la Mare, Stewart, Morley, Crawley and Kennerley – and then doing it again with du Sautoy and Monteith in the post-war years. This is what really gave the firm its staying power. When Geoffrey died in 1961, the firm could carry on without a stumble; it had never been a one-man show.

Two decades later, the firm was in danger of losing its relevance. Once again, it was a brilliant recruit – Robert McCrum – who brought back editorial flair. Needless to say, I was delighted to learn of the (small but important) role my mother Penny played in his arrival. She died before Robert's full impact had become apparent, but I remember her excitement about Milan Kundera and Mario Vargas Llosa in particular. Probably the most important realisation that writing this book has brought home to me is that a firm like Faber can never just sit back and relax on the cushion provided by the great writing of its past; it has to combine commitment to its authors with regular editorial renewal.

A continuous stream of excellent books would not have been enough, however, if Faber had carried on sharing the income they

generated with a paperback publisher. So I must also give credit to
the prescience of the people running the firm – first in the 1950s,
later in the 1980s – who saw that Faber had to publish both hardbacks and paperbacks. This was the crucial business decision that
really marked it out from its competitors, and the reason it was able
to survive when they could not.

The ability to survive is one thing; resisting the temptation to sell
is another. And that brings me back, in the end, to the Faber family,
and its role as owner. Geoffrey Faber had been scarred by his experience with the Gwyers. He was determined never to cede control to an
outsider, and he passed that determination on to his children, in particular my father, culminating in the family's decision not to take the
millions that were undoubtedly on offer in 1990, but instead to create a shareholding structure that effectively gave up that possibility.

Employee share ownership was the original reason for the Holding Company giving up control, but it had to be abandoned within
a few years. Today, the Holding Company, now renamed 'Geoffrey
Faber Holdings' and still controlled by the Faber family, owns exactly
50 per cent of Faber & Faber; an exactly equal shareholding is held in
a trust set up by Valerie Eliot. Both shareholders want the company
to remain independent; when required, they have been able to share
the burden of additional investment. Short of a catastrophic failure,
or a fundamental change in the nature of publishing, it is hard to
imagine any circumstances under which Faber would be sold – and
that is because of the arrangements put in place in 1990.

That decision to create a structure that safeguarded Faber from
sale may have been rooted in emotion, but it was also inherently
rational. It is true that, being relatively small, Faber & Faber will
have more variability in its financial performance than its larger
competitors, but as a private company with sympathetic shareholders it can be reasonably relaxed about that. The really important
point is that Faber's independence makes a fundamental difference to
how it publishes. Its culture remains vibrantly focused on great lit-

erature in a way that would be impossible to maintain if it were just a division in a larger company. Some of the best people in publishing are attracted to work there. On the verge of its ninetieth birthday, the firm is nimble, with an entrepreneurial spirit that belies its age. Readers recognise that the Faber brand actually means something. Most of all, Faber's independence is part of what makes it a natural home for some of the world's most significant writers. Faber & Faber is worth more to us, its private owners, than it could ever be as part of a conglomerate.

And what if I'm wrong? Perhaps there is a purchaser somewhere who would be prepared to pay a sum so large it defies economics. Well, I think my father was right to suppose that an extra bit of money probably wouldn't make his descendants much happier for very long. Every day, on the other hand, we can enjoy the way Faber & Faber lies at the heart of Britain's literary life. It is quite something to be able to be proud of your name.

# Appendix:
## Faber & Faber Sales and Profit History,
### 1929–1990

Most of the columns below should be self-explanatory. I have included one for 'gross dividend' because it is probably the best short-hand way of showing how prosperous the firm felt at the time as well as the return to the shareholders. The final column shows sales as predicted in Frank Morley's 1931 *jeu d'esprit*, 'Dr Morley's Parabolic Prediction or Futurity Revealed'. This noted how sales from 1926 to 1931 had followed the curve, $y = 2x^2+t$, where x was the number of years since 1926 and t was the actual sales in 1926.

| Year | Actual Sales (£'000) | Pre-tax profit/ (loss) (£'000) | Gross dividend (£'000) | 'Dr Morley's' predicted sales (£'000) |
|---|---|---|---|---|
| 1926 | 16 | N/A | N/A | 16 |
| 1927 | 18 | N/A | N/A | 18 |
| 1928 | 24 | N/A | N/A | 24 |
| 1929 (full year) | 34 | N/A | N/A | 34 |
| 1929 (Apr to Dec) | 25.4 | (2.6) | 0 | |
| 1930 | 50.9 | 2.4 | 0 | 48 |
| 1931 | 51.5 | (2.2) | 0 | 66 |
| 1932 | 56.6 | 0.0 | 0 | 88 |
| 1933 | 55.2 | 1.1 | 0 | 114 |
| 1934 | 61.8 | (2.3) | 0 | 144 |
| 1935 | 76.5 | 4.6 | 0 | 178 |
| 1936 | 94.9 | 3.5 | 0 | 216 |
| 1937 | 73.4 | (2.0) | 0 | 258 |
| 1938 | 76.9 | (1.5) | 0 | 304 |

| | | | | |
|---|---|---|---|---|
| 1939 | 83.8 | 3.1 | 0.6 | 354 |
| 1940 | 82.8 | 3.7 | 1.2 | 408 |
| 1941 | 133.4 | 19.6 | 4.9 | 466 |
| 1942 | 224.6 | 52.6 | 3.7 | 528 |
| 1943 | 364.3 | 95.9 | 6.2 | 594 |
| 1944 | 316.5 | 83.4 | 6.2 | 664 |
| 1945 | 357.6 | 94.4 | 6.2 | 738 |
| 1946 | 406.8 | 78.3 | 8.2 | 816 |
| 1947 | 310.7 | 9.5 | 5.6 | 898 |
| 1948 | 308.3 | 10.3 | 5.6 | 984 |
| 1949 | 277.8 | 8.9 | 5.6 | 1,074 |
| 1950 | 297.5 | 7.5 | 5.6 | 1,168 |
| 1951 | 338.2 | (6.5) | 0 | 1,266 |
| 1952 | 362.2 | 11.1 | 6.2 | 1,368 |
| 1953 | 358.5 | 10.3 | 5.6 | 1,474 |
| 1954 | 380.3 | 13.3 | 5.6 | 1,584 |
| 1955 | 371.7 | 14.3 | 6.5 | 1,698 |
| 1956 | 395.1 | 7.6 | 5.0 | 1,816 |
| 1957 | 455.9 | 13.5 | 7.2 | 1,938 |
| 1958 | 510.7 | 21.3 | 8.7 | 2,064 |
| 1959 | 589.4 | 45.0 | 10.1 | 2,194 |
| 1960 | 667.8 | 36.9 | 9.6 | 2,328 |
| 1961 | 673.3 | 38.7 | 9.6 | 2,466 |
| 1962 | | 38 | 12.3 | 2,608 |
| 1963 | | 41 | 13.8 | 2,754 |
| 1964 | | 57 | 16.1 | 2,904 |
| 1965 | | 70 | 16.1 | 3,058 |
| 1966 | | 88 | 18.5 | 3,216 |
| 1967 | 1,616 | 87 | 18.5 | 3,378 |
| 1968 | 1,707 | 56 | 18.5 | 3,544 |
| 1969 | 1,814 | 55 | 18.5 | 3,714 |
| 1970 | 1,851 | 4 | 0 | 3,888 |
| 1971 | 2,147 | 63 | 9 | 4,066 |
| 1972 | 1,948 | 171 | 12.9 | 4,248 |
| 1973 | 2,087 | 178 | 13.9 | 4,434 |
| 1974 | 2,283 | 138 | 9.4 | 4,624 |
| 1975 | 2,562 | 8 | 0 | 4,818 |

| 1976 | 2,769 | 177 | 9.5 | 5,016 |
|---|---|---|---|---|
| 1978 (Dec to Mar) | 3,911 | 394 | 19.4 | 5,424 |
| 1979 | 3,928 | 566 | 27.0 | 5,634 |
| 1980 | 4,010 | 166 | 29.4 | 5,848 |
| 1981 | 3,932 | (61) | 24.0 | 6,066 |
| 1982 | 4,797 | 234 | 24.0 | 6,288 |
| 1983 | 4,575 | (110) | 0 | 6,514 |
| 1984 | 4,421 | (306) | 0 | 6,744 |
| 1985 | 5,432 | 382 | 48.0 | 6,978 |
| 1986 | 5,971 | 296 | 60.0 | 7,216 |
| 1987 | 6,996 | 484 | 72.0 | 7,458 |
| 1988 | 6,876 | 388 | 72.0 | 7,704 |
| 1989 | 7,966 | 568 | 72.0 | 7,954 |
| 1990 | 8,808 | 491 | 78.0 | 8,208 |

1926–9  Based on the actual sales figures for the book business used by Frank Morley to produce 'Dr Morley's Parabolic Prediction'. The year 1929 includes three months of such sales by Faber & Gwyer. It is impossible in these years to split out profits or dividends attributable to the books business alone.

1929–52  Based on a schedule prepared in 1953 for the purposes of a share valuation.

1953–61  Based on audited accounts for Faber & Faber Ltd, including a trading account that shows sales.

1962–6  Based on audited accounts for Faber & Faber Ltd, but with no sales information.

1967–90  The restructuring in 1968 meant that Faber & Faber changed its name to Faber & Faber (Publishers) Ltd, and became a holding company, with two main subsidiaries, Faber Music Ltd, and a newly formed Faber & Faber Ltd, which took over the book-publishing business. The results for these years are based on consolidated accounts for Faber & Faber (Publishers) Ltd and therefore include the results from both music and books publishing.

Until 1976 Faber & Faber's financial years ended in December. It then moved to a March year-end, so that there are no results for 1977, but a fifteen-month period ending March 1978.

# Acknowledgements

A book like this would not be possible without the Faber archive and my primary thanks must go to its archivist, Robert Brown, who has been unfailingly helpful both in his responses to my requests and in his suggestions of new potential sources, as has Nancy Fulford in the T. S. Eliot archive. Both these archives are private and are not generally open to public enquiry. My brother Matthew alerted me to gems as he came across them in family correspondence. Similar thanks go to Jane Kirby, the Faber archive's cataloguer, and to Robert's predecessors, the late John Bodley, Colin Penman (to whom I take this opportunity to apologise for being such a bad manager) and, above all, the late Constance Cruickshank (née Sheldon), whose careful stewardship lies at the root of the Faber archive's current health.

My wife Amanda initially urged me to write this book and the idea was reinforced in a conversation with Mary Cannam. It was then commissioned by Mitzi Angel, with the support of Stephen Page. Mitzi has very sadly now left Faber for the murky world of corporate publishing but I've been lucky that the task of editing me was taken over by Laura Hassan, ably assisted by Ella Griffiths. Laura's comments have immeasurably improved the book. Other important and supportive early readers have been Amanda (again), my stepmother Liesbeth van Houts, my sisters Polly and Henrietta, Alex Bowler, Robert McCrum, Peter Straus, Giles de la Mare and Sue Smithson (née Morley). All have been helpful and John Haffenden in particular has saved me from errors and has been generous with his own immense knowledge of T. S. Eliot and his work. Kate Ward is responsible for the beautiful text design and overseeing pre-press, including excellent copy-editing by Jane Robertson, proofreading by Peter McAdie and indexing by Sarah Ereira. Pedro Nelson is managing production and Eleanor Crow commissioned the lovely cover artwork from Elliot Elam and designed the endpapers. Katryna Storace took my author photo. Hannah Styles has been helping me with permissions and I am looking forward to working with Rachel Alexander and Josh Smith on publicity and with John Grindrod, Dave Woodhouse, Myles Poynton and the rest of Faber's sales and marketing team.

The theft of my laptop when I was about six months into my research could have been a disaster, especially when I then discovered that my online back-up service had stopped working about a year earlier. I was saved by the kind initiative of the Eliot estate and its then typist, Debbie Whitfield, whose magnificent assistance enabled me to recover all my lost work within a few weeks. The estate's trustees Clare Reihill and Judith Hooper have continued to be hugely supportive.

Among my sources were several unpublished memoirs or later letters and emails. I quote none of them explicitly in the way I do for contemporaneous documents, but attentive readers will notice the debt I owe to Enid Faber (who was also, incidentally, a wonderful grandmother), Geoffrey Faber, Charles Stewart, Frank Morley, Morley Kennerley, Andrew Franklin, Humphrey Beckett (who told me more about my Great-Aunt Gwynedd), Peter du Sautoy, Giles de la Mare (again), Peter Crawley, Sarah Goad (who told me about Thom Gunn's choice of clothing), Tom Faber and Robert McCrum (again). The only published source I have used that is not already highlighted in the text is Joseph Connolly's beautiful *Eighty Years of Book Cover Design* (Faber, 2009).

Finally, I wish to thank and acknowledge all the authors and estates who so kindly gave me permission to quote them in this book. I list them below in the order in which they are first quoted, together with the relevant copyright information where supplied, but note that all work published here for the first time will generally remain in copyright until seventy years after publication, or seventy years after the death of the writer, whichever is later. In particular, all the work written in the course of their employment by Faber employees or directors with service contracts remains the copyright of Faber & Faber.

Thanks to: Lady Baker (material written by members of the Faber family), The Eliot Estate (© Set Copyrights Ltd), Fred Davidson (The Estate of Charles Whibley), Vince Freedman (The Estate of Barnett Freedman), Edward Mendelson (© The Estate of W. H. Auden), The Society of Authors as the Literary Representative of the Alison Uttley Literary Property Trust, William Pryor (The Estate of Gwen Raverat), Jonathan Lloyd at Curtis Brown (Spencer Curtis Brown), Curtis Brown Group Ltd, London, on behalf of The Beneficiaries of the Estates of C.P. Snow (Copyright © C.P. Snow 1939, 1947, 1949), Gerald Durrell (Copyright © Gerald Durrell 1952, 1953) and Lawrence Durrell (Copyright © Lawrence Durrell 1956), The Society of Authors as the Literary Representative of the Estate of Philip Larkin, Oluyinka Tutuola (The Estate of Amos Tutuola), Stephen and John Monteith (Charles Monteith), the Warden and Fellows of All Souls (The Estate of John Sparrow), Judy Carver and the Golding family (Copyright © William Golding Limited. All rights reserved), Jan Morris, Edward Beckett (The Estate of Samuel Beckett), Clive Wilmer and August Kleinzahler (The Estate of Thom Gunn), Carol Hughes (The Estate of Ted Hughes), Frieda Hughes (The Estate of Sylvia Plath), Carol Heaton at Greene & Heaton (Elaine Greene), Clare Flook and Jane McLeod (The Estate of P. D. James), Madeline McGahern (The Estate of John McGahern), Tom Stoppard, Colin Matthews (© Britten–Pears Foundation), the Heaney family (The Estate of Seamus Heaney), Douglas Dunn, John Carey, Currey & Co, The Estate of John Seymour, Paul Muldoon, Peter Carey, Kazuo Ishiguro, Michael Berkeley (Deborah Rogers), Milan Kundera, John Lloyd, Maggie Gee, Wendy Cope, Vikram Seth, Paul Auster, Hanif Kureishi, Antony Harwood. The letter from Virginia Woolf is extracted from *The Sickle Side of the Moon: The Letters of Virginia Woolf: Volume V 1932–1935* by Virginia Woolf published by

Chatto & Windus. Reproduced by permission of The Random House Group Ltd. © 1982. Excerpts from unpublished letters written by Bob Giroux to T. S. Eliot. Copyright © 2019 by Farrar, Straus and Giroux. Printed by permission of Farrar, Straus and Giroux. Excerpt from letter #135 'To T. S. Eliot' Thanksgiving [November 25, 1948] from *The Letters of Robert Lowell* edited by Saskia Hamilton. Copyright © 2005 by Harriet Lowell and Sheridan Lowell. Reprinted by permission of Farrar, Straus and Giroux. Excerpt from an unpublished letter written by Robert Lowell to Charles Monteith dated 26 February 1965. Copyright © 2019 by Harriet Lowell and Sheridan Lowell. Printed by permission of Farrar, Straus and Giroux on behalf of the Robert Lowell Estate.

Every effort has been made to trace the estates of other people quoted, and the publishers would be pleased to hear from them so that they can be properly acknowledged in future editions.

# Index

Figures in **bold** refer to pages with illustrations.

AE Prize, 272
Aeschylus, 191
All Souls College: dining at, 2, 145, 157, 264; Eliot's election bid, 13, 27; estates bursar, 1, 11n, 132, 145, 168; fellows, 1–2, 13, 25, 29, 205, 211, 213, 326; lawn, **206**; Minsted estate, 167–8; subwarden, 145; surveyor, 11n, 179; warden, 170, 215
Allen & Unwin (UK publisher), 319, 339–40
*The Ariel Poems* series, 43, 68, **69**, 272n
Arthur Faber Trust Estate, 5–8, 29, 58, 62
Ash, Kathleen, 324
Asher, Aaron, 360, 372
Associated Book Publishers (ABP), 388–9
Atterbury, Jasmine (Cleaver), 296
Auden, W. H.: *The Ascent of F6 and On the Frontier*, 250; death, **332**; Eliot's view of, 42–3, 61; Faber party for, **256**; first contact with Eliot at Faber, 42–3; Geoffrey's view of, 120; *Iceland*, 110, 118; judge of New York poetry award, 244, 245, 246; *Look, Stranger!*, 118–19; *Poems*, 75, 85; published by Faber, 75, **86**, 110, 129, 143, 374, 388; wartime in New York, 143, **144**
Auster, Paul, 385–6
*The Authors Handbook* for 1935, 99–100

Balcells, Carmen, 366–7
Balcon, Jill, 336
Barnes, Djuna: *The Antiphon*, 346; *Nightwood*, 107, 109–10
Bawden, Edward, 84
Beckett, Eric, 42
Beckett, Samuel: censorship issues, 236, 238, 243–4, 279; Nobel Prize, 259, 303; *Play*, 279; *Waiting for Godot*, 236, 238, 243–4, 279
Bedford Estate, 22, 179, 189
Benn, Sir Ernest, 40, 42, 47

Benn, Tony, **376**
Benn Brothers, 40
Bennett, Alan, 299–300, 301–2
Berryman, John, 236–7, 325
Birrell, Francis, 93
Blackie & Son, 147
Blake, George (Faber editorial director): Faber role, 74, 87; Faber shares, 74, 87–8, 90, 95–6; Geoffrey's letter on wartime publishing, 140–1; *Strand* editor, 71, 74
Bland, David (Faber production director), 176–7, 183, **253**, 275, 294
Blond, Anthony, 285
Bodley, John (Faber editorial director), 348–9, 362, 382
Bodley Head (UK publisher), 95, 99, 333, 395
Bond, Michael, *A Bear Called Paddington*, 247–8
*Book at Bedtime*, 384
Book Committee: 'bearded stranger' at, **107**; cracker explosions, 101–2; du Sautoy's report to, 344; Eliot's reports to, 73, 76, 118, 119; Eliot's sketches, **253**; Eliot's withdrawal from, 222, 226; first meeting, 32; formation, 31; Geoffrey's retirement, 232, 233; lunchtime meetings, 83; McCrum's report to, 356; meetings during Three-Day Week, 336; membership, 31–2; Monteith's report to, 229; role, 104–5, 209, 329; response to memo on Book Pricing Policy, 326; wartime meetings, 155, **176–7**
Book Marketing Council, 370
Book Society Choice, 191, 199
Booker Prize (Man Booker), 387, 391n, **392**, **396**, 399
*The Bookseller*, 119, 147, 349, 374–5
Boston, Lucy, 295
Bottome, Phyllis, 182
Boyle, Robin, 392
Brace, Donald (US publisher at Harcourt Brace), 67, 101, 235

Bradbury, Malcolm, 352, 354–5
Brentford, William Joynson-Hicks, Viscount, 97
Brink, André, 367
Britten, Benjamin, 259, 279–80, 282
Brooksbank, Eileen, 346–7
Buck, Pearl, 126
Burdett, Sir Henry, 1, 113n
Burgess, Anthony, 262
Burns, Anna, 399
Butler, Rab, 134

Caetani, Marguerite, 43
Calder, Liz, 370
Carey, John, 304–5, 325, 330–1
Carey, Peter: Booker Prizes, 387, **392**, 399; *The Fat Man in History*, 354–5; *Illywhacker*, 377; *Oscar and Lucinda*, 387, **392**; published by Faber, 351, 353, 379; *War Crimes*, 351
Carl XVI Gustaf, King of Sweden, **373**
*Cats* (musical): book of the show, 363; development, 355, 382–3; Faber income from, 353–4, 362, 365, 374, 385, 387, 390, 392, 393, 395, 399; Faber investment, 360; lyricist's share of the royalties, 353–4, 394; publication of music, 365; success, 353–4, 363, 392
Cecil, Lord David, 325
Century & Co. (US publisher), 65, 77
Century Hutchinson (UK publisher), 395
Cerf, Bennett, 119
Chamberlain, Neville, 146
Chatto & Windus (UK publisher), 23, 103, 333, 350, 395
Churchill, Winston, 127, 146, 148, 181
Clarke, Desmond (Faber sales director), 370, 375, 376, 378
Coady, Frances (Faber editor), 353, 372, 377
Cochrane, Louise, 175
Cohen, Harry, 52, 61, 62
Colin, Rosica, 236
Colindale, Harry, *They Want their Wages*, 17
Colmer, Mrs (editor of *The Nursing Mirror*), 21, 24n, 40
Colt, Brace, 7, 8–9
Comfort, Sydney, 82
Cooper, Louise (literary agent), 370, 371
Cope, Wendy, 370, 378, 379–80
Corlett, John, 252
Costa Book of the Year, 399

Crawley, Grace, 268
Crawley, Peter (Faber sales director, succeeding his father): Book Committee, 326; character, 312; *Everywoman*, 305–6; Faber directorship, 271; Faber sale question, 312; Faber shares, 275; father's illness, 188; Geoffrey's retirement, 314; managing editor disagreement, 333–4; publicity for *Poetry Introduction 2*, 324; relationship with Matthew Evans, 328–9; relationship with Peter du Sautoy, 309; resignation, 335; search for new premises, 298–9; succeeding father as sales director, 271–2; successor, 337; visiting Enid, 309–10
Crawley, William (Faber sales director and children's book editor): Book Committee, **176–7**, **253**; children's list, 91, 266, 295; Faber directorship, 160, 208; Faber paperbacks, 252; illness, 188, 251; offices, 168; Pearl Buck publication question, 126; proposal of de la Mare as chairman, 257; recruitment, 400; report on *Old Possum* sales, 136; retirement, 188, 266, 268, **268–9**, 295; sales director, 91, 188, 220, 400; son, 188, 272
Cresswell, Helen, 295
Crime Writers' Association, 308
*Criterion* magazine: acquired by Faber & Gwyer, 12, 13, 34, 35; Eliot's editorship, 1–2, 10, 12, 13, 16, 32, 70, 77, 83, 122–3; financial backing, 35n; termination, 122–3
*Criterion Miscellany*, 70, 75, 97
Curtis Brown, Spencer (literary agent), 197–9, 215, 218–21

*Daily Express*, 243
*Daily Mail*, 243
*Daily Telegraph*, 282
Daish, Judy (literary agent), 370, 389
Davey, F. Noel, 250
Day-Lewis, Cecil, 105, 336
de la Mare, Giles (Faber editorial director), 42, 217–18, 314, **340**, 358
de la Mare, Katta, 160, 194, 309
de la Mare, Richard (Dick or dlM; Faber editorial director and chairman): achievements, 260; appearance, **33**, **261**, **340**; *The Ariel Poems* series, 43; art list, 65; Board of Faber & Faber, 66, 74, 208; Board of Faber & Gwyer, 31, 32, **33**, 47; Book Committee, **176–7**; chairman

of Faber, 200, 233, 250, 252, 254, 257–8, 311, 314–18; character, 15, 65, 233, 260–1, 312; contact with artists, 68, 77, 82–3, 84, 192–3; Crawley's directorship, 271; 'Faber & Faber' dinner, 70; Faber finance concerns, 204–5, 309, 310–11; farming list, 65, 139, 209, 346n; gardening list, 209, 346n; health, 281, 312, 317; joining Faber & Gwyer, 15, 17, 400; *Memoirs of a Fox-Hunting Man*, xiii, 50, 54, 56–7; Monteith's appointment, 211, 217; music publishing, 279–80, 282; porcelain collection, 310n; president, 311, 318, **340**; production manager, 31, 65, 71, 183, 208; publishing criteria, 178; recruitment, 400; relationship with David Jones, 82–3, 118; relationship with du Sautoy, 281, 303–4; relationship with Geoffrey, 42, 172, 228, 251, 252, 254; relationship with Gwen Raverat, 192–3, 194; relationship with Sassoon, 50, 54; resignation of chairmanship, 318; retirement question, 309–10, 311–18; salary and bonuses, 66, 260; shareholding, 275; son's career, 217–18, 314; *Swedish Iron Ore*, 135, 251; visiting Enid, 309; wartime experiences, 160; wartime paper rationing issues, **176–7**, 177–8; wartime plans, 153; wartime premises, 179, 181; wartime taxation issues, 171

de la Mare, Walter: honours, 228; illustrations by Gwen Raverat, 192; naming Faber & Faber, 64; *Peacock Pie*, 250; reviews of Geoffrey's poetry, 1; son's career, 15; work included in the *Ariel Poems* series, 42

Dibblee, George, 2

Done, J. J., 11, 167, 179

Dorling, Christopher, 344

Dorling Kindersley, 344–5, 399

Drummond, V. H., 218

du Sautoy, Peter (Faber director and chairman): assistant, 293, 303; Book Committee, **253**; censorship issues, 283; chairman of Faber, 315, 317, 318, 319, 327; character, 315; Eliot's view of, 208, **253**; Faber Board, **340**; Faber merger issue, 339; forward planning, 327, 328; joining Faber, 181, 182, 400; Queen Square offices, 319, 320; relationship with Dick de la Mare, 281, 303–4, 309–10, 314; relationship with Geoffrey, 188; relationship with Peter Crawley, 309, 333; relationship with Snow, 186–7, 191, 197–9, 303; relationship with Ted Hughes, 276; resignation issue, 304; retirement, 347; *Self-Sufficiency*, 344–5; Steiner's *Death of Tragedy*, 262; vice-chairman of Faber, 257–8; view of 'Faber Paper Covered Editions', **249**; view of Faber sale proposal, 312; view of shareholders, 379; visiting Enid, 309

DuBuisson, Peter (Faber non-executive director), 319, **340**, 367–8

Duff Cooper, 127, 213

Duke, Frances, 42

Dunn, Douglas, 300, 302

Dunne, J. W., *An Experiment with Time*, 250

Durrell, Gerald: agent, 215, 218–19, 220, 221; Faber's loss, 220–1, 303; *The Overloaded Ark*, 203–4, 215, 218; *Three Singles to Adventure*, 218–19, 220

Durrell, Lawrence: *The Alexandria Quartet*, 120, 331; *The Black Book*, 119–20, 242, 331; cover design concerns, 240–1, **241**; Eliot's view of, 185–6; Faber author, 388; *Justine*, 240–2, **241**; *Prospero's Cell*, 183; relationship with Pringle, 184, 203; reputation, 259

Eden, Anthony, 127

Editors Dining Group, 369–70

Edward Arnold (UK publisher), 319, 339

Edwards, Mrs, 24

Eliot, T. S. (Tom, TSE, Uncle Tom): address at Geoffrey's Memorial Service, 266–7; advice to Geoffrey, 134, 208–13; advice to young poets, 287; All Souls fellowship question, 13, 27; Alsina's response to his poems, 18, 20; appearance, **30**, 92, 165, **256**, **284**; appointment to Board of Faber & Gwyer (formerly Scientific Press), 12, 123; association with Scientific Press mooted, 3–4, 10–11, 12; background, 3–4; Book Committee, 80, **176–7**, 222, 226, **253**; Book Committee fireworks, 101–2; bust by Epstein, **284**; children's verse, 90; Classical Association presidential address, 166; copyrights, 394; correspondence with Fitzgerald, 22–3; correspondence with Joyce, 70–1, 76, 81; correspondence with MacNeice, 83, 96; Crawley's retirement, 268; *Criterion* editorship, 12, 16, 32, 34, 35, 70, 122–3; death, 286, 288; drawings, **78**, **253**; Faber author, 360, 367, 374,

388; Faber Board, 66, 74, 104, 254; *Faber Book of Modern Verse*, 100, 102; Faber leadership issue, 172, 177–9; Faber office, **286**; Faber role, xi, 65, 74, 104, 200–1, 212, 222–3, 358; Faber shares, 90, 205, 209, 210, 211–12; 'Faber & Faber' dinner, 70; Faber & Gwyer Board, 12, 32, 53–4; Faber & Gwyer role, 16–17, 28, **30**, 35, 49–52; fire-watching, **170**, 174, 201; first meeting with Geoffrey, 3, 223, 224; godfather to Tom Faber, 41–2, **78**, 79, 92, **124**, 136, 253; Harvard lectures, 90; health, 12–13, 16–17, 43; Kensington flat, **383**; lectures, 90, 167; marriage to Valerie, 242–3, 383; marriage to Vivien, 13, 17, 43, 79, 90; modern movement, 104, 129, 346; nickname, 103; Nobel Prize, 189, **190**, 201, 235; office, **286**; Order of Merit, 190, 235; presidential address to Classical Association, 166; publication of Joyce, 71–2, 75–6, 121–2, 127–8, **128**; publication of Marianne Moore, 93; published by Hogarth Press, 12, 92; reading aloud, 92; recruitment, 400; rejections of Orwell, 81, 175; relationship with Auden, 42–3, 61, 118–19, 143; relationship with cats, **78**, 78–9, 179–80, 201, 251; relationship with Geoffrey, xv, 43, 112–18, 129, 160, 165, 169, 195–6, 223–4, 266–7; relationship with Giroux, 185, 235; relationship with Hayward, 101–2, 103, 215n; relationship with Lowell, 189–90; relationship with Monteith, 201, 214–15, 237, 245–6; relationship with Morley, 65, 90, 91–2, 117, 141, 143, 177–9, 184; relationship with Pound, 54, **55**, 95, 100, 184; relationship with Spender, 73, 85, 125–6; report on *The Black Book*, 119–20; report on *Guide to Kulchur*, 119; report on *In Parenthesis*, 118; report on 'The Palm-Wine Drinker', 202; report on the poems of 'Mrs Mackay', 76; report on *The White Goddess*, 235; report on *Who Moved the Stone?*, 73; response to aftermath of Faber financial crisis, 207–10, 211–13; response to Berryman's work, 236; response to Larkin's work, 237; response to Steiner's *Death of Tragedy*, 262; response to Ted Hughes's work, 245–7; response to Thom Gunn's work, 239; salary, 12, 209, 212–13, 222, 257; secretaries, 153, 192, **193**, 222, 242; social life, 120, 163, 168; spoof letter from

Stewart, 111–12; spoof letters to Geoffrey, xv, 112–18, 195–6; Swedish visit, 167; Ty Glyn visits, 91–2, 152; view of Monteith, 213, 216–17; view of *Nightwood*, 107, 108–9, 110; wartime, 156–7, 169, **170**, **176–7**; works: *Burnt Norton*, 150, 168; *The Cocktail Party*, 192, 250; *Collected Poems 1909–1935*, 150, 248, 250; *The Dry Salvages*, 168; *East Coker*, 150, 168; *The Family Reunion*, 133, 150; 'Grizabella, the Glamour Cat', 355; *Little Gidding*, 167, 168; *Murder in the Cathedral*, 104; *Notes Towards the Definition of Culture*, 188; *Poems, 1909–1925*, 14; *Old Possum's Book of Practical Cats (Pollicle Dogs and Jellicle Cats)*, xiii, 105, 106–7, 123, 135, 136, 201, 251, 348, 353, 356, 400; *Poems* (1920), 4; *Poems, 1909–1925*, 14; *The Sacred Wood*, 4; translation of *Anabase*, 43; unpublished cat poems, 251, 355, 356; *The Waste Land*, 3, 4, 12, 14, 27, 109

Eliot, Valerie (Fletcher): *A Propos of Practical Cats*, 365; appearance, **193**, **361**; *Cats* development, 348–9, 355, 356; *Cats* royalties, 353–4, 394; Faber director, 397; Faber shareholder, 387, 394, 397, 401; Geoffrey's illness and death, 266; joining Faber as Eliot's secretary, 192; marriage to Eliot, 242, 383

Eliot, Vivien, 13, 17, 43, 79, 90

Eliot's Club, 111–18

Ellmann, Richard, 262

*Encounter*, 287

Eric Gregory Award Committee, 300

Evans, George Ewart, 293

Evans, Matthew (Faber managing director and chairman): appointment of poetry editor, 364–5; arrival at Faber, 293; assistant to du Sautoy, 293, 303; *Bookseller* pieces on, 374–5; *Cats* plans, 348, 355, 356, **361**; chairman of Faber, 354, 357, 362; cricketer, **394**; Faber directorship, 304, 318; Faber economies, 342–3; Faber merger issue, 339; Faber paperback strategy, 369, 390–1; Faber profitability concerns, 390–1, 393; Faber sales expenditure, 378; Faber shareholding issues, 388; forward planning, 328; at Frankfurt Book Fair, 293; *Guardian* interview, 375–6; managing director of Faber, 333–5, **335**, **340**, 347, 354, 357; news of Tom Faber's second marriage,

383; *Not the Nine O'Clock News 1982*, 362, 363–4; publishing Vargas Llosa, 366–7; publishing Vikram Seth, 380, 381; recruitment of Robert McCrum, 350; relationship with du Sautoy, 293, 303–4; relationship with Pete Townshend, 382–3; relationship with Peter Crawley, 328–9; relationship with Pinter, 389, 394, 395–6; relationship with Robert McCrum, 354; response to Faber becoming 'Publisher of the Year', 387; resignation from 'Editors Dining Group', 369–70; sales to American publishers, 303, 304; *Writings on the Wall* press conference, **376**

*Evening Standard*, 126–7, 353, 395

*Everywoman*, *see* Llewellyn-Jones

Ewing, Kenneth (literary agent), 278–9, 297–8

Faber, Ann (daughter of Geoffrey and Enid): Alan's death, 169, 244; birth and childhood, 1, **36**; correspondence with Ted Hughes, 244–5; engagement to Alan, 161; Faber employment, 244–5; health, 244; *The Image*, 244; marriage to John, 251; relationship with Alan, 142, 143; wartime life, 151, 154

Faber, Arthur (cousin of Henry), 5

Faber, Dorothy (sister of Geoffrey), 5, 6, 7, 8, 63

Faber, Enid (Richards, wife of Geoffrey): appearance, **36**, **341**; children, 1, 3, 34n, **36**; death of daughter's fiancé, 169; Dick de la Mare retirement issue, 309–10, 311, 316, 317; family background, 134; finances, 1, 121; Faber accounts issues, 293–4; Faber cash flow problem, 309–10; Faber directorship, 269–70, 301; Faber fiftieth anniversary party, 341; Faber music publishing, 279–80; Faber role, 93, 201–2, 267, 269–70; Faber sale proposal, 312; Faber shares concerns, 275–6; grandchildren, 252, 276; health, 3, 9, 53, 223; holidays, 49, 68, 195, 230; home in Campden Hill, 1; husband's death, 266, 267, 269; husband's illness, 251; marriage, 1; memories of retirement question, 64; relationship with Eliot, 136, 243; relationship with Gwyers, 58; report on *The Palm-Wine Drunkard*, 202; response to husband's knighthood, 228–9; sister, 150n; social life, 23, 192, 250; son Tom's

marriage, 252; son Tom's reports on Faber, 312, 333, 337; Ty Glyn retreat, 79; wartime life, 148, 151, 154, 156, 158–9, 163, 174

Faber, Florence (Colt, mother of Geoffrey), 5–8, 58, 60, 62, 159, 160

Faber, Geoffrey: achievements, 1, 66, 139, 212, 400; advice from Eliot, 134, 208–13; All Souls estates bursar, 1, 11n, 132, 145, 168; All Souls subwarden, 145; appearance, **59**, 93, 103; appointment of Monteith, 220, 221–2, 231; bicycling, 140, 141; Book Committee formation, 30–2; book publishing plans, 10, 16, 17–18, 36; *The Buried Stream: Collected Poems 1908–1941*, 160, 165; career, 1–2, 27–8; cattle breeding, 168, 184; chairman and managing director of Scientific Press, 2; character, 65–6, 266–7; children, 1, 3, 34n, **36**, 41–2, 196, 275; crossword setting, 127; death, 265–6, 269, 400; death of Charles Stewart, 180–1; death of daughter Ann's fiancé, 169; depression, 84; discussions with fellow shareholders (Scientific Press and Faber & Gwyer), xiii, 32–5, 38–41, 44–50, 56; Eliot's appointment, 12–13; *Elnovia*, 1, 18, 34, 52–3, **59**; Faber launch, 64; Faber president, 257–8, 266; Faber shares, 310; Faber & Faber name choice, 66–7; finances, 1, 5–9, 29, 34, 52–3, 58, 62–3, 64, 80, 121, 139; fire-watching, **170**, 174; first meeting with Eliot, 3, 223; godfather to Giles de la Mare, 42; grandchildren, 252, 266; Grosvenor Place lease, 179, 181, 182; health, 34n, 148n, 204, 250, 251; holidays, 9, 49, 53, 68, 91, 195, 230, 231; homes, 1, 79, 158, 167–8, *see also* Ty Glyn; investment in publishing (Scientific Press), xi, 5–9; knighthood, 200, 228–9, 230; lapses of judgment, 183, 199; letter to Joyce, 122; lifestyle, 13, 34; liquidation of Faber & Gwyer, 62, 64; managing director of Faber & Gwyer, 61; marriage, 1, 267; Memorandum on Finance, November 1929, 72; Memorandum to the Board, 29 June 1954, 231–2; Memorial Service, 266–7; Monteith's approach, 205–7, 214, 215–17; nickname, 103; *Nursery World* project, *see Nursery World*; obituary, 65–6; offers directorship to Blake, 74; *Oxford Apostles*, 85, 92; paper rationing, 145, 146, 150, 161–2, 165, 169–70, **176–7**;

poetry, 130, 160, 165; political connections, 134; psychoanalysis, 34n; Publishers Association (P.A.), 98, 110, 132, 139, 140, 141, 145, 147, 150, 181n; raising money to buy shares, 5–9; recruitment of Faber team, 64–6, 86–7, 200–1, 217, 400; rejection of Stopes poems, 129–30; relationship with Dick de la Mare, 42, 172, 228, 251, 252, 254, 260–1; relationship with Eliot, xv, 43, 112–18, 129, 160, 165, 169, 195–6, 223–4, 266–7; relationship with Gwyers, 1–2, 15–18, 20–1, 33, 36–41, 46–9, 50–1, 52–4, 57, 401; relationship with Morley, 132–3, 142, 171–2; relationship with Snow, 122, 141–2, 197, 199; retirement as chairman of Faber, 200, 231–3, 256–7; Russell Square premises, 11, 13; salary, 26, 66, 139, 232, 257; secretaries, 134; social life, 23, 35–6, 70, 71, 93, 103, 120, 141, 163, 168; solicitor, 270, 310; stroke, 250, 251; support for Eliot's All Souls election, 27; translations, 80–1; trust, 310, 313, 314; Turkish baths, 43, 70, 159; view of 5-year clauses in contracts, 98–9; view of independent publishing, 136–7; view of Monteith, 231; view of *Nightwood*, 109; wartime experiences, 142–3, 146–50, 151–60, 163, 173–5; wartime work, 139

Faber, Henrietta (granddaughter of Geoffrey) 266, 276, **341**

Faber, Henry (father of Geoffrey), 5, 6–7

Faber, Ishti (widow of Arthur), 5–6, 8, 9, 58, 60

Faber, Matthew (grandson of Geoffrey), **341**

Faber, Penny (wife of Tom), 252, **341**, 349, 373, 400

Faber, Polly (granddaughter of Geoffrey), **341**

Faber, Richard (Dick, son of Geoffrey and Enid): birth, 3, 9, 223; career, 196–7, 311; childhood, **36**, 169; unmarried, 252; wartime, 151

Faber, Thomas (Tom, son of Geoffrey and Enid): appointment of Matthew Evans as chairman, 357; appointment of Matthew Evans as managing director, 333–5; birth, 34n, 36; career, xii, 275, 349; chairman of Holding Company, 347, 365–6, 372–3, 387, 392–3; childhood, **36**, 78–9, 92, 105, **124**, 136, 169; children, xii, 252, 276; christening, 41–2; correspondence with

mother, 309–10, 311, 312–13, 333, 337; Dick de la Mare retirement question, 309–10, 311, 313–18; Faber cashflow problems, 309–13, 318; Faber company image, 365–6, 372–3; Faber fiftieth anniversary, **341**; Faber independence question, 327–8; Faber merger question, 333, 339–40; Faber Music, 392–3; Faber profits from *Cats*, 365, 392; Faber role, xii, 275–6, 293–4, 301, 325–6, **340**, 347; Faber sale question, 311–12, 315, 395–6; Faber sales, 387, 392; Faber share concerns, 275–6, 333, 394; godson of Eliot, 41–2, **78**, 79, 92, **124**, 136, 253; marriage, 252; mother's directorship of Faber, 269–70; Pinter reassurance, 395–6; second marriage, 383; Simon Jenkins's report on Faber, 353; wartime, 151, 158, 181; wife Penny's death, 373

Faber, Toby (grandson of Geoffrey), xii–xiii, **341**

Faber & Faber: accounts department, 254; air raid preparations, 130, 139; appointment of Monteith, 200–1, 220, 221–2, 231; archive, xii–xiii, 120, 135; art director, 375; art list, xiv, 65, 182, 209, 218, 355; assessment of firm in 1980, 353; author's position, xii–xiii; backlist, 72, 388, 400; bank overdraft, 260, 309, 310–11, 318, 343, 392; bestsellers, 73, 194, 260, 319, 320, 322, **345**, 385; Board: (1929–1935), 66, 74, 87; (1936–1939), 104, 133–4; (1945–1950), 189, 196; (1951–1960), 208–9, 212, 231, 257–8; (1960–1970), 269, 301, 314–15, 318; (1971–1979), 319, 333–4, 337, **340**; (1980–1986), 362, **384**; Board minutes: (1945–1950), 189, 196–7; (1951–1960), 226, 257; (1960–1970), 266, 271, 274, 299, 301; (1971–1979), 336–8, 343, 347–9, 351; (1980–1986), 360, 362–3, 367–8, 385; (1987–1990), 396; Book Committee, *see* Book Committee; breadth of publishing in late 1930s, 125–7; bridge list, xiv, 347; British Empire publishing, 68–9; catalogues: (1929–1935) 71–2, 75, 85, 86, **94**, 100, 101; (1936–1939), 105, 110, 127–8, 135–6; (1939–1945), 150, 168; (1945–1950), 183, 186, 187, 188, 191; (1951–1960), 234, 242, 248–9; (1960–70), 259–60, 270, 283–4, 307; (1971–1979), 322, 331; (1980–1986), 367; censorship issues, 71–2, 81, 95, 97–8, 236, 243–4, 259, 272–3, 275, 279,

283; chairman: (Geoffrey Faber), 66, 71, 81, 101–2, 178, 197, 200, 231–3, 256–7; (Dick de la Mare), 200, 256–7, 266, 274, 299, 311–18; (Peter du Sautoy), 318, 319, 328, 333–4, 347; (Charles Monteith), 333–4, 347, 357; (Matthew Evans), 354, 357, 362, 395, 396; children's list, xiv–xv, 91, 295–6, 338, 347; colophon, 362, 365, 368; computers, 337, 368, 381; cookery list, xiv, 259, 347, 349; copyright issues, 126–7, 374; crossword, 127; design, xi, 65, 163, 260, 280–1, **289**, 295, 338, 354, 362, 365, 368, 375–6; dinners, 70, 79; directors: (1929–1935), 74; (1936–1939), 133–4; (1939–1945), 160, 172, 175; (1951–1960), 208–9, 218, 220, 231–3, 257; (1960–1970), 259, 260, 266, 269–70, 271–2, 301, 304, 312; (1971–1979), 327, 333–4, 337, 343; (1980–1986), 362, 375, 379, **384**; (1987–1990), 393; distribution department, 178; distribution director, 362n, 393; dividends, 64, 121, 145, 173, 319, 333, 403–5; editorial department, 328–9, 349, 353, 358; editorial directors, 301, 329, 366; editors: (1936–1939), 105, **128**; (1939–1945), 150; (1960–1970), 259, 260, 271, 295–6; (1971–1979), 320, 328, 343, 349–50, 400; (1980–1986), 353, 354; electricity emergency, 336; Eliot's role, xi, 65, 74, 104, 200–1, 212, 222–3, 358; Employee Share Ownership Plan (ESOP), 387, 393–4, 396, 401; farming list, 65, 139, 183, 209, 346n; female directors, 259, **384**; fiction list, 72, 353, 359, 380, 381; fiftieth anniversary celebrations, 319, 341; financial position: (1929–1935), 64, 80; (1936–1939), 104, 119, 125; (1939–1945), 145, 165, 166, 169–70, 173; (1945–1950), 182–3, 189; (1951–1960), 204–5, 208–10; (1960–1970), 260, 274, 310–11, 313–14; (1971–1979), 333; (1980–1986), 385; (1987–1990), 387, 390–1; formation, 64, 230; future of (1989), 397; gardening list, xiv, 209, 346n, 347, 349; Geoffrey Faber Holdings, 401; government interference, 319, 348; Grosvenor Place lease, 179, 181, 182; Harlow warehouse, 254, 258, 259, 337, 387; hereditary principle, 40, 188, 196–7, 217, 272, 313; Holding Company, 301, 314, 334, **340**, 347, 353, 360, 365, 372, 387, 392, 393–4, 397, 401; independence, xi–xii, 136–7, 258, 318, 319, 327, 339,

387–8, 391, 396–7, 399–402; jacket designs, ix, 76, 240–1, **241**, 280, 285–6, 294–5, 338, 368; jokes and spoofs, xv, 104, 111–18, **144**, 195–6, 364; logo, 375; management issues, 393; medical list, xiv, 64, 65, 305, 319; merger proposals, 313, 319, 333, 339–40; 'Minimum Terms Agreement', 374; music department, 282–3; name, 64, 66–7, **94**, 141, 354; office stationery, 362, 365–6, **366**; paper rationing, 138, 146, 150, **151**, 161–2, 165, 169–70, **177**, 182, 191; paper shortages, 337; paperbacks: (1951–1960), 200, 248–50, **249**, 252, 401; (1960–1970), 274, 288, 291, 292; (1971–1979), 322, 328, 338, 347; (1980–1986), 354, 369, 401; (1986–1990), 387, 390–1, 401; play list, 271, 368, 381; poetry list, 74–5, 100, 244, 364–5, 376, 380; position in 1970, 303–4; president, 257–8, 266, 311, 318, **340**; principal directors, 74, **131**, 257, 301; prizes, 399, see also Booker, Nobel; production costs, 337–8, 343; production department, 176, 178, 183, 204, 208, 209, 307, 309, 365; production directors, 65, 309; public company suggestion, 327–8; Publicity Committee, 133; publicity and promotion department, 343, 371, 384; Publisher of the Year (1990), 387; Queen Square offices, 299, 319, 320, **321**, 336, 349, 353, 365, 381; redundancies, 343; restructuring, 301, 387, 393–4, 396, 401; Russell Square offices, 104, 153, **164**, 168, **170**, 173–5, 179, 180, 182, 189, 298; salaries, 66, 87, 134, 192, 196, 213, 222, 231–2, 257, 319, 351; sale of company discussed, 275–6, 312–13, 387, 395, 396; sales: (1929–1935), 70; (1936–1939), 104; (1945–1950), 182–3, 187, 191; (1951–1960), 252; (1960–1970), 259–60, 273, 303–4; (1971–1979), 329, 343, 347; (1980–1986), 368, 372; (1987–1990), 387, 391; sales and profit history, 403–5; sales department, 76, 209, 240, 303, 329, 371, 378; sales directors, 91, 182, 188, 208, 272, 328, 354, 368n, 378, 387, 393; sales and marketing department, 329, 354; sales and marketing directors, 328–9, 375, 378; sales managers, 70, 82, 87, 95, 220; sales predictions, 104, 387, 403–5; science fiction, xiv, 250; shareholders: (1929–1935), 64, 65, 66, 74, 88, 90; (1936–1939), 113n; (1939–1945), 145; (1951–1960),

205, 208–10, 222; (1960–1970), 260, 270,
275, 301, 311, 316, 317; (1971–1979), 319,
327–8, 333, 334, 339–40; (1980–1986),
379; (1987–1990), 387–8, 393–4, 397, 401;
staff photo album, **193**; staff recruitment,
349; staff reductions, 320, 343; taxation,
139, 146–7, 150, 151–2, 159, 161, 165,
166, 170, 171, 173, 260, 393–4; team,
64–6, 86–7, 200–1, 217, 312, 329, 337, 393,
400; telegraphic address (Fabbaf), 141;
telephone costs, 343; typeface, 163, **249**;
'vertical integration' strategy, 390, 391;
wartime issues, 130, 138–40, 145, 146–7,
149–50, 152, 160–1
Faber & Gwyer: advertising manager,
29–30; Autumn Announcements, 43, 54;
Board, 12, 32, 38, 44, 47–8, 53–4, 56, 58;
Book Committee, *see* Book Committee;
book-trade dispute, 17–18; directors, 12,
28, 31–5, 44, 47; Eliot's appointment,
12, 123; financial position, 28–9, 38, 45,
48–9, 57–8, 61–2, 405; foundation (from
the Scientific Press), 13, **14**, 98, 230, 319;
General Strike, 25–7; liquidation, 62, 64;
list, 14, 35, 51, 54, 57, 64, 98; manager,
31; managing director, 61; *The Nursing
Mirror*, **45**, 57–8, 62; *The Nursery World*,
28, 34–5, 39; production, 20; production
manager, 31; receptionist, 270n; Russell
Square offices, 11, 13, 15, **22**, **30**; sales,
20–1, 60; sales manager, 20–1, 29, 31;
shareholders, 32–4, 38–9, 44, 46, 49, 62,
65, 113n, 379
*The Faber Book of Modern Verse*, 100, 102,
109
Faber family: Arthur Faber Trust Estate,
5–8, 29, 58, 62; Enid's directorship, 270,
301; Faber fiftieth anniversary party,
**341**; Holding Company, 301, 334, 401;
independence of company, 401; share of
Faber ownership, xii, 275–6, 401; trusts,
310, 313, 314, 340
Faber Music, 282–3, 301, 319, 334, 365,
392–3, 405
Fama Ltd, 182, 301
The Fantasy Press, 227
Farrar, Straus and Giroux (FSG, earlier
Farrar, Straus and Young), 235–6, 350,
353, 366, 367
Filchner, Wilhelm, 126
*Financial Times*, 261, 312
Fine Art Engravers Ltd, 182, 301, 311, 318, 319

Fitzgerald, F. Scott, 22–3
Fleur, Elizabeth, 41, 42
Forster, E. M., 168, 234
Frankfurt Book Fair, 293
Franklin, Andrew, 96
Franklin, Cecil, 95, 96
Freedgood, Anne, 380
Freedman, Barnett, 76–7

Gallimard, 360
Gamelin, Maurice, 146, 148
Gardner, Helen, 262
Gee, Maggie, 371, 388, 389, 390
Geering, Captain, 181
General Strike (1926), 25–7
*Gentlemen's Quarterly*, 279
Gide, André, 117
Gilbert, Stuart, 72
Giroux, Robert (Bob), 185, 235–7, 350, 353,
366
Goad, Rosemary (Faber editorial director):
Faber director, 259, **340**; Ishiguro work-
in-progress, 358; presentation of toy
pig to financial expert, 367–8; pub-
lishing Stoppard, 298; relationship with
P. D. James, 264–5, 271, 294, 298, 307;
relationship with Tom Paulin, 340–1
Goad, Sarah (Lambert), 296
Golding, Ann, **373**
Golding, William: Faber author, 259, 360,
367, 375; *Lord of the Flies* (originally
*Strangers From Within*), xiii, 224–6,
**225**, 227–8, 229, 230–1, 234, 250, 252,
399; Nobel Prize, **373**; punctuation, xiv;
reputation, 259, 360, 367
Gollancz, Livia, 395
Gollancz, Victor, 47, 49, 81, 122, 240, 395
Gordon, Giles, 298
Gottlieb, Robert, 359
Grand, General, 251
*Granta*, 370
Grass, Günter, 399
Graves, P. P., 75
Graves, Robert, *The White Goddess*, 187, 235
Greene, Elaine (literary agent), 263, 271,
294, 307
*The Guardian*, 375, 384
Guedalla, Philip, 57
Gunn, Neil, 125, 181
Gunn, Thom, 239, 245, 263–4, 290
Gwyer, Alsina (Burdett; director and
shareholder of Faber & Gwyer):

accountant's examination of book-publishing business, 54, 57–8; attitude to sale of shares, 5, 39–40, 44; Book Committee, 32; character described, 29, 58; Eliot's letter, 49–50; Faber & Gwyer Board, 32, 52–4; financial concerns, 61–2; health, 18; persuaded to appoint Eliot, 3, 4; relationship with Geoffrey, 1–2, 15–18, 20–1, 39–41, 46, 53–4, 57, 401; relationship with husband, 58–9; response to *Nursery World*, 15, 21, 25, 39; Scientific Press inheritance, 1–2, 41; shareholding, 9, 32, 39, 41, 60, 62; view of Eliot's work, 18, 20

Gwyer, Maurice (shareholder of Faber & Gwyer): accountant's examination of book-publishing business, 54, 57–8; All Souls fellow, 1; attitude to sale of shares, 5, 46; character described, 58; financial concerns, 28–9, 38, 48–9; financial news during strike, 26–7; knighthood, 53n; persuaded to appoint Eliot, 3, 4, 28; relationship with Geoffrey, 1–2, 33, 36–8, 46–9, 50–1, 52, 57, 401; relationship with wife, 58–9; response to *The Nursery World*, 10, 14, 20, 23–5, 34–5; shareholding, 9, 32, 39, 41, 60, 62; shareholding issues, 32–4; views on Board of Faber & Gwyer, 44, 47–8; wife's health, 18

Hadfield, James (psychotherapist), 34n
Hall, Donald, 251
Halliwell, Kenneth, 271
Hampton, Christopher, 294
Harcourt, Alfred, 67, 127
Harcourt Brace (US publisher): Giroux's career, 185, 235; Morley's career, 132, 143, 171, 172; turning down Snow, 149; view of Faber, 67
Hardy, Thomas, 42
Hare, Cyril, 263
Hare, David, 307, 342
Harris, Rosemary, 295
Harris, Wilson, *Palace of the Peacock*, 253–4, 255
Harrod, Roy, 141
Hartley, George, 237
Harwood, Antony, 389–90
Hayward, John (friend of Eliot, Faber and Morley): Book Committee visit, **107**; conversation with Sparrow, 216, 221; friendships, 101, 103, 216n; 'Man

in White Spats', 124; nickname, 103; wartime life, 147

Heaney, Seamus: correspondence with Monteith, 286–7, 290, **291**, 302–3, 306; *Death of a Naturalist*, 290; helicopter tour project, 375; Nobel Prize, 399; poems in *New Statesman*, 320; poetry reading, **332**; recommendation of Muldoon, 306, 327
Heath, Ambrose, *Good Food*, 84
Heaton, Carol, 307
Heinemann (UK publisher): publishing Plath, 254, 277–8, 279, 280–1, 288; publishing Snow, 122
Hemingway, Ernest, 86
Hesse, Max René, *The White Flame (Partenau)*, 81–2
Higgins, Sydney, **376**
Higginson, Gordon, 242–3
Higham, David, 68
Hitler, Adolf, 127n, 163
Hoare, Sam, 168
Hodder & Stoughton, 5
Hodgson, Ralph, 123–4
Hogarth Press (UK publisher), 12, 92, 125
Hoskyns, Sir Edwin, 250
Huebsch, Ben (American publisher at Viking Press), 110, 111, 159
Hughes, Ted: appearance, **256**, **332**, **383**; *The Hawk in the Rain*, 244–7, **246**, 280; helicopter tour plans, 375; *The Iron Man*, 295–6, 382–3; jacket design concerns, 280–1, 285–6, 294–5; marriage, 247, 276; New York City Poetry Center prize, 244, 245, 246; reputation, 259, 290; Sylvia Plath's works, 252, 254, 277–8, 279, 280–1, 285–6, 288–9; Whitbread Book of the Year, 399; *Wodwo*, 294–5
Hunt, Phyllis, 295–6
Hutton, Barbara, 87, 155
Huxley, Julian, 168
Hynd, J. B., 184

International Thomson, 388
*Introduction* (anthology of new writing), 274
*Introduction 2* (anthology of new writing), 274, 276, 278, 299
*Introduction 7* (anthology of new writing), 354, 355, 359
*Introduction to Astronomy*, 252
*Irish Times*, 291

Isherwood, Christopher, 43, **86**, 143, 250
Ishiguro, Kazuo: 'Best of Young British
    Novelists' inclusion, 370; Booker Prize,
    387, **396**; first approach to Faber, 352;
    Nobel Prize, 399; *A Pale View of Hills*,
    357–8, 359, 363; paperback concerns,
    391; *Introduction 7* inclusion, 355, 359;
    relationship with McCrum, 353, 354, 355,
    357–9, 363; *The Remains of the Day*,
    387, **396**

Jackson, Melanie, 377
James, P. D. (Mrs White): *Cover Her Face*,
    264–5, 271, 294; *A Mind to Murder*, 294;
    relationship with Rosemary Goad, 264–5,
    271, 298; *Shroud for a Nightingale*,
    307–9; Silver Dagger award, **308**; US
    publication, 294
Jeal, Tim, 342
Jenkins, Simon, 353
John Llewellyn Rhys Memorial Prize, 342
Jonathan Cape (UK publisher): Cape-Chatto,
    319, 333; dropping Barbara Pym, 287, 324;
    merger issues, 333; post-war sales, 198;
    publishing T. E. Lawrence, 80n; publishing
    Walcott, 366; Random House takeover,
    395; summer campaign, 26; wartime
    taxation, 170, 173
Jones, Brian, 300
Jones, David, 82–3, 118, 346
Joyce, James: *Anna Livia Plurabelle*, 70–1,
    75–6; appearance, 79; Faber author, 346,
    360, 367; *Finnegans Wake* (previously
    'Work in Progress'), 96–7, 121–2, 127–8,
    **128**, 191; *Haveth Childers Everywhere*,
    75–6; *Letters of James Joyce Volumes II
    and III*, 283; *The Mime of Mick, Nick and
    the Maggies*, 96–7; poem for Faber, 76;
    reputation, 108–9; social life, 79, 117n;
    *Ulysses*, 71, 72, 81, 95, 109, 283, 331
Joyce, Lucia, 96–7
Joyce, Nora (Barnacle), 79

*Kaleidoscope*, 384
Kapp, Edmond X., *Minims*, 18
Kay Scott, C., *Siren*, 17, 18, 20
Keillor, Garrison, 378–9, 384, 385
Kennerley, Jean, 87, 147, 155
Kennerley, Morley (Faber editorial
    director): arrival at Faber, 86–7, 400;
    Book Committee, **176–7**, 222, **253**; Book
    Committee fireworks, 102; character, 208;

confusing Durrells, 204; 'deputy' director
    to Frank Morley, 133, 172; dictaphoning,
    166; directorship question, 133, 172, 208;
    Monteith's arrival, 220; news of wartime
    taxation, 143; on Eliot's description of
    Valerie, **193**; photograph of bomb hole,
    **154**; relationship with Seymour, 324;
    responsibility for publicity, 87, 172, 220;
    shooting in Wales, 157; Thanksgiving
    dinner, 120; view of Monteith, 232–3;
    wartime health, 165; wartime social life,
    147, 155
Keynes, Maynard, 141, 142
King, Caradoc, 378–9
Kingsolver, Barbara, 399
Klavans, Jody, 354
Knopf, Alfred A., 356, 359
Kundera, Milan: *The Book of Laughter and
    Forgetting*, 359–60, 368; Faber author, 361,
    367, 379; *The Joke*, 360, 368; McCrum's
    rejection and acceptance, 356, 359–60;
    Penguin paperbacks, 368; Penny's response
    to, 400; relationship with McCrum, 361,
    363, 368, 372, 373–4; *The Unbearable
    Lightness of Being*, 372, 373–4
Kupfer, Steven, 354
Kureishi, Hanif, 381–2, 386

Lane, Allen, 99–100, 106
Larkin, Philip: attitude to poetry readings,
    336–7; Faber author, 388; Faber contract,
    227; Faber hoping for another novel, 187,
    195, 226–7; Faber offering to publish
    poems, 267, 277; Faber rejection of poems,
    187, 237; *A Girl in Winter*, 184–5, 186,
    226, 237, 277; *Jill*, 277; *The Less Deceived*,
    237–8, 276; paperback edition, 332;
    recommending poets, 300; relationship
    with Monteith, 226–7, 237–8, 267, 276–7,
    292–3, 303, 332, 336–7; trying to persuade
    Faber to publish Barbara Pym, 287–8,
    292–3, 324–5
Latimer Trend (UK publisher), 160, 182, 301,
    316, 318, 319
Lawrence, D. H., 97
Lawrence, T. E. (T. E. Shaw): All Souls
    fellowship, 1; *Revolt in the Desert*, 80;
    *Seven Pillars of Wisdom*, 173
Layton-Bennett, Kenneth (accountant), 54,
    56, 57–8, 60–2
Léger, Alexis St-Léger (pen name St-John
    Perse), 34, 259, 261–2

Leigh, Gertrude, 113
Léon, Paul, 121–2
Levine, Ellen, 384
Lewis, C. S., *A Grief Observed*, 270, 283–4
Lewis, Wyndham, 85
Lidbury, Sir Charles, 181
Liddell Hart, B. H., 126
*Listener*, the, 302, 307, 384
Lister, Mrs (caretaker at Russell Square), 175
Llewellyn-Jones, Derek, *Everywoman*, 305–6, 322, **323**, 347
Lloyd, John, 377, 379
Lloyd Webber, Andrew, 348, 354, 355, 356, 360, **361**
*The London Magazine*, 252
*London Review of Books*, 302
Longman, 158, 254, 312, 315
Lopokova, Lydia, 141
Lowell, Robert: Eliot's advice, 185; *Lord Weary's Castle*, 185; *Poems, 1938–1949*, 189–90; relationship with Eliot, 189–90, 288
Lucie-Smith, Edward, 287n, 290
Lutterworth Press, 202

McConnell, John, 362, 365, 375
McCrae, Fiona, 353
McCrum, Michael, 350, 381
McCrum, Robert (Faber editorial director): adding Garrison Keillor to Faber list, 378–9, 384, 385; adding Vargas Llosa to Faber list, 366–7, 400; appearance, **376**; background and career, 349–50; editorial flair, 320, 400; Faber appointment, 320, 349–51, 353, 400; Faber Board, 362; interest in Hanif Kureishi, 382, 386; rejection and then acceptance of Kundera, 356, 359–60, 400; relationship with Caryl Phillips, 370, 371–2, 381, 389–90; relationship with Hanif Kureishi, 386–7; relationship with Ishiguro, 352, 353, 354, 355, 357–9, 363; relationship with Kundera, 361, 363, 368, 372, 373–4; relationship with Maggie Gee, 371, 388, 389, 390; relationship with Paul Auster, 385–6; relationship with Peter Carey, 351, 353, 354–5; relationship with Vargas Llosa, 377; relationship with Vikram Seth, 380–1; reports to Book Committee, 356; response to *Spitting Image*, 377, 379; stake in Faber, 388, 393
McDouall, R. P., 262–3

McGahern, John, 265, 272–3, 275
Mackay, Mrs (poet), 76
Mackle, Henry, 226, 384
Mackle, Joanna, **384**
MacLeod, Joseph Gordon, 75
Macmillan (UK publisher), 199
Macmillan, Harold, 134
MacNeice, Louis, 83, 96, 101, 110, **256**
Macpherson, Dugald (Faber family solicitor): advice to Geoffrey, 270; advice to Tom Faber, 313, 314; letter to bank, 318; relationship with Dick de la Mare, 309, 313, 314, 317, 318; role in Faber trust, 310; successor, 339n
Marquis, Don, *Archy and Mehitabel*, 250
Mars-Jones, Adam, 356, 370
Marvell Press (UK publisher), 237, 267, 276
Maschler, Kurt, 182, 301
Maurice, Colonel George, 4–5, 8, 12
Maurice, Olive (Burdett), 4–5, 8
May, Derwent, 300
*Memoirs of a Fox-Hunting Man, see* Sassoon
Metalious, Grace, 292
Methuen (UK publisher), 91, 126, 389, 395–6
Midland Bank, 95
Milford, Humphrey, 28
Miller, Henry, 101, 331
Miller, Karl, 302
Millin, Mrs, *The Glass House*, 162–3
Millington, Mrs ('Milly'), 148, 165
Milosz, Czeslaw, 234
Ministry of Labour and National Service, 163
Ministry of Supply, Paper Control, 161–2
Minsted estate, Sussex, 167–8, 175, 184, 250, 257
Mirrlees, Hope, 156
Mitchell, Donald (founder of Faber Music): Britten contact, 279; career, 282; Faber Board meetings, **340**, 362; Faber Music, 282, 334, 392
Mo, Timothy, 391
*The Modern Health Series*, 16
Monteith, Charles (Faber editorial director and chairman): appearance, **206**, **253**, **291**, **340**, **373**; appointment of McCrum, 350; arrival at Faber, 200–1, 220, 221, 222, 231–3, 400; background and career, 205, 206–7, 211; Book Committee, 226, **253**; contacting James (later Jan) Morris, 228, 229, 233–4; contacting John Osborne,

239; correspondence with John Carey, 304–5, 325, 330–1; correspondence with Ted Hughes, 247, 252, 254, 276, 278, 279, 280–1, 286, 288–9; Eliot's view of, 216–17; response to Heaney's work, 286–7, 290; response to *Lord of the Flies* (then titled *Strangers from Within*), 224, 226, 228, 230–1, 399; Faber chairman, 333, **340**, 347; Faber directorship, 231, 232–3, 257; Faber party for Auden, **256**; health, 221, 357; impact on Faber, 200–1, 232–3, 259; interest in Berryman's work, 236–7; interest in Dunn's work, 302; interest in McGahern's work, 265, 272; interest in Muldoon's work, 306–7, 320, 324–5, 326–7; interest in Orton, 271; interest in Plath's work, 252, 254, 278, 279; interest in *Waiting for Godot*, 236; jacket design issues, 285–6, 294–5; meeting Ishiguro, 359; Pearson takeover question, 312; publication of *Ariel*, 280–1, 285–6, 295; publication of *The Barracks*, 272–3, 275; publication of *The Bell Jar*, 288–9; publication of *Death of a Naturalist*, 290; publication of *Forty Years On*, 299, 300, 301–2; publication of *The Hawk in the Rain*, 247; publication of *The Iron Man*, 296; publication of *Lord of the Flies*, 229, 230–1, 234; publication of *The Violent Effigy: A Study of Dickens' Imagination*, 330–1; publication of *Waiting for Godot*, 238, 243–4, 279; relationship with Eliot, 201, 214–15, 237, 245–6; relationship with Geoffrey, 200–1, 205–7, 211, 213–15, 217, 219–20, 233; relationship with Heaney, **291**, 302–3, 306; relationship with Larkin, 226–7, 237–8, 267, 276–7, 287–8, 292–3, 300, 303, 332, 336–7; relationship with Thom Gunn, 239, 262–4; relationship with Wilson Harris, 255; response to Barbara Pym's work, 290–2, 325; response to Ishiguro's work, 358; response to Ted Hughes's poems, 245–7; retirement, 353, 357, 364–5; Sparrow's view of, 215–16, 221; Stoppard offer, 297; view of art list, 355; wartime experiences, 221, 359
Moore, Lorrie, *Self-Help*, 377
Moore, Marianne, 93, 100, 244–6, **284**
Morgan, Charles, 192
Morgan (cat), 179–80, 201
Morison, Frank, *Who Moved the Stone?*, 73, 250, 252

Morley, Frank (FVM; Faber editorial director): appearance, 103, **107**; background and career, 65, 77, 103; character, 68, 103; correspondence with Geoffrey, 142, 145, 146–50, 151–3, 157–60, 165, 167, 168–9, 170–4, 179–81, 201; 'Faber & Faber' dinner, 70; Faber directorship, 74, 133, 142, 172; Faber investment question, 67; Faber offer (1943), 171; Faber principal director, 74; Faber recruitment, 65, 77, 400; Faber role, 65, 66; impact on Faber, 65; leaving Faber for Harcourt Brace in New York, 132–4, 139; National War Labor Board work, 170–1; in New York, 14, 125, 142, 143, 149, 185; nickname, 103; niece, 175; Paterson's resignation, 89, 91; publishing game, 120; refusal of Faber offer, 172, 177–9; relationship with Eliot, 65, 90, 91–2, 117, 141, 143, 177–9, 184; relationship with Giroux, 185; relationship with Morley Kennerley, 86–7, 133, 172; response to *Nightwood*, 107–8, 109; response to *Tropic of Cancer*, 101; return to London (1947), 185; sales predictions ('Dr Morley's Parabolic Prediction or Futurity Revealed'), 104, 387, 403–5; social life, 71, 103, 120; view of Spender, 73
Morris, Jan (formerly James), 228, 229, 233–4
Muldoon, Paul, 306–7, 320, 324, 325, 326–7
Murphy, Richard, 302

Nash, Paul, 68, **69**, 272n
National Book League, 319, 341, 342
National Westminster Bank, 312, 315, 318
*New Statesman*, 287, 320
New York City Poetry Center, 244, 246
*New York Herald Tribune*, 93
*New York Sun*, 103
*New York Times*, 184
Nichols, John, **340**
Nobel Prize in Literature: Beckett, 259, 303; Eliot, 189, **190**, 201, 235; Giroux and Faber winners, 236, 366; Golding, **373**; Grass, 399; Heaney, 399; Ishiguro, 399; Milosz, 234; Pamuk, 399; Pearl Buck, 126n; Pinter, 399; St-John Perse, 34, 259, 261–2; Szymborska, 399; Vargas Llosa, 366, 399; Walcott, 366, 399
*Noctes Binanianae*, 103
*Not the Nine O'Clock News 1982*, 361–2, 363–4, 377

*The Nursery World*: ceasing publication, 39; circulation campaign, 36–7, 39; criticisms of, 21, 23; disagreements over, 23–5, 34–7, 39–41; editorship, 24n, 40, 41; financial position, 28, 37, 41; launch, 15, 18, **19**; plans for, 10, 14–15; printing difficulties, 27; progress report, 20; sale to Benn Brothers, 40–1, 44

*The Nursing Mirror*: accountant's recommendations, 57–8; advertisement for *Nursery World*, **19**; editorship, 21, 24n, 40; income from, 26, 37, 44, **45**, 46, 50, 64; printing strike, 27; sale, 61, 62; Scientific Press publication, 1–2, 15

*Nursing Times*, 305

*Observer*, 57

Octopus, 389

Orange Prize for Women's Fiction, 399

Ortega, Daniel, 395

Orton, Joe, 271

Orwell, George (Eric Blair): *Animal Farm*, xiii, 175; *Down and Out in Paris and London*, 81

Osborne, John, 239

Ossietzki, Carl von, 111

Oxford University Press (OUP), 2, 28n

Pamuk, Orhan, 399

Parsons, Ian, 102

Pasteur, Tom, 392–3

Paterson, A. J. B. ('Pat'; Faber sales director): Book Committee, 31; career after Faber, 95, 96; departure, 87–91; overdraft guarantee issue, 95–6; report on sales (1929), 70; sales manager, 21, 29; statement on Smithers, 29; successor, 87, 91

Paulin, Tom, 340–1

Pearson group, 312, 315

Penguin Books: Caryl Phillips publication, 390; Faber paperback agreement, 338, 369; foundation, 106; Kundera offer, 368; Pearson takeover, 312; Stoppard offer, 297, 298; success, 248

Pentagram, 354, 362, 365, 368, 375, 380

Perse, St-John, *see* Léger

Phillips, Caryl (Caz), 370, 371–2, 381, 389, 389, 391

Phillips, Jayne Anne, 379

Phillips, Peter (Faber production director), 337, 338, **340**

Pierre, DBC, 399

Pike, Frank (Faber editor): contact with Ted Hughes, 277–8; correspondence with Hampton, 294; correspondence with Stoppard, 274, 276, 284–5, 299; correspondence with Stoppard's agent, 278–9, 297–8; Faber role, 259, 271; Ishiguro work-in-progress, 358; report on Orton, 271; view of Dickens book, 330

Pinter, Harold, 389, 390, 394–6, 399

Plath, Aurelia, 256

Plath, Sylvia: *Ariel*, 280–1, 285–6, 295; *The Bell Jar*, 254, 288–9, **289**; children, 295; *The Colossus*, 280–1; death, 276; at Faber party, 256; marriage, 247; poems, 252, 254, 277–8, 279, 280–1

Plutarch, 191n

Pocock, Tony (Faber sales director and vice-chairman), 337, **340**

*Poetry Introduction 1*, 300, 302

*Poetry Introduction 2*, 306, 320, 324

*Poetry Introduction 3*, 340

Porpoise Press, 74, 148n

Pound, Ezra: *A Draft of XXX Cantos*, 86; Faber author, 346, 388; *Guide to Kulchur*, 119; 'mentally unsound' verdict, 184; relationship with Eliot, 54, **55**, 95, 100; *Selected Poems*, 54, 92

Presses de la Cité, 395

Price Commission, 319, 348

Pringle, Alan (Faber editorial director): eye problems, 337, 342; Faber career, 184, 213, 220; *Finnegan's Wake* publication, **128**; illustrations for *Overloaded Ark*, 204, 214–15; relationship with Gerald Durrell, 203–4, 215, 218, 220–1; relationship with Larkin, 184–5, 186, 187, 226; relationship with Lawrence Durrell, 184, 203; relationship with Tutuola, 202–3, 342; retirement, 342; title for *Lord of the Flies*, 229

*Private Eye*, 354

Publishers Association (PA): delegation to US, 181n; Geoffrey's presidency, 110, 132, 139, 140–1, 145, 147; police raid issue, 98; war issues, 140–1, 147

*The Publishers' Circular and Booksellers' Record*, 136

Publishing News, 387

Pullein-Thompson, Diana, 236

Pym, Barbara, 287–8, 290–3, 325

*Radio Times*, 384

Raine, Craig (Faber poetry editor), 364–5,
    370, 378, 379–80
Random House (US publisher), 143, 380,
    395
Rankin, Nick, 389
Raverat, Gwen, 192–4
Read, Herbert, 61
Really Useful Company, 362
Redwood Burn, 348
Reinhardt, Max, 315
Reitz, Deneys, *Commando*, 68
Richards, Gwynedd (Enid Faber's sister),
    150, 155
Rickman, Alfred, *Swedish Iron Ore*, 134–6,
    251
Ricks, Christopher, 304
Ridler, Anne (poet and secretary to T. S.
    Eliot), 153, 163, 185, 192
Robarts, David, 318
Roberts, Kilham, 99
Roberts, Michael, 100, 102–3
Robinson, Stanley, 9, 113n, 145, 161
Rogers, Deborah (literary agent), 358–9, 377
Rooney, Brian, 307
Roosevelt, Franklin D., 159, 170–1
Rosen, Andrea, 356
Rothermere, Lady, 36
Routledge, 95, 96, 388
Russell, George (AE), **69**, 272n

Saroyan, William, 250
Sassoon, Siegfried: *Memoirs of a Fox-
    Hunting Man*, xiii, 50, 54, 56–7, 60, 62,
    260, 399; illustrations by Nash, 68; poetry,
    42, 54, 68; relationship with Dick de la
    Mare, 50, 54, 56–7
Scientific Press, the: foundation, 1; Geoffrey
    appointed chairman and managing
    director, 2, 29, 230; Geoffrey buying
    shares, 5–8; medical list, 64; name
    changed to Faber and Gwyer, **14**, 230,
    *see also* Faber & Gwyer; long-standing
    employee, 29; premises, 11; profitability,
    2; publications, 1–2, 58, 64; shareholders,
    1–2, 4, 113n; shareholders' views on
    future, 4–5
Scribner, 294, 307
Second World War: Air Raid Precautions
    (ARP), 139–40, 157; bombs, 138, 153–6,
    **154**, 157–9, 173, 174–6; book trade, 138–9,
    140, 146–7, 149–50, 151–2, 158, 161;
    demand for books, 138; end, 182; Excess

Profits Tax (EPT), 139, 165, 166n, 170,
    171, 173, 182; Finance Act (1940), 139,
    152; flying bombs (doodlebugs), 174–6;
    German invasion of France, 146; outbreak,
    138; paper rationing, 138, 146, 150, **151**,
    161–2, 165, 169, **177**, 182; preparations,
    130, 139; purchase tax, 139, 146–7, 150,
    151–2; War Risks Insurance Act (1939),
    140
*Self-Sufficiency, see* Seymour
Sequana Limited, 97–8
Servire Press, 96
SET Copyrights, 394, 397
Seth, Vikram, 380–1
*Sex and Life* (Steinach and Loebel), 158–9
Seymour, John: return to Faber, 322, 324;
    *The Complete Book of Self-Sufficiency*,
    320, 344, **345**, 399
Sheed & Ward, 169–70
Sheldon, Constance (Cruickshank), 134, 153,
    **176–7**
Short, Lionel G., *A Flower in Rain*, 17
Sillitoe, Alan, 289
Silvia, Queen of Sweden, **373**
Simmons, Leslie (Faber company secretary),
    204, 205, 242, 312
Simpkins (wholesalers), 17, 51
Simpson, Peter (Faber finance director), 381,
    385
Sitwell, Edith, 23
Sitwell, Osbert, 79
Smallwood, Norah, 350
Smith, Anthony, 274
Smith, Nicholas, 339
Smithers, H. E., 29–30
Snow, C. P.: *The Light and the Dark*, 186–7;
    *The Masters*, 142, 197, 198–9; move
    from Faber, 199, 221, 303; move to Faber,
    142; relationship with Geoffrey, 122,
    141–2, 199; sales, 187, 191, 197–9, 303;
    *Strangers and Brothers*, 142; *Time of
    Hope*, 191
Society of Authors, 374
Sophocles, 191n
*Spain in a Two-seater*, 16
Sparrow, John (warden of All Souls), 215–16,
    221
*Spectator*, 237
Spender, Natasha (Litvin), 163, 168
Spender, Stephen: appearance, **86**, **256**, **332**;
    career plans, 85; Eliot's view of, 73, 85;
    Faber author, 129; judge of New York

poetry award, 244, 245, 246; Morley's view of, 73; plans to change publisher, 125–6; *Poems*, 85; relationship with Eliot, 73, 125–6; social life, 163, 168
*Spitting Image*, 377, 379, 385
Squire, J. C., 57
Stapledon, Doris, 143
Steiner, George, 262, 383
Stephenson, Derek, 320
Stewart, Charles (Faber director): appearance, **131**; assistant, 15; Book Committee, 31, **177**; career, 2; character, 31–2, 180; children, 147, 160; correspondence with Alison Uttley, 127, 128–9, 131; death, 180–1; employment of Wolpe, 163; Faber & Faber Board, 66–7, 74; 'Faber & Faber' dinner, 70; Faber & Faber role, 65, 74, 180, 400; Faber & Gwyer Board, 31–2, 44, 47, 52; general manager of Scientific Press, 2; joke correspondence with Eliot, 111–18; managing directorship proposal, 61; nickname, 131, 160n; recruitment, 400; relationship with Dick de la Mare, 17, 172; salary, 66; successor, 181; war preparations, 130; wartime life, 147, 153, 174, **177**
Stockhausen, Karlheinz, 333
Stopes, Marie, 129–30
Stoppard, Tom: novel proposal, 278–9, 284–5; publication in *Introduction 2*, 274, 276, 278–9, 299, 300; *Rosencrantz and Guildenstern are Dead*, 296–8, 299
Strachey, Lytton, 93
Straus, Roger (American publisher at Farrar, Straus and Giroux), 350, 366–7, 390
Street, Arthur (A. G.), *Farmer's Glory*, 140, 192, 252
Strong & Co., 1
*Sunday Times*, 353, 384; Book Exhibition, 93
Swan, Ethel, 270
Szymborska, Wisława, 399

Tate, Allen, 67
Taylor, George, 368
Taylor, T. M., 32, 52
Thomson, George Malcolm, 148
Thorne, Ray, 307
Thwaite, Anthony, 267
*Time Out*, 384
*The Times*, 82, 111, 166, 228, 229, 233–4, 242, 303, 341, 353, 384

Times Book Club, 187
*Times Literary Supplement*, 82
Tony Godwin Prize, 350
*Town* magazine, 278
Townshend, Pete, 354, 382–3, **383**
Travellers' Club, 262–3
Truby King, 23–5
Tucker, Shirley (Faber cover designer), **289**, 295, 338
Tutuola, Amos, 202–3, 342
Ty Glyn: Eliot's visits, 91–2; expenses, 80, 121; Geoffrey and Enid's house in Wales, 79; sale considered, 121; sold, 167–8; staying at, 79, 85, 87, 92, 132, 151, 166; wartime difficulties, 168

Unwin, Rayner, 333, 339–40
Uttley, Alison, 127, 128–9, 131

van Houts, Liesbeth, 383
Vargas Llosa, Mario, 366–7, 377, 379, 399, 400
*Verse and Worse*, 250, 252

Wagstaff, A. R., 362
Walcott, Derek, 366, 367, 399
*Wall Street Journal*, 382
Walpole, Hugh, 92–3
Watt, Alan (son of Bill Watt): death, 169, 244; engagement to Ann, 161, 244; Geoffrey's relationship with, 125, 127; private secretary proposal, 132, 133; relationship with Ann, 142, 143, 161
Watt, A. P.: *Book at Bedtime*, 384; Garrison Keillor representation, 378–9; Geoffrey's correspondence with, 98–9, 162–3; Larkin's relationship with, 276–7
Watt, Peter, 184, 187, 276–7
Watt, William (Bill; literary agent), 98–9, 125, 127, 132n, 162
*Western Daily Press*, 274
Whibley, Charles (writer who introduced Geoffrey Faber to T. S. Eliot), 2, 3–4, 12, 223
Whitbread Book of the Year, 399
White, Terence de Vere, **291**
*Who Moved the Stone?*, *see* Morison
Wilmers, Mary-Kay (MKW; Faber editor): correspondence with Dunn, 300; departure from Faber, 302; Faber role, 259; *Forty Years On*, 299, 302; Frankfurt Book Fair, 293; response to Heaney's work, 290; response to *The Iron Man*, 296

Wodehouse, P. G., 83
Wolpe, Berthold (Faber cover designer):
  Albertus typeface, 163, **249**; anti-Nazi
  refugee, 153; employment by Faber, 163,
  **164**; employment permit, 163; jacket
  design issues, 240–1, **241**, 285–6, 294–5;
  retirement, 338, 362; treatment as enemy
  alien, 153, 163; typographical designs, 163

Woolf, Leonard, 12, 13
Woolf, Virginia, 12, 13, 92–3, 156n
Writers' Guild, 374
*Writings on the Wall* (anthology), **376**

X (quarterly magazine), 265

Yeats, W. B., 100, 102, 262